Albania at War, 1939–1945

The Second World War in Europe has generated more literature than perhaps any other event in modern history. Much of the interest has focused on military history, occupation policy, puppet governments, and resistance movements in Europe's principal states. Often ignored in this flood of material, however, are the small nations of southeastern Europe. Yet in the small states the human suffering was no less profound, the destruction no less devastating, the heroisim no less laudable, the treachery no less despicable, and the impact no less profound.

Albania at War is a comprehensive history of Albania from the Italian invasion in 1939 to the accession to power of the Albania Communist Party and the establishment of a "people's democracy" in 1946. Fischer analyses in great detail Italian goals and objectives in Albania and explains the eventual failure of Rome's policy, the subsequent German invasion of the country, and the rise of organised resistance movements against the Axis Powers.

This pathbreaking book is a vigorous and thought-provoking reassessment of competing external interests in Albania and explores the great obstacles that the Albanian people faced in regaining their independence at the end of the war.

BERND J. FISCHER is professor of history at Indiana University at Fort Wayne. His previous works include *King Zog and the Struggle for Stability in Albania*.

Albania at War, 1939–1945

Bernd J. Fischer

Hurst & Company, London

Published in the United Kingdom by C. Hurst & Co. (Publishers) Ltd.,
38 King Street, London WC2E 8JZ
under licence from Purdue University Press,
West Lafayette, Indiana, U.S.A.

Copyright © 1999 by Purdue Research Foundation. All rights reserved.

ISBN: 978-1-85065-531-2 (paperback only)

Printed and bound in Great Britain by
Marston Book Services Limited, Oxford

This work is dedicated to my mentor, Dimitrije Djordjevic, and to my parents, Gertrud and Emil Fischer.

Contents

Acknowledgments / ix
Foreword / xi
Abbreviations / xiv
Note on Place-Names / xv
Maps / xvi

Introduction / 1
1. Count Ciano's Invasion of Albania / 5
2. The Construction of an Italian Albania / 33
3. Italian Greater Albania / 61
4. Italian Repression and the Beginning of Resistance / 89
5. The Growth of Resistance and the Collapse of Italy / 121
6. The German Invasion and the Construction of a German Albania / 157
7. Resistance to the Germans / 189
8. German Retreat and the Construction of a Stalinist Albania / 223
Conclusion / 257

Note on Sources / 275
Notes / 285
Bibliography / 321
Index / 329

Acknowledgments

I am greatly indebted to many friends and colleagues without whom this work would have been considerably more flawed than it is, and to the various institutions who helped to make this work possible. The encouragement of my friend and mentor, Professor Dimitrije Djordjevic, I will always gratefully acknowledge. Professors Stephen Fischer-Galati, Peter Sugar, and Nicholas Pano and my colleague Professor Clifford Scott read part or all of this work and provided continuing encouragement through their useful comments and suggestions. My Albanian publisher, Brikena Çabej, and my friend Altin Rraxhimi also gave generously of their time to read the manuscript and offer important suggestions. Gabe Downs helped with the index and Elmer Denman with the photographs and maps. I would also like to acknowledge Debra Fehman and Barbara Blauvelt, whose encouragement and help were most welcome. Finally, I would like to thank the many individuals who provided assistance at the National Archives in Washington, D.C., the British Public Record office in Kew, the Nash archives at the School of Slavonic and East European Studies at the University of London, and the Auswärtiges Amt in Bonn.

Many institutions provided the financial assistance that made travel to the various archives possible. These include the National Endowment for the Humanities, the American Council of Learned Societies, Wenatchee Valley College, the University of Western Ontario, the University of Hartford, Indiana University-Purdue University Fort Wayne, and the West European Studies Center and the Russian and East European Institute, both at Indiana University, Bloomington.

Foreword

Albania and its people have coursed this century in relative obscurity. That they have attracted so little attention stems in part from the country's small size, population, and economy. Another reason is that Albania is the only nation-state in all of central Europe to have remained neutral in both world wars. Its abstention stemmed in large part from its immaturity as a political entity.

At its creation in 1913, it was in many respects an artificial state, inspired by Austria-Hungary's determination to block Serbia's access to the sea, rather than by the natural evolution of a common national identity, political culture, or centralized institutions. As a result, it did not actively participate in the ruthless, high-stakes competition that has determined the fate, identity, and agenda of the region's other nations. At the Paris peace conference of 1919 it neither shared in the spoils awarded to Greece, Italy, Romania, and Serbia, nor in the punishment meted out to Austria, Bulgaria, Hungary, and Turkey. Instead, Albania and its people entered the interwar period together with an assortment of emerging pre-national peoples, like the Croats, Slovenes, Bosniaks, Slovaks, and Ruthenes, who were caught in a kind of limbo between winners and losers. Without the leverage to represent their national interests, their fate was entrusted to those neighbors which had been enfranchised by the Paris peace settlement. Whereas the results were hardly catastrophic, this indifferent stewardship gave them a common interest with the Great War's defeated nations.

The discontents of the region's defeated and disenfranchised nations were readily exploited by opportunistic European powers, most notably by Fascist Italy and Nazi Germany, prior to their defeat and replacement by Stalin's Soviet Union. Professor Fischer shows how the two Axis hegemons exploited Albanian dissatisfaction with the country's ethnically imprecise frontiers. Italy pandered to these frustrations both through anti-Greek rhetoric and Albania's territorial expansion, first by border rectifications in the early 1920s, then by aggression against Greece and Yugoslavia in 1941. When Italy collapsed two years later, the German occupiers easily co-opted the Albanians. They readily forged a common front against the Serbs, both by showcasing their commitment to a "Greater Albania" and by assiduously promoting Albanian cultural development in Kosovo. Unlike the Italians, however, they also met more immediate needs by retaining better-qualified political leaders from each of the country's confessional groups, as well as by utilizing the greater experience and sensitivity of Austrian Germans who had served in the region under the Habsburgs. Most remarkable of all was the respect that the Germans showed for Albania's independence and neutrality.

Fischer's narration and analysis of the German occupation rectify a half-century of amnesia and mythmaking by Marxist and nationalist historians by increasing our understanding of the reasonably constructive relationship between the Third Reich and wartime Albania. Moreover, his case study raises questions that might be usefully applied to other defeated or disenfranchised peoples of the interwar period whom Nazi Germany both helped and used for its own ends. Yet Hitler's embrace proved fatal for his wartime collaborators. In Albania, traditional elites, nationalists, and even the proto-democratic forces that the Germans tolerated were judged guilty by association with the Nazi scourge. Like so many of the defeated or disenfranchised nations of interwar Europe, they were readily abandoned in favor of short-term advantages offered by the Allies' wartime partners. In Albania's case, this meant not only the Greeks, but the Communist partisans who had fought virtually alone against the Axis occupation; as in Tito's Yugoslavia, Albania was readily consigned to a half-century of Communist rule, even though the Red Army had played no direct role in its liberation.

For Albania, World War II may have been a catastrophe in terms of immediate wartime suffering and a half-century of totalitarianism. But, as Fischer demonstrates, it was the nightmare of World War II that transformed it overnight into a state with substantial centralized governmental institutions and a broadly based national identity. Once it has completed the turbulent transition from Communism, its transformation will be complete.

Or will it? Watching the incremental progress of European nation-building has been like listening to a Bach fugue, with different groups of people raising their voices in succession. The French, Spanish, and British were the first, in a process completed by the end of the eighteenth century. Then came the Germans and Italians in the middle of the nineteenth century. Over the next half-century the "subject peoples" of the Ottoman empire, Austria-Hungary, and Tsarist Russia's Baltic littoral raised their voices. The outbreak of World War II began what should prove the final passage of this chorus of nàtions. It has been turbulent and unpredictable, though hardly more so than the first three stages. It has featured Croats, Slovaks, and Albanians during World War II and, more recently, Macedonians and Ukrainians. Nor should we overlook the region's two "confessional" peoples—the Jews and Bosniaks—both of whom have built national homelands in the aftermath of a bloody partition. Surely we are near the completion of this final stage. But we have yet to hear from the large number of Albanians who remain denizens of other nation-states. An appreciation for the continuity between past and present suggests that they will someday complete the process by making themselves heard.

—Charles W. Ingrao

Abbreviations

AA	Auswärtiges Amt (Germany)
CGR	Captured German Records (National Archives)
CIR	Captured Italian Records (National Archives)
CAB	British Cabinet Papers
DDI	documenti diplomatici italiani
FO	Foreign Office (Great Britain)
OSS	Office of Strategic Services (United States)
USDS	U.S. Department of State
WO	War Office (Great Britain)

Note on Place-Names

Albanian place-names have both a definite and an indefinite form. As is often done in English works dealing with Albania, I have used the definite form in place-names ending in vowels and the indefinite form with place-names ending in consonants. Since much of Kosovo was added to the Albanian state during the war years, the Albanian spelling, "Kosova," is used throughout.

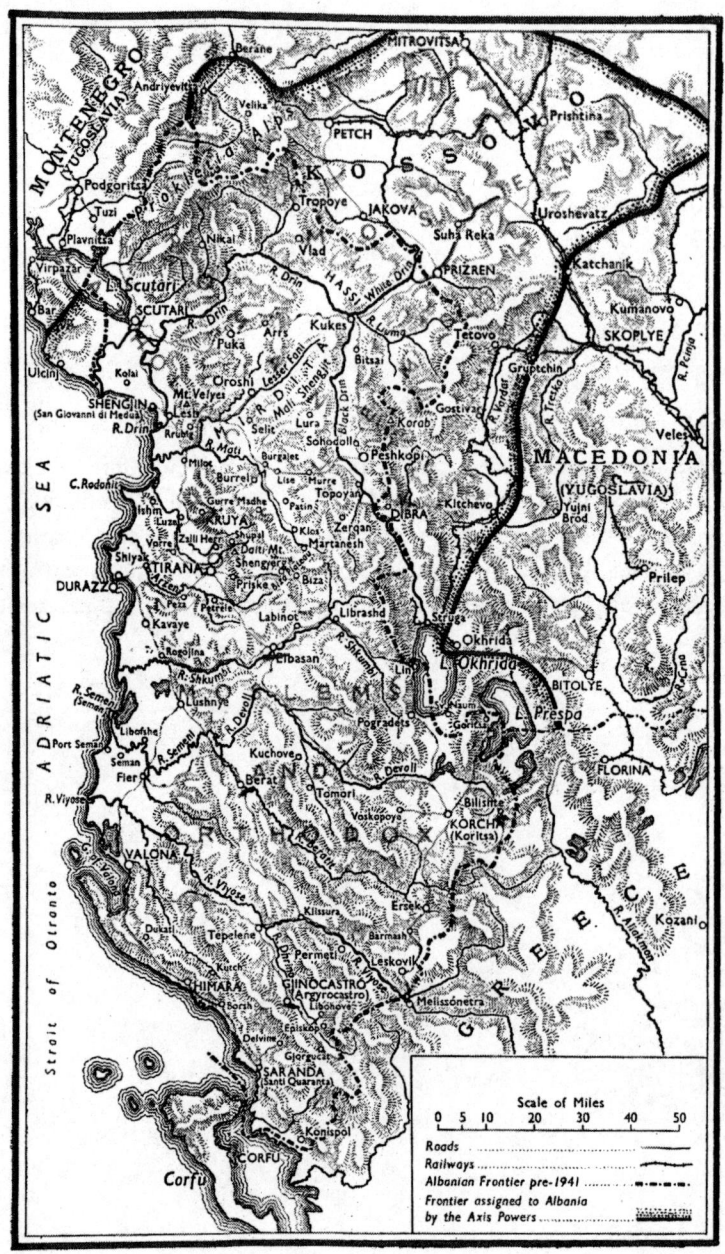

Albania, 1913–1941
(from Julian Amery, *Sons of the Eagle*)

Southern Europe and the Balkans
before World War II
(from Hermann Neubacher, *Sonderauftrag Südost*)

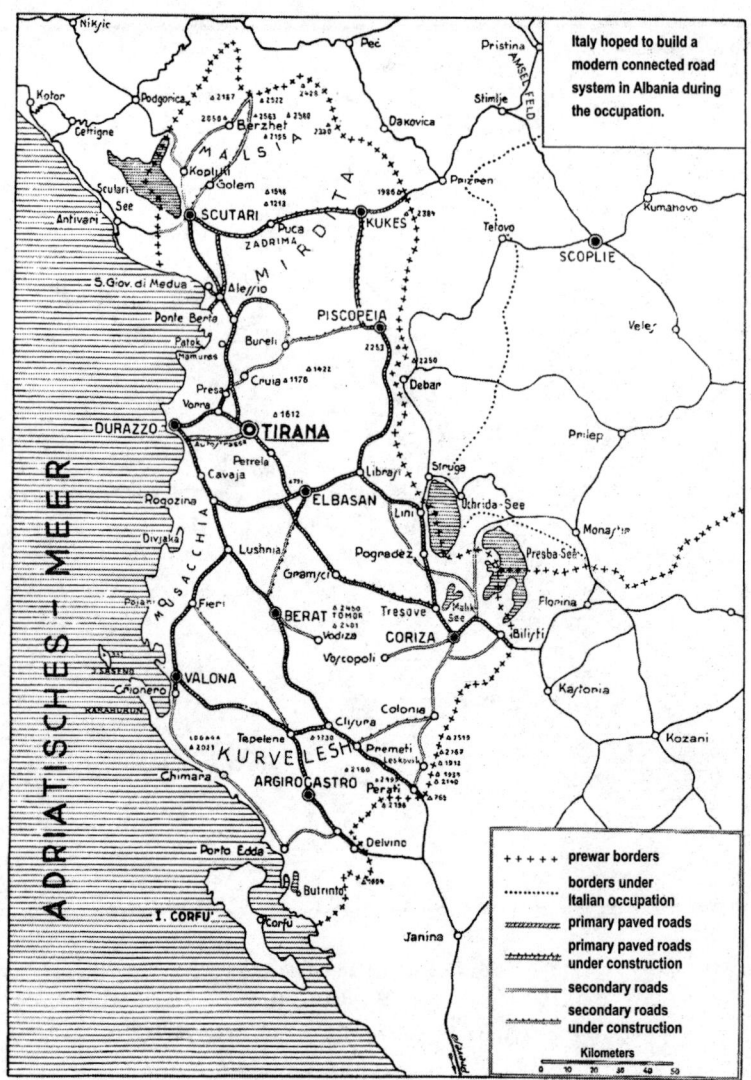

Road Construction in Albania
(from Erich von Luckwald, *Albanien*)

The Axis Division of Yugoslavia
(from Hermann Neubacher, *Sonderauftrag Südost*)

The Republics of Federal Yugoslavia
(from Hermann Neubacher, *Sonderauftrag Südost*)

INTRODUCTION

It is becoming increasing difficult to justify yet another book dealing with some aspect of World War II. Of all the armed conflicts of past centuries, World War II has engendered the most interest as well as an exhausting amount of written material. The opening of the Soviet archives and the recent commemoration of the fiftieth anniversary of the many defining moments of the war have resulted in yet another spate of books and films that examine the conflict in retrospect. But most of the research and interest naturally concentrate on the major theaters of war and the major figures involved. Little wars are often overlooked. Yet in the small state the human suffering was no less pitiful, the destruction no less devastating, the heroism no less laudatory, the treachery no less despicable, and the impact no less profound.

Albania counts as one of these forgotten theaters, in which the struggle was on a smaller scale, although it did not seem that way to the Albanians. The struggle was long and intense, and for the Albanians it was disturbingly familiar. The Albanians have known more than their share of war, often invaded but perhaps never fully conquered. In World War I alone, the newly created state of Albania was invaded and occupied by no fewer than six different foreign armies. Enver Hoxha—Albania's Stalinist dictator until his death in 1985—was fond of repeating the often quoted adage that Albanians have hacked their way through history with a sword in hand in order to build socialism with a pickax and a rifle. The reference may be overly colorful, but there is a certain truth to the assertion, particularly in the context of World War II. Although not as dramatic as it was elsewhere, the war began earlier and lasted longer in Albania. The Italians invaded and occupied Albania in April 1939, well before the German invasion of Poland and before World War II officially began, though it did not seem that way to many Albanians.

In a certain sense the war in Albania can be seen as a microcosm of the war in the rest of the Balkans and in Europe as a whole. Albania suffered from all of the same complexities, if not more. In the short run, the Italian invasion and the subsequent German invasion were unsuccessfully resisted by the brave few. Collaborators were found to fashion puppet governments, and resistance was organized to punish the traitors and expel the invaders. As is true of other areas of Europe, this resistance fragmented along political lines. The Allies found it difficult to decide which group to support, but nevertheless played an important role in terms of leadership and supplies. The invaders were finally expelled and the collaborators liquidated, as in other areas of Europe. At the end of the war in Albania, in late 1944, the communists found themselves unchallenged and assumed both military and political leadership.

But Albania's unique internal conditions produced significant variations in the theme, and below a familiar surface the complications become endless. During the Italian occupation the fragmentation among the resistance, for example, was much more severe than in other parts of the Balkans or in Europe. To complicate matters, many of these resistance groups proved to be inconsistent, occasionally cooperating with the invader, then turning to resistance, then reverting to cooperation. This vacillation can be explained, at least partially, by the lack of a fully developed sense of nationalism. As a result, the reaction of individual groups often depended principally on a regional, tribal, and local considerations. This lack of a fully developed nationalism also determined the response of many of the tribal chieftains to the invaders; they looked to play the various forces off against each other and thereby achieve some advantage for their areas. It is simple to judge many of these Albanian leaders in light of Vidkun Quisling and label them as traitors, but that would attribute to them a level of nationalist sophistication that they did not yet possess.

Many aspects of Albania's experience under German occupation are also unique. Albania's peculiar internal conditions, as well as German needs, allowed for the creation of a surprisingly independent occupation regime. This government, by doing away with most outward signs of fascism and following a reformist political and economic policy, managed to attract a significant amount of genuine popular support. Much of this came as a surprise to both the Germans and the Allies, sending them scrambling for information upon which to construct an effective policy. In the long run neither side succeeded in understanding the Albanians, and both failed to effectively control the situation.

Although both the Allies and the Axis failed, the impact of their struggle was crucial for the Albanians. In the short term the Axis powers relied on and temporarily bolstered the prewar political and social structure, and they provided some immediate economic relief. But as the war dragged on, the prewar political structure was destroyed and the social structure was undermined while the early economic advantages quickly dissipated. The Allies provided the Albanian resistance not only with an ideology but also with a considerable part of the material resources required to conduct effective resistance.

The war's long-term impact—as in other areas of Europe—was profound and often paradoxical. The war changed everything. Axis policy was principally responsible for guaranteeing that the prewar political and social structure could not be resurrected. The war, in general, pulled Albania out of one form of isolation but propelled it into another. Prior to the war, Albania was arguably the most isolated country in Europe. The wartime experience forcibly brought Albania into contact with foreigners, their ideas, and their guns. But while the Albanians were exposed to the outside world, the experience of the war strongly reinforced a traditional xenophobia for which the Albanians are legendary, a xenophobia reinforced and exploited by Hoxha's Stalinist government in the postwar world. Enver Hoxha found that Albania's experience during the war was his most useful tool in maintaining power based upon what has been called a state-of-siege or garrison-state mentality, which emphasized the danger that foreigners represented.

Under Hoxha's iron hand a powerful resistance myth was created, in which the Albanian people heroically defeated and expelled the fascist invaders. This myth became the common bond, and Albania's wartime experience dominated all aspects of existence in Albania until the collapse of communism in the early 1990s. Writers, including the country's preeminent novelist, Ismail Kadare, used the war as the major theme of many of their works; Albanian art and drama, even its currency, concentrated on the resistance; Albanian education was not allowed to separate itself from the antifascist struggle. Every aspect of Albanian civilization was measured by the wartime experience. It is not possible to understand the Albanians—something that is rapidly becoming more necessary with the recent opening up of Albania to the rest of the world—without a clear understanding of Albania at war. World War II might be an overexploited topic, but in this case an understanding of Albania from 1939 to 1945 is crucial if the Albanians of the late 1990s are to be dealt with intelligently. As Albania strives to become part of Europe in a real sense for the first time and is thrust unprepared into the international spotlight because of the continuing tragedy of the Balkans in the 1990s and Albania's own near collapse in 1997, an understanding of the war years, which did so much to shape the state and nation over the past fifty years, is valuable. It is hoped that this work will contribute to that understanding. It is further hoped that *Albania at War* will provide some moments of interest for Balkan and European specialists and some small enlightenment and enjoyment for the general reader.

This color painting is a fine example of the Albanian version of Stalinist-realist art depicting the Albanian partisans defeating a contingent of fascist troops. From the cover of Mehmet Shehu's book *On the Experience of the National Liberation War.*

CHAPTER 1

COUNT CIANO'S INVASION OF ALBANIA

The Italian invasion of April 1939, which began the war in Albania, was the culmination of centuries of Italian interest and twenty years of direct, if unsuccessful, economic and political involvement in Albania, principally under Benito Mussolini. The Straits of Otranto, which separate Albania and southern Italy by forty miles of the Adriatic Sea, have always served more as a bridge than a barrier, providing escape, a cultural span, and a convenient invasion route. The proximity between the two areas facilitated numerous connections, including classical Roman and Venetian contacts and the establishment of large Albanian colonies in southern Italy following the defeat of Gjergj Kastrioti Skënderbeg, the fifteenth-century Albanian national hero who held off a succession of Ottoman invasions. During the last quarter of the nineteenth century, following the creation of the United Kingdom of Italy, more active Italian interest transformed these occasional encounters into increasingly significant involvement.[1]

The motivation behind Italy's interest seems clear. Albania is important from a strategic standpoint in terms of defense and offense. With control of Vlora, or even simply the island of Sazan in the Bay of Vlora, the Italians could dominate the Adriatic Sea. Italian naval specialists, recognizing that Italy had no suitable base for naval operations on its Adriatic coast, eyed Vlora with considerable interest.[2] In offensive strategic terms, Albania could provide Italy with a bridgehead into the Balkans. Further, the Italians had vague ideas about Albania offering Italy territory upon which to settle excess population. It was also assumed in Rome, although the Italians never produced adequate geological charts, that natural resources, particularly oil and chrome, could be found in abundance in Albania. As nationalism and imperialism became more attractive to Italian politicians and citizens alike, Albania loomed as a lucrative prize, there for the taking.

Italy's first opportunity to finally take offensive action in Albania came during the course of World War I. Although not yet a belligerent, Italy occupied Sazan and Vlora in October 1914 without incurring the wrath of either side because all the major powers courted Rome. Italy's eventual entrance on the side of the Allies concluded a period of rather cynical bargaining, leading to the secret Treaty of London. In exchange for a military contribution against Austria, Italy was pledged extensive territories in Albania, although Rome was required to agree to an eventual division of the remainder of Albania between Montenegro, Serbia, and Greece.[3] During the course of the war, the Italians succeeded in occupying half of the newly formed state (Albania had declared its independence from the Ottoman Empire in 1912) but were forced out in 1920 because of Woodrow Wilson's refusal to recognize the Treaty of London, mounting domestic problems following World War I, armed Albanian opposition, and the Conference of Ambassadors' decision to reestablish an independent Albania. The conference mitigated Italy's Albanian disaster by officially recognizing Italy's prominent interest in Albania.[4]

Still, the removal of Italian forces proved to be unfortunate for the Italians and, at least to a certain extent, for the Albanians as well. The Italian government lost some prestige, and this issue was effectively exploited by Mussolini, providing him with an important stepping stone on his road to power. The Albanians came away from this experience believing that they had ejected the Italians by force of arms and that they could easily do so again. This impression, exploited by Albanian politicians, did much to color the future relations between the Albanians and the Italians.

Mussolini Assumes Power in Italy

With the advent of Benito Mussolini in 1922, Italy's interest in Albania was renewed. Mussolini chose to begin with economic penetration and found a willing partner in Ahmet Zogu, who dominated interwar Albanian politics first as prime minister, then president, and then after 1928 as King Zog. Zog eventually constructed a nonabsolutist monarchy, which was successful in some ways. He was able to forcibly reduce the chaotic lawlessness of the highlands and bring together some of the country's divergent elements. The independence that the northern tribes had enjoyed for centuries was at least partially lost. Many tribesmen were forced to give up their weapons, significantly reducing brigandage and the traditional scourge of Albania: the blood feud. By the 1930s the central government was recognized in all parts of the country, allowing Zog's administration to collect taxes and draft recruits for his army, something that would have been considered impossible immediately after World War I. This degree of political stability, limited though it was, did much to create an environment necessary for the growth of an Albanian national consciousness. Zog significantly contributed to the process of replacing tribal loyalty and local and regional pride with a rudimentary form of modern state nationalism.

But Zog failed miserably in terms of economics. This was partially due to the desperate economic conditions that faced Zog when he came to power in Albania, but his inability to understand modern economics must also be considered a factor. As a result, he found it necessary to rely on foreign aid to survive. When the League of Nations refused to grant a loan, that left only fascist Italy with enough strategic interest and financial resources to make the decidedly poor investment in Zog's regime. Zog asked for aid and Mussolini's government obliged, on the assumption that economic aid would lead to economic and political control and provide Italy with its long-sought Balkan foothold.

The first loan came in the form of an Italian-sponsored company for the development of Albania's resources. The company, called SVEA, loaned the Albanian government a significant sum to be guaranteed by Albanian customs receipts. The company also dictated how the money was to be spent.[5] The cost included an onerous pact of friendship and security that restricted Zog in terms of foreign policy and virtually allowed for Italian intervention in internal affairs as well.[6]

Zog felt that he could take the Italian money and strengthen the Albanian economy to create unity, yet, through subversion, deny the Italians the type of political control they coveted. Zog was not entirely unsuccessful: he received the money, and he kept control of the state. But if this was a victory, it certainly was a Pyrrhic one. First, the money was used unwisely. The roads and bridges constructed from the funds were built primarily for Italian military purposes. The buildings constructed were principally of nonessential types, including ostentatious fascist government buildings and a palace for Zog. Albania's pressing needs, including drainage and canalization and the development of indigenous industry, were completely ignored.[7] In the process Albania effectively became an economic colony, with the Italians exercising considerable political influence as well.[8]

But if nothing else, Zog was a nationalist, and he refused to give in completely to Italian pressure. Mussolini tried threats and more bribes, but Zog stood firm. Ironically, Zog's refusal to surrender Albanian political independence convinced the Italians that the only way they could ever expect to truly possess Albania was through outright invasion. In a sense, then, Zog's successful defense of Albania's political independence ultimately cost Albania its freedom. The task of destroying that independence was left to Count Galeazzo Ciano, the new Italian foreign minister.

In June of 1936, Count Ciano assumed control at the Palazzo Chigi, the Italian Foreign Ministry. The new foreign minister was responsible for infusing the Foreign Ministry with the *tona fascista*—a new aggressive spirit—but also for developing and carrying out an approach to what the Italians were beginning to refer to as the "Albanian problem."

The count was not particularly well suited for the job, being inexperienced and rather irresponsible. He was something of a playboy, not a hard worker, and some ambassadors found him difficult to take seriously. He could not seem to concentrate on any one problem for more than a few moments. His lapses of taste and manners alienated even Hitler, who referred to him as "that disgusting boy."[9] Indeed, Ciano gained the respect of few in the diplomatic field, chiefly because of his exhibitionism, vanity, and lack of discretion. One of Ciano's girlfriends frequently passed important facts immediately to Lord Perth, the British ambassador, and the count's favorite haunt, the Roman Golf Club, was well known to journalists as the best place in Europe for information leaks.[10]

Why Mussolini chose Ciano is clear. Ciano was married to the Duce's daughter, and he did what he was told. He was less subtle and less clever then Mussolini, but showed deference to the Duce as one would to a superior being. The count was so taken with Mussolini that he copied his mannerisms, his deportment, and even his handwriting. The sound of the Duce's voice on the radio would bring him to tears.[11]

This emulation naturally carried over into the conduct of foreign affairs, where the count not only followed Mussolini's orders to the letter (at least until 1943) but worked to instill the ministry with Mussolini's spirit. Like the Duce, Ciano disliked reading dispatches, relying instead on newspapers and spies for the information upon which to base policy. He kept his ambassadors completely in the dark, to the point where Ambassador Dino Grandi in London looked to the British Foreign Office for clues about the direction of Italian foreign policy.[12]

Although the count was rather flippant and inconsistent in terms of policy, he was able to find one project that held his interest and that he eventually came to consider his private reserve: Albania. Ciano's Albanian flirtation began shortly following his first trip to Tirana, the Albanian capital, in April 1937.

Count Ciano Plans the Invasion

The visit itself was rather uneventful, except as an indication of the count's style and boundless energy. Again in an attempt to ape Mussolini, Ciano dramatically flew his own four-motored airplane to Tirana, taking with him a bevy of Foreign Ministry officials and photographers. During his three-day stay, Ciano had numerous audiences with Zog, attended a myriad of banquets, placed a wreath on the tomb of the queen mother, laid cornerstones, and visited villages.[13] More significant, it was during and immediately after this visit that Ciano's plans for Albania began to take shape.

The count's initial actions were quite tame; he did not know exactly what he wanted out of Albania except that a greater Italian presence must be the first step. In August of 1937 Ciano wrote: "I have persuaded the Duce to give sixty millions to Albania over the next four years, for work of various kinds. My visit to Tirana convinced me of the necessity for taking good care of this sector of the front. We must create stable centers of Italian influence there. Who knows what the future will hold in store? We must be ready to seize the opportunities which will present themselves." The count then added significantly: "We are not going to withdraw this time, as we did in 1920. In the south [of Italy] we have absorbed several hundred thousand Albanians. Why shouldn't the same thing happen on the other side of the Adriatic?"[14]

By the beginning of 1938, Ciano seems to have decided that even waiting for opportunities was no longer a reasonable approach; opportunities had to be created. The foreign minister noted that "our penetration is becoming steadily more intense and more organic. The programme which I had traced after my visit is being carried out without a hitch. I am wondering whether the general situation, particularly the *Anschluss*, does not permit us to take a step towards more and more complete domination of this country which will be ours."[15]

It was while Ciano was in Albania attending the wedding of King Zog to the Hungarian countess Geraldine Apponyi in April 1938 that the count finally decided that a radical solution to the Albanian problem was needed.[16] Zog was too clever to fall into a political protectorate through economic pressure; the only way Albania would ever truly become part of Mussolini's resurrected Roman empire was through invasion. Having come to this irrevocable conclusion, Ciano and a large staff of advisers and experts drew up an extensive plan, while still in Tirana, to be presented to the Duce for his approval.

The report, discussed on 10 May 1938, was a well-prepared, detailed analysis of Italy's historical role in Albania, as well as a catalog of what Italy could expect to gain from the action proposed by Ciano. In his report Ciano took advantage of the Duce's weakness for flattery, appealed to him on a rational basis, and played on his worst fears.[17]

The report began by presenting Albania as a worthwhile objective for Italian expansion, based upon highly dubious economic figures. The count described vast opportunities in agriculture, livestock raising, forestry, the fishing industry, and mineral deposits. Here he was clearly playing on the Duce's not particularly successful attempt at autarchy, making Italy self-sufficient so that in case of war it would want for nothing. Ciano also noted that in ancient times Albania had been heavily populated; now it was practically uninhabited, but with proper Italian organization and management the country could provide a home for up to two million Italians.[18]

Ciano assured the Duce that the Italians would be welcomed in Albania because of the unpopularity of Zog's regime, which was described as money grubbing and riddled with nepotism. The flashy extravagance of the royal sisters and the massive expense of the royal wedding were much resented, Ciano reported, and clearly emphasized the vast division between the rich and the poor and the court and the people.

The count contrasted the ill feelings that most Albanians harbored for Zog with the popularity of the Italians. Ciano maintained that apart from the pro-Zog faction at court, "it is worthwhile to underscore that the people of the capital, of the ports and whoever comes in contact with us, are instead in every class and without reticence, pro-Italian. Also in the army, with a few exceptions, the sympathies are with Italy."[19] Ciano's assessment of the Albanian army was true enough, particularly as the Italians had long since taken control of the supply and training of Zog's military. Ciano's comments regarding the rest of the population were absurd, and how he came by them remains a mystery.

Next, the count raised the specter of German hegemony in the Balkans, one of Mussolini's greatest fears. It was known that the Hungarians had shown interest in Albania, and the count pointed out that it ought not be forgotten that Budapest had often been the vanguard of Germanism. He further noted that it would be a mistake to overlook the strong traces of former Austrian influence in Albania and the danger that Germany, reinforced by the *Anschluss* (the German annexation of Austria), presented. Germany might attempt to take and expand the political and economic position that imperial Austria once held.[20]

Ciano was careful to play upon Mussolini's need for glory with several references to Italy's poor military record, and he speculated on how Mussolini was about to bury these bad memories with the proposed action in Albania. The count argued that "in Albania, which belonged to us every so often in history, we seek and we find the natural road to our expansion in the Balkans. . . . In the sixteen years of Mussolinian policy it had been newly joined to Italy by bonds of great importance. This work . . . must find at the opportune moment its culmination in the annexation of Albania by Italy."[21]

Ciano concluded by presenting Mussolini with three options. First, Italy could continue to tighten its economic ties, but, the count suggested, the goal of political domination could not quickly be achieved by this method. The second option, which the count considered personally unsatisfactory, was Albania's partition among its neighbors. The third, and clearly his choice, was outright annexation, which could be easily achieved by playing on the dissensions between the Crown and the masses, fomenting a rebellion or internal crisis, and moving in to restore order.[22]

Ciano's diary tells us that Mussolini immediately agreed about the necessity for a radical solution, and the count noted that the Duce was prepared even to go to war as long as Albania was secured by Italy. Ciano had done well: the specter of Germany frightened the Duce, and the count's theatrics had appealed to him. At one point Ciano had handed the Duce a specimen of copper ore from the mines of Lezhë with the words "here are the Carthaginian figs."[23] Mussolini was forced to take Ciano's word concerning Albania's vast mineral wealth, because, true to the general disorganization of fascist Italy, in all the years Italy had been involved in Albania no one had bothered to conduct a proper geological survey.

Full approval of the plan, however, required a major decision, something from which Mussolini always shied away. He would rather make small, unimportant decisions, for these would not leave him paralyzed by doubt. The Duce, then, seems to have approved the plan in principle but wavered when a final irrevocable decision concerning implementation was needed. While Mussolini agonized over whether or not to invade, Ciano moved ahead with plans to subvert the Albanian government.

In order to reduce the possibility of armed resistance once the full plan was set in motion, the count initiated a program designed to rapidly and substantially increase Italian control over every facet of Albanian life. First, the number of Italian military instructors was to be discreetly increased "with the specific mission to create annexationist cells in the Albanian army."[24] Under the direction of the Italian minister Francesco Jacomoni and Giovanni Giro, an Italian fascist official who was sent to Albania to organize Albanian youth on the fascist model, economic and cultural infiltration was also to be intensified. The number of Albanians on the Italian payroll was to be increased, and the most important people, particularly the tribal chieftains, were to be won over "on a personal basis with expressions of mutual interest, with promises and with corruption."[25]

By June 1938 Giro reported that he had a considerable element of the country under his control. He added that public opinion was steadily rising against Zog and that Italian intervention in the event of a disturbance would meet with no opposition. The common people, Giro continued, would welcome with joy any improvement in material conditions, and the Italians could expect to destroy the desire to resist within three days.[26]

Overjoyed by this news, and not bothering to check the veracity of this extremely overoptimistic information, Ciano proceeded to draw up the next phase of his plan with characteristic fascist vigor. The physical removal of Zog played a key role in this phase. Ciano's first attempt may have been an effort to kidnap both the king and the queen. In early December the royal couple put to sea, along with the minister of foreign affairs and other high officials of the government. Zog had promised Geraldine a short honeymoon trip and felt secure enough to leave the country for a brief time, so they decided to sail to Venice. The vessel and the crew were Italian, something that the count had been adamant about supplying for Zog in June to "guarantee the impossibility of his escape in any eventuality."[27]

Soon after they left the harbor, Geraldine, who was already with child, became ill because of the bad weather, and the doctor who was attending her strongly recommended that the ship return immediately to Durrës, Albania's principal port. The queen, who was in her cabin, recalled, in interviews conducted in the early 1980s, that a good deal of noise and commotion on deck followed this decision and that Zog himself became very nervous. Geraldine maintained that it became known afterward within the royal circle that the Italians had hoped either to murder the king on board or to keep both of them in Italy.[28]

Although no strong evidence exists to support Geraldine's contentions, it is clear that Ciano and Jacomoni did come up with a detailed plan for the assassination of Zog. Jak Koçi, one-time private secretary to the king and the man responsible for procuring women for Zog while he was still a bachelor, offered to carry out the deed for ten million lire.[29] During the 1920s and into the 1930s Koçi was involved in building the relationship between Albania and Italy, and it seems he took his job somewhat too seriously. Ciano met personally with an unnamed Albanian, who certainly was Koçi, on numerous occasions to finalize the plan.[30]

After Zog was dead, so Ciano's scenario ran, the Italians would provoke street fighting and the rebellion of the mountain tribes. The population would turn to Italy to restore order and in gratitude offer the crown to the Italian king, Victor Emmanuel III. Following the offer, Ciano planned to finalize the annexation by conducting a plebiscite, similar to the one conducted by Hitler in Austria at the time of the Anschluss. Jacomoni guaranteed that all this could take place at a month's notice.[31]

The plan was so carefully prepared that Ciano longed to put it into operation. The foreign minister presented the scheme to Mussolini for final approval in early December 1938. The Duce again approved of it in principle but out of rationalism or doubt put a temporary lid on the overzealous count. The international ramifications of such an act did not escape Mussolini. He knew that if the plan were carried out, Italy would most likely drive Yugoslavia into the waiting arms of the Germans. Ciano was forced to slow down and turn his efforts to working out some kind of a partition deal with the Yugoslav prime minister, Milan Stojadinovic.

Although Jacomoni reported after the war to the High Court of Justice that Ciano let the idea of assassination drop at this point, the queen recalled two separate attempts on Zog's life during this period, which, she insisted, were inspired by the Italians. Sometime in early 1939 she was told of an incident in which a rifle had been found on the roof of one of the buildings that lined the park behind the palace.

Geraldine also told an interesting story that apparently involved Koçi, whom she accused of having bribed her Hungarian cook. The rather shaken woman immediately informed the king, who told her to keep the money. Zog thereupon apparently invited the offender to lunch and had the cook make one of Geraldine's least favorite dishes, something on the order of cabbage strudel. The queen took one bite and gasped, whereupon the unfortunate Koçi jumped up, demanding to know what they had eaten. The king, who had not lost his taste for manipulation, exposed the culprit and, somewhat uncharacteristically, spared his life in view of earlier service. Geraldine later said that Zog had Koçi thrown out of the country, although he would later return and serve the Italians.[32]

Zog announced publicly that a plot to overthrow the government and kill the king had been discovered and that the leader, Giovanni Giro, had been asked to leave the country. Giro, whose principal role was as organizer of the fascist "Dopolavoro," or after-work, program, was still unsuccessfully trying to organize an Albanian youth organization along Italian lines. He had long made no secret of his hostility to the regime. It came to the attention of the Albanian government that he had also been organizing those who were disaffected with the monarchy into fascist action committees like the "Lupi di Roma." These groups, principally active in the south, fashioned themselves after the Italian *squadristi* and clashed in the streets with supporters of communism.[33] Perhaps Giro's greatest sin in Zog's eyes, however, was his correspondence with certain Albanian émigrés in Paris, including Zog's old opponent Mustafa Kruja, who with Italian help had attempted to overthrow a government of which Zog was a part in 1922.[34]

Zog ordered his interior minister, the ruthless Musa Juka, to break up the pro-Italian groups. One of Giro's henchmen, the fascist journalist Vasil Alarupi, was detained in Durrës.[35] Four Italophile Albanians were arrested, and gendarmes were dispatched to various areas throughout Albania, including Tepelena and Shkodra. As a final gesture, the king called out the army reservists and loyal tribesmen. Jacomoni, who was not always subtle, warned the king not to interfere in Italian plans.

Zog Becomes Alarmed

By this time, of course, the king was growing alarmed and agitated, having noticed that his relations with Italy had taken a turn for the worse. There had, of course, always been tension between the Albanians and the Italians. Rome regularly sabotaged or strictly directed the loans that had been made to the Albanians, while Zog obstructed the Italians at every turn. Zog was using Italian money to buy goods from the Japanese, and as Mussolini had feared the king had asked the Germans why their economic drive had overlooked Albania.[36]

These dynamics were more or less routine, however, so when Ciano's personal policies began making themselves felt, Zog knew the Italians were up to something and quickly moved to stop them. Zog reasoned that if the Italians were indeed trying to kill him, they would eventually succeed and therefore realized that his only alternative was to attempt to placate them, something that he had been considering. In October 1938 he sent a rather pathetic message to Ciano proclaiming that "Albania now is in Italy's hands, for Italy controls every sector of the national activity. The king is devoted. The people are grateful. Why do you want anything more?"[37] Now, in March 1939, the king called in Jacomoni and declared that he wished to reestablish the most cordial relations with Italy. The Italian minister reported to Ciano that he felt this was just a maneuver to gain time to permit the king to come to some sort of understanding with third powers.

That kind of dealing was, of course, exactly what the king had planned. He mentioned to the British minister Sir Andrew Ryan, in confidence, that he was thinking of turning to the Germans.[38] Geraldine maintained that soon afterward Zog sent personal envoys to Hitler on two occasions and was told each time that only through Mussolini could Zog expect to maintain a free Albania. Aware that he was running out of options, the king, in anger, accused Hitler of not being a patriot, "for no patriot would tell another patriot to go and sell his country."³⁹ Ciano was concerned about Zog's agitation and wanted to move more quickly, particularly because by the middle of February circumstances had allowed him to return to his favorite plan of annexing Albania outright with no compensation for its neighbors.

Following Mussolini's suggestion, the count had gone to Milan Stojadinovic during the middle of January. Ciano had hoped to convince the Yugoslav leader of the advantages of an Italian takeover in Albania, a plan that included a number of northern frontier corrections in Yugoslavia's favor. He argued that after such an action Albania would cease to be the focus of nationalism, thereby reducing the problems concerning Kosova, the Albanian-inhabited area of Serbia. The count also was prepared to promise a military alliance and Italian support for any move Yugoslavia might make against Thessaloníki to assure itself an outlet to the Aegean.⁴⁰

Stojadinovic, who had been forewarned of Ciano's purpose by Bozko Hristic, the Yugoslav minister in Rome, was unhappy with the talk of "correction of frontiers"; he wanted partition. He spoke specifically and covetously of Shkodra, Shëngjin, and more extensive Yugoslav access to the Adriatic, which would be made possible only by the cession of the northern provinces of Albania and the completion of a railroad line.⁴¹

When the Yugoslav regent, Prince Paul, discovered that his prime minister was treating with Ciano concerning the partition of Albania, he was incensed. He was appalled that neither the cabinet nor the regent had been included on such a critical matter, something that would have definitely put Yugoslavia in the Axis camp. More important, Paul, like King Alexander before him, had no desire to increase the size of the Albanian population in Yugoslavia. "We already have so many Albanians inside our frontiers and they give us so much trouble," Prince Paul complained, "that I have no wish to increase their number."⁴²

Stojadinovic, for this and other reasons, was quickly forced out and replaced by Dragisa Cvetkovic, who was not only much closer to the regent and his foreign policy but, more significant, was not known for his friendly attitude toward Italy. After the dust had settled, Ciano was forced to reevaluate his position. He came to two conclusions: first, "to go ahead just the same, with Stojadinovic, partition of Albania between us and Yugoslavia; without Stojadinovic[,] occupation even against Yugoslavia."⁴³ The count also decided that it was now imperative to move as quickly as possible on his Albanian project, and he hoped to begin the project by the first week in April.

Ciano's new urgency stemmed primarily from the knowledge that the Yugoslavs now knew the plan, and he feared that rumors regarding the undertaking would spread far and quickly. The count also feared that the pro-Western Cvetkovic might move closer to Britain and France and perhaps attempt to come to some understanding with the Albanians.

Jacomoni presented additional reasons for quick action, including the increased demands for payments from tribal chieftains with which he was being besieged. The Italian minister also suggested that the local leaders might become suspicious of Italian hesitation and use the knowledge of their subversive activities to force Zog to change his mode of governing. Finally, Jacomoni argued that a number of exiles were about to be allowed back into Albania, and Italy should move before they could effectively build a patriotic movement of resistance against the Italians.[44]

Mussolini agreed with Ciano's assessment concerning the Yugoslavs but would not be hurried into the Albanian project. The Duce would not move without the successful conclusion of the Spanish Civil War and the signing of a pact with the Germans. Mussolini's decision must have come as another disappointment not only because Ciano's plan was again delayed but also because by mid-February rumors of some impending Italian move were becoming rather widespread, causing Ciano no little embarrassment. To counter these stories the foreign minister decided, "We must spread the most varied rumors; like the octopus we must darken the waters."[45]

Ciano could do little else but wait for another opportunity to convince the Duce that to hesitate any longer was not in the best interests of the Italian empire. The German occupation of Prague on 15 March 1939 finally offered the count another chance. Mussolini's initial reaction to the German move was a combination of uncertainty and fear.

Ciano, on the other hand, perceived the German move as a cause to take Albania. Germans troops in Prague led the count to one of his first outbursts of indignation against the Germans, asking rhetorically at one point "Is it worthwhile to deal loyally with such people?" He added, "It is useless to hide that all this bothers and humiliates the Italian people. It is necessary to give them satisfaction and compensation: Albania."[46]

By 23 March the count had finally convinced the Duce to support an immediate drastic change in Italy's relationship with Albania. Ciano was able to do this by resurrecting the specter of the German menace as well as by presenting Mussolini with notes of a meeting between Zog and Jacomoni in which the king implied that he might be willing to grant Rome further concessions.

The last remaining holdout to Ciano's "final solution" was Victor Emmanuel. The Italian king informed Mussolini frankly that he was not in agreement with the new policy on Albania because he did not see the point of risking such a venture in order to "grab a few rocks." Perhaps Victor Emmanuel simply did not approve of the dethroning of another king, although he had already participated in the process once in Ethiopia and had once referred to Zog as little more than "the better bandit," unworthy of a member of the House of Savoy as a bride. Either way, the Duce, who was now confirmed in his decision, ignored Victor Emmanuel, informing Ciano that "if Hitler had to deal with a nincompoop of a king he would never have been able to take Austria and Czechoslovakia."[47]

Although Mussolini had finally agreed to Ciano's basic idea for a solution, he would not support unadulterated annexation. He hoped instead to attempt to subordinate Albania by the construction of irreversible political, economic, and military bonds between the two countries. The Duce himself drew up the form of the ultimatum to Zog, which Ciano described as "very brief consisting of three dry clauses which gave it more the appearance of a reprieve than of an international pact."[48] The count, in conjunction with Leonardo Vitetti, director general of the Office of General Affairs in the Foreign Ministry, came up with his own proposal, which had the advantage of being couched in courteous terms. The Duce eventually approved.

The count's document consisted of eight major sections, including (1) a rigorous defensive alliance, (2) the promise of Italian military aid in case of any external threat to Albanian territory, (3) permission for the Italian government to intervene to restore public order, (4) the concession to Italy of free use of ports, air fields, and communication lines, (5) the elevation of the status of the Italian Legation to embassy, (6) provision for Italian financial and technical assistance in each Albanian ministry, (7) the dismantling of customs barriers between the two nations, and (8) the extension of the rights of Italian citizenship to Albanians and vice versa. Ciano further required concessions regarding fascist organizations in Albania, as well as the introduction of Italian organizers into the gendarmerie.[49]

Ciano believed that Zog would likely capitulate. He noted cynically in his diary: "There is, above all, a fact on which I am counting: the coming birth of Zog's child. Zog loves his wife very much, as well as his whole family. I believe that he will prefer to insure to his dear ones a quiet future. And frankly I cannot imagine Geraldine running around fighting through the mountains of Unthi or the Mirdizu in her ninth month of pregnancy."[50]

Meanwhile in Albania, because of continuing rumors of troop movements and ultimatums, Zog and his government were confronted with ever increasing requests for information, primarily from the diplomatic corps. Albanian government officials denied that the situation was serious; most of them did so honestly because Zog handled these negotiations personally. Zog was aware that most of those around him were being paid by the Italians. As late as 30 March, the Albanian minister of foreign affairs would not admit that there were any serious problems between Albania and Italy or that Albania was menaced. He would not even speak of financial difficulties. Jacomoni informed the British minister, Sir Andrew Ryan, that although financial difficulties existed, Italy's best course would be to respect Albanian independence and to work with and through the Albanian regime.[51] All of this seems to have convinced Ryan that there was little cause for alarm.[52]

The king, too, probably for reasons of fear, had become much quieter since his complaints against Italy, and Giro in particular, in February. On 25 March, during a formal audience with Ryan, he said only that he intended to pursue a "good" policy toward Italy, subject to two things: independence and integrity.[53]

This was, of course, exactly what Ciano hoped to seize from Albania with his ultimatum. Zog could not accept, yet he feared Italian reaction if he did not. The king fell back upon one of his favorite tactics: playing for time. On 28 March Zog informed Ciano that he supported the demands but that his ministers refused to go along, an obvious ruse that did not fool even Ciano. By 31 March, the Italian foreign minister decided that Zog had indeed refused to sign.[54]

The count, however, was prevented from initiating his long-hoped-for hostilities by military considerations, of which he became aware on 31 March. Military preparations had begun shortly before the ultimatum was presented to Zog. Four regiments of *bersaglieri* (specially trained mountain troops), one regular infantry division, air force detachments, and all of the first naval squadron had been ordered mobilized and concentrated at Apulia. Soon thereafter an additional division as well as a battalion of tanks were ordered mobilized at the suggestion of Marshal Pietro Badoglio, past and future chief of the general staff, who nevertheless continued to oppose the invasion.

Despite the impressive numbers, the deficiencies of this force soon became clear to both Ciano and Jacomoni after talks with General Alberto Pariani, the chief of staff, and General Alfredo Guzzoni, who was to commander the invasion forces.[55] It appears that organizational problems prevented the Italian army from gathering something as simple as a battalion of trained motorcycle troops. Unforeseen problems with disembarkation further complicated the enterprise and forced Ciano to take another look at the entire undertaking.[56]

Apprehensive about the possibility of either an unsuccessful or a badly executed landing, Ciano moved closer to the option of taking Albania with Zog rather than against him. In conjunction with the Duce, the count drew up a new set of conditions that Zog was expected to accept, since they supposedly allowed the king to save face. These new demands were somewhat less onerous than the first set and included (1) control of all ports, communications, roads, and airfields in the event it appeared that Albanian independence was in danger; (2) an Italian organizer in each Albanian ministry who would have the rank of minister ranking immediately below the Albanian minister; (3) Italians in Albania would have equal civil and political rights with the Albanians; (4) the raising of the Italian Legation in Tirana and the Albanian Legation in Rome to the status of embassies.[57]

Following the presentation of these demands, Jacomoni made it clear to Zog that the situation was now extremely serious. The king was given a simple choice. If he accepted the demands, Ciano would go to Tirana to attend the solemn ceremony of signing the treaty, accompanied by a strong squadron of planes to emphasize the new relationship. If he refused, disorder would break out on 6 April, followed by the landing of Italian forces on 7 April.[58]

The king, recognizing that the Italians had taken a step backward, or perhaps fearing that the time had come for international help, finally broke his silence, informing the American minister not only of the Italian demands but of his specific reaction to these demands. In regard to the first demand, Zog had informed the Italian minister that only after previous agreement and in case he, the king, requested it, would he agree to the landing of Italian troops in Albania. Zog refused the second demand, and as to the third, he agreed only to extend civil rights to the Italians. He would not consent to allow Italians to be elected to Parliament or to own land. The king saw no difficulty with the fourth point. Zog further mentioned, however, that because some of his ministers had asked that he reconsider, he had asked Jacomoni for more time.[59]

The tense situation had, in the meantime, slowly made itself felt among the population of Tirana. On the evening of 1 April there was a demonstration in Tirana, nationalist and anti-Italian. On the night of 2 April, a larger, probably less spontaneous, and more definitely pro-Zog and anti-Italian disturbance took place. The king had clearly decided by this time that Italy meant to invade, and he hoped that the demonstrations would encourage the Italians to reconsider or at least generate substantial nationalist resistance to the invader. Within two days, Zog ordered general mobilization and the evacuation of the Durrës civilian population, which apparently was never fully achieved.

Although somewhat pessimistic about the possibility of a negotiated settlement, Zog nevertheless intended to keep all possible channels open and worked feverishly to come up with an acceptable set of counterproposals. Motivated by the new slim hope of saving Albania, and by the fact that Queen Geraldine was on the verge of giving birth to his heir, Zog presented Ciano with a revised plan on 2 April, incorporating the few acceptable points of the Italian ultimatum. The king agreed to certain demands but still refused to accept any proposal that he deemed incompatible with the independence and integrity of Albania. Finally, the king asked that General Pariani, the only Italian who had gained the respect of the Albanians, be sent to Albania to discuss the question at issue. Pariani had served as military attaché in Albania in the 1930s and was one of the few Italian officials who had made a good impression.

Zog's proposals were ignored. Despite the continuing military difficulties, Ciano had regained his nerve and it only remained to create the proper impression internationally. In the pursuance of this end, the foreign minister directed that all Italian civilian personal and their families prepare to leave Albania. Ciano announced to the world that such a move had become necessary because Italian lives were in danger, a claim so blatantly ridiculous that it was greeted with scorn by the diplomatic community in Tirana. The Duce shared Ciano's impatience with Zog, and as a result he decided on 2 April to proceed with the invasion if Zog remained intransigent.

From an international perspective, the time was right for Mussolini; Madrid had fallen, and although Mussolini had not yet concluded his pact with the Germans, Hans Georg von Mackensen, the German ambassador in Rome, reacted favorably when informed of the invasion plans.[60] British prime minister Neville Chamberlain's actions in March and early April confirmed Mussolini's ideas concerning Western inertia. On 23 March the Duce received a letter from Chamberlain expressing concern and requesting the Duce's aid in maintaining international peace. Chamberlain's statement in Parliament on 6 April served to significantly build the confidence of the fascist leadership.

The prime minister noted that with regard to Albania, the British government had "no direct interest, but a general interest in the peace of the world."[61] Despite reports now arriving from many quarters concerning Italian mobilization, Chamberlain did not feel that it was a propitious time to draw the attention of the Italian government to the fact that the occupation or annexation of Albania would violate the Anglo-Italian Agreement of 1938, which called for the maintenance of the status quo in the Mediterranean. To emphasize his lack of concern, the prime minister left on the evening of 6 April for a ten-day holiday in Scotland.

The same morning Zog had been presented with a personal telegram from Mussolini fixing the expiration of the ultimatum at noon. The king refused to accept but referred the matter to his ministers and a committee in Parliament. The Italians gave him six more hours. While he waited he granted the American minister an audience, which had been set up some time before. Zog seemed by this time to have resigned himself to his fate. He referred with bitterness to the fact that the Italians decided to launch their offensive at the very moment when his wife was giving birth. Minister Hugh Grant noted that the king gave the impression of a man who felt bitter disappointment for what he considered a gross betrayal by the Italians as well as the rest of the world. On 5 April, he had appealed to the democracies and on 6 April, to the Balkan Entente, all, of course, to no avail.[62]

During the course of 6 April, warships appeared off Durrës and Vlora to embark the last of the Italian civilians. In the afternoon dozens of Italian planes passed over Tirana, dropping leaflets instructing the population to refuse obedience to their government and not to resist the Italians. The leaflets added that Italian forces would remain as long as necessary for the reestablishment of peace, order, and justice. While the planes were flying overhead, a tremendous demonstration by a crowd of several thousand Albanians was staged in the principal square in Tirana. Hundreds of young men cried for arms with which to defend the country. According to Geraldine, Zog refused, fearing that much innocent blood would be shed. In the evening a special cabinet and parliamentary meeting voted to reject the Italian demands and to resist with force the landing of Italian troops, while at the same time appealing to the Italians for further talks.[63] But the atmosphere was one of gloom. Independence would be lost in either case.

Mussolini, who continued to vacillate, had not yet given up hope for a negotiated settlement, although it could now only be achieved after the initial landing. The Duce told Zog to send his negotiators to Guzzoni once the Italian force had landed in Albania. Late on 6 April he sent the following orders to Guzzoni: "If tomorrow morning a spokesman for Zog presents himself at the moment of disembarkation, listen to him and notify me by telegram. If instead no one asks to confer with you, execute the disembarkation smashing whatever resistance."[64] Meanwhile the general was ordered to proceed with the invasion.

The Italian Invasion of Albania

At 5:30 on the morning of 7 April, Good Friday, some twenty-two thousand troops supported by some four hundred aircraft, three hundred small tanks, and dozens of warships attacked Durrës, Vlora, Shëngjin, and Saranda.[65] With few exceptions, the Albanian army did not respond, but this should not be surprising; it was small and underequipped. Officially, it consisted of fifteen thousand in 1938, but it is doubtful that more than eight thousand were in uniform at any given time, a figure further reduced to four thousand during the winter. This numerical weakness was exacerbated by the fact that by 1939 most of the army's training personal were Italians, who had effectively removed the desire to fight. Still, major fighting took place at Durrës, where the townspeople and a small contingent of troops sent from Tirana opposed the invasion. Some of these troops consisted of members of the three-thousand-man gendarmerie, who seemed more eager to resist, possibly because they were trained and led by retired British officers until the late 1930s.[66] The defenders, led by Durrës gendarmerie commander Abaz Kupi, although vastly outnumbered and limited to fifty rounds of ammunition per man, managed to beat back the Italians.

After the invaders had retired, the ships opened fire using shrapnel to disperse the resistance. Instead of retreating, Kupi and his men moved forward and lined a parapet closer to the water's edge. Their courage was to no avail, however, since the attackers landed again in larger numbers with a flanking party. Kupi and his men were overcome by sheer weight of numbers, and after inflicting a good many casualties they retreated into town.

For two or three hours street fighting occurred throughout Durrës, although it was soon brought to an abrupt end after a transport disembarked a large number of small tanks. By nine o'clock all effective resistance in Durrës had ended, and the Albanian survivors were either having coffee in civilian clothes in the cafés or making their way along the road out of the town toward Tirana in the hopes of finding somewhere a few more rounds of ammunition with which to shoot another Italian or two before the inevitable end.[67]

Reports on the number of casualties differed rather significantly. The townspeople of Durrës maintained that the Italians lost four hundred. Although Italian propaganda claimed that Italy lost only twelve men in the entire invasion, it is possible that approximately two hundred Italians were killed at Durrës alone and that they may have lost as many as seven hundred in all.[68] Albanian casualties may have been higher.

There was no important resistance at the port of Vlora, but Italian cyclists were ambushed on the road outside the town and suffered some casualties. A party of some forty men opposed the landing at Shëngjin with no more than six or seven casualties on each side. The road to Tirana was open on all sides.

During the afternoon, however, Guzzoni's triumphant march ground to a halt and had to be delayed for six hours, much to the chagrin of Mussolini and

Ciano. Indeed, Ciano was horrified that the delay would result in the impression that the Albanians had stopped the Italians.[69] But the Italians themselves were responsible. Despite Guzzoni's able improvisations, the serious weaknesses in the Italian military machine had made themselves felt and it became clear to all involved, including the Duce, that had it not been for the lack of organized resistance, the Italians might have been faced with a military disaster. As Ciano's chief assistant, Filippo Anfuso, who accompanied the count on his flight over the battle zone for campaign medals put it, "If only the Albanians had possessed a well-armed fire brigade, they could have driven us back into the Adriatic."[70]

The organization of the entire expedition had been inadequate, partially because the commanders were given little time to prepare. Pariani was told on 29 March that Albania would most likely be invaded and the operational commander, General Guzzoni, was not told until late in the day on 31 March. Even more remarkable, the air force did not receive its orders until two days before the invasion. As a result of these serious oversights, once the Italians reached Albania, they were seriously handicapped by badly trained, inadequately equipped, and poorly led men.

Guzzoni was forced to mobilize his own corps during a hurried train trip down to Brindisi. As a result, the conscripts to be used were given no more than a few hours' notice, not enough time to learn how to operate the weapons that they were expected to use. Many conscripts were attached to motorcycle companies without knowing how to ride, while others joined signal units without knowledge of Morse code.[71] A British observer gives us an interesting picture of the Italian troops sent to Albania. While they apparently behaved well, they were sad specimens. Very young and in poor physical condition, the troops were at least imperfectly trained. Their uniforms, rifles, machine guns, and tanks were of poor quality.[72] The Albanians were overwhelmed but hardly impressed.

A paucity of important information both before and during the invasion added to the difficulties. Although the Italians had built the port installations at Durrës, the naval commanders were not told that the main harbor could not accommodate deepwater ships. Radio communications were so defective that the senior air force officer had to fly back and forth between Albania and Italy carrying messages to explain what was going wrong. He reported with astonishment on the lack of unity of command, adding that if the authorities had remembered to use air reconnaissance first, the Italians would have learned that little resistance was to be expected.[73]

The Italian propaganda machine was thrown into action to mask the blunders. Official accounts reported that the attack would remain in history as a classic masterpiece of efficiency, organization, power, courage, and political sense. Colonel Emilio Canevari, the best known of the military commentators, reported the brilliant attack of nonexistent motorized formations in close contact with the air force, and he explained that all observers were impressed by the clockwork precision of a carefully studied and brilliantly executed plan.[74]

All of this naturally came as a pleasant surprise to the operational commanders, who might have expected court-martials. They were delighted to learn that fascism expected no better of them.[75] Many people were aware of the bungling, however, and Mussolini was forced to make a frank statement to the leadership, explaining that the expedition had nearly failed because the organization and the people at his disposal were so defective. In one sense at least, the bungled invasion did the fascist leadership a great service; it made clear to them how totally unprepared Italy was to fight a major war.

Fortunately for the Italians, their mistakes were met with inactivity on the part of Zog, his government, and his army. No serious preparations for resistance were made; no leadership was offered. Zog behaved less than capably in this final crisis. The king's first concern on that fateful day was for the safety of his family. Initially it had been suggested by members of Geraldine's family that the queen and her two-day-old son, Crown Prince Leka, seek refuge in the American Legation. Hugh Grant, the U.S. minister, was approached and readily gave his consent.[76] There was some question about the queen's health, because she had not fully recovered from the cesarean birth of Leka.

At the last moment, Geraldine was pronounced healthy enough to travel and was sent off in an ambulance at 4:00 A.M., one and one-half hours before the invasion. The caravan of cars that accompanied the royal family snaked its way slowly through southern Albania toward the Greek frontier.

After the queen was safely away, Zog moved to his prime minister's residence and from there broadcast a radio message to his subjects, urging them to continue to fight until every drop of blood was exhausted. Few Albanians owned radios, so few heard the appeal; even fewer were willing to die for Zog. In the meantime, the king made a final effort to come to a negotiated settlement with the Italians, sending emissaries to Guzzoni as Mussolini had suggested. Close to noon, Zog sent Rrok Geraj, minister of national economy, as well as Colonel Sami Koka, under the protection of the Italian military attaché, to talk with the Italians at Durrës. After these last talks proved fruitless, the king made a fateful decision; he would follow his wife into exile.

The queen informed me that Zog had planned to withdraw into the hills to continue resistance activities on a guerrilla warfare level, despite the suggestion on the part of the government that he save himself by leaving the country. The king was persuaded to abandon the idea, however, once the Yugoslav position had been made clear. According to the queen, Belgrade informed Zog that if he withdrew into the hills they would not only block his retreat but would actually step in to stop Albanian nationalist agitation on their borders.[77]

Although Geraldine may have overstated the case somewhat, the dubious attitude of the Yugoslav government certainly played a role in the king's decision. Knowing that organized resistance could be sustained for only a short time, the king would eventually have been forced to escape into Yugoslavia. If Belgrade closed its frontiers, which was more than likely, the king and his supporters could easily have been rounded up. Geraldine told her biographer that a decisive factor in Zog's flight was Parliament's decision that Zog leave. Robyns writes that "it was not his decision but parliament's."[78] If nothing else, this contention demonstrates a lack of understanding of Zog's dictatorship.

The fact that Albania was capable of little more than token resistance must also have been considered by Zog. The army, because of the substantial Italian influence and the fact that Rome had always emphasized numbers rather than quality, could not be counted on to be of much use to either side. Indeed, as we have seen, the Albanian military seems to have played only a minor role in the invasion.

This left only the tribesmen to carry on the fight, many of whom Zog had disarmed and who would have been, as a result, not only outnumbered but also vastly outgunned. Although some of them might have fought for Zog—certainly his own tribe of Mati—it soon became clear, given the handicaps for which Zog himself was primarily responsible, that the severe shortage of guns, ammunition, and organization would have quickly crippled Albania's organized resistance capabilities. It is also at least conceivable that Zog, after years of sparring with the Italians, with no help in sight, simply did not have enough energy to carry on the fight. Clearly he was not dedicated to the idea of resistance. Although this decision certainly saved a great many lives, it created a good deal of controversy.

The Aftermath of the Invasion and Foreign Reaction

The king's critics have roundly condemned him for his flight to Greece, accusing him of deserting his country. German documents even maintain that Zog may have spread rumors that Tirana was to be bombed, in order to clear the streets and cover his escape on horseback.[79] Whereas this is likely, it is perhaps an exaggeration to claim, as does socialist Albanian historiography, that he fled only after undermining preparations for armed resistance.[80] The act of fleeing was damaging enough. It is clear that whatever popularity he had had was lost by this uncharacteristic act. Had he remained and appeared, for example, at Durrës, or had he put up some token resistance in the hills, he might have welded the Albanians together, although the wide social and economic gap that blocked the development of the cohesive social order required to withstand invasion made this unlikely.[81] And he would have been overcome in the end by the numerical superiority of the Italians in any case. Still, any hostile action toward the invader would have at least allowed King Zog to make a more positive impression on Albanian history. As it was, with their country invaded and their king gone, most Albanians resigned themselves to the inevitable.

The disappearance of the king and the collapse of resistance allowed the Italians, moving inland from their beachheads in four columns, to take Tirana on the morning of 8 April, basically without firing a shot. The Albanian garrison in Tirana had deposited its weapons in the garden of the Italian Legation.[82] At about 10:30 A.M. Italian soldiers on motorcycles followed by small tanks entered the Tirana square. There were few people in the streets and even fewer in the various ministries, since most of the government had left with the king. Only the doorkeepers and a few subordinate officers, who did not try to conceal their bitterness, remained behind awaiting the invader.

Ciano, displaying his usual, presumably fascist inspired, energy, flew to Tirana shortly after the arrival of the Italian advance troops, eagerly expecting the festive welcome that he had been guaranteed by one of his personal agents. He was disappointed, for only a few turned out to welcome him. He was met at the airport by General Guzzoni and the air force chief, General Giuseppe Valle, who were anxious to explain what had gone wrong with the attack. Jacomoni was there as well, because the Italians had been so confident of success that they had not bothered to evacuate their mission. Accompanied by General Zef Sereqi, King Zog's chief aide and the last Albanian minister to Rome, Ciano arrived at Tirana city hall at noon and was met by Dr. Mihal Sherko, secretary general of the Albanian Ministry of Foreign Affairs as well as Xhafer Bey Ypi, the former prime minister and chief inspector of the court. The thoroughly disreputable former archbishop of the Albanian Orthodox Church, Vissarion, whom Zog had fired for leading a scandalous life, gave a short speech to a small crowd gathered in front of the city hall and urged cooperation with the Italians.[83] His talk was not well received.

Italian propaganda reported that the Albanians were wildly enthusiastic about the Italian invasion, an assertion that has no foundation in fact, although there were some Albanians, including those who met Ciano on his arrival, who deserted their country. Other notable examples of treachery include the case of the ex-prefect of Durrës, Marco Kodheli, who fled to Bari on 6 April to broadcast statements condemning Zog and calling for a warm welcome for the Italians. Kodheli returned to Albania on the day of the invasion to resume his duties.[84] The king's own aide, General Sereqi, resigned his post as minister in Rome shortly before the invasion and returned to Albania in the company of Ciano. Sereqi had been promised a significant role in the Italian puppet state.

There were also, of course, many petty opportunists who saw the coming of the Italians as a means by which to make a few lire. A particularly distressing example of this sort of individual must be the Durrës tailor Reuf Xhuli, whom Ryan discovered making Italian flags out of calico on the day the Italians marched in.[85]

But there were as many examples of individual heroism. Abaz Kupi, who was never a staunch supporter of Zog, not only led the resistance in Durrës but went on to organize a respectable guerrilla movement that the Italians were never able to completely destroy. Showing equal bravery, but in another way, the ex-prime minister Mehdi Bey Frashëri took it upon himself to broadcast scathing attacks against the invasion as well as address a remonstrance to Mussolini. Following the departure of the government from Tirana, he urged young men with revolvers to distribute themselves to preserve order. When the invading troops were at the gates he sought asylum in the Turkish Legation, continuing to refuse to sign a declaration in support of the Italians. His personal courage impressed even the German minister, who successfully appealed to Rome to allow Frashëri to return home unmolested.[86] Despite Italian guarantees, Frashëri was soon arrested and interned in Italy.

Apart from these few exceptions, general public opinion in Tirana varied from indifference to open resentment. Many Albanians may have opposed Zog's regime but it does not follow that they would welcome Italian rule, particularly since one of their general grievances had always been that Zog had given too much away to the Italians. Privately, Ciano was not oblivious to the attitude of the Albanians, noting in his diary, "There is a certain amount of coolness, especially among the high school students. I see that they dislike raising their arms for the Roman salute and there are some who openly refused to do it even when their companions urge them. . . . I see the eyes of some patriots flaming with anger and tears running down their faces. Independent Albania is no more."[87]

With the invasion accomplished, Mussolini's next move was to do whatever he could to defuse international opposition and justify the invasion. Virginio Gayda, Mussolini's unofficial mouthpiece opened the campaign in his paper the *Giornale d'Italia* with a personal attack on Zog:

> And more and more the King governed like a feudal lord, inconsiderate of the most elemental needs of the people, greedy of money for his personal whims, ambitious, irresponsible and fomenting both internal discord and international intrigue. The implacable enemy of all Albanians not members of his political clientele, he had in large measure, transformed the generous Italian policy of financial and economic assistance into a quasi-exclusive preserve to be doled out again by way of his personal exchequer.
>
> Notwithstanding the treaties and the frequent Italian complaints, the Albanian people were the last to profit from Italian generosity. The protests of Albanian patriots and the attempts at revolt of the poor and needy populace were alike silenced by the threat of arms.
>
> A general discontent ranged around the royal house in Tirana. In these last days King Ahmet Zog had requested from the Italian government new gifts as well as personal protection and the dispatch of troops to garrison certain points in Albania. But at the last moment, the Italian government learned that these forces were intended to serve for a foolish coup de main of the King against Kosovo with the evident intent of disturbing the tranquility and cordiality of Italo-Yugoslav collaboration.[88]

The editor of the *Lavoro fascista* attempted to rationalize the invasion on the basis of state security, arguing that "at a time when all the democracies are extending and attempting to extend their frontiers in all the regions of Europe and Africa, where no real and natural interest calls them, Italy could not neglect for her safety's sake, the adjacent coast."[89]

In the same vein, the *Popolo di Roma* commented that "it is enough to look at a map of Italy to understand what supreme necessity of legitimate defense obliges Italy to take her precautions in the Adriatic. . . . In the case of war against anyone, the sure military possession of the Albanian coast is for Italy a question of life and death."[90]

Italy's official explanation, as presented by Ciano in a forty-minute speech before the Chamber of Fasces and Corporations on 15 April, merely restated the comments of the press. In the presence of Reichsminister Hermann Göring, as well as a number of Albanian delegates, the count, beginning sometime prior to the Punic Wars, traced the historical ties between the Italian and Albanian people. Relations were described as very friendly until the advent of Zog. In spite of Zog's constant animosity, Mussolini had been good enough to continue the flow of goods, services, and goodwill to the ever grateful Albanian people. The count was careful to itemize the various benefits that Rome had bestowed on Tirana.[91]

Ciano argued that it was Zog himself who, realizing that disorder and dissension within the country had reached too great a level, had asked the fascist government for troops and arms to quell the unrest. Popular opinion, not Italian soldiers, had forced Zog to flee, according to the count. Less than a week earlier Ciano had tried to convince Lord Perth that Zog had asked Rome for aid in order to launch an attack on Yugoslavia.[92] Sir A. Noble at the Southern Department of the Foreign Office minuted on Perth's report, "Count Ciano is a liar, and a clumsy liar at that."[93]

None of this was, of course, taken very seriously, and the only support Ciano received, both for his speech and for his invasion, came from quarters from which little else could have been expected. The Hungarian press took a purely Italian view of the events in Albania. *Pester Lloyd* even went so far as to comment that Zog bore a heavy responsibility for the fate of his unhappy Hungarian wife. The Vatican's *Osservatore romano* fully supported the move, and the apostolic delegate to Albania asked Sir Andrew Ryan, who was a Catholic, if he was not pleased now that Albanians could convert to Catholicism without fear of government pressure.[94]

The Germans lent Italy full support, despite Italian attempts to conceal the operation from Berlin until the last minute. An editorial in the *Völkischer Beobachter* on 8 April accused Zog of ill-treatment of his people and the exploitation of Italian generosity, which was, of course, quite true. But much was made of the story that Zog was planning to use Italian troops in a move against Yugoslavia, in spite of the fact that the German minister in Tirana reported to Berlin that the story of Zog's projected attack on Yugoslavia was pure fiction.[95]

The official German communiqué released on the same day noted that "Germany had the fullest understanding for the protection of Italian interests in this area and would not be able to understand or approve if the Democratic Western Powers, who have no interest there, should wish to interfere in the juridically unexceptional position and action of our Axis partners."[96]

Albania's Balkan neighbors, although less willing to accept Italian explanations, were too frightened to offer open opposition. Yugoslavia was given twelve hours' notice and took the time to ready two divisions but remained quiet during and after the invasion, seemingly satisfied with the Duce's pledge that Italy was disinterested in the Albanians of Kosova. The Greek minister in London, Charolambos Simopoulos, refused to accept any of Ciano's explanations, expressing complete skepticism about the stories of Zog's project to attack Yugoslavia and of important Albanian chieftains' having asked Mussolini to intervene.[97] Because the Greek government was concerned about Corfu, however, no strong reaction was forthcoming.

Only the Turks refused to accept the new situation and continued to grant the usual diplomatic privileges and immunities to the Albanian minister and his staff. The Turkish government took the view that Zog's rule had only been interrupted, because he had not abdicated. Apart from Turkey, the invasion was met with little more than gloom and misgivings in the Balkans.

In the West, the denunciation of the Italian action was widespread and noisy. Newspapers of the Right, Center, and Left alike condemned with extreme severity the attack on Albania. Without exception they considered it a brutal and cynical act of unprovoked aggression in direct violation of the Italo-Albanian Agreement of 1927 as well as the Anglo-Italian Agreement of 1938.

In Paris the invasion was considered a menace both to France and Great Britain, especially for the latter in view of the Anglo-Italian Agreement. As a result, both the newspapers and the government showed, as they had in the past, a definite tendency to look to London for some sort of a lead. Several papers, including the Social Radical *Ere nouvelle,* criticized Great Britain for its complacent attitude toward Italy in the Mediterranean.[98]

This criticism was not misplaced, for London proved that Mussolini's lack of concern for the reaction of the democracies was well founded. The first British reaction seems to have been embarrassment that they had been taken by surprise. Despite some Secret Intelligence Service (SIS) hints, on 3 April Sir A. Noble still believed that Italy was not about to move against Albania, and two days later in a cabinet meeting Foreign Secretary Viscount Halifax agreed. Following the invasion, Chamberlain took the Italian action personally, writing his sister, "It cannot be denied that Mussolini had behaved to me like a sneak and a cad."[99]

The official Foreign Office reaction turned out to be a good deal milder than the indignation expressed in the Western press. Both Lord Perth and Lord Halifax advised against a strong reaction, fearing that Italy would only be driven into greater reliance on Germany as a result.[100] The prime minister, who hurried back from Scotland for the occasion, approved this attempt to appease Mussolini and as a result allowed the Anglo-Italian agreement to remain in force without even denouncing Italy's violation of it. The mild British reaction surprised even Ciano, who noted in his diary that the memorandum from Lord Perth to the Italian government might have been composed in the offices of the Italian Foreign Ministry.[101]

Ciano noted happily in his diary on 10 April, "Reaction abroad begins to lessen. It is clear above all that the British protests are more for domestic consumption than anything else."[102] As a final step in Britain's acceptance of the Italian action, London applied to the Italian government for an executor for a new consul general on 31 October 1939 and thereby gave de facto and de jure recognition to the Italian invasion.[103] Still it is an overstatement to suggest, as Enver Hoxha does in his memoirs, that the British encouraged Italy to occupy Albania.[104]

Although the Italian invasion violated the sovereignty of Albania, guaranteed by the League of Nations Covenant, the reaction of that body to the outrage made it amply clear how completely impotent the league had become. Because no nation complained to the league, the issue was not even discussed until the Albanian chargé in Paris, Mehmed Abid, who had been instructed by Zog to do so, sent a letter denouncing the aggression and requested an immediate meeting of the Council of the League to decide about aid to be given Albania.

The secretary general, Joseph Avenol, answered that because the request had not come either from the Albanian government itself or through its accredited representative in Geneva, he could not consider it as an appeal under the covenant. On 13 May, the secretary received a letter from King Zog, who asked for help in the reestablishment of Albanian independence. Avenol read the letter to the Council of the League and "added that the reading of the letter constituted the action he intended to take with reference thereto."[105] Under Italy's direction, Albania withdrew from the league on 14 April 1939.

Despite the difficulties that the Italians had encountered during their invasion of Albania, the leadership was delighted with the outcome and immediately looked to the future. To the German ambassador and the visiting Hungarian premier and foreign minister, Ciano exuberantly described Albania as a great bulwark from which Italy would dominate the Balkans. Mussolini immediately began to lay plans for using Albanians to stir up unrest among their conationals in Yugoslavia and Greece, in anticipation of a more aggressive foreign policy in the Balkans. By May 1939 the Duce seems to have focused this new enthusiasm on Greece, whose defeat he saw as a means by which to further expand his new Roman empire, as well as to drive the British from the eastern Mediterranean. Just as the subjugation of Albania had created an Italian lake out of the Adriatic, so the fall of Greece would turn the eastern Mediterranean into an Italian sea.[106]

Western European leaders seem to have interpreted Ciano's invasion in a similar light. Despite initial widespread complacency, Zog and the Albanian people seem to have been the last victims of appeasement, for the West drew something of a line at this point. A few days after the invasion, President Franklin Roosevelt made his first serious intervention into European politics by inviting Hitler and Mussolini to give assurances that they would not attack a list of twenty-nine countries for ten years. More important, Britain and France immediately moved to guarantee Greece and Romania against aggression. In Athens the British ambassador delivered to the Greek government unconditional guarantees that London would not allow Corfu or any other part of Greece to be taken by the Italians.

Ten days later the British announced the introduction of compulsory military training, a move that seemed to mark a fundamental change in London's foreign policy. Soon after this significant development, London signed a pact with Ankara. In a sense, then, events in Albania marked an important stage in the process by which a coalition gradually developed to destroy fascism.[107] It can be argued that Albania's sacrifice was not in vain, although the Albanians would probably not have been consoled by the knowledge.

CHAPTER 2

THE CONSTRUCTION OF AN ITALIAN ALBANIA

The Albania of 1939, which Ciano intended to make bloom and Mussolini hoped to use as a bulwark, presented a considerable challenge. There certainly had been some development since independence in 1912, particularly in terms of political stability and internal cohesion. But Zog's limited constructive talent, his inability to grasp modern economics or find advisers who could, and his failure to comprehend the true magnitude of the peasant problem left his country far behind the rest of the continent. In 1939 Albania remained the poorest, most isolated, and most backward state in Europe.

Agriculture and animal husbandry were the occupation of more than 80 percent of the population, though no more than 11 percent of the land was arable. Zog's ineffective attempts at land reform left most of the land in the hands of religious orders and feudal Moslem landowners. A full three-fifths of the arable land in Albania was owned by 150 landowners. At least 40 percent of the peasants were landless, living in grinding poverty. Agriculture and stockbreeding techniques remained medieval, with iron plows found only in the south and primitive crop-rotation systems requiring that 20 percent of the arable land lie fallow. Albanian peasants, as a result, were the least productive of all Balkan peasants, who in turn were the least productive of all European peasants.[1] Consequently, large quantities of wheat, corn, and rice were still being imported (accounting for 23 percent of total imports in 1938) in an attempt to meet the basic needs of the Albanian people.[2]

Like agriculture, Albanian industry lagged far behind even the rest of the Balkans. In 1938, industry accounted for only 4.4 percent of the national income.[3] There were no large industrial establishments, and what industry did exist was principally of the cottage variety, fulfilling some basic household needs. Each of the half dozen leading towns in Albania had a flour mill and three or four additional factories such as dairies, distilleries, breweries, cigarette factories, fish canneries, and wagon works.[4] Virtually all needed manufactured goods, therefore, had to be imported, insuring that during the 1930s export values never exceeded 50 percent of import costs. Both the expansion of this limited industrial base and the effective exploitation of Albania's not inconsiderable timber and mineral wealth were severely hampered by a limited and primitive transportation network. In 1939 Albania possessed forty miles of narrow-gauge railroad and perhaps five hundred miles of surfaced road.[5] The rest of the transportation network consisted of cart tracks and paths that virtually disappeared in the winter.

Social conditions remained almost as primitive as economic conditions. In the north the Gegs, who made up close to two-thirds of Albania's approximately one million people, remained tribal, still susceptible to the ravages of the blood feud, although here Zog had made some progress since the 1920s. In the south, home of the Tosks, impoverished peasants were still treated essentially as serfs by their feudal Moslem landlords. Only three towns, Durrës, Vlora, and Tirana, in any way resembled European cities, with Albania as a whole just over 15 percent urbanized.[6] Tirana, which was named Albania's capital shortly after World War I, had grown rapidly as a result, but still possessed just over thirty thousand inhabitants in 1939. The dirty streets of the capital presented the usual Balkan contrast of cheap modern structures interspersed with hovels. The Italians had superimposed a series of rather ostentatious government building in the center of town, along with the modern Hotel Dajti, and just outside the city in the middle of a wooded park, the yet unfinished tall yellow royal palace.[7] General living conditions in Tirana and elsewhere were poor; the people suffered from a bad diet that made them vulnerable to disease. Public health services were nonexistent, and education was still rudimentary. Albania had no university, few high schools, and an illiteracy rate of 85 percent, the highest in Europe.[8]

But these problems would have to wait; the first priority was the creation of an Italian Albania. Count Ciano, who had been responsible for the political preparation for the invasion, was also primarily responsible for the absorption of the newly conquered territory. Curiously, Ciano slowly developed a certain paternalistic affection for the Albanians, which manifested itself in keen interest not only in the planning for the integration of Albania into Mussolini's new Roman empire but also in the implementation of this policy.

Ciano was guided by one basic principle—the annexation of Albania, based upon what he called a policy of justice and force, without the international complications that this might cause. He wanted a colony without it appearing to be a colony. Ciano was keenly aware of the promises of independence and territorial integrity that he had indiscriminately handed out both to foreign governments, as well as to the Albanians themselves. Not to engender undo alarm, therefore, Ciano paid particular attention to both the pace and the form of the annexation. The opposition that he encountered came from numerous directions, including the Albanians themselves, Victor Emmanuel III, and Mussolini. Ciano achieved some initial success, although constant readjustment was required, indicating significant problems in the process. Ultimately, of course, as with most military occupations, the hearts and minds of the Albanians were not won over.

The creation of a new political structure was first on the agenda and proved to be quite simple, because Ciano was able to use the existing ruling class. Although Ciano found little sympathy among the population, as we have seen, there was no shortage of collaborators. Ciano rapidly constructed a provisional administration, finding many willing to serve. He initially called on those who had been politically marginalized by Zog, most with long-standing contacts with Italy.[9] Ciano also attracted many of the secretaries general of the previous ministries.[10] All of Zog's ministers, with the exception of Rrok Geraj, the minister of national economy, who had been sent to talk with Guzzoni and in the old Roman tradition simply followed in his troop, had left with Zog. This provisional government was headed by its most distinguished member, Xhafer Bey Ypi, a former prime minister and chief inspector of the court up to the time of the invasion. Ciano had originally planned to name Serreqi,[11] but Ypi was clearly a bigger fish. Others in this provisional government included the previous press chief and Mihal Sherko, the general secretary for foreign affairs. This provisional government followed a simple plan laid out by Ciano, who, of course, hoped that his moves would be perceived as being domestically inspired. On 8 April, both in Tirana and privately to the British ambassador to Italy, Lord Perth, Ciano again explained that the Italians were determined to respect Albanian independence and territorial integrity.[12] This was of course a ruse and fooled only a few. On 9 April Ciano told Lord Perth that Italy's further intentions would henceforth depend upon the Albanians themselves, a clue to his future moves.[13]

As the rather transparent plan ran its course, Ypi, on 10 April, sent a message to Mussolini reaffirming the loyalty of the Albanian people, who confidently awaited the carrying out of Ciano's program, which promised "order, prosperity, political and social justice within the solemn frame of Fascist liberties." Lord Perth noted sarcastically that he was not aware there was such a thing as Fascist liberties.[14] On the same day, to complete the first phase of the plan, Ypi broadcast a speech admitting the incapacity of Albanians to govern themselves and stated that under Zog Albania had been nearing a breakup, which the Duce had prevented. Ypi appealed to the Duce to save the country.[15] This is, of course, what Ciano had intended when he had announced two days earlier that his next steps would depend on the Albanians themselves. The Albanians, at least to the satisfaction of Ciano, had spoken.

On 9 and 10 April, Ciano, working with what he called "some jurists and other picayune professionals" laid out his plan for the annexation of Albania, without the outward forms of annexation, liberally bribing former Albanian officials to win their cooperation. His first task was to subvert Mussolini's plan to construct some form of regency, presumably with a prince of Savoy at the helm.[16] This being done, and with the acquiescence of the "professionals" who told Ciano that his plan would not look like aggression, Ciano gained Mussolini's approval on 10 April and immediately set his scheme into operation.

The first step required that Ypi call a constituent assembly, scheduled to convene on 12 April. Although touted as a "national" assembly, the body of 159 consisted of 68 large landowners, 25 tribal leaders, and 46 business people, as well as clerics from all denominations, a few intellectuals, officials, and officers.[17] Among this collection of prewar elite were found many who had served both Zog as parliamentary deputies—apparently only a few former deputies who had stayed in Tirana were unwilling to take part—and the Turkish authorities before him. Those former deputies who had left the capital were initially hard to find, with many having to be brought to Tirana aboard Italian planes.[18] Some of the delegates were apparently chosen quite arbitrarily at a moment's notice. Ryan reported that one delegate from Durrës was simply instructed the day before to go to Tirana to attend an important meeting dealing with local affairs.[19] Many of the deputies chosen in this fashion were rather sorry figures, distinguished only by the level of their servility toward the Italians.[20]

The Vërlaci Government

The constituent assembly, under the leadership of Ypi, was assigned a very simple task: to follow the design set down by Ciano. The assembly performed its role quickly and without much discussion. First it announced that as of 12 April, "the year 17 of the Fascist Era," the Zog dynasty was deposed and the Constitution of 1928, which constructed Zog's monarchy, was abrogated. Next, it announced that a close bond would be established between Albania and Italy in the form of a personal union under Victor Emmanuel III, who would be asked to assume the Albanian throne. At the same time Albanian sovereignty and national freedom were proclaimed, and the population was encouraged to believe the Italians, who had promised Albania its national freedom, own language, national flag, peace, and justice.[21] Albania was to officially become an autonomous constitutional monarchy hereditary in the House of Savoy. Finally, a new government was formed with the great landowner and ardent foe of Zog, Shefqet Vërlaci as prime minister and head of the first of the five puppet regimes constructed by the Italians.

The government included mostly nonentities, among them Xhemil Bey Dino as foreign minister, whose only redeeming qualities seem to have been that he was the son-in-law of Vërlaci and that while serving as Albanian ambassador to Bulgaria under Zog (he had earlier been minister in London but was forced to resign after his lover committed suicide on the steps of the legation) he had sent Mussolini a congratulatory telegram during the course of the invasion of Albania. Fejzi Bey Alizoti was chosen as finance minister. He was described as a strong Italophile who supplemented his meager income during the 1930s by accepting a subsidy from Italy. He was said to be corrupt and described as a gross creature physically and morally, with a certain amount of low cunning.[22] Andon Beca was chosen as minister of agriculture and domestic economy by virtue of the fact that he was a loyal hanger-on of Vërlaci's and was injured in a Zog-inspired attempt on Vërlaci's life in 1927. As a deputy from Elbasan, he raised the cry of "Long Live Italy" at the opening of the Albanian Parliament on 15 October 1938, evoking no response.

Maliq Bey Bushati, who would play an important role in later collaborationist governments, was chosen to serve as minister of the interior. Bushati was described as a man of character but no great intelligence who, although admitting to having plotted against Zog with the Italians, was dismayed by the lengths to which they went and resented their representing him as one of those who had invited their intervention.[23] Bushati would later claim that he participated in order to save what could be saved, in order to resist through collaboration, a policy technique at which Albanians were particularly adept, after some four centuries of preserving their nationality by a balance of warfare against and diplomacy with the Turks.[24]

Perhaps the most distinguished of this otherwise uninspiring group was the new minister of education, Ernest Koliqi, one of Albania's foremost writers and intellectuals. Described by one author as Italy's "gray eminence" in Albania, Koliqi's reputation suffered from his compromise with the Italians, particularly among many of his youthful followers who opposed the Italian invasion.[25] His reputation would have suffered even more had his supporters known that he was on Ciano's personal payroll.[26]

Even Ciano was not overly impressed with the new regime, noting in his diary on 12 April after his first meeting with Vërlaci that "I did not know Vërlaci, had I known him I would have opposed his nomination. He is a very surly-looking man, and will give us a great deal of annoyance."[27] Overall, Vërlaci would turn out to be less trouble than Ciano had anticipated. However, Vërlaci's nature is perhaps best characterized by his request in December to be allowed to assassinate King Zog. Vërlaci, whose daughter had been jilted by Zog in the 1930s, was determined to see Zog dead, as demanded by traditional Albanian blood feud law. Both Ciano and Mussolini refused to allow this, reasoning that Italy could expect no benefit from such a move, only blame. Perhaps Ciano's ultimate statement regarding this new Albanian elite was recorded in his diary following a reception at the Albanian royal palace in early 1941. Ciano noted rather ironically that the Italians were "missing eight cigar lighters, a silver case, 60 knives and forks. As a debut on the part of Tirana high society, that's not bad."[28]

Still, Ciano needed these people because they supported his vision without hesitation, unlike others in both Italy and Albania. Ciano arrived in Tirana on the day the constituent assembly met and immediately encountered opposition to aspects of his program. Many Albanians, who were cooperating with the Italians, were concerned about the concept of a personal union under Victor Emmanuel III. These leaders, principally chiefs from the Shkodra region, understood that giving the crown to the Italian king signaled the end of Albanian independence. These chiefs would have preferred a prince of the house of Savoy, or as Ciano modestly noted in his diary, Count Ciano himself.[29] Ciano, in long discussions with the chiefs, repeated the myth that his plan did nothing to threaten the form or the substance of Albanian independence. The chiefs eventually desisted, either as a result of Ciano's soothing words, or because of the copious quantities of Albanian francs he liberally distributed, and many of them declared the traditional Albanian *besa*, a pledge of peaceful coexistence. A *besa*, which can be given to an individual or group, allowed the Italians to travel freely through specific regions, where, they promised, they would do no harm.[30] Although northerners are reasonable in arguing that this was not collaboration, the policy can be described as a form of passive cooperation.

On 13 April the Italian Fascist Grand Council approved the union proclaimed by the Albanian constituent assembly, and three days later a law was announced in Italy authorizing and proclaiming Victor Emmanuel's acceptance of the crown of Albania.[31] On 15 April Vërlaci headed an Albanian delegation of forty-nine to Rome to officially present the Albanian crown to Victor Emmanuel III. Few of the persons included seemed to count for much

The Construction of an Italian Albania

in the country, indicating perhaps that there was not much of a rush to participate in this final humiliation. The most distinguished member of the delegation, next to Vërlaci, was the ex-archbishop Vissarion, whose removal from his see in 1935 cleared the way for the creation of the autocephelous Albanian Orthodox Church. As we have seen, Vissarion resurfaced with the Italian invasion and went out of his way to welcome the invaders, exposing himself to universal contempt.[32]

The scene, as described by Ciano, was a curious one. The small group of visibly depressed Albanians seemed lost in the great halls of the Quirinal Palace.

> Vërlaci especially appears depressed as he pronounces, with a tired air and without conviction, the words he has to say in offering the crown. The King answers in an uncertain and trembling voice; decidedly he is not an orator who makes any impression on an audience, and these Albanians who are a warrior mountain people look with amazement and timidity on the little man who is seated on a great gilt chair beside which stands a gigantic bronze statue of Mussolini.[33]

In Victor Emmanuel's acceptance speech and in Mussolini's talk the day before, the Albanians listened anxiously for the word *independence,* but they did not hear it. Mussolini, who sensed this, promised Ciano that he would talk to them about national independence and sovereignty before they returned home. The fiction needed to be preserved for the sake of Albanians as a whole and for the sake of the collaborators in particular.

Ciano continued to pursue his plans at his own slow, steady pace and continued to encounter frequent opposition. The Duce now wanted to move faster; as early as 13 April he wanted to abolish the Albanian Foreign Ministry. Ciano was again able to prevail, writing that "we must proceed gradually unless we want to antagonize the rest of the world. So far matters have run as smooth as oil because we have not had to use force. On the other hand, the Ministry of Foreign Affairs is of use to us in order to have a new state of things legally acceptable without having to pass through an interminable polemic of recognition. Later it can be quickly suppressed."[34]

The 1939 Constitution

The constitution that institutionalized the personal union between Albania and Italy sealed the fate of Albanian independence. The constitution was handed to another visiting delegation of Albanians on 3 June. Ciano sugar-coated the pill with compensation of a personal nature, such as nominations to the Italian senate and ambassadorial titles. Vërlaci was made an Italian senator, Dino became an ambassador, Koliqi was given a professorship at the University of Rome, and Serreqi was finally rewarded for his betrayal by promotion to the rank of general of division.[35] These awards seem to have been enough, because Ciano noted that, for the first time since the invasion, the Albanians seemed to be visibly satisfied. Ciano too was satisfied and noted, "The operation to emasculate Albania without making the patient scream—the annexation—is now practically realized."[36]

The constitution has been described by an American legal scholar as typical of the new order that the European dictators imposed on conquered states. "The whole political power is concentrated in the hand of the dictator. His executive officers are the department chiefs of the ruling state and a governor general. At the same time the governor general exercises control over a puppet regime which serves as buffer between the authorities of the ruling state and the population of the subjugated country."[37] The tone of the new relationship was set by the constitution's introduction. There was not even the semblance of an expression of the popular will by having it voted on by the constituent assembly; rather, it was conferred by the sovereign authority of Victor Emmanuel III in the same way that Abdul Hamid II introduced the Constitution of 1876 to the Ottoman Empire. This decision seems to have been made at the last moment, however, because as late as the middle of May Jacomoni informed the German minister that the document would be laid before the Albanian assembly in order to document Albanian participation in the process.[38] The release of the constitution was accompanied by at least one positive development: according to Ryan, the rather sickening use of the expressions *independent, independence,* and *personal union* were finally dropped.[39]

The document itself was known as the Statuto Fondementale and was composed of forty-five articles in seven chapters. Despite the veneer of constitutional monarchy, what it created was a fascist military dictatorship—authoritarian, hierarchical, highly centralized, and antidemocratic. It invested the executive power of the state (which was exercised by Mussolini) in the king,[40] who was to be represented in Albania by a lieutenant general. The lieutenant general was responsible for the control of the puppet regime by appointment and through permanent Italian counselors attached to each ministry.

On 23 April Francesco Jacomoni, the Italian minister, who had recently been elevated to ambassador, was appointed the first lieutenant-general. The appointment of Jacomoni, who was described as indefatigable but lacking in sincerity, came as a surprise to some and a disappointment to others. It had long been assumed by many in collaborationist circles and among the diplomatic community that a prince of Savoy (with the Duke of Bergamo as the favorite) would be appointed. The German minister suggested that the chief reason a member of the house of Savoy was not appointed was because Zog's new palace was not yet ready and Tirana boasted no residence worthy of a prince.[41] Whatever the housing situation, the appointment was a mistake and helped to undercut Ciano's careful attention to sending the correct signals. The appointment of so secondary a person as Jacomoni created the impression that he was little more than a high commissioner in a conquered territory.[42] Seemingly aware that Jacomoni's appointment might cause a problem, Rome hoped to raise his comparatively low status by having the Albanian government confer upon him the title of Altesse Serenissme. And needless to say, his elevation had been preceded by the obligatory spate of telegrams to Mussolini and Ciano requesting his retention and promotion to a higher position.[43] To his credit, though, Jacomoni, unlike most Italian officials in Albania, treated the Albanians as backward but not inferior.[44]

To complete the chain of command, Ciano constructed an undersecretariate for Albanian affairs at the Foreign Ministry, to which Jacomoni would report. The undersecretariate controlled a variety of Italian authorities in Albania, including the Office of Civil Engineering, Office of Highway, Tramway, and Automobile Transportation, and Offices for Railroads and Public Works, as well as directorates of the Italian Day Dispensary in Tirana, Albanian youth, and after-work recreation centers, or Dopolavoro.[45] Much of this bureaucracy essentially created a parallel structure, because the Italian inspectorate of public works was independent of the Albanian ministry of public works, and so on.

As undersecretary Ciano chose Zenone Benini, whose principal qualification for the post seems to have been that he knew Ciano as a boy and served with him in Ethiopia. He had joined the party in 1920 and had become a *squadrista*, which, of course, appealed to Mussolini. But he had no training or experience as a diplomat or a government minister, having taken a degree in pure mathematics. Even the official Italian press had a difficult time in explaining his appointment. The Stefani Agency's announcement concluded with an almost apologetic "also very competent in corporate and syndical questions."[46] Ciano's justification was that the situation required a technical expert because it would be necessary to quickly develop a program of public works.

Through Jacomoni, Benini, Ciano, and Mussolini, the king, then, had extensive authority. The king declared war and peace and commanded the Albanian armed forces. The king was made responsible for issuing administrative ordinances and appointing officials. The constitution's construction of several judicial and legislative branches was simple eyewash, since these two branches were mere administrative units, subject to the will of the executive.[47] Justice emanated from the king and was administered in his name by judges whom he appointed.[48]

In general, the Italians retained the old judicial organization of the Zog regime, which included a justice of the peace attached to every municipal office; the courts of prefectures with an attorney attached; and the courts of appeal, which heard appeals on penal and civil questions from the lower courts of the prefectures. Political offenses were taken before a special court, and military crimes were tried before military tribunals.[49] The laws that these courts carried out came principally from the Italian Criminal Code of 1930, most of which was introduced by Jacomoni's decree on 6 January 1940. The code dealt in detail with all forms of crimes against the state. Personal freedom did not exist under the Italians in Albania, because any citizen could be jailed as a result of the decision of special committees of police internment. These committees, one in Tirana and several in the provinces, were staffed by representatives of the Italian police and fascist militia.[50]

Special laws against acts of sabotage—particularly those directed at roads and telecommunication services—were introduced in late 1942 to supplement the penal code. According to the decree, all inhabitants of villages within a five-mile radius of an act of sabotage were considered collectively responsible. Heavy fines and imprisonment of the heads of all families were imposed by the special police internment committees.[51]

The legislative branch, also similar to its Zogist predecessor and its Italian counterpart, was a sham. The statutes specified that the interpretation of laws rested exclusively with the legislative power, but this claim was meaningless. The legislature, called the Superior Fascist Corporative Council, had sixty to seventy deputies made up of members of the newly created Central Council and Directorate of the Albanian Fascist Party and members of a body called the Central Council of the Corporative Economy. The latter body, which was not constructed until March 1940, was composed of four sections representing agriculture, industry, commerce, and the professions and arts. The members of the Superior Fascist Corporative Council, fourteen of whom were Italians, possessed virtually no legislative power. The body, appointed entirely by the king, was convoked and prorogued by the king. No subject could be placed on the agenda without the king's consent. The king, in fact, issued decrees that later came before the council for formal adoption. As if this were not enough, the king also had veto power over the decisions of the council.

The collaborationist government was, of course, entirely controlled by the

Italian authorities. The prime minister and his cabinet (restricted to ministers of agriculture and forests, industry and commerce, justice, interior, finance, public works, and public instruction) were appointed and dismissed by the king and responsible to the king, not to Parliament. Although all the ministers were Albanians, each had a permanent Italian counselor ranked next to him. The Italian counselors supervised all the offices of the ministries and their staffs, and had the right to sign all the acts issued by the ministries. Thus the Italian advisers directed all the work of the ministries, acting on the orders of the Jacomoni.[52] The role of the Albanian ministers was never completely defined, although this did not seem to make much difference.

Conspicuously absent from this list of Albanian ministers were a foreign minister and a military representative. Ciano had decided by June 1939 that he had waited long enough and that he could now safely suppress the Albanian Ministry of Foreign Affairs as well as the remnants of the Albanian military and security forces. Ciano noted in his diary that he decided on 25 May to close the Albanian Ministry of Foreign Affairs. This was followed by the inevitable announcement that the Albanian government had decided to suppress its own foreign ministry.[53] The event itself was quick and anticlimactic. On 3 June Xhemil Dino flew to Rome and signed a treaty with Ciano at the Palazzo Chigi providing for the unification of the diplomatic and consular services of Italy and Albania. Foreign ministries were given a specific amount of time to apply for permission to open consulates general. Some states—including the United States, France, and Turkey—refused and liquidated their legations. Others—including Greece, Yugoslavia, Bulgaria, Rumania, and Great Britain—acceded to the Italian demands.[54] The British hoped to avoid criticism for this official recognition of Italy's military aggression by asking the Italians not to give the event undue publicity. The *Giornale d'Italia* complied and announced the recognition with little prominence.[55]

The small Albanian army, which had demonstrated its insignificance during the invasion, was reorganized by a series of Italian decrees promulgated a few days before the introduction of the constitution. On 10 May a degree from Jacomoni announced that the three-thousand-strong Albanian gendarmerie would henceforth be absorbed into the *carabinieri* and commanded by an Italian general of carabinieri, General Cristino Agostinucci (affectionately known as the "Stuffed Lion" by Albanians), assisted by Italian and Albanian subcommanders. As a military unit, it would come under the jurisdiction of the supreme command of the Italian armed forces in Albania while cooperating with the Ministry of the Interior and the local police.[56] The same degree announced that the frontier guard would come under the command of Colonel Enrico Palandri of the Royal Guard of Finance.[57] On 26 May the government of Vërlaci "proposed" the merging of the small Albanian army (estimated at this point at six battalions with a total strength of about sixty-five hundred men)[58] into that of Italy's. This move was approved by Italian law on 13 July and confirmed by a decree from Jacomoni in December.[59] To regulate the number of officers, it was announced, on 22 May, that officers and noncommissioned officers of the army, gendarmerie, and frontier guard who had not returned to service by midnight 10 May would be considered to have resigned. An active list of eight hundred officers was eventually developed, of whom only about two hundred were retained.[60] The Italian military command, still under General Guzzoni, was never subjugated to Jacomoni, a situation that was to cause considerable subsequent problems.

Other levels of authority not directly regulated by the constitution included the administration of local government. The Italians did little to change the general structure of the administration of the Zog regime. The form and content, developed over a period of years, was authoritarian enough to fit right into the plans of the fascist occupier. In any case, Italian advisers had already been at work for many years, so that many aspects of the administration already closely resembled their Italian counterparts.[61] As under the Zog regime, local government had no inherent powers, except when dealing with the tribal powers of the north. Local officials were not elected but appointed by the central government and controlled by the Ministry of the Interior. The same was true of the advisers and the advisory councils of local officials. The country was divided into ten prefectures headed by prefects. Further subdivisions in descending order included subprefectures, municipalities, communes, and, in certain districts, villages, headed respectively by subprefects, municipal heads, commune heads, and elders. The most important local official was the prefect, who wielded much administrative and police power as well as considerable authority over local officials. The smaller communes and villages were still presided over by their own local officials, but these officials were now appointed by the central government.[62] It was only on local and relatively minor matters that Albanians possessed any real decision-making powers.

The Albanian Fascist Party

Second only to the military as a power base outside the constitution, and the third element of what for a time became a three-way power struggle (the other two contenders being the Italian army and the Office of the Lieutenant General) was the Albanian Fascist Party, the only political party in Albania. As in Italy, the party was constructed to parallel the state and was able as a result to gain considerable influence for its parent, the Italian Fascist Party.

True to form, Ciano arranged on 11 April for a group of Albanians with recognizable names to "request" the formation of an Albanian Fascist Party.[63] By the end of April the Italian government had graciously consented. On 23 April Achille Starace, the secretary of the Italian Fascist Party, arrived in Albania, accompanied by considerable ceremony (including the exchange of nineteen-gun salutes) and two warships to announce the foundation of the Albanian Fascist Party. Whether due to Ciano's caution or traditional bureaucratic delays, the party did not receive its constitution until 6 June 1939 and was not presented with an organized directorate and a central council until March 1940.[64]

Once its complex structure was finally agreed upon, it came as a surprise to only a few that the real power in the party rested with Giovanni Giro, a personal friend of Mussolini who had created a series of diplomatic incidents by attempting to construct a youth movement in Albania during the last years of Zog's reign.[65] Giro, as inspector general of the party, directed the activities of the Albanian secretary general, Tefik Mborja.

Mborja, who was appointed by Victor Emmanuel in conjunction with Starace and Vërlaci, was a lawyer and former deputy in the interwar Albanian Parliament. He had supported Fan Noli, the Albanian democratic leader and staunch opponent of Zog, and had represented the Noli regime in Rome in 1924. Ryan described him as a respectable person with a considerable amount of energy.[66] But as with other officials appointed by Ciano, Mborja's principal qualification was that he had been a friend of the Ciano family in the 1920s. As head of the party Mborja sat in the Albanian cabinet as an ex-officio member and in so doing exercised some influence. The press account of his selection also mentioned that he would have some part in the direction of the Italian party, although this was never spelled out clearly. What was spelled out clearly was the Albanian party's dependence on the Italian party, as demonstrated by the provision that the Albanian party could only modify its own statutes with previous agreement of the parent party.[67]

The statutes provided for a central council under the minister secretary, provincial administrations under federal secretaries, *fascios*, (a form of national leagues), regional groups, and nuclei. These groups, at least on paper, possessed considerable authority. The central council of the party formed one of the two elements of the Albanian Parliament. The party as a whole held considerable influence in local administrations and controlled various ancillary organizations. The latter included a fascist youth movement called Albanian Youth of the Lictor, as well as other youth organizations, university fascists—of whom there were only a few because Albania had no university—female fascists, and the Ente Assistènza Fascista, an assistance society.[68] In exercising these political, educational, welfare, and economic roles, the party commanded considerable power over the Albanian population. Still, the Italians maintained an absolute veto over any of the actions of all Albanian organizations.

The rank and file of the party was made up of native Albanians and Italian residents in Albania. The statutes expressly excluded Jews and, as a sop to Albanian sentiment in a passage defining the prerequisites for membership, included fidelity and courage, "qualities characteristic of the people of Albania."[69] Members swore allegiance to Mussolini, described as the founder of the empire and the creator of the new Albania, and pledged to serve the cause of the fascist revolution with their lives, if necessary. The membership automatically constituted a voluntary civil militia in traditional black shirts. The militia was divided into four legions, which supervised ten cohort commands. The apparent goal was the recruitment of two thousand members, or two hundred for each of the ten cohort commands.[70]

Nominally, there was no compulsion to join the party, but methods were found to make life difficult for those who demonstrated reluctance, particularly Albanian government officials. As a result, the party was, of course, made up of many people who joined for personal gain rather than any sense of doctrinal conviction. Albania failed to produce nearly the number of ideological partners for the fascists as did Romania or Croatia. Many who joined did so as a mere formality. Accustomed to the system of graft and corruption that prevailed under the Turkish Empire and under Zog, many of the Albanians, not known for mastery of Western ideas of political morality, regarded the Fascist Party as just another chance for the Italians to get rake-off. Philosophically accepting the occupation of their country, many collaborated without any recognition of the ideological betrayal involved. As we shall see, many would later head for the hills once they realized what their collaboration would mean in the long run.[71] It is perhaps unjust to roundly condemn as traitors those who had yet to fully develop a concept of modern Western nationalism.

A bungled attempt was even made to recruit Albanians from outside Albania for membership in the Albanian Fascist Party. In May 1940, Mborja sent two emissaries to Thessaloníki with the hope of forming an Albanian fascist organization in Greece. The two, a parliamentary deputy and a journalist, interviewed leading Albanians and attempted to convince them of the brilliant achievements of fascism in Albania. The Greek Albanians advised them to leave, which the emissaries readily consented to do.[72]

Italianization of the Financial Structure

Italianization of the economy was also an important early priority. The Italian government had for some time attempted to force a customs union on King Zog in order to gain full control of Albania's foreign trade and the economy in general. Zog had successfully resisted, but soon after the invasion the Italians moved quickly to institute this long-standing goal. Jacomoni, as one of his last acts as ambassador, negotiated the far-reaching union with Vërlaci and announced the agreement on 22 April. Henceforth Albania and Italy were to be considered, for customs purposes, one territory under the Italian customs system. Italian and Albanian goods would be considered domestic goods and traded freely between the two countries. All Italian export and import restrictions and all other international agreements now applied to the customs union. All Albanian agreements with other states were considered null and void. All administration and preventive services would be carried out by the Italian customs service.[73]

The agreement also pegged the Albanian gold franc at 6.25 lire (one-half of the franc's actual worth) and extended to Albania the whole Italian system of exchange control. Albanian currency would henceforth be covered by Italian gold or notes through the Bank of Italy and printed by the Italian state press or the press of the Bank of Italy. The Italian government took full financial responsibility for the Albanian budget, the agreement having destroyed Albania's ability to raise revenue through customs. Italy promised Albania fifteen million gold francs a year, rather generous since Albania averaged about half that sum in customs revenue. Finally, the agreement set up a mixed committee to implement the various provisions, made up of representatives from the Istituto Nazionale per i cambi con l'èstero (National Institute for Foreign Exchange), the Bank of Italy, the National Bank of Albania (which had already for some time been dominated by Italians), and the foreign ministries of both countries.[74]

The impact of the agreement was substantial and largely unanticipated by the Italian authorities. With regard to foreign trade, the effect was expected. Albania's small export trade had been dominated by Italy for years, so little changed here. In terms of imports, prior to the invasion Italy was responsible for perhaps one-third of Albania's imports, with Germany, Austria, and Czechoslovakia providing perhaps one-sixth. As a result of the treaty Albania would receive all of its needed imports from Italy or at least through Italy.

Of more significance for the average Albanian, however, was the provision dealing with currency regulations. As a developing society, Albanians were just in the process of developing confidence in paper money. Although Zog was no financial genius, he had been very careful to build this trust by supporting his currency with gold and by issuing and circulating gold coin. Under Zog's regime, the National Bank of Albania readily exchanged paper money for gold or foreign currency. The value of the Albanian gold francs, therefore, remained stable, and because of the constant need to change notes for gold, the amount in circulation was kept at a minimum. In the ten years before the invasion, no more than 11 million to 14 million gold franc notes circulated. At the end of 1937 that amount was covered by no less than 7.6 million in gold and 15 million in foreign currency.[75]

The introduction of Italian currency into Albania and the doubling of the franc against the lira destroyed faith in Albanian currency. Albanians as a result began to hoard gold, which could have been put to good use in the development of the country. As the Italians would soon discover, their program for Italianization of Albanian currency would have further negative effects as well.

The remaining independent bank, the Agricultural Bank, was fused with the Bank of Naples on 12 May. All functions were transferred to an agricultural credit section of what was described as the Banco di Napoli, Albania. The indication here is that the Bank of Naples had created an Albanian subsidiary. The transfer of this bank completed the Italian takeover of Albania's financial structure.

Propaganda

During the same short period of seemingly frenzied activity, Jacomoni and Vërlaci signed an agreement giving Italians in Albania and Albanians in Italy the same civil and political rights they enjoyed in their own countries. This became possible following the startling discovery by Italian racial experts that the lowly Albanians were actually of Nordic stock, just like the Italians.[76] Ciano made special note of this agreement, suggesting that it was as important as the annexation itself.[77] The implications of this move were clear to all. The Italians had finally gained the right to own land in Albania. The German minister commented that it was assumed that as a result the Italians, whom he considered more energetic than the Albanians, would beat the Albanians out of the most valuable land and that in a few years only the unfruitful and inaccessible mountains would still be peopled with Albanians. He remarked further that it was clear that for the Albanians, this recognition of equal rights in Italy was practically worthless.[78]

The Italians also paid particular attention to the control and diffusion of propaganda. This included silencing the Zogist press and replacing it with more cooperative papers. The two Tirana daily papers, *Drita* and *Shtypi*, were closed and replaced by a new paper, called *Fashizmi* and edited by Alizoti, which became the official organ of the Albanian Fascist Party. About a quarter of the first issue appeared in Italian. The paper was not well received for a number of reasons. First, the high illiteracy rate certainly had an impact. But equally important, the Albanians in Tirana quickly identified *Fashizmi* for what it was, a vehicle for the dissemination of unadulterated Italian propaganda. Recognizing this handicap, the Italian authorities, in March 1940, tried to make the paper more palatable by renaming it *Tomori*, after the highest mountain in Albania. At the beginning of April, Qemal Vrioni, a member of a well-known wealthy family who had been involved in a major revolt against Zog in 1935, took over editorship. At the same time the paper ceased to be a party organ.[79] These cosmetic changes did nothing to diminish Italian control. To complete their control of Albania's rather limited news organizations, in January 1940 the Italians decreed that the Albanian Telegraphic Agency would henceforth be limited to Stefani Agency messages.

In order to disseminate propaganda in the cultural field, the Italian authorities established the Skënderbeg Foundation, with its main office in Tirana. Divided into two sections, the first, the Institute of Albanian Studies, hoped to develop the "philosophical, literary, artistic, and historic culture in Albania." It members were appointed by Jacomoni, and its membership was open to Albanian, Italian, and even foreign scholars. The second section, the Italo-Albanian Skënderbeg Club, hoped to facilitate social relations between Italians and Albanians and was open only to Italians and Albanians.[80] Despite a substantial budget, the impact of the Skënderbeg Foundation was marginal.

Education

Of considerably more concern in terms of Italianization was the Albanian educational system. In this matter the Italians could not fail to act decisively. Zog had considered education a priority, but it seems that there were always more urgent priorities. The primary problem was a lack of qualified teachers and a lack of funds. Ordinary teachers received subsistence-level pay and in most cases possessed no more than a primary-school education themselves. The result was that although there had been some improvement during the interwar period, when the Italians invaded, Albanian education was still in a rudimentary form.

The Italians found in existence some 663 elementary schools (for those aged six to eleven)—up from 560 in 1930—and 19 intermediate schools (for those aged eleven to thirteen), with a total of 1,595 teachers and 62,971 pupils. There were also schools of the lycée type at Shkodra, Korça, and Tirana, as well as the Ecole Normale at Elbasan, where full secondary education for those aged eleven to eighteen was available. The dearth of secondary schools was indicative of Zog's belief that it would be a mistake to have too many secondary schools because they would produce a "white-collar" class. Accordingly, preference was given to the development of agricultural and technical education. By 1939 there were 13 industrial schools, 1 technical institute, and 2 training schools for teachers. There was no university in Albania, and there would not be one until 1957, but Zog's government did provide a limited number of scholarships (over two hundred by 1939) to enable some students to finish their education abroad. Most students went to Italy, but some of the Greek-speakers from southern Albania finished their education in Athens. Unfortunately, the most qualified were not always chosen, because the selection process for scholarships abroad, much like most other benefits, was based on favoritism.[81]

Not surprisingly, the most effective educational institutions during the Zog years were run by religious organizations or by foreigners. In the north Jesuits and Franciscans ran a number of schools that enjoyed good standing and filled, to a certain extent, the local need. The Americans supported a technical school and two agricultural colleges, which they staffed and financed. From the technical point of view, the Italians were the most helpful, for they founded four arts and crafts schools to train mechanics and artisans.[82]

In southern Albania the educational situation was less discouraging. An educational system dating back many hundreds of years was still in existence. The schools were good, the teachers fully qualified, and the standard of education relatively high. Whether Greek propaganda, as was asserted by many nationalists, took the form of subsidies distributed secretly for the upkeep of these schools, or whether the relative prosperity of the south resulted in public-spirited endeavors on the part of the local population, there existed in southern Albania a state of educational well-being, which was unknown in other parts of Albania.[83]

While Zog must be credited with some improvement in the Albanian educational system, he did considerable damage as well. Ever suspicious of the Italians, Zog was convinced in 1933 that the Italians were using their schools to influence Albanian students politically and culturally. Zog's minister of education convinced him that in some instances portraits of Mussolini and Victor Emmanuel had replaced those of Albanian heroes. The minister further argued that the Italians had actually built more schools than were needed in certain areas of northern Albania. Although some of these complaints were not entirely unjustified, Zog's fear of the Italians ran away with him. Convinced that the Italians were making insidious advances to the entire Catholic north in an attempt to undermine his influence among the tribes and replace it with their own, Zog struck a blow for nationalism.[84] Unfortunately the blow was also aimed directly at Albania's already meager educational system. Zog closed all foreign schools. Had the Albanian school system been somewhat stronger, the departure of the foreigners may not have had such a resounding impact. As it was, the entire system was thrown into chaos and did not begin to recover until some of the foreign schools were allowed to reopen several years later, in 1935. This conflict with the Greeks was never fully resolved.[85]

When the Italians arrived in 1939 they first closed the schools in order to carry out a general evaluation of their priorities for both the students and the teachers. The latter were a particular concern, since it had not escaped the Italians that teachers were perhaps more likely than any other influential subordinate class in the country to include a fair number of patriotic idealists. Extensive weeding out and retraining commenced immediately. Most non-Italian foreign schools were closed, and the number of secondary schools was reduced even further. This last development was justified, by the Albanian minister, on the same basis as Zog's argument that these schools did little but increase inordinately the number of candidates for official employment. The secondary school in Korça was closed primarily because it was the chief center of French culture in the Albanian educational system. Minister Koliqi suggested that the school was responsible for the dissemination of subversive ideas.[86] To counter this and other foreign influences, both Albanian and Italian were taught and new textbooks boasting politically correct historical interpretations were hurriedly introduced.

Controlling the educational establishment proved less arduous than controlling the students. The Italians attempted to supervise the students by setting up a series of fascist youth organizations. The Federazióne della Gioventù Albanese del Littorio was formed. Girls were organized into the Gioventù Femminile del Littorio, and boys under fourteen were assigned to groups of Balilla. Italian authorities would soon discover, however, that winning the hearts and minds of Albanian students was not as simple as they had hoped.

Religion

Establishing control over Albania's diverse religious hierarchies proved to be a much simpler task. Albania had always been something of a religious anomaly in the Balkans, with its 70 percent Moslem majority. The remaining Albanians were divided between the Orthodox Church (20 percent) prominent in the Hellenized fringe in the south and the Catholic Church (10 percent) prominent in the area around Shkodra in the north. Although Albanians have never been considered religious fanatics, the existence of three religious communities (not to mention the various subdivisions among them) was considered by Albanian nationalists as an invitation for foreign intervention. Elsewhere in the Balkans religion often served as a unifying force; in Albania it proved to be divisive. Because this division constituted a block to the development of a national community, twentieth-century nationalist leaders, particularly Zog, who was not a religious bigot and not even very religious, hoped at least to remove control of Albanian churches from the hands of foreigners.

The Moslem faith in Albania, with most of the faithful belonging to the Sunni branch, separated itself from any outside control in 1923. The other two churches proved to be more of a problem. Zog turned first to the Orthodox Church, arguing that ties with the ecumenical patriarchate in Istanbul should be severed.

The first step in this direction had been taken as early as 1921 by Fan Noli, who had already played a leading role in the formation of the Orthodox Church among Albanian émigrés in the United States. He and a few associates, undeterred by the fact that the mass of the Orthodox faithful seemed to be out of sympathy with their aims, proceeded to open a vigorous campaign in favor of religious independence. They received the support of successive Albanian governments, which looked favorably on a movement whose organizers preached liberation from alien control.

In September 1922 the Congress of Berat was called by the government to deal with the question. The congress, made up of various delegates chosen in no organized fashion, declared the Albanian Orthodox Church to be autocephalous and ruled that Albanian instead of Greek should be used for liturgical purposes. In addition, the congress constructed a council headed by V. Marko, one of Noli's aides, to control the church and appoint bishops to an Albanian synod. The Congress further appealed to the patriarch to legalize the projected severance.[87] The decisions of Berat remained largely inoperative, however, because of the lack of a hierarchy. Albania did not have a single Orthodox bishop after World War I. The mission sent to Istanbul to discuss matters with the patriarch failed to convince the patriarchate to recognize the autocephalous character of the church.

Zog reopened the negotiations in 1926, but by 1928 the position of the church remained what it was in 1921. Having decided that the patriarch was nothing more than an instrument of Greek propaganda and was purposely delaying in the hope of imposing upon the new church restrictions to secure the supremacy of Greek influence, Zog decided to take matters into his own hands.

In February 1929, a meeting took place in Zog's villa for the purpose of creating a synod. The only bishops available were unfortunately of questionable character. Archbishop Vissarion, described earlier, who had been educated and ordained in Greece and consecrated at Kotor by two Russian bishops, became the first head of the church. He was assisted in the organization of a council by Bishop Victor, a Serb by birth and citizenship, who was for some time in charge of the small Serbian colony at Shkodra and who was consecrated bishop in Belgrade in 1923 by the Serbian patriarch. Upon returning to Shkodra, Victor began acting in an episcopal capacity, illegally in the eyes of the patriarchate, because he was technically part of the Serbian Church, which had no jurisdiction over Albanian territory.[88]

Zog prevailed upon these two prelates to consecrate three uneducated country priests in order to fill the remaining seats on the five-man synod. Istanbul immediately excommunicated all but the Serbian bishop, hoping that Belgrade would independently condemn Bishop Victor, but to no avail.

Thus the autocephalous church was established with a certain semblance of legality. But the solution brought little immediate tranquility in its train, since the new synod was distrusted by the rank and file of the Orthodox Church. Incidents that revealed hostility toward it led to petty acts of persecution on the part of the authorities. Although he professed contentment, Zog was fully aware of the blemishes and continued to search for a lasting solution.

The rift between the Albanians and Istanbul remained unresolved until 1937, when Zog relieved Vissarion of his duties, apparently because the latter had continued to live a scandalous life. Zog found a certain Kristopher Kissi, who had been a bishop before the war but was without a see, to replace Vissarion.[89] As a result of Kissi's appointment as Orthodox metropolitan of Tirana, and because the other bishops were also replaced by more acceptable candidates, the patriarch finally, on 13 April 1937, recognized the Albanian Orthodox Church as autocephalous.

Although the Catholic Church claimed the smallest number of adherents, in many ways it was the most susceptible as a conduit of Italian influence. Like the Orthodox in the south, the Catholics (with the exception of the great Catholic tribes) were urban, often middle-class and foreign-educated, and as a result were more influential than their numbers would merit. The clergy, with its effective educational system, provided the natural leadership for this community. Zog, himself a Moslem, was perhaps more suspicious of the Catholics than he needed to be, but this can be explained by the church's obvious connection with Italy and his ever increasing reliance on Italian financing. There was, of course, no question of creating an independent Catholic Church, so Zog was limited to attempting to control it through the force of state power. Zog was frightened by the Catholics and their connections with the Italians but felt it was important, on occasion, to demonstrate his independence from Catholic and Italian influence. He was successfully able to do this on a number of occasions which helped him to maintain some measure of control over the Catholics.

Zog's first major conflict with the Catholics in Albania and their protectors involved the institution of a new civil code in 1927, which called for civil marriage and divorce. By implementing this code Zog hoped to end the shooting of faithless wives, a custom generally accepted in Albania. The Vatican objected strenuously, and the Italian minister pointed out that domestic reaction among the Catholics in the north might result in the organization of an opposition party. Zog stood his ground, informing the archbishop of Shkodra, the spiritual leader of Albanian Catholics, that he would not tolerate protests from the church and that "any priest whose enthusiasm ran away with him beyond proper bounds would soon be provided with a tree with adequate strength to support his weight."[90]

Zog's warning was taken seriously, since he had demonstrated in 1926 that he was willing to take drastic measures against Catholic leaders. In November a revolt had broken out among Catholic tribesmen of Dukagjin, who were subsidized but not encouraged by the government in Rome. Zog, with overwhelming firepower, quickly crushed the insurrection and arrested and sentenced to death many Catholics, including a number of priests. Rome asked that they be spared. This put Zog in a rather awkward position, for if he reprieved the priests who had openly confessed their guilt, he would have been attacked by the Moslems, who remembered that some years earlier he had hanged several Moslem clerics for complicity in a revolt. He would also have been accused of being a slave to the Italians. Further, it seems that Zog actually wanted them dead, commenting to the British minister "I do so much want to hang them as they deserve."[91]

The problem was finally solved by use of Zog's odd, and brutal, system of checks and balances. Zog bowed to Italian pressure and commuted the sentences of the priests who had proudly confessed to having participated in the revolt. In order to satisfy the domestic demand that he hang a priest, however, he brought forth one who few knew had been arrested and quickly hanged him. In this way Zog was able to remind the Catholic hierarchy that despite an occasional need to compromise, his power was considerable. Although Zog's relationship with the Catholic Church in Albania was never cordial, demonstrations of this sort allowed him to effectively mitigate what he perceived as a potential for foreign influence and disunity.

Zog had created, if not compliant, at least quiet religious communities, particularly at the upper levels of leadership. This made Italy's task after the invasion much simpler. With this background, the Italians had remarkably little trouble with Albania's religious communities. Still, Mussolini was clearly uneasy about the Moslem religious community and desperately sought out methods by which to tie them to Rome. Perhaps his most novel suggestion was the construction of a large mosque in Rome. Victor Emmanuel supported the idea, although this is hardly surprising, since the king enthusiastically supported any program that struck at the church. The Vatican, of course, was horror-stricken, and Ciano's intervention was required to smooth the ruffled feathers. Ciano correctly assumed that the way to win over the Albanian Moslems was not by building mosques but rather by increasing the wages of Albanian Moslems.[92]

Ciano felt so confident about the Moslem organization that he went so far as to replace the nominal head of the church, who had recognized the Italian regime in Albania, with an even more easily controlled "Moslem Committee." The Moslem community at large accepted this change with little complaint. Indeed, in a remarkable full-page analysis in the first edition of *Tomori*, a leading Moslem cleric concluded that the terms *fascism* and *Islam* were essentially synonymous.[93] The one exception was the Bektashi dervish organization, much of whose leadership never fully accepted the Italian invasion and remained in opposition.

Although no solid evidence exists, it is highly likely that the Italians finally tired of this constant opposition and had the head of the Bektashi sect, Nijaz Deda, murdered. The German minister reported that the aged head of the sect, as well as a Dervish who hurried to his rescue, was killed on 28 November 1940, Albania's independence day. The outrage occurred at about midnight in a cloister just outside of Tirana. Five fascist policemen outside the complex did nothing, and the murderers, when caught, had thirty thousand francs with them. Jacomoni ordered a state funeral and ordered top-level party and government people to attend.[94] The Italian authorities released the story that the motive for the killings was robbery, but few were convinced. For Jacomoni the important point, of course, was that the entire Moslem religious hierarchy either support the occupation or at least remain neutral. By exhibiting the same degree of ruthlessness that Zog had, Jacomoni was able essentially to achieve his goal.

The Orthodox hierarchy proved compliant as well. Vissarion's unashamed boot licking has already been mentioned. His motivation was, presumably, to ingratiate himself in order to be offered a new official position within the church leadership. Vissarion might have succeeded in this were it not for the fact that the existing hierarchy supported the invasion as well. The head of the church, Archbishop Kissi, and his three bishops expressed formal approval of the invasion in 1939.[95]

The Catholic Church and many Catholics, not surprisingly, proved to be quite supportive of the invasion. Even today many older Albanian Catholics remember the Italian occupation with fondness. Italy brought them priests and took their children to seminaries. The Italian troops behaved well and had after all gotten rid of Zog for them.[96] There were, however, many exceptions to the rule of Catholic cooperation with the Italians, particularly among the village priests. Most of these priests had been trained in Albania and were quite nationalistic. A number actually left the country after the invasion. The hierarchy, on the other hand, often found it difficult to contain their enthusiasm. The apostolic delegate, L. Nigris, saw the invasion as a very positive development that allowed all those Albanians who wished to become Catholic greater freedom to do so.[97] The Albanian hierarchy, with its two archbishops and four bishops, was given immediate tangible evidence of its members' increased significance.

Much of this evidence was, of course, monetary. In the first Italian budget for the annexed Albania, religion in general received considerable attention. Zog's last budget had allotted 50,000 francs to the Moslems and 35,000 to the Orthodox Church. The Italians allotted 375,000 to the Moslems, 187,500 to the Orthodox Church, and 156,000 to the Catholic Church. Although all the religious hierarchies did very well in comparison, given the numerical 7 to 2 to 1 division in Albania the Catholics were treated with considerable generosity.[98]

As further evidence of the Italian bias in favor of the Albanian Catholics, in February 1940 Jacomoni began pushing the Uniate Movement, but under Catholic supremacy. Zog had traditionally discouraged this position because of potential religious conflict but the Italians seemed unconcerned about this possibility. They correctly assumed that a great deal could be done with money.

Archbishop Kissi of the Orthodox Church, not known for his incorruptibility, was apparently offered money.[99] Although this Italian program experienced little success in the long run, its institution helped to guarantee the loyalty of the Catholic hierarchy.

Italian Albania, in terms of its structure, proved to be little different from its Zogist predecessor, at least in the early years. Zog had created a non-absolutist, monarchical dictatorship with the cooperation of the old feudal aristocracy, made up of the great landowners of the center and south, with the cooperation of the major northern tribal chieftains. Power remained with Zog, but he could never afford to alienate his constituency. Many of them, particularly the chieftains of the north, were kept in line with favors and simple graft. An often used formula was to commission a chief as a colonel in the Albanian army and then provide him with enough gold on a monthly basis to support a certain number of nonexistent troops.

The Italians were quite experienced and comfortable with this system of graft. Ciano, in particular, considered himself to be something of an expert in the art of the bribe. The Italians recognized that the chiefs were not politically significant on a national scale, since they could rarely afford to leave their areas for any length of time. In light of this realization, the Italians seemed more willing to give the chiefs even greater freedom in their own areas. This, of course, encouraged local loyalty at the expense of state loyalty. Here, Italian policy did considerable damage to the budding Albanian nationalism Zog had carefully and painstakingly sought to instill during his reign. Of the great landowners who cooperated with Zog, some left with him. Most of these, however, soon returned. In any case, the Italians were not required to look too far to find individuals from good families who had been alienated by Zog. Zog had started his career as a minor chieftain. His road to power was littered with the bodies of those who opposed him. By Albanian custom, killings of this nature required the imposition of the traditional blood feud. By the 1930s it was estimated that some six hundred such blood feuds haunted Zog, often making him a prisoner in his own palace. Many of these people, too, were more than willing to cooperate with the Italians. The invasion produced little in terms of radical political or social shifts. Internal rivalry and struggle between these people remained of a personal rather than a political or social nature. The power, or lack thereof, that the traditional feudal elite exercised was also very similar. As under Zog, these people had limited real power. This arrangement changed little under the Italians.

As Luan Omari, perhaps the leading socialist Albanian legal historian, tells us, the Italians did not change much structurally and really did not need to. While Italian Albania was certainly more centralized, the judicial and legislative structure possessed the same lack of independence as under Zog. Although Zog conducted the occasional election for his Parliament, with advantages of extensive electoral interference along with the very high illiteracy rate, it would be absurd to speak in terms of democracy under Zog. The elective principle, insofar as it existed, was abolished entirely under the Italians. Omari argues that the new constitution resulted from a merger of the Italian and Zogist constitutions. This seems a fair characterization. What we have here is a miniature Italy grafted onto a Zogist frame. The operation was performed slowly and occasionally with tact. The result was a nonabsolutist, fascist, military dictatorship in the guise of a constitutional monarchy. The next step was to try to sell it to the Albanians.[100]

The wedding of Zog and Geraldine, 28 April 1938. (Jacomoni)

Zog's representative Rrok Geraj meets with General Guzzoni at Durrës on the day of the Italian invasion. (Jacomoni)

Xhafer Ypi offers Italy a personal union with Albania following the Italian invasion, 12 April 1939. (Jacomoni)

Ceremony at the Quirinale Palace in Rome—the Albanian crown of Skenderbeg is offered to the Italian king, Victor Emmanuel III, 16 April 1939. (Jacomoni)

CHAPTER 3

ITALIAN GREATER ALBANIA

Ciano was willing to exaggerate Italian popularity in Albania in order to convince Mussolini to invade. Ciano could delude Mussolini, but he found self-deception, particularly following his first visit to Albania after the invasion, more difficult. Rather than receiving the warm welcome his agents had assured him, he saw overt hostility. Once the Italians had established their occupation, therefore, Ciano made every effort to improve the dismal reputation the Italians had traditionally experienced and to win over the populous, or at least, some of the populous. A carrot-and-stick approach was adopted, with, at least during the first year, considerably more emphasis placed on the former. With this initial altruism, the Italians hoped to improve both their political and economic position in Albania.

In a sense, Italy's conciliatory attitude began to make itself felt on the very day of the invasion. Observers noted that the Italian naval gunners at Durrës refrained from using high explosive shells and restricted their fire to the extent that surprisingly little damage was caused. Once ashore, Italian troops behaved with restraint and even friendliness, despite some determined Albanian resistance. While many examples of fraternal behavior can be found, very little overtly harsh action was reported.[1] Ciano's diary tells us that he personally gave orders that Albanian soldiers, particularly the officers, were to be well treated.[2] Once the fighting, what little of it there was, had stopped, the Italians demonstrated increased restraint and caution. Andrew Ryan reported on the good-natured naïveté of the Italian soldiers sent to guard the British mission in Durrës.[3] It is likely that this attitude stemmed partially from the basic nature of the recently drafted Italian peasants, who had nothing against Albanians, and partially from official policy.

Ruth Mitchell, a long-time British resident of Albania, wrote on 26 April 1939, "The pain being taken not to offend or annoy the people, not to give the slightest feeling of conquest or superiority is really remarkable."[4] Indeed, the Italians were careful to avoid the impression of occupation. The port of Durrës was free for anyone to walk around. One saw an occasional sentry guarding a dump of rifles or a vessel unloading oil, but only small garrisons were found in both Durrës and Tirana. And the road between these two principal towns of Albania was left entirely unguarded. Where security patrols did exist, the Italians made certain, at least in the early months, that they consisted of one Italian carabinière and one Albanian soldier—although rumors naturally circulated that the Albanians had guns but no bullets.[5] Even as large numbers of troops and much war material arrived, both were quickly sent to outlying regions. The troops who had participated in the invasion were quickly replaced by fresh troops who had no connection with actually shooting Albanians.[6]

Winning the Hearts and Minds: Social Development

Ciano hoped to reinforce an impression of benevolence with a number of initial gestures aimed more at public relations than at addressing any of Albania's profound social and economic problems. One of Ciano's first moves was to distribute food and clothing in some of the many poor areas and to release those prisoners who had not already been set free.[7] Ciano, who greatly enjoyed playing the savior of the Albanians, did much of this in person. He personally distributed 190,000 gold francs to the needy in Tirana, Shkodra, Vlora, Gjirokastra, Saranda, Korça, and Kukës. Because the money was given directly to the poor, bypassing the usual bureaucracy, it did some good. Although Mussolini had not been informed, Ciano soothed his ire by reporting that Italian generosity had resulted in demonstrations in recognition of Italy and the Duce.[8]

Italian largess was followed by a well-orchestrated anti-Zog campaign. Ciano recognized that Zog maintained the support of some Albanians, and many others at least equated the memory of the king with an independent Albania. The campaign included changing all those street names in Tirana and elsewhere that were associated with Zog and his family. As usual, Ciano and his agents used excessive zeal. The southern port of Saranda, which had recently been renamed Zogaj, was now called Porto Edda, after Ciano's wife, Mussolini's daughter. The giant inscriptions "GZ"—for Geraldine and Zog—and "ZOG" on the great bluff behind Zog's summer residence in Durrës were cleverly transformed into "REX." The compound itself was turned over to the Italian "Dopolavoro" organization to serve as a holiday camp for Albanian and Italian workers. Accommodation was provided for hundreds at a time for a two-week period at the cost of two francs per head per day.[9] In announcing this new benefit *Fashizmi* alluded to the orgies that Zog had hosted there.[10] To remove Zog's picture from wide circulation, all Albanian currency was recalled but quickly released once Zog's features had been obliterated.[11]

The Italian press and the Italian-controlled press in Albania heaped scorn on Zog and his sisters for their extravagance and lack of concern for the average Albanian. Much was made of the story, which the Germans repeated in their documents, that Zog, on the evening of 7 April, had manufactured the rumor that Tirana would be bombed, in order to screen his and his government's flight. Whether the story was true or not, by the end of April it was generally believed. In July, the announcement of the sequestering of his property was accompanied by a further barrage of anti-Zog sentiment. This was probably unnecessary, since Zog had been remarkably effective in discrediting himself—he needed little help from the Italians. To the credit of the Italians, Geraldine escaped this campaign. Indeed, Rome even went so far as to offer to return her wedding gifts. She refused.[12]

The Italians hoped to contrast Zog's unpopularity with at least the appearance of popular support for their actions. Much publicity was given to messages of welcome from the heads of Albania's various religious communities. Some were disgustingly obsequious. The Italians, like Zog, paid a great deal of attention to the tribal leaders because of their important regional influence. Groups of them were brought by car and airplane to Tirana and were received by the lieutenant general to extend a *besa* and to swear their allegiance to the new king. Particular attention was paid to the chiefs from Mati—Zog's own clan—as well as to a large body of some 250 chiefs, including the leaders of the powerful Catholic Mirdita tribe. This latter group was headed by the principal Mirdita chief, who was honored with the title of "prince."[13] The remainder received more conventional honors, including regional appointments and sacks of money. Ciano's diary tells us of distributing bundles of Albanian francs to initially recalcitrant chiefs.[14]

Similar methods were used to demonstrate a groundswell of popular support when auspicious occasions demanded it. Ciano's visit to Durrës in August 1939 serves as a good example. He was greeted by some thousands of peasants who had been brought in from outlying districts, paid, and provided with small Italian and Albanian flags. There was little real enthusiasm except from a band of enterprising peasants who tapped a large barrel of wine that had been left in the street. After having consumed considerable quantities, they proceeded to utter fascist slogans with a fervor that would have satisfied even the most exacting organizer.[15]

But the Italians were ready to do more than engage in propaganda to improve their image. Having learned from their mistakes in Ethiopia, they were ready to offer widespread tangible benefits to the Albanians. One of the more successful programs initiated to win the hearts and minds of the masses was the sending of Albanian children to summer camps. The program, sponsored by the Gioventù Italiana del Littorio, was originally greeted with such hostility and suspicion that the first posters announcing the plan disappeared and many of the first children who traveled to Durrës and Vlora were accompanied by hysterical parents who were certain that they would never see their children again. The parents cried that when the Serbs came, they took the children, when the Turks came, they took the children, and now the Italians were doing the same. One mother gave her small son her glass eye, saying "When you are a man and perhaps free, you will come back and look for me. If you see a woman with one eye of this color you will know it is your mother."[16]

Their fears were unjustified, however. Upon arrival in Bari, the ten thousand children sent in July and August were given colored disks to wear around their necks, and their clothes were taken for disinfection and kept for the return journey. The children were bathed; sent for medical inspection; and given new clothes, a toothbrush, and toothpaste—the last of which most ate immediately. Next, they were served dinner, given postcards of Mussolini and the king, and then sent off for a month to Ravenna. The organization was reported to be excellent at every step, down to a personal visit by Mussolini on 29 August. On their return, after a fine time in the open air, the children looked healthy and happy. Every effort had been made to impress these children favorably with the benefits of the new regime, to good effect.[17] The program proved to be good propaganda and provided tangible benefits to thousands of children.

Opportunities to study abroad and tours of various types for adults, with the same intended goal, were also arranged. In July 1939, Professor Koliqi, the Albanian minister of education, announced that there were more than 400 Albanian students studying abroad. Of these, 150 held full scholarships from the Ministry of Education and 40 from the Ministry of National Economy. All of the 190 scholarship recipients, as well as 50 percent of the remaining 210—who were self-supporting—were studying in Italy.[18] Many of these students were enrolled in the Battaglioni Scanderbey in cooperation with the Italian Gioventù Universitària Fascista, a politically inspired student organization. At the same time, the Italian government introduced a program allowing teachers and pupils from Albanian schools to tour Italy and Libya.[19]

Even more tangible, the Italians dispatched a number of "missions" to see to the improvement of health standards and general living conditions in Albania. With considerable publicity, in May 1939, a dental mission arrived from Rome—forty people in 10 groups of four—to tour Albania. Although they only stayed for ten days, the Italian authorities announced that a permanent dental center was to be established in Elbasan. Mussolini instructed Jacomoni to eradicate malaria in six months as well as to begin a campaign against VD and TB, which although perhaps not epidemics, took a considerable toll among Albanians and Italians.[20] Jacomoni made considerable headway. He appointed an Italian doctor as technical councilor to the Albanian Department of Health and, more important, saw to the construction of a number of hospitals in Tirana and other towns.[21]

In July a well-equipped sanitary mission arrived and toured various provincial centers, announcing that permanent establishments would be set up in some of these centers. In August Count Ciano arrived to attend a ceremony in honor of the completion of the first phase of a scheme to provide Tirana with an adequate water supply. As part of this phase, water was pumped from the bed of the Tirana River and transported in pipes to the city. The second phase included the construction of a reservoir at a higher level, which would provide the necessary pressure for distributing water to each household. Similar improvements were planned for Durrës, Vlora, Korça, and Gjirokastra.[22] The local *fascio* in each town also provided a number of services. They dealt summary justice to swindling or profiteering shopkeepers, arbitrated local disputes, and arranged through their women's organization for midwifery service and home nursing. They even helped with house repairs.[23] Ciano summed up Italian policy in his diary, noting "it will be necessary quickly to carry out a program of public works. Only this way will we definitely link the people to us and destroy the authority of their chiefs, showing that only we are capable of doing what they have not been able or did not want to do."[24]

Winning the Hearts and Minds: Economic Development

While all of this activity was received favorably by most Albanians affected, the Italians believed that they could make the greatest immediate positive impact in the economic sphere. At the same time, they hoped to garner substantial benefits from Albania's natural resources, agricultural potential, and pool of cheap labor. The first priority was to produce an accurate study of Albania's prospects, since, despite Italy's long-term economic involvement, this seems not to have been done. The figures that Count Ciano presented to

Mussolini on 10 May 1939, stressing Albania's vast agricultural and mineral potential, were extremely optimistic estimates. When Ciano handed Mussolini a chunk of Albanian copper ore, proclaiming it to be the Carthaginian figs, he was demonstrating able showmanship but very little else.

The task of gathering the required information fell to Zenone Benini, Ciano's undersecretary for Albanian affairs. Benini issued his report in October 1939, and though not as exaggerated as that of Ciano's, it too was overly optimistic. In terms of iron ore, Benini reported that Albanian deposits were sufficient for Italian requirements for ten years. Further, Albania was said to possess enough sulphate of copper and bitumen to take care of Italian requirements indefinitely. Oil production would increase, and some 500,000 acres of land would soon be drained for the cultivation of cotton, oil seeds, and maize.[25] While he did not mention Italian colonization in this published report, informed observers hardly needed to be reminded that this had long been a priority. Ciano had long predicted that Albania—Italy's *quinta spónda*, or fifth shore—could become home to millions of surplus Italians, although as with most of his statistics he seems to have just pulled this number out of a hat.

To facilitate this exploitation, Benini ordered the complete overhaul of Albania's weak infrastructure. Work was begun on thousands of miles of roads constructed by the Italian firm Aziènda Strada Albanìa. New airport runways were constructed, harbors were enlarged and modernized, and railroad construction was begun. Although the latter was not completed under the Italians, significant progress was made, to the extent that the Tirana-Durrës line could be opened in 1946. Postal and telephone service was upgraded.[26] Yards and warehouses were constructed in anticipation of the bounty that careful Italian planning and technological advancement would produce.

Many of Benini's conclusions had merit, but on the whole he too had exaggerated. On the agricultural front Albania was and would continue to be a drain on Italian resources. Rather than producing a surplus to feed the army of occupation, even in the best of times Albania required the annual importation of 20,000 to 30,000 tons of cereals.[27] This need was hardly offset by the modest exportable surplus production of some 2,000 tons of olives, 1,500 tons of dried beans, and about 2,000 tons of assorted dairy products and some livestock.

Albania's mineral resources proved to be much more impressive. While the effective exploitation of iron ore, bitumen, and copper would have to await the completion of an adequate road network—which in 1939 was a long way off—Albanian oil and chrome reserves were of immediate importance to the Italians. Crude oil was produced at wells in the Devoll Valley near Berat and carried by an Italian-built pipeline to Vlora for shipment to Italy. In 1939 shipments amounted to 175,000 tons and an increase to 200,000 tons was expected by 1940. There seems to be some confusion as to what percentage of Italian needs this quantity could fill. The British Ministry of Economic Warfare suggested in December 1940 that Albania provided about one-third of Italy's oil imports. Other, and more numerous, sources suggest that the figure was much lower, even below 10 percent.[28] There was general agreement, however, that the oil would be expensive, since its quality was not particularly good — having an asphaltic base and high sulfur content. The difficulty of extraction and shipment added to the cost, including, of course, the need to ship it to Italy for refinement and return it to Albania as motor and aviation fuel.[29]

Chrome, important in the production of steel, was perhaps Albania's most significant mineral resource for the Italians. Like oil, it was already being extracted and exported. Unlike oil, Albanian chrome reserves provided Italy with 100 percent of its needs. This would become particularly crucial once Italy entered the war, since Albania possessed the only source of chrome available in the territories controlled by Italy.

The Italians, then, hoped that extensive investment in Albania would bring both economic and political benefits. Despite a weak domestic economy, Mussolini guaranteed the Albanians the sum of 22 million pounds over five years for economic development, considerably more than the 8.2 million Rome had spent since the early 1920s.[30] Initial reports of Italian activity were quite favorable. Ruth Mitchell commented at the end of April 1939, "What a great improvement there is in the condition of the people already. . . . The whole atmosphere had become brisker and more enterprising; now at least there is hope."[31] Even the German minister Eberhard von Pannwitz, who was perpetually critical of the Italians, commented favorably on the Italian tempo, which he likened to the Nazi tempo in Austria after the *Anschluss*.[32]

It is clear that the Italians did much initial economic good and many Albanians benefited, particularity merchants and the vast lower class. The new construction projects brought in large amounts of capital and employed many Albanians. Although most of the firms handling the contracts were Italian, most of the foremen were Italian, and many of the workers were imported from Italy, unemployment, which had been a problem under Zog, ceased to be a problem. Principal among the new projects was road construction. By the middle of May the Italians had already renovated the road between Tirana and Durrës, reducing car travel time from one and a quarter hours to fifty minutes.[33]

On 25 May 1939 *Fashizmi* announced a program for the construction within two years of fifteen hundred kilometers of modern roads, soon supported by an Italian law authorizing 800 million lire in funding, 150 million of which was allocated for the first two years. The program consisted mostly of widening and reconditioning existing roads. And despite Mussolini's personal order that the roads be planned in such a way as to lead to the Greek border, many served important commercial functions.[34] By the end of August seventeen thousand Albanian laborers and five hundred Italian foremen were employed on the project. By early 1940 it was reported that some thirty thousand workers, supported by Italian engineers, were building roads and bridges in Albania.[35]

Other high-profile projects included land reclamation, for which the Italian government set aside 1,200 million lire to be spread over eight years. Ciano visited Durrës on 19 August 1939 and inspected the first reclamation plans. More than thirteen thousand hectares were to be reclaimed in the Durrës area by the end of 1941. As early as mid-May 1939 twenty-five hundred Albanians, under the direction of ten Italians, were busy enlarging the runways of many Albanian airports from one to two kilometers.[36] Harbor construction was also a major priority. After the embarrassment of April 1939, when naval commanders were unaware that Durrës could not handle ocean-going vessels—despite the fact that Italian engineers had worked on the harbor for Zog—the Italian authorities determined that Albanian ports, particularly Durrës, would be enlarged. The government in Rome also allotted 200 million lire for the first stage of railroad construction connecting the oil fields with the port of Vlora, as well as a line from Durrës to Elbasan, near the Greek frontier.

Considerably less useful but also a source of some employment for the Albanians were the large fascist buildings in Tirana, which Italian authorities felt necessary to demonstrate Italy's imperial glory. Amidst the huts of Tirana the Italians built marble palaces for the Fascist Party, the fascist youth movement, and the Instituto Fascista Albanèse pégli infortuni sul Lavóro, the fascist social services.[37] Not only were the buildings unnecessary, but they proved to be less than functional, with large facades but remarkably small interiors. More useful were the warehouses and barracks built throughout Albania. And in February 1940 the Ente Turìstico Alberghièro Albanìa was established to construct and operate hotels in Vlora, Shkodra, Korça, Elbasan, Berat, Gjirokastra, Porto Edda, Tirana, and Durrës. The announcement was welcomed not only as a means to stimulate Albania's nonexistent tourist industry but also to alleviate the chronic hotel shortage in the capital. It had not been possible to find a hotel room in Tirana since the invasion.[38] Within one year of the invasion there were approximately 140 different Italian enterprises functioning in Albania. They dominated Albanian finance, public works, agriculture, mining, industry, communications, and transportation—every vital sector of the Albanian economy.[39]

All this activity had a considerable immediate impact on many Albanians. The Italians provided many jobs, possibly too many. As more and more projects were inaugurated, more and more agricultural laborers abandoned their previous jobs, leaving an agricultural labor shortage. The attraction, of course, was primarily financial, because the Italians had doubled the wages of unskilled workers on public projects from one to two francs a day. Albanian workers were also afforded unemployment insurance along modern lines. And civil servants were not overlooked in this spasm of generosity. Those who were cooperative had their pensions and even their back wages paid. By May 1939, civil service salaries had increased by 22 percent.[40]

The increase of salaries itself in troubled times does not, of course, guarantee a higher standard of living. But the Italians seem to have taken that into consideration as well. Italian authorities fixed prices, including rents as well as the cost of wheat and other cereals. The cost of such services as water supply, electricity, transport, and hotels was regulated, and the vendors were required to display prices. The government provided regulation and arbitration of disputes.[41]

Although these measures were unpopular with some merchants and property owners, they came as a relief to the vast majority of people. The National Bank of Albania testified to the new economic activity and the general higher standard of living by reporting in April 1940 that (1) the increase of banknotes in circulation from 12 million francs at the time of the invasion to 20 million at the time of the report—since inflation was not yet high—was evidence of a real increase of Albania's wealth and (2) both ordinary and company accounts held by the bank had increased.[42] Ciano commented, perhaps overoptimistically, in May 1940: "There is no question that the mass of the Albanian people have been won over by Italy. The Albanian people are grateful to us for having taught them to eat twice a day, for this rarely happened before. Even in the physical appearance of the people greater well being can be noted."[43]

If Albanians did not notice by themselves that they were better off, the Italians and their Albanian puppets were ever ready to remind them. *Fashizmi*, on 19 January 1940, published an article comparing the tax burdens of various countries. Readers were told that taxes in dollars per head per year were lower in Italy than anywhere else in Europe. The figures quoted were Italy: 30.9; France: 54.5; the United States: 107.5; Great Britain: 107.8; Germany: 109.7. The author invited Albanians, in a spirit of self-congratulation, to consider their own comparative immunity from taxes. Of the total annual revenue of 26 million francs, taxation—direct and indirect—accounted for 11.8 million. Taxes listed included a house tax, a tithe on agricultural products, the poll tax on livestock, the tax on certain articles of consumption (alcohol, tobacco, sugar, coffee, and flour), the yield of state monopolies, and official fees. This equaled about 11.8 Albanian francs per head, or 3.7 dollars, which was claimed as the world's lowest rate of taxation. The article also noted the Albanian government's pledge to reduce taxation if possible, or at least not to increase it. Albanians were implicitly reminded, further, that they were getting a lot for nothing.[44]

Winning the Hearts and Minds: Irredentism

But Ciano believed that the Italians could engender the greatest goodwill by pursuing Albanian irredentism, something that happily coincided with Italian plans for Balkan conquest. When Albania's state boundaries were delineated by the Conference of Ambassadors in London in 1913, many Albanians were left outside of the new state. The largest group of unredeemed could be found in Kosova, which had served as the cradle of Albanian nationalism in the nineteenth century but, following the Balkan Wars, became part of Serbia. A much smaller number of Albanians was found in Macedonia, and even smaller numbers inhabited Montenegro and the region of Çamëria in northern Greece.

Zog, although he titled himself "King of the Albanians" to help establish his nationalist credentials, had not pursued an irredentist policy for a number of reasons. Kosovar chieftains were among his most dangerous rivals. It is also possible that he had made an agreement with the Yugoslavs to leave Kosova to them in return for the support they gave him in forcibly returning to power in 1924. He may also have come to the sensible conclusion that his other problems precluded expansion. Maintaining power was far more important to Zog than a dangerous foreign policy that could have led both to war with a much stronger neighbor and to internal conflict.

Despite Zog's reluctance to pursue irredentism, the issue did not die, particularly in light of Serbian repression of Albanians in Kosova. The Italians, though they had not pushed the issue prior to the invasion, decided to take full advantage of irredentism once Albania was part of the imperium. In June 1939 Ciano, in referring to Kosova and Çamëria, noted that Mussolini defined irredentism as "the little light in the tunnel," the ideal spiritual motive to keep the Albanian nationalism spirit high.[45] He believed that it was simple for the Italians to increase their popularity by becoming champions of Albanian nationalism, and he was encouraged to learn—from the Albanian ex-minister in Belgrade—that the 850,000 Albanians of Kosova were "physically strong . . . morally firm and enthusiastic at the idea of union with their mother country."[46]

First, however, Ciano reassured Greece and Yugoslavia of his disinterest in their Albanians. In the case of Yugoslavia, he took advantage of a meeting with Foreign Minister Jovan Markovic on 22 April 1939 in Venice to do so personally. The day before, Ciano noted in his diary that "for the moment we must not even allow it to be imagined that the problem is attracting our attention; rather"—he wrote in his usual rather colorful fashion—"it is necessary to give the Yugoslavs a dose of chloroform."[47] This is apparently what Markovic was administered.

Assuming that his personal assurance of disinterest was enough, Ciano next launched a clumsy and transparent campaign to keep the flame of irredentism alive in Albania. For the most part, the campaign took the form of what was made to look like a series of spontaneous outbursts of nationalist enthusiasm from Albanians in the puppet government and among the population at large. There was, of course, the occasional hint from an Italian official. Ciano had himself inaugurated the campaign on 13 April 1939, when, in addressing the staff of the soon-to-be-disbanded Albanian Foreign Ministry, he noted that Italy wished to enlarge Albania's frontiers and help it realize its national aspirations. To help him in this process, Ciano created the Office for Irredentism at the Undersecretariate for Albanian Affairs. Ciano asked Koliqi to draw up a program on irredentism based upon Ciano's three-stage priority: (1) general broad propaganda laying stress on culture and religion, (2) same as to the management of public welfare, and (3) clandestine military organization to be ready for the moment when the inevitable Yugoslav crisis came to a head.[48]

Other Italian officials quickly became involved in adding fuel to the fire of irredentism. In the middle of June in a speech at Korça, the Italian minister of public instruction, Giuseppe Bottai, compared Albania with Piedmont and spoke of its enlargement in two or three years. The Yugoslav consul complained, and the local Albanian papers suppressed the passage. Later in the month, the Greek minister in Tirana reported to his foreign minister that Marshal Badoglio, who was on a tour of Albania, promised his audiences greater prosperity and the extension of Albania's frontiers. Jacomoni made similar references during the ceremonies welcoming the marshal.[49]

Next, Ciano arranged for extensive direct Albanian involvement. During his visit to Albania in mid-August 1939 his efforts to mobilize Albanians met with some success. In his welcome address, the prefect of Tirana expressed his desire for the unity of all Albanians and the creation of a greater Albania with the help of the fascist imperium. Ciano promised that Italy would see to it that Albania realized its deepest desires, and he ended his short talk with "Viva la Grande Albania." Ciano was also greeted with numerous posters, banners, and maps of an enlarged Albania put up by Italian blackshirts. Favorite slogans included "Duce, we think of all Albanians in the world" and "Duce, think of our brothers." Albanian demonstrators—who the German minister reported had been organized several days in advance—met Ciano with signs and banners that proclaimed, "We are Albanians from Kosova" and "Long Live Kosova."

While *Fashizmi* took no part in this irredentist outburst in August, a violent article did appear in October. When both the Yugoslav and Greek ministers complained, the Italian director general of press propaganda and tourism disclaimed responsibility, maintaining that a young student—who would henceforth be watched—was the responsible party.[50] Ciano's strategy was clearly to keep the issue alive, without ever pushing it too far at any single instance.

These occasional references to Albania's unredeemed increased throughout 1940 as Mussolini came closer to making a decision about further military action in the Balkans. During the months before the Italian invasion of Greece, most public pronouncements by either Albanian or Italian officials were accompanied by some "spontaneous" demonstrations followed by a pointed reference by the speaker concerning the inevitable union of unredeemed Albanians with the mother country. In March, for example, Mustafa Kruja gave a series of speeches, relayed by loudspeaker and printed and circulated, in which he made references to Albania's unredeemed territories. He referred to Albania's frontiers as "clearly traced and admitting to no doubt but not corresponding to the effective extension of Albanian rights, either of priority of possession, ethnical affinities of population or common aristocracy of origin." In case this verbosity left the audience confused—which it undoubtedly did—someone in the audience was quickly prompted to shout, "Kosova!" Senator Kruja answered: "There is a war on in Europe now. When it is over you will find that all your hopes are realized."[51]

The principal irredentist demonstrations, however, accompanied Ciano's frequent visits to Albania. In the middle of May 1940 the count conducted another well-publicized photo opportunity tour of Albania, giving away money and reviewing parades. His visit was accompanied by the now-obligatory banners that carried inscriptions saluting Kosova and Çamëria. Ciano was convinced that these constant references to irredentism were winning over the Albanians. After the May 1940 visit he noted in his diary "a warm welcome.

The Albanians are far on the path of intervention. They want Kosova and Çamëria."[52] At the same time Greece and Yugoslavia were being reassured. Mussolini, in his speech declaring war on the Allies in June, guaranteed Greece and Yugoslavia safe from invasion. So the Albanians might not misunderstand, however, Piero Parini, Jacomoni's deputy, assured Vërlaci in the presence of the German minister, Pannwitz, that one must listen to the tone of the speech rather than the content.[53]

In light of Hitler's successes elsewhere, Mussolini moved ever closer to the determination that Italian imperial glory required action in the Balkans. Ciano's role, as with the invasion of Albania, seems to have been decisive. Although action in the Balkans certainly fit into the Duce's overall ambitions, the timing and direction remained rather vague. Mussolini had a hard time with decisions; Ciano's destiny seems to have been to continue helping him make disastrous ones. By April 1940, Ciano began turning his attention to Greece in earnest. Because of political considerations, particularly German pressure, Ciano decided that Kosova and Yugoslavia would have to wait.

The pattern of events had much in common with his approach to the invasion of Albania. Without any word from Mussolini, he began gathering information, laying the groundwork, and experimenting with possible scenarios. During his visit to Tirana in May 1940, Ciano took the opportunity to question the general commanding Italian forces in Albania, General Carlo Geloso, about how many troops would be needed to invade Greece. Geloso, who estimated that ten or eleven divisions were required, and seemed to show little enthusiasm for the project, was immediately removed and replace by Sebastian Viscounti Prasca, who would not make the same mistake. Viscounti Prasca demonstrated boundless enthusiasm for the project and did not bother about assembling an adequate army. Jacomoni added to Ciano's confidence by reporting on the magnificent spirit of the Albanian fascist militia and their burning desire to fight for the expansion of Albania and the Italian empire.[54] Ciano, meanwhile, indulged in his usual penchant for spies and saboteurs, ordering that Albanian irregulars from both sides of the Greek frontier be recruited to cause unrest in Çamëria. He even toyed with the idea of having an Albanian assassinate the king of Greece, frighteningly reminiscent of the plans to murder King Zog.[55]

But this was about as far as the plans went for the moment, as Mussolini was naturally preoccupied with Italy's declaration of war on the Allies and his usual vacillation about where to attack next. In terms of the Balkans, Mussolini seemed to be leaning toward Yugoslavia, but Ciano was determined to further his Greek plans. Ciano's enthusiasm was redoubled by an intercepted

Greek message in which General John Metaxas, the Greek strongman, referred to Ciano's "brutal and boorish manner."[56]

To insure that the Duce would not forget Greece, Ciano, through Jacomoni, manufactured a series of border difficulties that showed Italian propaganda and diplomacy to be remarkably inept and lent considerable credence to Metaxas's unflattering assessment of Ciano. Ciano decided to focus on an incident in June when unknown assailants, possibly Greek police, killed and beheaded Daout Hoxha, a leader of the Albanians in northern Greece.[57] It has been suggested that Hoxha on occasion may have worked as an Italian agent hired to foment unrest in Çamëria.[58] The Stephani news agency—later repeated by the official German news bureau—portrayed Hoxha as an Albanian freedom fighter and patriot treacherously murdered by Greek agents who then cut off his head and passed it from one Albanian village to another in Çamëria to intimidate the population.[59]

The Greek news agency refuted every point, maintaining that Hoxha was a notorious criminal who for twenty years had been sought by Greek authorities for robbery and murder. The Greeks reported that far from being in a state of agitation, the few Albanians in Çamëria were happy with the paternalistic Greek regime. To placate the Italians, Athens arrested two Albanians for the crime and held them in anticipation of extradition requests from Italy. The Italians, most likely because of the usual slovenliness demonstrated by the Foreign Ministry, never requested extradition.[60]

On 10 August Ciano presented Mussolini with the Italian version of the Daout Hoxha story, effectively bringing the rather fickle dictator's attention back to Greece. Mussolini, seemingly incensed, called for an "act of force, because since 1923 [the Corfu Incident] he had some accounts to settle and the Greeks deceive themselves if they think that he has forgotten."[61] On the next day the Duce called for more particulars on Çamëria and ordered a Stephani dispatch that was to start agitation on the question. Within a day the Italo-Albanian press poured forth with bold headlines deploring Greek oppression in Çamëria, which had some basis in fact—the Greeks had generally treated the Albanians of northern Greece deplorably.[62] Mussolini also ordered Jacomoni and Viscounti Prasca to report to Rome to discuss his new determination to launch a surprise attack on Greece by the end of September. On 12 August 1940 Mussolini told Ciano, Jacomoni, and Viscounti Prasca that unless Corfu and Çamëria were yielded without a fight, Italy would "go the limit." Jacomoni and Viscounti Prasca, according to Ciano, announced that the action was possible, even easy.[63] War came one step closer when an Italian submarine sank the antiquated Greek cruiser *Helli* in Greek waters on 15 August. As an indication of the level of confusion in Italian policymaking at this time, Ciano knew nothing of this incident, commenting only that "I consider the intemperance of Di Vecchi at the bottom of it."[64]

By this point Berlin became alarmed and informed Ciano and Mussolini in no uncertain terms that the status quo in the Balkans must be maintained. Mussolini meekly acquiesced but allowed preparations to continue just the same. Viscounti Prasca busily moved Italian units to the Greek frontier while Jacomoni armed and trained Albanian guerrillas to spread terror and disrupt the Greek rear. Italian officials even took to encouraging one another. Jacomoni sent frequent messages to Ciano detailing the supposed miserable and grave conditions endured by the Albanians in Çamëria, while directing the Albanian press and radio to continue the exaltation of Daout Hoxha.[65]

In his growing enthusiasm for the projected invasion, Jacomoni went so far as to suggest that the operation should begin with a mock attack by Albanian irregulars on an Italian border post to serve as a pretext. This, of course, was little more than a rehash of Heinrich Himmler's rather transparent raid on the Gleiwitz radio station in August 1939 immediately preceding the German invasion of Poland.[66]

If German objections momentarily convinced Mussolini to suspend plans for an invasion, German action in Romania encouraged Mussolini to act immediately. When on 12 October 1940 German troops entered Romania, Mussolini was livid, complaining to Ciano that "Hitler always faces me with a fait accompli. This time I am going to pay him back in his own coin. He will find out from the papers that I have occupied Greece." Although there was still some resistance from the general staff, particularly from Badoglio, Mussolini dismissed it by boldly proclaiming that "I shall send in my resignation as an Italian if anyone objects to our fighting the Greeks." Ciano himself was equally convinced that the operation would be "useful and easy."[67]

Reports from Albania were all positive. Jacomoni announced that the Albanians of Çamëria were favorable to the Italians and drew up plans for their immediate assistance.[68] More important, Jacomoni reported, Albanian youth, who had always been reserved, now made open manifestations of approval. They awaited the invasion keenly and enthusiastically. Overreaching himself, Jacomoni claimed that all the Albanian patriots and troops were burning with the desire to liberate Epirus (northern Greece) once and for all. He was hardly able to prevent the Albanians from crossing the frontier on their own. Mussolini, apparently convinced by this nonsense, was actually afraid that extensive military participation on the part of the Albanians might convince them that the inevitable victory over the Greeks was primarily the result of Albanian arms.[69] He need hardly have been concerned.

With all these excellent reports, added to his rage at the Germans, on 13 October Mussolini fixed 26 October as the day of the invasion. Although this was something of an innovation—in the past he had simply issued directives—on 15 October Mussolini summoned a council of war to announce his decision and receive direct reports from his ministers and generals. Present were Ciano, Viscounti Prasca, Jacomoni, Badoglio, and General Mario Roatta, deputy chief of staff of the army. Conspicuously absent were naval and air force representatives. Jacomoni repeated that the Albanians were enthusiastic and the Greeks depressed.[70] Ciano, despite evidence to the contrary from Emanuele Grazzi, his minister in Greece, supported Jacomoni's position, arguing that the economic polarization in Greece made the lower classes "indifferent to everything including our invasion."[71]

From a military standpoint Mussolini was assured that all was in readiness. Viscounti Prasca announced that he had prepared the operation down to the smallest detail—it was now as perfect as humanly possible. He confidently told Mussolini that he expected to oppose a Greek army of thirty thousand (the actual figure turned out to be about ten times that many), which would be taken by a series of quick envelopments. After an hour and a half, Mussolini concluded that the problem had been examined from every angle and that there was nothing left to be said.[72]

On 22 October Ciano drew up an ultimatum to be presented to Metaxas. It was similar to the one that he had offered Zog the year before and was intended to leave Greece "no way out, either occupation or war."[73] Greece was required to immediately agree to Italian occupation of some strategic bases. As a further example of carelessness of method, Grazzi, when asked, was unable to inform Metaxas which strategic bases the Italians had in mind.[74] Metaxas, without consulting his government, answered with his now famous "Oxhi!" or "no." Jacomoni was then allowed to set his Albanian irregulars to work and had them attack an Italian border installation. The net result was the wounding of two unfortunate Italian carabinieri. The ruse fooled no one.[75] Oddly enough, surprise was on their side, however. The Greeks did not believe the Italians foolish enough to attack so late in the year.

The Italian Invasion of Greece

On 28 October, with eight divisions—some 140,000 men—under torrential rain, the Italians invaded Greece along a 150-mile front. The operation was rather haphazard, with no attempt to take Corfu or to bomb any of the vital centers of Greece's military and administrative activity. Instead, the Italians launched a series of surprisingly inadequate sporadic air raids on the civilian population. The hastily prepared invasion force was poorly equipped, poorly trained, poorly supported, and led by rank-conscious incompetents.[76] Still, on the coast the Italians experienced considerable success, penetrating ten miles by 9 November. But in the center Viscounti Prasca was stopped. Ciano, becoming uneasy, flew to Tirana to encourage the Italian generals. His fears were temporarily allayed by the continued optimism of Viscounti Prasca, who reported that despite difficulties, his troops were behaving well and that even the Albanian blackshirt militia battalions were demonstrating high morale. One of the wounded Albanian heroes was reported to have announced in pidgin Italian, "We all die, so that Duce pass."[77] The Italian press contributed to this volume of misinformation by reporting that the Greeks were welcoming the Italian soldiers and were thankfully accepting imitation bronze busts of the Duce, which fascist agents were distributing.[78]

In reality the Italian military situation became very desperate very quickly. By 6 November Ciano admitted that the initiative had passed to the Greeks. The Greeks had counterattacked in western Macedonia and routed the best of the Italian Albanian troops, the one-thousand-man "Tomori" Battalion. Badoglio ordered reinforcements but to little avail. The Battle of Metsovo on 11 November served as a model for subsequent Greek victories. The crack Italian Alpine "Iulia" division, counting on tanks and air cover, had advanced along the valleys toward Metsovo, taking no notice of the high ground to the rear. Greek mountain regiments, which were actually disobeying orders, made a forced night march and occupied the high ground. At dawn they attacked and after some hard fighting, the Italians broke and fled.[79] The tanks could not function in the rough terrain, and despite Italian air superiority, the rain and cloud cover prevented them from flying. When they did the Greeks were prepared, having obtained the Italian air force codes and operational instructions, leading to interception and high Italian losses.[80]

On 14 November General Alexandros Papagos, chief of staff of the Greek army, with forces that now slightly outnumbered the Italians, began a general counteroffensive. His troops, better equipped, supplied, and motivated, not only drove the Italians out of Greece but soon were in control of large sections of Albania. Korça, the third-largest town in Albania, fell on 22 November, a blow to Italian prestige and a boost to Greek hopes. At this battle alone the Italians lost two thousand men captured, as well as thirty-five artillery pieces and six hundred machine guns. As a final humiliation, at Menton in France, just beyond the Italian frontier, posters appeared proclaiming, "This is French territory, Greeks, do not advance further!"[81]

Viscounti Prasca, who blamed everyone but himself, was replaced and Badoglio resigned, but the Italian collapse continued. By December the Greeks had taken Gjirokastra, Pogradec, and Porto Edda, along with approximately 25 percent of Albania. Panic gripped the Italian leadership. General Ubaldo Soddu, Viscounti Prasca's replacement, concluded that military action was impossible and that the situation could only be handled through political intervention. Ciano quoted Mussolini as admitting, in despair, "There is nothing else to do. This is grotesque and absurd but it is a fact. We have to ask for a truce through Hitler."[82] The Duce was only saved from this humiliation by the weather, which stopped the Greek offensive and created a virtual stalemate.

Over the next few months, Mussolini sought desperately to break the stalemate. Soddu was replaced in late December for general incompetence and after Mussolini discovered that he spent his evening hours composing music for films.[83] In January Mussolini, to restore morale, ordered ministers, high party officials, and members of the Chamber of Fascis and Corporations under forty-five years of age to serve on the front in Albania. The bewildered and irate fascist elite—without servants or suitcases—were sent to struggle in the mud, rain, and snow of the Albanian mountains. Dino Grandi, a leading fascist, commented after the war that in the muddy trenches of Albania he made contacts and outlined the resolution that would later topple Mussolini.[84] Finally on 9 March the Italians, with Mussolini present, launched a powerful counteroffensive with some twenty-eight divisions, over 300,000 men, nearly one-third of the entire army.[85] Despite numerical superiority and better organization, little came of it, and after five days it was discontinued. By this time the fighting morale of the troops was irreparably damaged, and Mussolini was forced to wait for the Germans to come to his rescue. Italian losses were extensive, and included 14,000 dead, over 50,000 wounded, 25,000 missing, and over 12,000 maimed during the frozen winter months.[86]

The blame for this disaster could be and was spread widely. Zenone Benini—and Mussolini in conversations with Hitler—blamed the Albanians.[87] And indeed, despite misplaced high hopes on the parts of Ciano, Jacomoni, and Viscounti Prasca, the Albanians demonstrated a marked lack of enthusiasm for either side.[88] Albanian armed forces played only a minor role in support of the Italians. Mussolini claimed that two Albanian battalions were attached to each Italian division that invaded Greece. While this is certainly an exaggeration, at least two battalions of Albanian fascist militia, the "Tomori" and the "Taraboshi," saw action against the Greeks in the Korça area.[89] Mussolini later noted that through March 1941, fifty-nine Albanians had been killed and seventy-eight wounded.[90] The complete story is somewhat less glorious. The Albanian Fascist Party was made up principally of opportunists who expected to benefit materially from their connection with the fascist occupier. When faced with the hard reality of a mountain campaign against a determined enemy, Albanian units either deserted or defected in droves.[91] Those who remained did so poorly that they were ultimately withdrawn and confined to a concentration camp in central Albania.[92] Had the Italians used them in the Albanian areas of Çamëria rather than in the Orthodox areas of Korça, perhaps the militia might have demonstrated more enthusiasm.

Irregular Albanian cooperation with the Italians was also quite limited. Despite the large sums that Jacomoni spent for "political" purposes, the return was pitiful. Albanian spies, in attempting to provide him with what he wanted to hear, convinced him—among other things—that the Albanians in Greece would rise. Some even suggested that the Greeks themselves would rise in favor of the Italians. Once the Greeks had taken parts of Albania, these agents were to operate beyond Italian lines, providing sensitive intelligence and were to harass the Greek forces. There is some evidence of sabotage, particularly interruptions of military telephone and telegraph services, and news reached Athens that some saboteurs were being shot.[93] All this activity was of a limited nature, however, with little effect. These spies and saboteurs were rather uncommitted—the principle motivation was, of course, money. Their collective ineffectiveness is perhaps best illustrated by the fact that at no time were they able to locate Greek army corps headquarters, which the Italians hoped to bomb.

Despite the claims of socialist Albanian historiography to the contrary, the Albanians did little more to help the Greeks.[94] By early November reports surfaced that Albanians were interfering with Italian military efforts, cutting telephone communications, seizing ammunition, harassing the Italians with hand grenades, and providing intelligence to the Greek army.[95] Although this aid may have been more substantial than that given to the Italians, it still must be considered minimal, and it came primarily from the Greek minority in southern Albania, who warmly welcomed the arrival of the Greek troops.[96]

Why the Albanians refused to help the Italians is clear. The Italians were perceived as invaders, and irredentism was not as all-pervasive as Ciano had hoped. Many Albanians took the view that if they were unable to preserve their former small and independent country, revisionist aspirations were merely ridiculous. Even those who took an active interest in their conationals beyond the frontiers questioned whether an extension of the Italian puppet regime to include these elements was really a desirable development.[97]

That the Albanians did not support the Greeks more extensively can also be explained. The government in Athens made a number of errors in political warfare. Official statements and actions did little to alleviate the traditional mutual mistrust between the Greeks and Albanians. Soon after the Greeks had begun driving the Italians back into Albania, General Metaxas announced that Greek forces were fighting for the liberation of Albania, but he said nothing about the independence of Albania. Elaborating in private, he said that he did not want Albania and would gladly see it free and independent, but that the future settlement had to secure certain strategic points to Greece to protect it against further attack.[98] The British ambassador in Athens reported to London that "They [the Greek government] have never stated exactly what they have in mind but I have little doubt that they have their eyes on Northern Epirus. I don't know what precise boundary they hope to fix. . . . I doubt they have thought this out except that it must include the southern lateral road."[99] Although the Albanians were naturally not privy to these communications, the ambivalence of Metaxas's statement about liberating Albania was not lost on the Albanians, and had it been, the Italians were there to interpret it for them. As if this were not enough, the BBC, in an Albanian-language independence-day broadcast, stated, "The Greeks are not out for any expansion at our expense or anyone else's." Pearson Dixon, head of the Albanian Section of the Southern Department at the Foreign Office, fumed that the BBC ought to be on the lookout for this type of Axis propaganda.[100]

In terms of occupation policy, the Greeks, for the most part, followed normal procedures in occupied territories in times of war. Papagos ordered, for example, the continued operation of the Albanian civil courts whenever possible and the application of Albanian law insofar as it did not conflict with the interest of the occupying forces.[101] The director of the Albanian state bank presented further evidence of the correctness of Greek behavior. He informed the German minister that all reports of atrocities were simply propaganda, adding that once the Greeks had pulled back he found the safes in the state bank still intact. Indeed, the Greeks had not even tried to open them. Even the pictures of Mussolini and Victor Emmanuel could still be found—they had been neatly stacked in the back of the bank.[102]

Still, some Greek actions did much to reinforce the impression that Greek aims included territorial acquisition. Upon driving the Italians out of Korça, the Greek military apparently received instructions from Athens to inhibit Albanian independence-day celebrations on 28 November. The military ignored the instructions and was reprimanded. The military command at Gjirokastra received similar orders and proved more diligent in carrying them out. Fear was further exacerbated when the Greeks set up a municipal council in Korça consisting of eleven Greeks and four Albanians under an Albanian mayor.[103] Perhaps the most telling reason why Albanians did not participate more extensively on the Greek side was because direct offers of aid were often refused. Laird Archer, director of the Near East Foundation in Athens, notes in his diary a series of conversations with Frederick Nosi, the former interpreter at the American Legation in Tirana. Nosi expressed perplexity over the Greek refusal to accept him as a volunteer or to accept similar offers from large groups of Albanian exiles in Greece.[104] The Greeks clearly wanted to be careful to avoid the impression that non-Greek Albanians had anything to do with ejecting the Italians from southern Albania. The Greeks were perhaps too concerned with long-term political thinking at the expense of practical short-term military considerations.

Apart from blaming the Albanians, the Italians blamed each other as well. Mussolini blamed both his military and political advisers — he was right, of course, but he was the one who surrounded himself with incompetence. Of Viscounti Prasca, Mussolini concluded, "every man must make one fatal error in his life — mine was listening to Viscounti Prasca.... The human material I have to work with is useless, worthless."[105] These sentiments were certainly shared by some who served under Viscounti Prasca. A captured Italian officer — a philosophy student from the University of Rome — described the invasion as grotesquely mismanaged with farcical strategy and nonexistent tactics — units were put into the line in a haphazard manner, a division at a time, wherever a break occurred.[106]

Ciano came under fire as well, for spreading misinformation. Indeed, it is reasonable to suppose that Ciano would have lost his job had the Italians been pushed into the sea. There can be no doubt that Ciano received and passed on ludicrous information. One reason for this was Ciano's irrepressible penchant for using spies and intrigue to gather information and conduct policy. Ciano was completely misled by his Albanian spies concerning the attitude of both the Greek and Albanian population near the frontier and about the Albanian attitude toward the invasion.

Perhaps the best example of Ciano's carelessness was his assumption that the Greeks would not fight because of the bribes he had distributed to the Greek military leadership. The money was apparently taken to Metaxas, who told his officers to keep it but redouble their efforts to resist the Italians.[107] For his part, Ciano preferred to blame the soldiers, commenting "Our soldiers have fought but little and badly. This is the real fundamental cause of all that has happened."[108] This is at least partially true, although the principal reason seems to have been unpreparedness. Incredibly, two weeks before the invasion, Mussolini, without consulting the chief of the general staff, ordered a large-scale demobilization, sending some 600,000 trained soldiers, or about half of the army, home. This process could not be halted until 10 November, so many of those who participated in the attack had just been called up and were essentially untrained.[109] This practice, it seems, continued into 1941. On 22 January Ciano forwarded to Mussolini a letter he had received from a professor at Livorno who complained that his eighteen-year-old son had been mobilized on 17 January and sent to Albania the same day, without knowing what a firearm was. Ciano noted in his diary, "This explains so many things."[110] Badoglio recognized the deficiencies, and his evaluation of the problem was essentially correct, though he refused to confront Mussolini. He was quoted by Ciano as remarking just before he resigned: "There is no doubt that Jacomoni and Prasca have a large share in the responsibility of the Albanian affair, but the real blame must be sought elsewhere. It lies entirely in the Duce's command."[111]

The Germans, meanwhile, watched the Italian disaster in Albania with irritation and alarm, partially, one would suspect, because they might have been able to stop it. As a result of information from numerous sources, including the reports from Pannwitz, the German Foreign Ministry was convinced by 18 October that the Italians planned to invade Greece. Despite this knowledge, Hitler was unwilling to alienate Mussolini by asking him a direct question about his plans.[112] But German anxiety and anger increased as reports of the full extent of the debacle began to arrive. Pannwitz in Tirana cabled that Italian expectations of Albanian involvement were completely unfounded and unrealized. General Enno von Rinteln, the German military attaché in Italy, who toured Albania in early November, added further reasons for the Italian failure. At least one — the severe weather — could not be entirely blamed on Italian planning and execution. The Italian command in Albania, not surprisingly, heavily emphasized this factor in its own reports.[113]

But Rinteln had found other problems as well. He concluded that the Italians were entirely unprepared for the attack. He noted the transportation problem, for which he saw no immediate solution. He commented that supply of munitions and food to the front was inadequate, suggesting that corruption in the rear might be one of the explanations.[114] He might have added that Albania had but one port — Durrës — that could handle large quantities of heavy equipment and that the port was filled with vessels unloading marble for the pointless fascist buildings being constructed in Tirana. Those who planned the campaign were convinced that a division could be disembarked in a single day at Durrës. The Italian Navy, not consulted until after the campaign had begun, later announced that rather than one day, one month would be needed.[115]

After being asked for help, the Germans attempted to control the damage militarily and diplomatically. By 9 December fifty Junker 52S transport planes had been transferred to Rome and were flying between Foggia and Albania.[116] At the same time, preparations were made for what was called "Operation Cyclamen," the dispatch to Albania of a German corps, including the First Mountain Division and armored forces. The task of this unit was to assist the Italians in breaking the Greek line and to support a frontal assault on Greece itself by General Siegmund List's army from Bulgaria. But Hitler ultimately gave up on the plan in consideration of the enormous transportation problems and because German troops in force in Albania might warn the Allies about the impending move against Greece.

Simultaneously, the Germans considered a diplomatic solution through a separate Italian-Greek peace, with Greece being awarded some Albanian territory. Much to the anger of the Italians, the Germans never broke diplomatic relations with Greece, so they were in an excellent position to conduct negotiations. But this too came to nothing when the 27 March 1941 coup in Yugoslavia toppled the regent Prince Paul and those who had signed the Tripartite Pact. This event convinced the Germans that Axis prestige could only be restored through a successful military campaign.[117] The Italians were finally saved by the Germans in April 1941 with the invasion and rapid defeat of Yugoslavia and Greece.

The Italians took no part in the war, fearing the considerably stronger Yugoslav army. Italian commanders informed the Germans that they would attempt to hold the Albanian frontier against the Yugoslavs but in the end were unable to do even that. The Yugoslavs foolishly crossed into Albania but were required to withdraw after only three days in an attempt to stop the Germans, who had already entered Kosova from the east.[118] Of course it was to no avail, and the Yugoslavs were rapidly defeated.

The Greeks suffered a similar fate. Greek forces, even those in Albania, as a final gesture of contempt for the Italians, made a point of surrendering to the Germans. The Germans proceeded to establish a brutal occupation regime in Greece and simply dismembered Yugoslavia, resulting in the creation of powerful resistance movements.

The Creation of Greater Albania

Although it was clear to all that the Italians had failed to humble the Greeks by force of arms, Ciano hoped at least partially to redeem Rome's tattered reputation in the eyes of the Albanians by effecting a favorable territorial settlement. He was still hoping to make the most of irredentism. By now, of course, the situation was somewhat more complex—he had the Germans with which to deal. In August 1941 Victor Emmanuel was able to declare the creation of "Greater Albania," which would come close to including all Balkan Albanians. On the surface, it seemed that the Italians had lived up to their promise. In reality, however, the circumstances surrounding the declaration did much to undermine the positive effects on Italo-Albanian relations that the Italians might have expected from such a development.

With the collapse of Yugoslavia, the Italians hurried to construct a case for enlarging Albania and present it to the Germans. Ciano had really not expected that Italian Albania would actually find itself in possession of Kosova; rather, he had used the issue as propaganda to fire up the Albanians and threaten the Yugoslavs. This is evidenced by the fact that it was not until the end of April that he called four Albanian specialists to Rome to formulate claims. A maximum and a minimum program were drawn up. The maximum program was a Greater Albania of two and a half million to three million people, including Podgorica, Novi Pazar, Ohrid, Bitol, Florina, Ioannina, and Arta, in other words besides Kosova, large sections of Montenegro, Macedonia, and Greece.[119] That this Greater Albania remained a suggestion and never became a demand indicates that the Italians recognized that this maximum program was unobtainable. Albania, never having been an empire, had no historical claims to much of the territory the Italians hoped to receive, and Albanians made up only a minority in much of these areas. With the maximum program, Albania would have become a multinational state, with an Albanian majority of only 55 percent. In any case, the Germans, encouraged by the Bulgarians, refused to consider these excessive claims.

The minimum program still increased the population of Albania (which stood at somewhat over 1 million) by between 500,000 and 850,000 people, primarily from Kosova and the Dibra area of Macedonia, and a small strip of Montenegro.[120] This plan left less than 20 percent of the population of new Albania as minorities, a much more manageable figure. Although the addition of these Kosovar Albanians would significantly increase the Moslem majority, Italy hoped to command their loyalty as citizens of Albania. The Italians also hoped that the addition of large numbers of Moslems would force the Orthodox and Catholic Albanians into closer collaboration with the puppet regime.

Once the goals were established, the campaign began. Jacomoni encouraged the leaders of a Kosova irredenta movement—which included Rexhep Mitrovica and Bedri Pejani—to telegraph Mussolini requesting the liberation of Kosova. He need hardly have made the suggestion, because many of

Albania's more extreme nationalists feared that the Italians would not press the Albanian case with proper vigor.[121] But Ciano, who continued to view Albania as his own private fief, energetically lobbied the Germans. On 21 April he met German Foreign Minister Joachim von Ribbentrop and carefully presented the military, economic, and ethnic reasons for pushing Albania's frontiers to the east and south. After their third meeting on 24 April, a compromise—later confirmed by the Vienna Awards—was reached. Albania was awarded most of the territory Ciano had requested, with a few exceptions. Bulgaria was awarded the region around Ohrid, which the Bulgarian foreign minister had assured the German minister in Sofia was sacred to Bulgaria. King Boris had reinforced Bulgarian claims at a private audience with Hitler on 19 April, two days before Ciano got to Ribbentrop. Hitler told Boris that his request seemed reasonable.[122]

Bulgaria thereby established control over extensive ethnic Albanian-inhabited land in Macedonia. Italian Albania and Bulgaria now shared a frontier that became the cause of considerable Italo-Bulgarian friction and the subject of almost constant incidents, which often degenerated into armed conflict between Bulgarian troops against Italians supported by some Albanians on both sides of the new frontier. Although the Bulgarian occupation of the Slavic areas of Macedonia was reasonably benevolent, at least for a time, treatment of the ethnic Albanians was uniformly harsh. Later in the war the Bulgarians decided to resolve the issue by simply driving the Albanians out of their portion of Macedonia.[123]

Although the Italians gained some control over Çamëria, including the districts of Ioannina, Thesprotia, and Preveza, with some 300,000 inhabitants, and hoped to annex this territory to Albania, the Germans would not allow it. Albanian enthusiasm, despite all the earlier propaganda, was much less than had been expected.[124] Although the Italians went so far as to choose Xhemil Dino as high commissioner for Çamëria, this area remained under the control of the military command in Athens. A small district at the southeast end of Lake Prespa, between Florina and Bilisht, did come under the administration in Tirana, so far as police and customs were concerned.[125]

Ciano's biggest disappointment, however, and the cause of long-term Italo-German friction, concerned certain Albanian areas of Mitrovica, which the Germans retained for themselves. The principal German motivation was to control the iron ore deposits at the mines of Trepça. The situation became considerably more complex, however, when the Germans proceeded to construct a model occupation regime. General Eberhard, commander of the German 60th Motorized Infantry Division, met with Albanian leaders and signed a series of agreements. These agreements allowed considerably more autonomy than the Italians were willing to grant the Albanians in Greater Albania. The Germans allowed for the construction of a council, many of whose members came from Kosova and "old Albania" (which is what pre-1941 Albania came to be called). The Germans allowed village elders to direct most of their own affairs and even constructed dozens of Albanian-language primary schools. Even Prime Minister Vërlaci was heard to note that the Germans seemed to be doing very well in Mitrovica.[126] German policy certainly contrasted sharply with the Serbian administration of old Yugoslavia as well as with the Italian puppet regime in Kosova.[127]

The German general, who had a particular sympathy for the Albanians, also saw to the construction of an Albanian gendarmerie of one thousand men and managed to recruit officers and men from Kosova and old Albania.[128] The troops wore the emblem of Skënderbeg and flew the old Albanian flag. This was particularly disturbing to the Italians, since they had created a fascist Albanian flag. The Italians were also concerned that the name of Prince William of Wied—a German prince who had served as Albania's first ruler in 1914 and had never abdicated—was frequently heard in public. It did not escape the notice of the Italians that Wied's son was an officer with the German army in Romania. Perhaps most galling of all, the German commander in Mitrovica seemed quite tolerant of anti-Italian activity. Gestapo agents had even gone so far as to contact members of the growing Albanian resistance.[129]

Although undoubtedly unaware of the Gestapo contacts, by November Ciano had enough reasons to be concerned. In a strongly worded protest to German ambassador Mackensen, Ciano accused the Germans of deliberately fostering an autonomous Albania under German leadership that would serve as a focal point for opposition to the Italians. The new state would eventually be led by Wied's son, who would construct a government made up of anti-Italians and a militia that would take an oath directly to Hitler. As a solution to the problem, Ciano suggested that, as a gesture, Hitler might want to cede Mitrovica to Albania.[130] The German Foreign Ministry conducted a full investigation and found that some of Ciano's claims were true. The Foreign Ministry cabled Belgrade and Tirana, making it clear that Mitrovica must, under no circumstances, become a source of tension between Italy and Germany. Mackensen was instructed to tell Ciano that there was no truth to the allegations that the German military was consorting with anti-Italian Albanians. German interest in Mitrovica was defined as restricted to maintaining peace and quiet, which was being fostered by the granting of local cultural autonomy. Mackensen was further instructed to ignore Ciano's call for the inclusion of Mitrovica into Albania and, if he should bring the topic up again, to refer him to the Vienna Awards.[131] This seems to have satisfied the Italians temporarily, allowing them time to absorb Kosova and to attempt to benefit from its inclusion into Albania.

The absorption of Kosova proceeded with some energy and provided Albania with considerable benefit. Iliaz Agushi, who was placed in charge of Kosova as minister of liberated territories, installed a regime dependent on Tirana and initiated a number of policies that benefited both the population of Kosova and that of old Albania. The great Kosovar landowners who had been dispossessed by the Serbs were to be placated by being paid one-quarter of the income from their former estates.[132] And one source suggests that to match Serb policies during the interwar period, between 70,000 and 100,000 Serbs were forced out of Kosova,[133] many of whom ended up in concentration camps in Prishtina and Mitrovica. These Serbs were apparently used as labor on fortification works in Italian Albania and as workers in the Trepça mines for the Germans. The Serbs most vulnerable were those brought in by the Yugoslav government between 1918 and 1940 to settle some of the 154,287 acres of land seized from Albanians and whose settlement was accompanied by forced expulsions of Albanians.[134]

The Albanian puppet government launched an ambitious educational program that included the opening of 173 Albanian primary and many secondary schools, the first in forty years.[135] Albanian schools in Kosova were shut down in 1918 in order to "Serbianize" the population. By 1921 Serbian authorities had decided to deny the Albanians access to any education, in an organized effort to keep them ignorant and illiterate. A Serbian official wrote in 1921 that "the Albanians will all remain backward, unenlightened, and stupid; nor will they know the state idiom [Serbian], which would help them to fight against us. It is in our interest that they remain at the present level of their culture for another twenty years, the time we need to carry out the necessary national assimilation in these areas."[136] Under these circumstances, it is hardly surprising that many Kosovars viewed the Italians, with their 20,000 occupation troops and their Albanian puppets, as liberators.

But old Albania clearly benefited from this addition as well. Apart from the considerable subsoil wealth, Kosova provided a substantial agricultural surplus, badly needed in old Albania. The National Bank of Albania reported in 1942 that the Kosova regime, despite a one-fifth decline in wheat sown as compared to before the war, was producing as much as old Albania. Total maize production was also about one-half of that produced in old Albania.

Because Kosova contained no more than two-thirds of the population of old Albania, a surplus was produced. In 1942 twenty thousand tons of grain and thirty thousand tons of corn were shipped to old Albania from Kosova; two-thirds of the maize and one-third of the wheat could also be exported from Kosova to Albania without depleting the resources of Kosova in any way.[137] The union solved the problem of chronic lack of cereals.

Those committed to the fascist regime made the most of the acquisition for the purposes of propaganda. And indeed the annexation of Kosova was a popular move both in Kosova and in old Albania. Albanian socialist historiography admits that "a section of the population fell victim to this nationalism."[138] But it was not enough enthusiasm to win any lasting support for the Italians. By the time Kosova was annexed in 1941, the Italians had already lost the battle to win the hearts and minds of the Albanians; in fact, some have suggested that the adventure that ultimately brought Greater Albania about—the Italian invasion of Greece—ruined all that the Italians had done in Albania by contributing to the collapse of the relative stability of the early period of the Italian occupation. In a way, then, the achievement of Albania's territorial dreams directly coincided with the beginning of the end for the Italians. The negative impact of Italian policy vastly outweighed the positive. This is perhaps best illustrated by the steady rise of disenchantment and resistance.

CHAPTER 4

ITALIAN REPRESSION AND THE BEGINNING OF RESISTANCE

The Italians made many mistakes in Albania, not the least of which was assuming that they could win over a majority of Albanians at all. The Albanian attitude toward the Italians in 1939 ranged from indifference to suspicion to passive antipathy to hatred; by late 1940 the latter was the prevailing emotion. Unlike with their feelings about the Germans after 1943, the Albanians never respected the Italians, although with increased repression came fear. The Albanian attitude toward the Italians was guided in part by the mistaken assumption that Albanian arms had actually driven Italian armies into the sea in 1920. This national myth had been fostered by Zog and did the Albanian nation a disservice because it encouraged Albanians to underestimate the Italians and often not to take them seriously.

Growing Italian Unpopularity

This overly negative attitude about the Italians was reinforced during the 1920s by the impression left by a few hundred Italian artisans and small merchants who had been abandoned in Albania after World War I and who begged soldi to survive. Mussolini's restructuring of the Italian government and his military exploits in Spain and Ethiopia did little to alter the impression of many Albanians. Educated Albanians considered the Italians to be parvenu in the European community of nations, newcomers who were really not in a position to bring culture or economic well-being. There were intangible considerations as well. Albanians did not like the entire Italian Weltanschauung, and they disliked what they considered the weak, nonmasculine way the Italians carried themselves and behaved. Many Albanians believed Italians to be liars and dissimulators.[1]

The vast sums of money the Italians spent in Albania did little to alter this attitude. This was partially the case because many Albanians believed that

Italian money was not really meant for Albanian development but rather for Italian interests exclusively. Many Albanians believed that the Italians hoped for Albania's financial destruction under Zog and saw to the squandering of large sums of money to help bring this about. After the invasion some Italian policies were based to a certain degree on altruism, but even these seemed to misfire. Add to this background the blunders and mismanagement, and it is not difficult to imagine how the Italians became increasingly unpopular. Even those Albanians who had initially supported the Italians—either out of a sense of saving what could be saved or out of simple venality—began to turn away as the excesses of the fascist movement began to have an impact. As Italian mistakes multiplied, Albanian opposition grew. As opposition grew, resistance increased. The Italians responded by grasping for a policy, but settled for increased repression, tempered by sporadic and often erratic concessions.

The Italian administration of Albania was not successful, and many of Rome's problems were self-imposed. On the whole, the Italians behaved badly. After an initial burst of activity they settled into disorganization, lack of direction, corruption, and a preference for form over content. Corruption was widespread and reached the highest levels of the administration. Albania, and the vast sums that Rome spent there, provided a unique opportunity for countless Italian adventurers and con men, as well as a temptation for contractors and suppliers who might otherwise have remained legitimate. Because the sums were so vast, a considerable bureaucracy grew up to administer the money. The fascist bureaucrats did much to secure jobs for their friends and contracts for firms in which they had a personal interest. The marble buildings that the Italians constructed for various fascist organizations have been mentioned. It is not surprising that Mussolini's private secretary was intimately connected with the marble quarries at Carrara.[2] Ciano himself became involved. With the large secret funds at his disposal for miscellaneous expenses in Albania, Ciano initiated a vast network of corruption. When the Italian police discovered it, they determined not even to inform Mussolini.

This is not to suggest that corruption was something new and shocking to the Albanians. But under Zog it had been more or less limited to the court and its immediate vicinity. With the Italians it became much more widespread and very obvious. Albanians quickly became aware that high Italian government and party people had financial interests in specific projects and that enormous prices were paid for particular construction projects and deliveries, far in excess of their actual worth.

Giovanni Giro, the inspector and real power behind Albanian fascism and the Albanian youth movement, proved to be another high official implicated in the vast corruption schemes. He was responsible for the collection of large sums from rich merchants for party work, funds that he personally controlled. Giro's Italian opponents and competitors—including Jacomoni—made public his indiscretions and arranged to have him removed from his post, which Giro heard about only by listening to the radio. Few lamented his passing; the Albanians in the government found him boorish, fanatical, and unsophisticated, with a penchant for employing and raising to power many thoroughly disreputable Albanians. Giro was also heartily disliked for his barely concealed contempt for all Albanians, which led him to try to Italianize everything, including the Albanian language, which he referred to as a "meaningless dialect." Giro became an embarrassment to Jacomoni by his corruption as well as by his tending to disregard the lieutenant general's authority.[3]

Giro was not alone in his contempt for the Albanians. Ciano complained particularly about the Italian middle classes, who, he maintained, "treat the natives badly and who have a colonial mentality. Unfortunately, this is also true of military officers and, according to Jacomoni, especially their wives."[4] The German minister, further, reported about incidents in which Italian soldiers and workers not only harassed and insulted Albanian women, but also were caught stealing both in villages and in Tirana.[5]

The Giro affair pointed to another Italian problem, namely, the often bitter rivalry between the various levels of Italian authority. Rumors of disagreements between soldiers and civilians—even between Jacomoni and General Guzzoni—began within a month of the invasion.[6] With the arrival of Giro, the struggle seems to have become three-way. The replacement of Giro by Piero Parini, who retained his positions as adviser to the Albanian prime minister and secretary general to the lieutenant general, removed one complication but by no means solved the problem. Since the very nature of Italian fascism encouraged interdepartmental friction and personal jealousy, it is perhaps only surprising that those attributes took as long as they did to surface in Albania. In a note to London describing the increase in rivalry, the British consul general commented that as the internal Italian hostilities increased, Jacomoni's wife began taking intensive English lessons.[7]

Giro's annoying style, which corresponded to Ciano's *tona fascista* and was often referred to as *dinamismo*, was evident in many Italian actions. This general attitude of nervous haste did much to further alienate the Albanians. A period of quiet reform and abstinence from provocative manifestations might—at least prior to the invasion of Greece—have assured Italy of valuable support. Instead, the Italian authorities pushed forward with little concern for Albanian sensibilities, assuming that only rapid results could maintain Italy's imperial pride. Much of Italy's activity was really smoke and mirrors, and it was often perceived by the Albanians as little more than a series of public relations stunts. For many Albanians, the grand new fascist buildings in downtown Tirana, large but essentially useless, stood as a symbol of the occupation.

The German minister pointed to the new Tirana stadium as another example of this principle of form before function. The stadium had twenty thousand seats, although Tirana itself at the time had a population of just thirty thousand. The parades for Ciano further illustrate the point. When he visited Albania for a triumphal tour in May 1940, uniformed Albanian girls were trotted out with 100 new bicycles, 100 tennis racquets, and 50 fencing masks and foils. But there was no tennis court or teacher, no fencing club, and no fencing instructor.[8] The reality was considerably different: Albania was soon worse off than it had been under Zog. Within a year of the Italian invasion the hospital in Tirana was in worse shape than it had been under Zog—when it was directed by a German doctor. Many of the apparatuses no longer functioned properly and were not replaced. After an initial spurt of activity, the construction of the much advertised road network slowed, and after a year—because of constant military and commercial traffic—the roads were actually in worse shape than they had been under Zog.

In some matters the Italians seem to have gone out of their way to alienate the Albanians. The new flag serves as an example. The Italians took the old flag, a black double eagle on a red field, and added a *fascis* on either side, looking as if they were about to crush the old symbol. To make matters worse, the Italians topped the eagle off with the crown of Savoy, which itself is topped by a cross. In a country where 70 percent of the people were Moslem, this was little more than woodenheadedness. When the Italians tried to explain that the *fascis* was the symbol of the old imperial Roman order and that it should be valued for its history, they were asked to explain why, in that case, it did not make up part of the Italians' own flag.[9] Ciano noted in his diary that Victor Emmanuel observed in a sarcastic tone that the new flag did not contain all the heraldic symbols of the house of Savoy, indicating that it could have been worse.[10] As we have seen, the new Albanian fascist flag became an even greater problem when the Germans allowed the Albanians of Mitrovica to use the original flag.[11]

Moslems were further outraged when Italian curfew restrictions began to interfere with the traditional fast of Ramadan. And the Moslems of Albania, through family connections, felt themselves very close to Turkey and Egypt, two countries that allowed Zog to maintain semiofficial missions for years. This was done partially out of courtesy to Europe's only Moslem ex-king and partially as an indication of displeasure with the Italians. Both states saw Italian imperialism as a direct danger. The attitude of Turkey and Egypt continued to influence many Albanian Moslems.

The most widely held complaints about the Italians, however, had to do with the rapidly deteriorating economic situation. An old Balkan saying admonishes that an empty belly burns a hole in the flag. After initial improvement, the extensive dislocation of the Albanian economy began having a negative impact, effecting Albanians at all economic levels. Following a temporary upsurge, because of the massive influx of capital, the period of the Italian occupation saw working and living conditions deteriorate both in the towns and in the countryside.[12]

The economic problems caused by the Italian presence, although often unavoidable, occasionally resulted from faulty Italian policy. The customs union proclaimed on 22 April 1939 did much to undermine the confidence in paper money that Zog had painstakingly attempted to build up during the years of his reign.[13] The customs union also harmed or bankrupted what little industry and homecraft the Albanians were able to produce, throwing many skilled workers out of work. Granted, the industrial base was minuscule by modern standards, accounting for little more than 4 percent of the national economy at the beginning of the war.[14] What little did exist, however, was destroyed by low-cost, often low-quality Italian imports.[15] Although the peasants saw some benefit from these low-priced goods, in general they too were worse off. Compulsory delivery of agricultural products at low prices, the expropriation of small farms by Italian banks, and the confiscation of thousands of acres of land for military needs further impoverished much of the peasant majority.[16]

The principal economic complaints, however, were produced by shortages and rising prices, and of the two the latter was clearly the most serious. Within less than a year of the invasion, prices for certain goods had risen sharply. By pegging the Albanian franc to the lira and by instituting rigorous currency control, the Italians quadrupled the price of a paper gold napoleon. Peasants and merchants reacted by raising prices to reflect the pre-occupation equivalence of Albanian paper and gold. One lek, which had bought seven eggs in April 1939, bought two in February 1940. The price of potatoes had risen by 200 percent, that of low-quality meat from three to eight leks per kilogram. The minimum daily wage for unskilled labor had been doubled by decree, which damaged the interests of small employers. They were further hit by the various obligatory contributions to the funds of Fascist Party organizations and to social services. But many of the "voluntary contributions" were simply passed on to the public in the form of higher prices. The cost of construction material rocketed with the housing crisis brought on by the Italian civilian invasion, and the extensive program of public buildings, roads, official residences, and fascist centers strained all available supplies and brought profit to none but Italian contractors.[17]

The Italian-controlled National Bank of Albania confirmed what every Albanian was experiencing and published the following index figures for the increase in foodstuff prices:

June 1937	51.9
June 1938	52.8
June 1939	55.2
Oct. 1939	62.8
Nov. 1939	67.7
Dec. 1939	72.1[18]

Shortages, too, caused new problems for the Albanians. By February 1940 wheat, maize, fish, flour, and firewood were all uncomfortably scarce. Tirana frequently suffered from bread famine, and bread could rarely be found in Durrës after 8 a.m. The common assumption was that the Italian garrison was being fed at the expense of the Albanian population. This was actually not the case. The requirements of the Italian army may have depleted supplies of certain local produce, such as vegetables, but almost all of the needed supplies were brought from Italy. In general, the Italian soldiers serving in Albania fared poorly. Since everything they needed—including meat, potatoes, pasta, oil, flour, hay, straw, gasoline, and grease—had to be sent from Italy, they were completely at the mercy of the feeble transportation system. As a result, they too suffered from food and supply shortages as well as from too few barracks and a shortage of drinking water. Often malnourished, they were particularly susceptible to malaria, dysentery, and typhus.

The shortages that affected the Albanians were often actually caused by a scarcity of labor and by the weather. The many thousands of Albanians employed on road construction reduced agricultural labor and, more notably, labor available for woodcutting. Most of the food shortage in late 1939 and early 1940 was caused by excessive rains. The British consul general in February reported that it had rained for twelve days out of every fourteen since the autumn of 1939 and that the farmers in much of Albania were in despair.[19] But whether they were responsible or not, the Italians were handed the blame.

It should also be noted that the complaints were subject to regional differences. The north did not experience as heavy an Italian presence and because the Italians favored the Catholics in any event, conditions were perhaps less severe. But this only meant that the complaints against the Italians were of a different nature. Because of the Italian policy of weapons confiscation, the northerners, for example, found it difficult to protect themselves from raids mounted by armed Montenegrins. The Albanians complained that the Italian carabinieri did nothing. The Albanians of Kosova had similar complaints about marauding Bulgarians.[20]

It seemed that no matter what the Italians did, their collective reputation suffered among the Albanians. Their outwardly beneficent measures for local economic reconstruction, including the reclamation of land and the mortgage and loan facilities for farmers, were perceived by the Albanians as mere preparation for extensive Italian colonization. The methods employed by the banks in granting agricultural loans and arranging mortgages seemed to Albanians to be designed mainly to acquire the best lands and the best olive trees for eventual distribution to Italian settlers, who, thanks to the new constitution, were now able to own land in Albania. The extensive business and infrastructure projects were seen in the eyes of many Albanians as pompous attempts at propaganda victories aimed at enriching Italian companies, exploiting Albanians, and paving the way for more Italian workers and colonists. By the middle of 1940, Italian civilians were arriving at the rate of two hundred to three hundred a day.[21] Between April 1940 and September 1941 more than fifty-one thousand Italian workers and colonists arrived in Albania.[22]

The Italians seemed to have rapidly alienated many important segments of Albanian society. Merchants complained of the restrictions of currency control and the system of obligatory import and export permits. These were granted or refused by the banks in strict accordance with Italian commercial interests; if Italy could supply the article, it was useless to apply for permission to import it from elsewhere. Those who had previously dealt with foreign companies in states other than Italy either went out of business or switched their business to Italian firms. Merchants, as was the case with most Albanians, were also unhappy about the new Albanian currency pegged to the lira. A currency black market quickly developed, and foreigners were offered twice the official rate for many Western currencies. Merchants imported anything they could find in their anxiety to hold goods of any kind rather than Albanian paper money.

Albanian businessmen of all types complained that they were being elbowed out and that it was impossible to obtain approval for any new Albanian enterprises. When an Albanian came up with a financial scheme, there was always an official to suggest that the plan should be Italo-Albanian in character and then to produce an Italian to organize it.[23]

The Greek minority in the south disliked the 1940 order that made Albanian instead of Greek the language of instruction in their schools. The Orthodox in general were concerned about the favor being shown to the Catholics, as well as the powerful pressure, usually in terms of bribes, put on their Archbishop Kissi—and he was quite susceptible to this type of pressure—to induce sympathy with the Uniate movement within his flock.

But the greatest distaste for the Italians and their methods was demonstrated by the professional classes, intellectuals, and students. Their opposition, although often exacerbated by the inconveniences in which their contact with the Italians inevitably resulted, was motivated primarily by principle. It is here where budding Albanian nationalism could be found, the newest nationalism in the Balkans, a twentieth-century phenomenon fostered and strengthened by Zog. And it was among this group that the resistance would find willing fighters.

Eventually the Italians alienated even those who had originally been willing to collaborate. They complained that the Italians did not understand or trust them, that the Italians hoped to disenfranchise them in their own state. The Albanian collaborators complained that they were being shut out of all major decisions, that Albanian patriots were being imprisoned, and that the Italians were involving themselves in every facet of Albanian administration, even in those areas where they had demonstrated nothing but incompetence. They further complained that the Italians often acted disgracefully, and that public safety had declined since Zog's day. Italian military incompetence in the war against Greece had resulted in the destruction of much of southern Albania, and it did much to drive Albanian collaborators to look to the Germans as more competent allies.[24]

But recognizing that their futures were linked to fascist Italy, the Albanian collaborators made a series of suggestions with a view to creating a more equal and perhaps stronger relationship. Albanian officials suggested that this might be possible if the Italians took a number of steps, including (1) stricter adherence to the proclaimed independent state of Albania within the structure of the personal union under Victor Emmanuel III, (2) increasing the power of the lieutenant general, who was too dependent on a long list of Italian officials other than the king (he was forced to listen to the undersecretary for Albanian affairs and in police matters to the general in charge of the carabinieri, as well as to the independent military secret police), (3) the creation of a new Albanian government with real power, (4) the creation of a real Albanian administration with real power, (5) the transfer of police powers to an Albanian administration, (6) the reduction of the number of Italian officials and the reduction of their responsibility, (7) the reduction of the number of Italian advisers in any ministry to five as well as the reduction of their power, (8) turning the Albanian Fascist Party over to the Albanians, and (9) genuine attempts to reduce the rampant corruption. Albanian officials complained that the Italians had refused to fulfill any of their promises and warned that to gain the support of even the most pliable Albanian, this was a prerequisite.[25] Albanian officials advised both Jacomoni and Ciano that the possibility of loyal cooperation was still there but that by the middle of 1941, time was running out. The Italians had to choose between true collaboration or a simple occupation.[26]

The Italians were willing to admit that mistakes had been made, that they had often attached themselves to the wrong people, and that they had dealt with Albania only as a plantation economy. Many admitted that the imposition of the Fascist Party might have been a mistake. The war against Greece had interrupted the reconstruction of Albania and damaged the Italian image.[27] Despite this limited self-criticism, however, little changed, at least while the Albanians remained quiet.

Early Nonviolent Resistance

But the Albanians did not remain quiet very long. Still, resistance in Albania began slowly after the Italian invasion of April 1939, because the average Albanian outside of the major towns successfully ignored the Italians, not a difficult task given Albania's rather primitive level of development. Poor transportation and communication facilities fostered localism. The number of radios in the country was estimated at two to three thousand and there were few newspapers. With Albania's illiteracy rate approaching 85 percent, more newspapers would have had only a limited impact in any case.[28] Albania's traditional society of clan chiefs and feudal beys further inhibited resistance.[29] The clansmen and peasants would not move without leadership, and their leaders, for the most part, were either cooperating with the Italian authorities or were at least reluctant to act against them. Many were hesitant to act against the Italians because the Italians, who hoped to work through them, actually increased their local authority.

Many, both leaders and led, were understandably awed by the number of Italian occupation troops, some seven divisions, by 1943.[30] And even if the Italian troops did not project the image of efficiency that the Germans would later project, their vastly superior number and their modern weapons clearly had an impact. The lone Albanian peasant with his outmoded Turkish long rifle could not help but be impressed. The Albanians, further, had been overrun by foreign troops so often—since the Balkan Wars of 1912 to 1913 they had seen Serbs and Austrians, Greeks and Montenegrins, Bulgarians and Italians—that many had persuaded themselves that the new Italian invasion, too, was just momentary. Peasants who had seen their houses burned down three times in three years by different invaders are slow to challenge new authority. So there was grumbling, but in the early months no organization of leadership—or overtly oppressive occupation policy—to bridge the gulf between grumbling and adventure.

Nevertheless, grumbling increased and isolated acts of nonviolent resistance, ranging from noncooperation to public acts of defiance, did begin immediately after the invasion and increased as the Italian occupation dragged on. Much of this early opposition involved a new, growing vocal group in Albania, the increasing number of intellectuals educated abroad and domestically educated students, who had a stronger sense of national identity than did the Moslem peasants, who were dominated by their feudal lords, or the illiterate tribespeople of the north. It is important to note that this opposition, while primarily directed against the Italians, was also directed against the traditional Albanian ruling classes, the feudal landlords and chiefs, who with Zog had obstructed social change in the interwar period and were performing the same function with the Italians.

The Italians took immediate notice of this growing unrest. Count Ciano, on his first official visit to Albania five days after the invasion, noted in his diary that some Albanians, particularly high school students, disliked raising their arms in the Roman salute, while some refused to do it at all.[31] This was only the beginning. In May Ciano noted that "there is a bit of a storm in the intellectual spheres of Albania, which explains why twenty or so people will immediately be sent to concentration camps."[32] But the demonstrations not only continued; they became more serious.

At the end of May 1939, a widely reported incident took place in Tirana's movie theater. During the showing of a film, Zog and his wife appeared in a news clip, and some in the audience rose and shouted, "Long Live Zog." The performance was stopped, and each member of the audience was asked whether he or she had taken part in the demonstration; two young men admitted participation, and their names were taken.[33] Although this incident certainly did not indicate a resurgence of popular feeling in support of Zog, it did demonstrate growing vocal hostility toward the Italians, particularly among the young. The Albanian flag day, 28 November, witnessed the most serious student demonstrations since the invasion. In Tirana older students refused to learn the fascist anthem, "Giovinézza," despite intensive instruction from the local fascists, and during the parade honoring the day, they sang Albanian patriotic songs instead. Despite the fact that in the parade they were positioned between the police and the military, they still burst out singing "Albania, Albania." Some observers reported shooting. After the parade student leaders were called to explain their actions, but were soon released.[34]

On the same day, similar demonstrations occurred elsewhere. In Shkodra a crowd of two hundred students and two hundred workmen singing patriotic songs failed to salute the head of the local Fascist Party. He complained and the local police investigated, finding that some of the workers claimed to be communists. Eight students, three of whom professed to be communists, were arrested and jailed. Officials in Korça and Vlora reported student demonstrations as well. It seems that many of the ringleaders, like those in Shkodra, were arrested and some, along with several schoolteachers, sent to concentration camps.[35]

But the students would not be discouraged. In January 1940 Ciano noted in his diary again that students and intellectuals were still causing trouble.[36] The diplomatic community too commented on the continuing student disturbances. The British consul general reported on 3 February that demonstrations had occurred in Korça and Shkodra. Failure on the part of the students in Korça to salute fascist officials with the requisite enthusiasm led to the intervention of the carabinieri. Carabinieri officials apparently visited the lycée attended by the offending students and despite the protests of the headmaster, entered the classrooms. Again the student's salute was unflatteringly slovenly. The headmaster selected two of the worst offenders and asked them what homes they came from: one was the son of the prefect of Pogradec and the other was the son of Xhafer Bey Ypi, the minister of justice. The headmaster led the carabinieri to the door and slammed it behind them. The minister of education was sent to investigate, and he closed the lycée.[37]

The Italians continued their crackdown by sending thirty to forty boarders on government scholarships home from the lycée at Shkodra. According to several eyewitness accounts, this action resulted in some three hundred irate students beating up some of their teachers, whom they considered to be creatures of Italian policy. The unfortunate instructors were apparently driven through the streets toward what the students considered to be their spiritual home, the local Fascist Party office.[38] The German consul general reported similar problems in April. He noted that pictures of Mussolini and Victor

Emmanuel were torn down or defaced, that Italian flags were being torn down, and that students throughout Albania were demonstrating and refusing to sing the "Giovinézza." Ramiz Ali, Albanian president from 1985 to 1992, personally remembers the growth of student demonstrations from 1939 to 1941 in Shkodra, Tirana, Korça, Vlora, and elsewhere, with some of his own professors arrested for antifascist activity.[39] The authorities reacted by again dispatching the minister of education, who before the invasion had had a reputation as a nationalist. He had attempted to maintain this impression by posing as the champion of nationalist youth and democratic ideas in a collection of poems published after the invasion. By early 1940, however, few were willing to accept him in this role and more often than not, he was received with shouts of "traitor."[40]

Other elements of Albanian society soon took up the example of the students and young intellectuals. Albanian socialist historiography makes much of this early dissatisfaction on the part of the workers. Although it is undoubtedly an exaggeration to suggest that they were significantly influenced by the growing Albanian communist movement or that they had, by this time, developed a class consciousness, worker's incidents occurred with increasing frequency. As early as June 1939 workers at the Vlora dockyards went on strike for higher wages, which occasioned the intervention of the carabinieri.[41] In October 1940 workers struck at the mines of Selenica, and twelve were imprisoned before the interior minister gave in to their demands.[42] These initial strikes spread to include foreign contractors. In April 1940 eighty workers struck at Ferrobeton in Vlora.[43] While these strikes may not have been entirely antifascist in character, refusal on the part of the workers and other employees, despite some pressure, to join the Fascist Party was reported to be widespread.[44]

Sabotage, both symbolic and actual, was reported by Italian authorities and foreign observers. The symbolic variant included continued defacement of the portraits of Italian leaders. Perhaps the most interesting variety of defacement was the smearing of honey on the chin of the Duce's portrait during the summer—which quickly gave the impression that Mussolini had a beard of flies. But Albanian socialist historiography reports more serious sabotage as well. Pollo and Puto claim that particularly after the Italian invasion of Greece, sabotage significantly reduced Albania's output of raw materials. Production at the petroleum works was reduced by 25 percent, and entire galleries exploded in Albania's chromium mines. This activity was accompanied by the appearance of anti-Italian flyers in the major towns, something that became common after the beginning of 1940.[45]

Early Armed Resistance

Incidents of armed resistance increased as the occupation wore on. It is true that early anonymous attacks on fascist policemen and officials were barely distinguishable from traditional Albanian brigandage. Soon, however, distinctions began to be made. In May 1940 the British consul general reported a sudden outbreak of robberies and housebreaking in Durrës and Tirana, carried out by armed gangs operating with cars. Ex-archbishop Vissarion was beaten and robbed, and a number of Italians, several soldiers, an officer, and a foreman were killed. What was noteworthy here was that housebreaking and this type of armed robbery had never been characteristic Albanian crimes.[46] It can be assumed, therefore, that the motive here might have been political—an attempt to embarrass both the Italians and their puppet Albanian regime.

The motive of the first organized uprising against the Italians is also questionable. The action occurred among the Catholic Mirdita tribe in the north in the summer of 1940. It is surprising only in that it occurred among Catholics, who benefited from Italian pro-Catholic policies, and that it occurred among the Mirdita in particular, whose chief had been a bitter foe of Zog's and actually lent the Italians considerable support. The revolt, which was easily suppressed, was undoubtedly occasioned by the fear that the Italians would conscript young men and send them to fight for the Italians in North Africa, which the Italians had been careful not to do.[47]

The motives of some armed resistance, however, were never in question. Enver Hoxha tells us that the armed struggle against the Italians began on 7 April 1939 and continued uninterrupted from that point.[48] Although this may have been an exaggeration, armed resistance motivated by patriotism was not uncommon during the early years of the Italian occupation. British newspapers, perhaps overoptimistically, reported in August 1940 that the large Italian army was having trouble. An Italian battalion had apparently been ambushed near Burrel, losing men and material. In another incident an Italian lieutenant colonel was killed. British ambassador Sir Ronald Campbell in Belgrade passed on reports that he received suggesting that the Italians were losing more than fifty men a day in ambushes.[49] Much of this might be considered wishful thinking—particularly since the Italians had declared war on Great Britain two months earlier.

As early as May 1940, the Italians began to report the operation of sporadic armed bands, often near the border regions and usually interpreted as organized criminal activity. Ibrahim Kupi, the brother of Abaz Kupi, is mentioned in this context. Although Ibrahim Kupi was originally reported operating north of Kruja, by August 1940 he was reported to have moved to border regions to coordinate his efforts with like-minded leaders on either side of the Yugoslav border. Also mentioned in these early reports are Murat Kaloshi, a former Zogist gendarmerie commander, and several Dibra bands—one led by Haxhi Leshi. The guerrilla fighters Myslim Peza and Muharrem Bajraktari, who would soon play important roles in organized band resistance, are first mentioned in these summer 1940 reports as potentially dangerous elements. Although these groups were perhaps not yet fully organized, they were credited with cutting wires, distributing anti-Italian leaflets, and committing minor acts of sabotage, which the Italians simply referred to as terrorism.[50] While these groups operated only sporadically and without much success until late 1942, they proved to be the beginning of what would become a serious challenge to first the Italians and then the Germans.

The Italians began to take more serious notice of this growing problem when, on 17 May 1941, an attempt was made on the life of Victor Emmanuel III, during his first official visit to Albania.[51] Ciano, in his diary, dismissed the incident, suggesting that the youth, Vasil Laçi, was a Macedonian Greek rather than an Albanian.[52] The Italian press described him as "under a spell of poetic madness." The Italian authorities hanged him in Tirana ten days later and stepped up repression in general. Albanian socialist sources reported that in May 1941 1,130 houses were searched, 21,131 Albanians were declared enemies of the state, and 5,270 were interned.[53]

German military representatives in Tirana reported to Ambassador Mackensen in Rome that as late as November 1940, they thought it unlikely that the quiet in the land would soon be disturbed. By the end of 1941 these same observers complained about the security situation in Tirana itself.[54] By that point the Italians had begun losing control of all but the main towns and communication routes. This can be explained, at least partially, by the mountainous terrain of most of the country, which for centuries provided refuge for Albanian tribesmen fighting the Turks and Albanian brigands plundering whomever they encountered. While Italian road construction was slowly making some of these areas more accessible to policing, Albanians were returning to their old habits faster than the Italians could build roads.

Early British Involvement with the Resistance

The British can rightly claim a share in initiating the first organized Albanian resistance against the Italians. As early as April 1940 British agents of military intelligence (R), a branch of the War Office that was involved with fomenting guerrilla warfare and/or Section D (which stood for destruction) of the Secret Intelligence Service (SIS) became interested in Albania. The British intelligence community, influenced by the overly romantic ideas of Englishmen who had been in Albania during the interwar period, was convinced that Albania was the ideal place for their first attempt to encourage guerrilla warfare in southeastern Europe. The same geographical features that allowed the Albanians to hold out against the Turks—the rugged inaccessible mountains—were deemed just right for resistance. In reality, however, Albania was perhaps less ready than its neighbors for this type of war. With its arrested political development; its rudimentary nationalist development, with no real recognition of territorial unity at even higher levels; its primitive social organization; and its inexperience with modern tactics, including aerial bombardment and mechanized columns, Albania was far from ready to develop a modern people's war.[55]

But these are things that the British learned only with experience. In April 1940 they rushed ahead with plans to initiate guerrilla warfare and eventually raise a rebellion against Italian rule. The scheme, set in motion in Yugoslavia, included collecting information, establishing contact with Albanian patriots in Kosova and Albania proper, and setting up organizations to smuggle in supplies for an eventual uprising.[56] British agents established contact with a number of loosely organized Albanian groups—most of which centered around a nucleus of a powerful family and its retainers—engaged in information gathering and maintaining a wide network of contacts. Principal among these groups was one led by the wealthy Kosova landowner Gani Bey Kryeziu and his brother Said Kryeziu. The Kryezius became the focus of British operations because of their pro-Western stance, because of their good relations with Yugoslav authorities, and because they wielded influence both in Kosova and in Albania.

Gani Kryeziu had been a bitter opponent of King Zog's—principally because Zog opposed Kosova irredentism and because Zog was responsible for the assassination of Kryeziu's brother Ceno Bey in 1927.[57] With the Italian invasion, however, Gani Kryeziu, as a patriot, had dropped his opposition to Zog and supported a broad resistance movement. It was on his suggestion that the British first made contact with Colonel Abaz Kupi, then in exile in Istanbul, who had led the Albanian resistance to the Italians at Durrës and would become the leader of the Zogist force of resistance.[58]

Kupi, an Albanian chieftain in the Ottoman tradition, spent thirteen years of his life as an outlaw in the mountains, fighting against the Turks in the Balkan Wars, against the Austrians in World War I, against Zog in 1923, and with Zog in 1924. In 1934, in typical tribal fashion, he accepted the position of major in Zog's gendarmerie, with responsibility for his home area in Kruja. Kupi was brave and generous, yet at the same time ruthless and cunning, with a rare capacity for making each man believe he was his friend. Physically he was rather short and looked a bit like Napoleon as first consul—particularly since Kupi combed his hair down over his forehead to cover a scar from a bullet wound.[59] Kupi's abilities as a fighter and Albanian-style diplomat were thought useful both by Kryeziu and the British. The promise of British support convinced Kupi to travel to Yugoslavia in late 1940 to work more closely with British intelligence and the Kryezius.

Kupi in turn enlisted other supporters of Zog while Said Kryeziu won over Mustafa Gjinishi, a member of Albania's small but growing communist movement. While communism had played only a minor role in Albania during the Zogist years, Said Kryeziu, whose opinions inclined to the Left, sensed that a growth of a radical movement in Albania was inevitable. Gjinishi's adherence to the budding resistance movement was considered fortunate by the British, in light of the generally negative attitude that other communists in Albania expressed toward the British. The British were unsure whether Gjinishi was following orders or acting on his own. Albanian socialist historiography and Enver Hoxha dismiss Gjinishi as a traitor, presumably because of his later opposition to Hoxha. In any case, relations between the once bitter enemies—Gani Kryeziu, Mustafa Gjinishi, and Abaz Kupi—apparently were quite cordial, even friendly. In an ominous and deadly accurate prediction of the future, however, the three agreed that once the Italians were expelled, they would have to fight among themselves for power in a postwar Albania.[60]

These initial British contingency plans received further impetus with Italy's entry into the war in June 1940. Military intelligence (R) and Section D agents in Yugoslavia began operations in Greece, where they contacted leading Albanian exiles, established dumps of demolition material near the Albanian frontier, and explored the possibility of acquiring agents on the Albanian side who could establish dumps at selected points in Albania.[61] In June and July 1940 reports reached Tirana of the activities of Kupi and Kryeziu, accompanied by the disturbing news that many Albanians were crossing the border to join them.[62] Although both the British Foreign Office and the Middle East High Command approved of Section D's plan for Albania, the agents were warned not to do anything that might provoke an Italian invasion of Greece. Repeated warnings about provoking the Italians stopped plans for an uprising in Albania. But secret preparations continued not only in Yugoslavia and Greece but elsewhere as well. The Foreign Office decided to construct a secret and unofficial Albanian central committee in London to coordinate the various Albanian organizations abroad. This group was to be headed by Sir Jocelyn Percy who had helped organize the Albanian police for Zog.

The Role of Zog

The Italian attack on Greece in October 1940 changed the situation again. Since the British War Office was convinced that an attack on the Italian rear by the Albanians would be of great help to the Greeks, plans were resurrected and this time the general reluctance to use Zog was even set aside. Following Zog's flight from Albania, he wandered for months in search of asylum, until it was finally granted him by England on the occasion of the fall of France. As soon as Zog arrived in England, he and his agents began lobbying for some role in the war. Because the British had officially recognized the Italian annexation of Albania and had replaced their minister with a consul general, Zog was admitted to England merely as a private citizen. Zog hoped to change his status and assume an active role in the war, out of patriotism and a shrewd understanding that this would legitimize him as far as at least some Albanians were concerned. Zog's active participation in the war, with British acquiescence, would have committed the British to the restoration of some form of Albanian independence after the war and possibly a role for Zog himself.

The British government, sensing that Zog lacked popularity in Albania, and wishing to maintain a free hand, refused to grant Zog any role and even required that before admitting him he agree to refrain from political activity of any kind. By the early fall of 1940 British policy toward Zog had changed very little, perhaps best summarized by a Foreign Office minute from Pearson Dixon, of the Southern Department. Pearson noted,

> I said that in our view it would be a mistake to put forward King Zog's name in any way as a figurehead for the recovery of Albanian independence. Not only was he largely discredited personally, but we did not want to commit ourselves as to the future status of Albania, which we should be bound to do to some extent if the ex-king was to be used. At the same time we should naturally not be adverse to letting Albanians abroad know that King Zog among others was behind an independence movement if this would really help.[63]

Zog had initially agreed to refrain from political activity but proved to be something of a problem regardless. The Italian government was concerned that he was admitted to England at all, particularly in light of the fact that some Moslem states, such as Turkey and Egypt, refused to recognize the annexation and allowed Zog's missions to remain open. (This of course was much less of a problem after Italy entered the war.) And Zog himself was far from inconspicuous. He brought with him to England some one hundred sacks of gold, possibly part of the Albanian state treasury, and installed himself on an entire floor of the Ritz Hotel. He was accompanied by thirty-six people, six of whom were listed as "H. M. Ordinance Officers." These officers turned out to be his personal bodyguard of Albanian tribesmen, who—much to the annoyance of Scotland Yard—carried sawed-off shotguns. In light of these problems, the Foreign Office decided—as it did with numerous politically undesirable people—to ship Zog off to the United States.[64]

At the last moment, after many of the arrangements had been made, the Foreign Office changed its mind. This change of policy was effected in part by the arguments of Zog's secretary Qazim Kastrioti, who, obviously encouraged by the king, suggested that the British would be making a serious mistake in expelling Zog. Kastrioti maintained that all Albanians, including formerly implacable opponents who had been exiled by the Zog regime, were willing to support the king's wartime leadership and if he left Europe their cohesion would be destroyed and their usefulness crippled. Only Zog had sufficient status to induce Albanians to take the risks involved in embarrassing the Italians. Finally, Kastrioti argued that Zog possessed great assets in his good relations with the Turkish government and in the high regard that the people of Islam had for the only Moslem king in Europe.

While recognizing that much of this argumentation was overstated, foreign secretary Lord Halifax reversed the earlier decision to expel Zog. He feared that Zog would spread stories of British inhospitality once in the United States. Lord Halifax was also unwilling to ask the United States to receive people like Zog, who would probably do no harm in England. The foreign secretary decided to reserve that option for those the government desperately wanted out of England. The Foreign Office's greatest fear, however, was that the government might be faced with criticism along the lines that it had lost an opportunity of pursuing the war more vigorously against the Italians if Zog were required to go.[65]

With the Italian invasion of Greece in October 1940, the British attitude toward Zog changed. Zog himself saw the invasion as an opportunity to again put his name forward and did so. Zog reminded Sir Andrew Ryan, the former British minister in Albania who acted as an unofficial liaison between the Foreign Office and Zog, that he could rally some thirty thousand supporters—many with

Italian Repression and the Beginning of Resistance 107

whom he had remained in contact—and equip them with ten thousand rifles, which, Zog maintained, were hidden in northern Albania, a claim that the British took seriously. The Italians believed the number of rifles to be even higher. Colonel Gabrielli, the Italian military attaché in Tirana, reported in May 1939 that some forty thousand rifles with ammunition remained at large.[66]

On 8 November 1940 Zog presented the Foreign Office with a concrete plan. He suggested that he himself go to Istanbul and organize the fourteen thousand Albanians there into a fighting force to be landed in Thessaloníki. This force was to be augmented by the Albanian community in Greece, which Italian intelligence reported had already organized a committee that was in contact with the British. From there he would initiate a small fighting front with the twenty officers at his disposal, while at the same time directing a general uprising against the Italians. He believed that a major revolt could be stirred up by the tribes of the north and among the Kosovars. Although the same could not be expected of the weaker, less warlike southern Albanians, they could at least be counted on to harass the Italians. To support his case, Zog noted that the Kosovars were ready to send a delegation to meet with him, and he produced a series of telegrams from the Albanian community in Istanbul requesting that he come and organize this proposed fighting force. Both Percy and Ryan lent their support to Zog's plan, concluding that with proper financing, Zog could direct a united Albanian effort sufficient at least to embarrass the Italians.[67]

Meetings were held between the Foreign Office, War Office, and the new Special Operations Executive (SOE), formed in July 1940 by the war cabinet in the process of reorganizing existing intelligence agencies. SOE, which was destined to play a leading role in guerrilla warfare in Albania, was designed to coordinate and carry out subversive activities under the direction of the minister of economic warfare.[68] All parties in principle accepted the idea of using Zog along the lines that he had suggested, with SOE displaying particular zeal in suggesting that Zog should be flown to Greece.[69] But before final arrangements could be made, the British hoped to determine the attitude of the various governments involved and the true extent of Zog's popularity inside Albania. Here the trouble began. The entire project was called into question almost immediately by the uncompromising attitude of the Greek strongman General Metaxas and the British minister in Athens, Sir Michael Palairet, who some in the Foreign Office had accused of having "gone native."

Metaxas argued that because of Zog's unpopularity, his presence in the Balkans would actually aid the Italians. This reaction was not unexpected by the British, and Metaxas's motives were quite clear. The Greeks, who had by this time driven the Italians back into central Albania, had not liberated Albania in order to hand it back to the Albanians. Metaxas was interested in retaining large sections of southern Albania, and he recognized that if he allowed Zog any role in resistance he would run the risk of committing himself to the restoration of an independent Albania under Zog's rule. Accordingly, Metaxas even refused to allow Zog to broadcast a rallying speech from Radio Athens on the Albanian independence day. Later, in February 1941, the Greek government went further and successfully blocked the broadcast of a BBC interview with Zog. The Greek government, among other points, objected to a remark made during the interview in which Zog hoped to see Albanians free and happy within their legal frontiers.[70]

Metaxas did, however, react favorably to the suggestion on the part of Istanbul Albanians who hoped to form a legion in Greece. Because the offer was not made dependent on Zog's leading it, Metaxas welcomed their participation, provided that they could equip themselves.[71]

The British, however, still believed that Zog could play a useful role in the resistance and even before discovering the attitude of the other parties involved, on the night of 23 November offered to fly him to Cairo as the first step in carrying out these plans.[72] The hope was to begin some sort of operation on 28 November, Albania's independence day. Zog was taken somewhat by surprise and decided not to be hurried in such a manner, at least not until he had been able to see either Winston Churchill or Lord Halifax. Zog was, of course, keenly aware that the British government would make absolutely no commitment regarding the future of Albania. He hoped that a meeting with either the prime minister or the foreign secretary would at least give him some measure of legitimacy, which might later be useful. Queen Geraldine, in her authorized biography, maintained that Zog met frequently with both Churchill and Lord Halifax and advised them on the conduct of the war, but British documents make clear that no such meetings ever took place.[73] Zog allowed the moment to pass.

Geraldine maintained that Zog was wise not to have gone, since the plane that would have taken him was shot down en route.[74] But even had he safely arrived in Egypt, Zog would have been unable to participate as he had hoped. Within days of the Foreign Office's offer to fly Zog to Cairo, telegrams began coming in advising that Zog be kept in England.

Every government or British office slated for some sort of participation in the project reacted negatively to the plan. The Turkish government made it clear that they would not welcome Zog in Istanbul. Of the other possible staging areas, Cyprus was disqualified because of Greek objections and Palestine was ruled out after the colonial office pointed out that it would be a mistake to admit a non-Jew. The British ambassador in Belgrade, Ronald Campbell, cabled that the Yugoslav minister of war had been informed by the general commanding the Third Yugoslav Army on the Yugoslav-Albanian frontier that the Albanians with whom he was secretly in contact were united in their opposition to Zog. This should not have surprised the British, since the Yugoslavs had no love for Zog, and the Albanians with whom the general was in contact were undoubtedly Kosovars, many of whom resented Zog's reluctance to pursue Kosovar irredentism.

Zog's resistance plan was finally killed by reports from the Cairo embassy and from the commander in chief Middle East. After soliciting a report from Colonel Wilfred Stirling, head of the commander's Albanian mission in Istanbul, General Archibald Wavell, the commander in chief, strongly advised against the project. The British minister in Cairo, John Lampson, concurred, adding that he felt it most unwise to send Zog to Cairo, since he doubted whether the Egyptian court or government would welcome his presence. Lampson further added that because Cairo was filled with so many doubtful legations, Zog's every move would be spied upon and reported to the enemy.[75]

SOE, with Foreign Office participation, continued to move ahead on the Albania plan — now without Zog — in the form of a northern rising centering around Gani Kryeziu. Kryeziu was slated to occupy Kukës and proclaim an Albanian national government, headed by himself, which would release a statement of hostility toward Italy and friendship toward Greece. The plan was again put before the Greeks, who again rejected it out of hand, Metaxas arguing in favor of coordinated activity of several small bands, something that did not include unwanted political implications. Palairet seems to have finally lost his patience, cabling caustically to the Foreign Office, "I hope that the zeal of the experts on Albania will not be allowed to outrun their discretion and that we shall not thrust any such ambitious but ill-considered schemes on the Greek government who are after all chiefly responsible for the conduct of the campaign in Albania."[76] Anthony Eden, who had replaced Lord Halifax as foreign secretary, became involved at this stage, noting that "SO2 [which is what SOE was referred to as in Foreign Office papers of the time] seems to have rushed ahead without much thought." And three weeks later, he stated, "One thing must be clear. SO2 do not and must not conduct foreign policy. They are our instrument and not we theirs."[77] Eden was perhaps being overly harsh, since Foreign Office functionaires participated at every stage of the planning. In any case, it is clear that Greek sensibilities were the principal factor determining British policy toward Albania at this stage, which would cause the British trouble in Albania later in the war.

Both the plan, in its various forms, and Zog were dropped at the end of December 1940. Zog was to be kept in what the Foreign Office referred to as "warm-storage."[78] It is possible that an important opportunity was missed. Although Zog's flight and the character of his family and regime made him unpopular in many circles in Albania, and although Lawrence Grafftey-Smith, the British consul general in Durrës, was correct in reporting that there was no substantial pro-Zog party in Albania, Zog could certainly still command considerable support. It is true that few in the Orthodox community in the south and in the Catholic community in the north, and few of the Kosovars, would have resisted the Italians for Zog. Still, to the Moslem majority—of which Zog was a member—he remained the only figure of national stature, and indications were that an active resistance posture on Zog's part would have encouraged resistance in Albania. It would also have done much to undo the damage to his own reputation that his flight had caused.

As it was, all the British planning and negotiation to encourage Albanian resistance at this early stage came down to one rather pathetic operation in April 1941, after Hitler decided that Mussolini needed to be rescued from the Greeks. Following the German invasion of Yugoslavia, in an effort to create a diversion to support the Yugoslav armies, a British officer led a small band of Albanians, centered around the Kryeziu group, on an abortive invasion of Albania. Lieutenant Colonel Dayrell Oakley-Hill, who knew something of Albania by virtue of his having participated in organizing Zog's gendarmerie, led a tiny force of some three hundred from Kosova into Albania, without radio communications, sufficient arms, air support, or even the promise of support or supplies from anywhere. Campbell in Belgrade, presumably out of a feeling of pity, cabled London on 22 March 1941 that in view of the planned operation it would be useful if the BBC mentioned Albanian independence, or better yet, if the group were provided with some weapons or something.[79] His suggestion seems to have fallen of deaf ears. Oakley-Hill and his group were on their own.

Once inside Albania the force was able to gather a few hundred supporters, but as soon as Yugoslavia collapsed, so did the lilliputian invasion. Enver Hoxha celebrates the collapse of the mission, arguing that its real purpose was to (1) create conditions in which Albania would enter the sphere of British influence in the future and (2) stifle the development of any other resistance center outside of British control.[80] As usual with Albanian socialist historians, Hoxha gives the British far too much credit in terms of an organized political policy. Hoxha's attitude toward this mission is important, however, since everyone associated with it became suspect in his eyes.

Of the leadership, Oakley-Hill surrendered to the Germans, an act ridiculed by Hoxha. The Kryeziu brothers were captured by the Italians and sent to a concentration camp in Italy. Mustafa Gjinishi managed to work his way south to join some of his communist colleagues in the Korça area, and Abaz Kupi made his way to his own area of Kruja and there built up one of the first permanent organized resistance forces in Albania.[81]

The First Permanent Guerrilla Bands

By the end of 1941 several permanent organized guerrilla bands were reported to be in operation. These first small groups centered around returned band leaders, such as Abaz Kupi, who developed a nucleus of family members and then slowly spread their influence. This family-tribal feature distinguishes them from the early resistance groups in the ruins of Yugoslavia and Greece, which tended to be more ideological and less personal. The individuals first mentioned in this more organized context included again Colonel Muharrem Bajraktari, who, after plotting against Zog, left Albania for Yugoslavia and then France in 1936. He returned to Albania after the Italian invasion and immediately began organizing a small band in the Lumë district of northeast Albania. Bajraktari was believed to cherish an ambition of becoming president of an Albanian republic, and in his more expansive moments, the leader of some form of Balkan federation. Apart from his rather vaulted image of his potential, he was also said to have a persecution mania that sometimes verged on insanity.[82] Still, he was to develop a good reputation as a resistance fighter.

Another figure to gain early prominence as a band leader was Myslim Peza, whom the Italians had already mentioned as a brigand. Like Bajraktari, Peza was also an early opponent of Zog, having left Albania in 1925 after Zog's return to power. Peza was active in central Albania near Tirana, in areas adjacent to those where Abaz Kupi was operating. Peza is the only one of these early resistance leaders who would develop a close relationship with the communists. Socialist historians report that even before the organization of the Albanian Communist Party, Enver Hoxha recognized the significance of Peza's movement and sent communists to organize his group for him, help that Peza gladly accepted.[83] Indications are, however, that this claim by historians is merely an attempt to predate active communist participation in the resistance.

Also included in this early group of resistance leaders was the Moslem Bektashi cleric Baba Mustafa Martaneshi, also known as Baba Faja, abbot of Martanesh, who operated in the vicinity of Elbasan and was able to gain followers by emphasizing the anti-Islamic nature of fascist Italy and the dangers that Italian imperialism posed for coreligionists in Turkey and Egypt. For his antifascist pronouncements, his occasional military activity, and his cooperation with the budding communist movement, Baba Faja became one of the most wanted men in Albania.[84]

What distinguished this new organized resistance from the earlier individual or small group activity was objective and impact. The new organized groups, rather than attacking individual soldiers often only for personal gain and cutting an occasional wire, attacked targets of economic importance to the Italians. In October, for example, the *New York Times* reported that the oil pipeline to Vlora had been cut.[85] In the following month it was reported, although not confirmed, that the important iron and copper mines in the Mirdita district of northern Albania were partly destroyed.

Although these acts posed no serious military threat to the Italians—at least not until late 1942—the mere existence of the groups and their continued growth were matters of concern. Some foreign observers were surprised at the growth of both vocal and active organized resistance. The British consul commented that "the apathy of Albanians towards the abuses of the Zog regime was deplored in a succession of dispatches from this post as the most disquieting feature of local political life."[86] To Grafftey-Smith, then, any vocalized discontent was a surprise, let alone organized violent resistance.

The Italians Respond

The Italians initially, too, seemed genuinely surprised at the growing opposition, given the vast sums of money—which they could ill afford—being thrown at the Albanians. Understandably, therefore, the Italians lacked a cohesive policy in response. What emerged was an uneven combination of increasing repression and further concession. Soon after the invasion Ciano laid down the broad outlines of Italian policy in Albania, suggesting that "there must not be the least sign of weakness, justice and force must be the characteristics of the new regime."[87] To be sure, the Albanians received as much justice as did the Italians themselves. The new constitution extended to the government extensive powers of detention and internment and severely restricted the personal rights and liberties of Albanians, not to suggest that Zog had been particularly conscious of these rights and liberties either.

Ciano was quick to use this power given to the authorities. Intent on dealing harshly with what he called troublemakers, Ciano personally ordered many deportations and internments. On 30 May 1939 former prime minister Mehdi Frashëri, who had sent a nasty telegram to Mussolini on the occasion of the Italian invasion, left his refuge in the Turkish Legation after receiving assurances that he would not be molested. He was forced—along with his family—to accept exile in Italy. Rrok Geraj, former minister of national economy, and Eqrem Bey Libohova, the former Italophile minister of foreign affairs, were detained in Rome. Arrests and exiles continued throughout the summer of 1939 and increased in number as the Italians began to realize how unpopular they were. Italian authorities had explained the occasional resistance and continuing violence of the first few months of their occupation by suggesting that the root cause was prisoners who had been released an 7 April by the Zog regime, running rampant and creating havoc. The Italians further rationalized that part of the problem stemmed from an increase in blood feud violence, which any change of regime in Albania engendered.[88]

By the summer of 1939 these arguments were no longer credible, and repression increased. In June 1939 *Fashizmi* published a series of warnings—one under the title "Draconian Punishment"—directed at those who failed to accept the new status quo.[89] The Italian secret police was given a freer hand and determined to limit or entirely sever contact between Albanians and foreign legations. By the end of the summer, through constant surveillance and intimidation, Italian military intelligence (Servizio Informazioni Militare, or SIM) agents effected a virtual total boycott of foreign legations in Tirana. Everyone was watched. The German consul reported that the Italians had hired an army of informants to discover who was critical of their policies. As with many other Italian initiatives, however, the Albanians quickly turned this program to their own use. Albanians denounced blood feud enemies and simple rivals, involving the Italian authorities and their puppets in all manner of private quarrels. The Italians eventually caught on and began taking these denunciations somewhat less seriously.[90]

None of these Italian measures had any positive effect on the problems they faced; indeed, the security situation continued to deteriorate. As it did, Italian pressure increased. In June 1939 decrees were issued ordering the arrest and deportation of persons deemed dangerous to the public law and order as well as orders demanding the surrender of arms and ammunition. In January 1940 further decrees condemned crimes "against the personality of the state."[91] A set of particularly harsh decrees were reportedly issued on 11 April 1940—which banned demonstrations, rallies, processions, and meetings—with severe penalties, including death, for those who defied the decrees.[92]

In 1942, following the beginning of organized resistance, a series of new draconian laws were enacted. In April the newspaper *Tomori* published a lengthy set of new decrees, which included (1) fascist military patrols were ordered to shoot any passers-by who did not stop when ordered to, (2) coffeehouses and various other establishments were ordered closed from 7:30 P.M. to 7:30 A.M., (3) a general curfew was instituted from 8 P.M. to 6 A.M., (4) women were forbidden to wear veils in the street, (5) those caught wearing unauthorized military uniforms were subject to the death penalty, (6) the riding of bicycles and motorbikes was forbidden, (7) closed vehicles were prohibited, (8) gatherings of more than five people were prohibited, and walking in groups was prohibited, and (9) those who had not declared the possession of stencils for printing signs were to be sentenced to five years in prison.[93]

In August *Tomori* reported further decrees, including "All prefects in Albania are authorized to fix by order the delay during which all rebels in the district of a certain prefecture must give themselves up under penalty of death for infringers. The families of those who do not surrender will be interned in concentration camps, their houses burned and their possessions confiscated. These measures will also be taken for military deserters and for recruits who will not respond to the calling-up orders."[94] A number of Albanian collaborators found these new restrictions too difficult to accept and resigned from the government.

And for those who were still not convinced to cease their opposition, rumors began to spread of assassination squads made up of Albanians hired by the Italians to silence Albanian patriots.[95] Although the existence of these squads is still in doubt, a number of prominent unsolved murders did take place. As we have seen, the most celebrated may have been that of Nijaz Deda, the chief abbot of the Moslem Bektashi sect on 28 November 1941, in a cloister about one and a half miles from Tirana. The abbot was guarded by a fascist military patrol, which apparently failed to intervene.[96] This outrage may have been meant as a warning, particularly in light of the fact that many members of the Bektashis were active in the resistance.

But as the German consul noted, along with the new whip came new helpings of sugar bread. Interspersed between increasing repression, the Italians made further concessions. The authorities had already demonstrated — with the removal of Giro — their willingness to jettison unpopular officials and programs. One of the least popular innovations for which the Italians were responsible was the creation of the Albanian Fascist Party, and this was one of the first organizations that the Italians were ready to rearrange. As early as January 1940, at the first official meeting of the party, Tefik Mborja, the Albanian secretary, spoke of mistakes, particularly in recruitment.[97] In March the Italians determined to start by reorganizing the party's official newspaper, *Fashizmi,* which had proven to be a complete failure. First they replaced the Italian editor with an Albanian. Then they severed the paper's connection with the party and renamed it. As mentioned in chapter 2, a new name, *Tomori* (the name of the highest mountain in Albania and an object of some patriotic reverence) was chosen. None of these changes seem to have done much good, however, since the few literate Albanians recognized from the start that the paper was a creature of the Italians and would remain so.

The Kruja Government

Because the changes in the party seemed to have little effect on Albanian dissatisfaction, the Italians turned to more significant administrative changes. In November 1941, the Office of the Undersecretary of State for Albanian Affairs was replaced by a mixed Italo-Albanian commission, which was intended to give the Albanians at least the impression of participation in decision making. Perhaps more important, in December the entire Albanian puppet government was replaced. Ciano noted in his diary that as early as June 1941 Jacomoni and Mussolini had agreed on some new directives for Albania in order to try to do something about declining support. The basic idea was, without eliminating the beys, to broaden the Albanian government by including new elements closer to the intellectual classes and the people. This was to be accompanied by more extensive autonomy for the government.[98] By November Jacomoni's plan was complete. He proposed replacing Vërlaci and some of his reactionary landlords with Mustafa Kruja.

Kruja, a man of relatively humble origins—his father was a retainer of Zog's uncle, Esad Pasha—had been active in Albanian politics since 1912.[99] An opponent of Zog and of the beys, Kruja rose to become prefect of Shkodra under the short-lived government of Fan Noli. He was described in a 1924 dispatch as "a man of considerable intelligence but . . . he is also a truculent ruffian who is notorious for having caused the assassination of a least two persons of note whose existence was politically inconvenient to him."[100] With the fall of Noli's regime, Kruja fled to Zara, where, while receiving a subsidy from the Italian government, he became a strong irredentist and a person of consequence among Albanian political refugees. He returned to Albania shortly after the Italian invasion and was rewarded for his steadfast support with the title of Italian senator.

But his appointment as Albanian prime minister caused a considerable stir; Ciano had reservations, and Vërlaci was livid. Ciano commented in his diary that Kruja's appointment "means a further concession to the extremists of Albanian nationalism. Up to now the results of this policy have not been good; things went better when Benini concentrated authority in Rome."[101] Vërlaci hurried to Rome and complained bitterly to Ciano and Mussolini. Ciano noted, "I saw Vërlaci who spat venom when talking about Jacomoni and this is natural because he was shown the door. . . . When he saw Mussolini Vërlaci behaved badly. . . . He naturally detests Kruja, but he does not have solid arguments against him. He confines himself by saying that the country cannot be governed by a man who is the son of a servant by whom Vërlaci himself had been served a cup of coffee in the home of Esad Pasha."[102] The budding resistance abruptly ceased its criticism of Vërlaci immediately after his ouster because he apparently began to subsidize the resistance in order to discredit Kruja with the Italians as a man who could not keep order.

Kruja's cabinet certainly included more of a cross section of Albanian society than had Vërlaci's. Most were strong nationalists intent on preserving Greater Albania. The cabinet included younger elements, such as Tahir Shtylla, who counted as a recognized scholar, and members of the Albanian intelligentsia. Kruja also included Hasan Dosti, who eventually became a leading member of the resistance, and Kostaq Kota, who had served as Zog's last prime minister. Kruja hoped that this cabinet, as well as achieving a promised restoration of some freedoms, would win the adherence of a substantial number of Albanians from all levels of society.

The Italians seemed willing to take a chance on Kruja. Even Ciano was won over, it seems, by Kruja, who convinced him that the situation was actually quite calm. Although this assessment agreed with that of Jacomoni, who like most fascist officials was hesitant to deliver bad news to Ciano or Mussolini, it was, of course, nonsense. Oddly enough, Vërlaci was the only one with Albanian experience to lay out the problems that Italy faced, informing Ciano that matters were troubled and the people dissatisfied, an honest approach that certainly played a role in his own dismissal. But Kruja's attitude did produce some results.

In his first meeting with Mussolini, the Duce promised to grant the Albanians a more liberal and autonomous local regime.[103] And Kruja was able to extract further concrete concessions. First Kruja was able to convince Mussolini to restore to Albania its old flag. On 4 May, after informing Victor Emmanuel, the crown of Savoy and the fasces that framed the Albanian eagle were removed.[104]

Kruja was also able to effect the release of a large number of antifascists

Italian Repression and the Beginning of Resistance

interned in Italy, extract an offer of amnesty for the bands operating against the Italians, and resurrect an independent Albanian gendarmerie, which had been dissolved soon after the invasion as being too Zogist.[105] The new militia was to be composed of three thousand men, whose task it would be to relieve the gendarmerie of their guard duties once a level of security was returned to the countryside. The thousand Albanians who were employed as assistant gendarmerie were to be integrated into the new unit. As a first step, Kruja called for the creation of a three-hundred-man volunteer force to police the area around Kruja, which happened to be the district in which Abaz Kupi was active.[106]

Kruja's policies achieved some initial success. German sources tell us he was able to make contact with some of the band leaders, many of whom he had personal relations with from their days of anti-Zog activity. Some were even won over—at least temporarily—including Myslim Peza, who accepted full amnesty and freedom of movement. Peza would not, however, come to Tirana to collect a promised subsidy because he distrusted the Italian authorities.[107]

Kruja's success, however, proved to be both superficial and temporary. Many of his policies backfired almost immediately. Many of the antifascists whose release he secured immediately fled into the hills to join the growing resistance movement, as did many of the Albanian recruits, who disappeared with their weapons.[108] The security situation, far from improving, deteriorated rapidly. Common crimes continued to increase, and ever larger sections of the country fell to the band leaders. The relative stability of the early period of Italian occupation was lost forever. Italian incompetence, the failure of the war against Greece, the worsening economic conditions, and the growing resistance movement insured that those early days would not return. Despite this dismal picture, however, the Italians were still fortunate in at least one respect: by the end of 1941 Albania had still not developed a truly national resistance movement. The band leaders were primarily tribal chieftains who could not and would not leave their areas for extended periods. In most cases they also defended their areas as jealously against one another as they did against the Italians and their Albanian puppets. But this benefit, enjoyed by the Italians, also proved temporary. With the maturing of the communist movement, something close to a national resistance movement was finally developed.

Italian reconstruction at the port of Durrës during the Italian occupation. (Luckwald)

Italian construction of the new Dopolavoro building in Tirana during the Italian occupation. (Luckwald)

Zog's palace, built by the Italians and then after the invasion turned into a military hospital on the orders of Victor Emmanuel III during the Italian occupation. (Luckwald)

Albanian youth march to school in new fascist uniforms during the Italian occupation. (Luckwald)

Mussolini meets with his commanders in Albania during the Italo-Greek war, March 1941.

Albanian prime minister Vërlaci and Victor Emmanuel III at the airport in Tirana, May 1941. (Jacomoni)

CHAPTER 5

THE GROWTH OF RESISTANCE AND THE COLLAPSE OF ITALY

By the end of 1941, German diplomats reported that the security situation in Albania was becoming difficult. By the early summer of 1942, they reported anarchy in the open land, with Italian control restricted to the major towns, the major roads, and military installations.[1] One year later the occupation system was in tatters, and by August 1943 it had collapsed entirely. A series of events explains these developments, with the most important occurring outside of Albania, involving the general course of World War II. But events inside of Albania did much to contribute to the Italian collapse. And the most significant was the rise of something close to a national resistance movement dominated by Albanian communists and aided by the British.

The Creation of the Albanian Communist Party

The story of the rise of the communist movement in Albania is as byzantine as it is remarkable. Beginning with no more that a few dozen fiercely independent adherents, the movement, in a matter of decades, gained power in a state where communism was little known and was juxtaposed or at least alien to many indigenous traditions. The communism that developed under these circumstances was naturally unique and often seemed indistinguishable from extreme nationalism. Tracing this story is often fraught with danger. Because Albanian socialist historians tended to be very selective in the materials they used, there are several versions of these events. Indeed, the formation and rise of the Albanian Communist Party and its relationship with the Yugoslav Communist Party have engendered more historical dispute that perhaps any other issue in modern Albanian history.

Communist activity in Albania dates from the early 1920s, when a group of Albanian nationalists were encouraged and then financed by the Comintern through its Balkan Communist Federation. Bajram Curri and his colleagues in the Kosova Committee, a group of northerners who sought the union of Albania and Kosova, were attracted by the federation's call for the readjustment of Balkan frontiers based upon the principle of national self-determination. The Comintern tried concurrently to establish a communist party in Albania, the only Balkan state that did not have one at that time. Although these efforts failed, interest in communism increased among some Albanians following the overthrow of the Fan Noli government in 1924. Noli and many of his followers fled, and some organized the Committee of National Liberation (KONARE), which by 1928 was essentially controlled by the Comintern. KONARE was instrumental in sending about twenty-four Albanians to Moscow for training.[2] These two dozen organized a diminutive Albanian communist party in exile and were directed to return to Albania to found an indigenous party.

The most active of these early Albanian communists was Ali Klemendi, who returned to Albania in 1930 and succeeded in constructing a few communist cells. Klemendi's influence was sporadic and limited, however, as was his presence. In prison from 1932 to 1935 and deported in 1936, he finally died in 1939 of tuberculosis in Paris, which had become a center for Albanian communists. In the meantime the Comintern sent Koço Tashko, who arrived in Albania in 1937 and discovered four squabbling groups with a combined membership of less than two hundred, who posed little or no threat to the Zog regime.[3] The groups included Zjarri (Fire), which was not orthodox; a group in Tirana; one in Shkodra; and one in Korça. Of the four, the Korça group generally supported the Comintern line, and it is here, therefore, that Tashko concentrated his energies. But the internal disputes went from bad to worse. In February 1939 most of the Shkodra group was arrested by agents of Zog— foul play on the part of the other groups has been suggested.

When the Italians invaded in 1939, the communists were too weak and divided to take any action, although Albanian socialist historiography reports that they all resisted with determination.[4] While some individual communists are said to have joined some of the small but growing resistance bands, there seems to be little evidence to suggest that the communists groups did anything more than organize a few demonstrations. In keeping with their inability to agree or compromise, the four groups developed different bases of support and different strategies for dealing with the occupation. The Korça group, which remained orthodox, had a better mix of intellectuals and workers than did the other groups. It had been active in the small but growing trade union movement and therefore had some contact with the masses. It called for general resistance against the invader. The remnants of the Shkodra group, which had greater contact with youth and the schools, endorsed a traditional working-class socialist revolution.[5] The Zjarri group, which was labeled Trotskyite and anarchist, argued that the fascist stronghold should be taken from within; in other words, some degree of cooperation with the Italians was required.[6]

Instead of facilitating the unity of the various groups, the invasion seems only to have caused further splits. A "Youth" group split off from the Korça group and took the position that because Albanian peasants were so conservative, no real basis for a party existed. The Yugoslav communists later condemned this group as a little more than a gang of thieves. The situation was further complicated when the Germans took France in 1940 and sent many Albanian communists back to Albania. The Italians allowed them to move around freely because many of them followed the prevailing Comintern line and denounced the war as imperialistic.[7] By early 1941, apart from some independent communists who had been returned from Paris, there were eight separate groups, two of them considered Trotskyite.

At this point, the Yugoslavs seem to have stepped in. The Communist Party of Yugoslavia (CPY) was probably motivated at least in part by the trouble it was having setting up cells in Kosova. In order to attract the Albanians there, the CPY, at its Fifth Congress in the summer of 1940, had reaffirmed its 1929 decision to support the principle of national self-determination in regard to Kosova. The party was a long way from power and had little to lose. But this move did not have the desired effect of gaining recruits among the Albanians of Kosova. It is likely that the CPY thought the construction of an Albanian party would be of help in this regard.[8] In any case, the Shkodra group appealed to the Yugoslavs for help in constructing a party. The German attack on the Soviet Union provided a new sense of urgency for Albanian communists. As Enver Hoxha was later to write, "the struggle didn't begin with the entry of the Soviet Union but at that point it became clear that the struggle would not be in vain."[9]

Following an initial failure, two Yugoslav emissaries, Miladin Popovic and Dusan Mugosa, convinced representatives of three of Albania's communist groups to meet with them in Tirana at the beginning of November 1941. After six days—and twenty years of struggle—the fifteen communists present at this meeting elected a provisional central committee of seven and in so doing founded the Albanian Communist Party (ACP). The most controversial question regarding the founding of the ACP involves the level of Yugoslav participation. Official Albanian socialist historiography fails to mention the Yugoslavs at all, giving credit to the Albanian leadership, which was spurred into action by the need to resist the Italians and by the German invasion of the Soviet

Union. At the other extreme some Yugoslav historians and émigré Albanians argue that the Yugoslavs were principally responsible for the creation of the Albanian Communist Party. Stavro Skendi, for example, argues that Popovic and Mugosa were sent to organize the party, choose the members of the central committee, and became the real leaders of the Albanian party. Stavro Skendi suggests that the ACP was little more than a branch of the CPY.[10]

But this conclusion may be an overstatement. Mugosa himself has written, "True, the movement was fragmented and lacked coordination. True we assisted in establishing proper discipline and cooperation among the various groups. Yet this should not be interpreted to mean that the Albanians could not accomplish this task themselves. They possessed capable leaders who would have, in time solved their administrative problems. We were invited to assist and did so."[11] The historian Nicholas Pano's assessment is the most reasonable. Pano argues that "while it is true that it required a world war, foreign occupation and Yugoslav assistance to achieve this goal, it should also be noted that the objective could not have been realized without the existence of a small, hardcore, native communist movement."[12]

The central committee of the new party chose Enver Hoxha as secretary. The choice was not an obvious one, but Hoxha had a series of natural advantages. First, although he was an active member of the Korça group, he remained outside of the top leadership. He was probably a compromise candidate. While he had not distinguished himself as a leader, he was respected, well educated, well spoken, and dedicated—a pleasant, good-looking young man of thirty-three.

Hoxha, who would dominate the party and Albania for the next four decades, was a Moslem Tosk from Gjirokastra in the south. He is perhaps best described as an nationalist first, then as a Stalinist communist, and finally as an intellectual.[13] Since his family was reasonably well off, Hoxha received as good an education as Albania had to offer, including one of Zog's scholarships to study abroad. Hoxha attended the University of Montpellier, where he studied natural sciences, although his real interests included history and political science. Here he further developed his leftism and patriotism, which had already become apparent in his lycée years in Albania. In 1934 he lost his scholarship and moved to Paris, where a large Albanian émigré community could be found. He apparently preferred the company of non-Albanian leftists, ignoring such organizations as KONARE. He later expressed considerable contempt for KONARE, writing "illegal work under Zog's repressive regime demanded great sacrifice which the leaders of the organization were not ready to make."[14]

While his contact with Albanian radicals in exile seemed limited, he did join the French Communist Party and established some connection with the party newspaper, *L'Humanité*—although what kind of connection remains unclear. The official histories use rather imprecise language in describing his relationship with the paper, including "he established connections with the editorial board of *L'Humanité*, . . . to which he contributed materials denouncing Zog's regime,"[15] and "in Paris he became involved in editing *L'Humanité*."[16] In any case, when he returned to Albania in 1936, without a degree, he was a confirmed Marxist, well versed in ideology and quite enthusiastic. Hoxha was hired to teach French at the lycée in Korça, where he joined the Korça group and became one of its active members but was not, apparently, within the leadership circle. In December 1939 he was fired by the new Italian administration for his radical views and was sent to Tirana by the Korça group to spread its influence. The tobacco shop that Hoxha ran soon became a meeting place for leftists, and Hoxha was ultimately forced to go underground to avoid arrest, at which point, he tells us, he became one of the principal forces behind the movement for unity.

With a secretary, a provisional central committee, and its Yugoslav advisers, the party was ready to meet its first challenges. Its problems were many. First it was virtually unknown, with an initial membership of 130, most of whom were young intellectuals and middle-class students—although there were some laborers and artisans in the movement as well. Many of these people, including Hoxha himself, were influenced primarily by Western intellectual traditions, alien to the majority of Albanians who were conservative, xenophobic peasants. The first goal, then, was to boost membership by direct recruitment and by the establishment of a program that might attract the average Albanian. Mugosa directed recruitment, while Popovic stayed with Hoxha to help organize the party and its basic program. That the Yugoslavs provided the pattern to follow for the Albanians is clear, including the adoption of the Yugoslav slogan "death to fascism, liberty to the people," as well as the red star on the cap.[17]

Hoxha moved quickly on both fronts. He based the party on traditional Marxist-Leninism and democratic centralism, denouncing both social democracy and Trotskyism. The communist groups were officially dissolved and were replaced by local cells and regional party committees run by a network of local party officials. Membership was open to all who expressed themselves ready to accept the discipline of the party, with early recruitment targeting young intellectuals and youth, chiefly high school students, artisans, small shopkeepers, and a few labor leaders, as well as a few petty thieves.[18] By January 1942, however, the party had grown to only some two hundred members, approximately the same number as claimed to be communists in 1937.

The initial growth of the party was modest for a number of reasons. First, Hoxha, despite dissolving the communist groups and warning of "groupism," was faced with ideological struggles both within and outside of the party. The Zjarri group, which had not participated in forming the party, continued struggling for its own unorthodox position. The official history of the party complains that party work was undermined by a "5th column of Zjarri chiefs."[19] Perhaps more troubling, however, were the remnants of the "Youth Group," which objected to expanding the party by taking in illiterate peasants. The dispute was serious enough to jeopardize the existence of the party. But by the summer of 1942, Hoxha, who had by this time begun to exhibit that relentless drive that would serve him so well, managed to purge these divisive and disobedient elements from the party. But their influence had spread, and it became necessary to dissolve the Gjirokastra district committee to destroy the "liquidatory" elements who controlled it.[20]

At the same time Enver Hoxha was able to censure both Koço Tashko and Mustafa Gjinishi for criticizing party direction. Hoxha tells us that these two were being uncooperative because of their lack of advancement within the party. But Hoxha was more likely motivated by the fact that both had more experience than he and could at some point threaten his position. Here he was taking a lesson from the rise of Stalin.

Although these purges by no means ended internal party strife, they did allow Hoxha to turn his attention to other significant priorities, including expanding popular acceptance of the party and its goals. These goals were set down in a twenty-eight-point program that included the slogan "to fight for national independence and a people's democratic government." The political line and communist propaganda envisioned workers and peasants being formed into military units that were to include all nationalists who truly wanted to fight, to prepare people for an armed uprising but not to neglect other forms of struggle until the uprising was practical, and to eventually create a people's army but until that was practical to rely upon band and partisan warfare. This struggle was to be linked to that of the Allies fighting the Axis, but the struggle of the Soviet Union was to be emphasized and the party was instructed in "developing love for the Soviet Union."[21]

While the communists were fairly successful in increasing growing opposition to the Italians and their Albanian puppets, they were much less successful in attracting wide-scale support for their movement. This is perhaps not surprising, since the party was dominated by intellectuals and middle-class students. Their natural constituency was rather small. In 1939 there were probably no more than two thousand to three thousand people who might be considered intellectuals in the country, and Albania certainly had the smallest middle class in Europe, when considered as a percentage of its population.[22] As for the communists' traditional ideological partner, the working class, one need only remember that in 1939 only 4 percent of the national economy could be considered industrial.

And the communists made an already difficult situation even more challenging. They handicapped themselves in that many of their more visible advisers were Slavs, who had always aroused suspicion and fear among Albanians. We are just now learning from the recently opened party archives how completely dependent Hoxha was on those advisers. In an internal discussion in 1944, Hoxha confessed that "when the Party was formed, our reliance on those two comrades, Miladin and Dusan, was great, because I was without experience and without clear views on organization and policy."[23]

To make matters worse, the communist approach to social issues left the impression that Albania would become part of some nebulous Slav-dominated Balkan federation. In an attempt to dispel some of these unfortunate impressions, the provisional central committee ordered that communist propaganda be deemphasized in favor of the struggle against fascism and the Italian invader.

Hoxha determined that the party would stimulate and then lead the resistance by example. As we have seen, resistance, even organized resistance, had already begun. In order to catch up with events, the party quickly began to organize its own resistance groups, which were expanded into active bands by December 1941 and early 1942. The informal resistance groups consisted of perhaps five to ten people who operated from their homes. They were responsible for various acts of sabotage and the spreading of propaganda in order to do damage to the enemy and to attract the attention of the masses.

As early as the fall of 1941, communist propaganda, whether it originated with the Albanians or not, was commanding the attention of many in Albania. The German consul reported that soon after the German invasion of the Soviet Union, communist propaganda handouts appeared in Tirana and several other Albanian towns. At the same time, the hammer and sickle appeared on the walls of various public buildings. Although the handouts included the letters *PKSh*, for Albanian Communist Party (which of course did not yet exist, although the consul was unaware of this fact), the German consul believed that the handouts were not of Albanian origin. He came to this conclusion based upon the language used, which he argued was alien to Albanian circumstances, and because of how the leaflets were randomly distributed. The consul entertained the possibility that the Italians themselves were responsible for the communist propaganda in order to use the occasion to arrest uncooperative Albanians. He reported that many Albanians seemed to think along the same lines. As another explanation, he argued that there were many communists among the Italian soldiers stationed in Albania.[24]

To lend credence to these assertions, the consul listed a series of incidents in which Italians were observed distributing communist propaganda. In Elbasan and in Korça, Albanian night security personal observed uniformed Italians on bicycles disseminating communist literature. In a small town near Durrës, Albanian police arrested a number of Italian carabinieri painting communist emblems on village walls. An Italian major was arrested attempting to smuggle communist material into Durrës, and two other Italian officers were caught and charged with the same crime in Tepelena.[25]

While these incidents are difficult to verify, it is clear that both the Italians and Kruja were quick to blame communists for their various troubles. As an example, in March 1942 in Korça, Skënder Çami, an Albanian major of gendarmerie, was assassinated. The German consul reported that, as usual, the perpetrators were unknown. *Tomori*, the government newspaper, however, immediately declared that the assassins were paid agents from Moscow. To support this claim, the paper frequently referred back to the communist propaganda handbill campaign that had occurred following the German invasion of the Soviet Union.[26] Kruja, too, from the beginning of his regime began labeling all in opposition to his government as communists who were being supported with foreign gold from Montenegro and Serbia.[27] This was a rather transparent attempt to convince all those Albanians not yet involved with the resistance that only foreign radicals or foreign paid radicals were in opposition to his government.

Regardless of how much of this early communist propaganda actually originated with the ACP, by the summer of 1942, the party was growing rapidly. Hoxha's attempt to deemphasize the social revolution was beginning to pay off. Many of the landless peasants in the south, who were Orthodox and labored on the estates of Moslem landowners, responded to the basic slogans of resistance to the foreigners and traitors and of land to those who till it. These simple slogans addressed the crucial issues in Albania: the national problem and the land problem. As the party grew, its bands grew and resistance grew. Other than the various demonstrations for which the communists were responsible, these first acts seemed to have been assassinations of collaborators and Italian officials. Young patriots, often armed with their own pistols, carried out these early attacks without giving up their jobs or their homes.[28]

As 1942, the fourth year of the occupation, wore on, the local press and foreign consulates began to report an increasing number of attacks. In May the chief of police of Tirana was gunned down. There were a number of attacks on Prime Minister Kruja, none of which were successful, although members of his family, including his son, were killed. During the summer an arms repair factory was attacked. Perhaps the most spectacular act of sabotage organized by the new communist bands was the interruption of all telephone and telegraph communications in June and July of 1942.[29] In August the party published the first issue of its paper *Zëri i Popullit*, which allowed the communists to widely disseminate—and often exaggerate—their achievements.

But while these communist activities were becoming increasingly annoying, the biggest problem facing the Italians remained the northern bands. By the summer of 1942, the Italians had virtually given up the north. The gendarmerie posts that still remained in place were concerned primarily with their own security and the gendarmes rarely ventured out. Even some of the main roads could only be used by well-protected convoys. Although many of the northern leaders, including Peza and Kupi, occasionally negotiated cease-fires with the Italians, Kruja's attempt to coopt them ultimately proved unsuccessful. While the influence of the chiefs remained regional, it was they who were considered Albania's resistance leaders both at home and abroad.

The communists were determined to change this impression and seize the initiative with a bold stroke. They hoped to create a popular front national resistance movement dominated by their own party. Still, there were divisions in the party on this approach. Popovic actually opposed the idea, suggesting that there was a genuine possibility that such a movement would merely result in the loss of time and in supplying scarce resources to criminals who would soon become traitors, such as the Yugoslav nationalist leader Draza Mihailovic. Popovic's position was initially supported by Hoxha, who feared that the leading role of the party would be threatened. But the veteran communists—including Mustafa Gjinishi, Ymer Dishnica, and Koço Tashko— called for a united front to include all who were willing to fight the Italians, and they prevailed.[30] Hoxha came around and eventually decided that this plan had the potential of thrusting him into the limelight, thereby helping him with his goal of a socialist Albanian under his leadership.

Formation of the National Liberation Movement

Accordingly, in September 1942 Hoxha invited the northern chiefs, the landowning beys of the south, and the old liberals and republicans who had opposed Zog to a conference at Peza. The spot was chosen carefully in an attempt to associate the party with Myslim Peza, who by now, like Kupi, had become something of a legend in Albania. About twenty people attended, including some band leaders, a few people identified as private patriots, and of course representatives of the Communist Party. Hoxha was undoubtedly relieved that the beys, liberals, and republicans declined to attend, leaving the communists as the only organized political party at the meeting. Although the official party history tells us that the delegates agreed to set aside political differences, it is clear that hard bargaining took place. Kupi was unhappy with the term *partisan*, the use of the red star, and some of the political decisions. Kupi ultimately gave in on these points and even agreed to make Zog's return dependent on the popular will. In exchange Hoxha mitigated some of the strident language associated with social reform.

Elements within the party later accused Hoxha of "sectarianism" for being unwilling to compromise further. Indeed, he was rather reluctant to cast his net too broadly and never included the diverse liberal elements that Tito accepted into his organization. Hoxha was clearly focusing on the postwar political structure, not wanting to burden himself with excess political baggage. Hoxha was a gambler, and he was clearly taking a big risk that other strong resistance organizations would not form outside of his control. He was taking a page from Lenin. But he did manage to attract Kupi, Peza, and Baba Faja, three of the principal resistance leaders in Albania.

From these various compromises, the Peza conference laid the basis for the Lëvizje Nacionalçlirimtare (National Liberation Movement, or NLM). Although socialist Albanian historiography makes no mention of it, British sources maintain that the old liberal Mehdi Frashëri, a former prime minister and one of the most distinguished Albanians, then interned in Italy, was chosen as honorary president.[31] His later collaboration with the Germans is likely at the root of the hesitation on the part of socialist historians to mention him in this light. A general council was established made up of seven communists, including Mustafa Gjinishi and Enver Hoxha, and three noncommunists: Abaz Kupi—who was persuaded to participate by Mustafa Gjinishi—Myslim Peza, and Baba Faja. But a British officer who later observed the working of this group reported that Baba Faja and Myslim Peza were middle-aged, rather old-fashioned, good livers, very heavy drinkers, and possessed of considerable personal charm and courage. They were, apparently, at the same time comparatively uneducated, lethargic, and somewhat incompetent. Because Kupi basically kept to his own area, the general council was not only dominated but controlled by communists.[32]

It should not be surprising, due to the council's composition, that the

General Council of the NLM adopted proposals set down by the ACP with regard to the conduct of the war and the rudiments of an administrative structure. The main points were incorporated into a basic platform that included the following points: (1) to wage uncompromising war against the fascist invaders and the traitors, for a free, independent, and democratic Albania, (2) to organize all true Albanians into a united national liberation front without discrimination as to class, political conviction, religion, or region of origin, (3) to set up national liberation councils everywhere as organs uniting and mobilizing the people in war and as organs of the people's power, and (4) to popularize and prepare for the people's armed uprising as the ultimate stage, the logical consequence of the partisan war.[33] The failure to mention radical social reform in the platform was intended to draw the support of noncommunists.

The general council supervised the national liberation councils and the partisan units. The councils—suggested by Enver Hoxha—in those areas yet to be liberated functioned as propaganda agencies, collected materials necessary for the war, conducted espionage, organized the economic struggle against the Italian capitalist companies, and sabotaged the accumulation of agricultural products by the fascists. In those areas already liberated by the partisans—once this became a reality—the councils were to function as the new state, or in Albanian socialist terminology, as "organs of the people's power." They were responsible for maintaining law and order; developing the local economy; overseeing the food supply and the sowing and harvesting of grain; managing trade; organizing education, culture, and the press; settling blood feuds; and maintaining readiness for war.[34]

The immediate concern, however, was to expand the small communist bands into larger and more numerous NLM bands, insuring that the party could maintain political and military control. And the organizational structure of the new bands did much to insure that this would be the case. The bands were constructed on the Yugoslav model and consisted of a nucleus of party members who had been forced to leave the towns. The bands were based in the countryside and survived with help from the peasants. The peasants, as the official history admits, were initially suspicious and even subjected these party members to mockery.[35] But slogans—like "land for those who till it"—and pressure brought many around, particularly as more students, artisans, employees, and workers joined the movement. The plan, as drawn up by the General Council of the NLM, envisaged bands of fifty to sixty, commanded usually by a nonparty member but advised by a political commissar. The commissar left military jurisdiction in the hands of the commander, except (1) when orders were at variance with the political line of the party, (2) when orders were at variance with the interests of the war of national liberation, or (3) when treason on the part of the commander was involved.[36] In other words, noncommunist commanders had the freedom to do exactly what they were told. The party, whenever possible, directed both politically and militarily. To strengthen control, each band had a party cell at its core, which usually held weekly meetings to deal with organization and theory issues. Both the cells and the political commissars were responsible to the regional committees of the party. Popovic, who attended the conference as an adviser, hoped to further strengthen party control by creating a general staff that would tie the various units together, but his suggestion was not adopted.[37]

These partisan units were supplemented by territorial units—irregular self-defense detachments made up of volunteers. These were planned for every larger village or one for two or three villages together. Their function was to protect the liberated zones and to serve as a source of replenishment for the regular partisan units. The recruitment program proved to be quite successful; the party history relates that by the end of 1942, there were some two thousand partisan fighters plus a larger number of territorial units and reservists.[38] These groups also had become active enough that the Italians mounted several drives against partisan forces and centers, beginning a cycle that was at least partially responsible for the partisan success. The partisans would launch an attack, and the Italians would respond. Because the Italians generally feared the Albanians, they usually responded only with large units, which rarely found partisan forces and therefore were restricted to conducting punitive reprisals, including the shooting of hostages, but principally the burning of villages. This naturally resulted in an increase in the number of homeless peasants who swelled the ranks of the partisan forces.[39]

Formation of the "Balli Kombëtar"

The liberals, republicans, and beys who had declined Hoxha's invitation to participate in the Peza conference, viewed these various developments with considerable concern. Many quickly concluded that in order not to be entirely shut out of power at the end of the war, they would have to demonstrate something more than mild dislike and noncooperation with the Italians. To facilitate a more active role, the liberal nationalists, some of whom nevertheless also established loose links with the NLM, in November 1942 formed a group called the Balli Kombëtar (National Front), or BK. This group hoped to provide a political and military organization for the moderates who distrusted the communists. The leaders of the BK claimed that the group was founded on the first day of the Italian invasion, and indeed, there probably was some informal organization among a few former politicians,[40] but the organization and its platform were clearly a direct reaction to the founding of the NLM. Albanian socialist historiography argues that it was put together by the reactionary middle class, big landowners, big merchants, reactionary clergy, rich peasants, and the Trotskyite Zjarri group, with the support of the fascist invaders.[41] While much of this is overstated, it does not go as far as Milovan Djilas, the Yugoslav politician and writer, who has described the BK as "Albanian minority fascists."[42] But when Hoxha suggested that the BK was formed not to fight the invader but rather to disrupt the political work of the Communist Party, he is not far from the truth.

As its leader, the BK chose the elderly and largely ineffectual Mithat Frashëri, a former diplomat and a cousin of Mehdi Frashëri. Mithat Frashëri enjoyed little of the respect that his cousin commanded, and he was described as an obstinate and romantic Tory who surrounded himself with people of questionable integrity. The central committee formed to conduct policy apparently had originally included some moderate and younger members, but because these elements were soon arrested by the Italians, the older, more conservative members—those prone to collaboration—were left in charge. This included a number of individuals from the so-called Paris group, anti-Zogists who had spent most of the interwar years in exile in France and had only returned after the Italian invasion. The most prominent among this group included Ali Këlcyra, who had an appearance and eloquence in the tradition of the old French Radical Party, but was a politician of the Zog school, and Rexhep Mitrovica, who would later head a collaborationist government under the Germans.

The programs that the BK leaders developed were not only in direct reaction to the NLM's program, but also had the disadvantage of being rather vague. The BK actually developed two programs, the "Eight Points" and the "Decalogue," which both sounded, at least superficially, like the NLM program. For example, both the BK and the NLM declared themselves to be above politics and open to all Albanians. But there were a number of important differences. The BK program sought to reestablish a "free, ethnic and democratic Albania," a clear reference to the desire to retain Kosova.[43] While this point attracted the support of many Albanians, the fact that the BK programs did not suggest fighting as a means to achieve an ethnic Albania, did not mention who had power, and did not even mention whom the BK was struggling against, was certainly a disadvantage. In essence, the BK program was passive. The leadership hoped to avoid useless destruction, wait for the defeat of the Axis before encouraging a national uprising, preserve Albania for the Albanians, and preserve the military strength of the BK for the inevitable confrontation with the communists.[44] But this is not to suggest that there was not actual resistance. Many of those who eventually associated themselves with the BK had resisted before joining and some continued to resist. In general, the BK was a much looser organization, which allowed the individual commanders of the *çetas*, the small resistance groups, to act independently. Many used this freedom to resist the invader.

The BK was able to construct what in many ways became a parallel organization to the NLM. Aside from the central committee, regional committees were constructed in many districts, and at least two publications appeared periodically. The BK put together its own youth organization called the Rinia Balliste. The BK attracted the support of numerous members of the Kruja government, including Fuat Bey Dibra, the minister of national economy, and Hasan Dosti, the minister of justice, as well as a number of important officials in the Gjirokastra area, including the prefect Faik Qyku. Much of this was very disturbing to the NLM, particularly as BK influence grew in the villages of southern Albania, where the BK agitated against the NLM and constructed BK organizations.[45] The BK was initially less successful in expanding its influence among the chiefs of the north. Although the chiefs certainly were more sympathetic to the program of the BK, their distrust of all central authority—and the fact that the Italian occupation had affected the mountainous north politically and economically to a lesser extent than the rest of the country—convinced the chiefs to remain aloof from both the BK and the NLM, as well as from each other.

And like the communist-dominated NLM, the BK established contact with similar organizations in Yugoslavia and Greece, or at least made an effort to do so. Some tenuous links were established with Mihailovic, but this contact proved to be of little value to either organization. Attempts to contact the Greek nationalist leader Napoleon Zervas were not made until May 1944, when Dhimitër Falo was sent to negotiate a general agreement. Included in the proposed agreement were provisions recognizing the territorial integrity, independence, and sovereignty of both states, provisions calling for military and economic cooperation, and Greece was to support Albanian demands to retain Kosova and Dibra. But this scheme came to nothing when Falo was caught, with his documents, by Albanian partisans and shot.[46]

There are some isolated reports from early 1943 of cooperation between BK and NLM units. This can perhaps best be explained by the loose BK structure and by the fact that months often went by without contact with the leadership. This is similar to the development of resistance in Yugoslavia, where, until the end of 1942, Tito and Mihailovic coordinated some of their actions and shared some supplies.[47] In general, however, relations between the BK and the NLM before the Italian collapse in the summer of 1943 were hostile but confined to a fierce propaganda war, indicating the concern both had about the mere existence of the other. Both had weaknesses readily exploited by the other. The BK naturally emphasized the communist core of the NLM, the proliferation of foreigners in its leadership, and the possibility of Albania's losing its independence to a Slav-dominated Balkans, or at the very least, the loss of Kosova. The NLM countered with charges that the BK leadership was little more than the old traditional ruling elite trying to maintain Albania as it was under Zog, only without Zog. Hoxha argued persuasively that the BK's opportunistic program allowed one to question its patriotism.

Hoxha wrote that "some are partisans of intrigue . . . some are partisans of alarmism, the third group are partisans of big words, but none are partisans of deed."[48] The NLM pointed out, correctly, that the preponderance of large landowners among the leadership led one to question the seriousness of its land reform proposals. But Hoxha was more than a little worried about the BK in January 1943; after all, its forces were more numerous than his own, having been more successful with peasant recruitment. But the partisans were better propagandists, so their actions were widely known, and as the Italians weakened and withdrew to the cities, the partisans gained access to more and more villages and were able to steadily increase their own peasant recruitment.[49] Still, socialist historians admit that the emergence of the BK in the political arena created significant problems for the NLM. The BK's ties to the "rural gentry," especially in southern Albania, caused many members of the NLM to "waver and hesitate," necessitating, once again, the dissolution of some NLM councils in the south.[50]

Hoxha wrote of the BK in 1943, "It is a great obstacle indeed, because we should not underestimate the individual influence of its adherents in Albania, always bearing in mind that they have succeeded in creating among the people the opinion that there exists a nationalist organization with which the communists should come to an understanding and agreement."[51] This popular pressure was augmented for Hoxha by directives from the outside. In December 1942 Mugosa finally returned to Albania with recognition for the party from the Comintern and orders that worried Hoxha. Hoxha was directed, most likely by Tito, to redouble his efforts in pursuit of popular front policies. As many upright patriots as possible were to be recruited both as fighters and as leaders. In the meantime, party propaganda was not to go beyond the bounds of the national liberation war. Hoxha had been ordered, in no uncertain terms, to come to some accommodation with the BK. As we will see, attempts at an agreement between the BK and the NLM were made.

The Continued Growth of Resistance

As both organizations grew, so did resistance—particularly that carried out by the NLM. Resistance had been stimulated by a number of factors. It was clear to many Albanians—through BBC and other sources—that the Axis, particularly after the battle of Stalingrad, was on the defensive. Albanians were further encouraged by the December 1942 declarations made by the principal Allied states (which will be discussed in more detail later in this chapter) calling for the reestablishment of Albanian independence after the war. The declarations had a particularly good effect on the resistance and they frightened Kruja, who held an emergency grand council meeting on Christmas Day to denounce the statements. One of the members made an anti-Italian speech and was immediately arrested.[52]

But the principal reason for increased resistance was the successful recruitment policy and the growing organization of the NLM. By early 1943 NLM bands began to coordinate their activities for the first time. Because of the efforts of the NLM, resistance in Albania became national for the first time, and the Italians were forced to adjust their military tactics as well as their political policy. By January it was estimated that there were three thousand to four thousand partisans in all, the bands growing as the reprisals became more onerous. Of particular help to recruitment was Kruja's decision to send government-equipped Dibra bands into southern Albania, where they behaved considerably worse than did the Italians.[53] In an interview with the German consul on 3 February 1943, Lieutenant General Jacomoni admitted that since the end of 1942 the attitude of the Albanians toward the Italians had taken a significant turn for the worse, and he went so far as to question whether Albania would remain part of the Italian kingdom. Ten days later the head of the Italian carabinieri admitted that much of the open land of southern Albania was in partisan hands. He argued that "energetic" methods were necessary. The Italians, he said, should follow the German example and shoot fifty Albanians for each Italian death.[54]

To make matters worse, multiband attacks on Italian positions increased, particularly in the Korça, Gramsh, and Vlora districts of the south. And in

March, after the first national conference of the Albanian Communist Party, bands were consolidated into the First Partisan Battalion, which included three or four bands. This further complicated the military situation for the Italians. In April some of these new units carried out assaults on Italian troop concentrations near the Selenica mines. In May partisans of the Korça district fought what came to be known as the Battle of Leskovik, in which the partisans claimed two hundred Italians killed and a dozen trucks and armored cars destroyed. In June a major engagement took place on the Struga-Dibra highway. At the outset of July major encounters took place at Përmet. After five days of fighting—during which the Italians, supported by aircraft, were forced to call in reinforcements from Berat, Gjirokastra, and Tepelena—the partisans withdrew but claimed five hundred Italians dead and dozens of vehicles destroyed.[55]

By June the partisans claimed to have ten thousand fighters in thirty partisan bands and twenty battalions. In addition, there were twenty thousand reserves made up of peasant bands of volunteers and the urban guerrilla units. At the beginning of July the General Council of the NLM decided to form the headquarters of the National Liberation Army, which the communist party had decided on in March. A general staff was established with Hoxha as commissar and Spiro Moisiu, a relative nonentity whom Hoxha could control, as military commander. District staffs were established and Albania's first brigade was formed, with Mehmet Shehu, the partisan's ablest military figure, as commander. When the first brigade was finally established in August, it consisted of four or five battalions with a total strength of five hundred men.[56] Despite these new organizations, however, the traditional character of partisan warfare—no frontal attack—was retained until late 1944.

While many of these Italian casualty figures are undoubtedly exaggerations and many resistance operations ended in failure, the Italians slowly began to panic, grasping for a more effective political and military policy. Still, despite the increasing problems throughout 1942, Ciano heard nothing but positive reports from his officials. Given the Italian experience with the invasion of Greece, he should have been more suspicious than he was. In March 1942 Ciano notes in his diary that Jacomoni reported that the situation was quite good. In April, continuing the general self-delusion, Jacomoni reported that the only problem was the shortage of material that prevented the Italians from continuing with their public works. By September Ciano began to hear about an undercurrent of discontent, but in October Jacomoni sent him another favorable report on Albania. The lieutenant general reported that the critical period—which he had neglected to mention—was now over and with some gesture of force against the rebels, it was possible to bring order and quiet back into the country. In December he seems to have sent Ciano yet another favorable report, and as late as January 1943 General Lorenzo Dalmazzo, commander of the Ninth Army in Albania, viewed "the Albanian situation with remarkable tranquillity."[57]

Although Ciano was clearly guided by what he longed to hear, he was clever enough to take some precautions. As early as March 1942 he complained: "But there is a matter that has attracted my attention, the insufficiency of our military forces [in Albania]. We have scarcely four divisions, each composed of two regiments and the regiments composed of two battalions; a small number of carabinieri, not one tank."[58] He took his concerns to Mussolini, who agreed to send a few more troops and some companies of light tanks. But this did not satisfy Ciano, who complained again in September about the lack of troops. "There are four divisions, but in name only, in reality 11 thousand men. Cavallera, to whom I communicated the alarm could do nothing more than give me fifty tanks; not enough."[59] It seems that Ciano had to wait for general cries of alarm before he could convince Mussolini and the Comando Supremo to reinforce the Italian garrison.

In January and February 1943, the extent of the problem seems to have convinced at least some of the Italian officials in Albania that Ciano and Mussolini needed to be told the truth. On the night of 17 January the police inspector of Tirana sounded the alarm. He sent a telegram to the Foreign Ministry complaining of a government crisis and growing rebellion, suggesting that the only solution was to hand the government over to the Italian military. Ciano seemed genuinely surprised, noting in his diary, "Now one thing is clear, either someone is too cool or too nervous."[60] After confronting Jacomoni on the phone on 18 January, the lieutenant general admitted, in a veiled way, that things were quite bad.

Italian Response

Ciano and the Italians began countermeasures. Jacomoni had already begun to act, apparently without the knowledge of Ciano. Indeed, that seems to have been the intention, for one of Jacomoni's early moves was to keep the growing opposition as quiet as possible. As an example, the Italians took pains to suppress any report that suggested that the countryside was experiencing unrest. *Tomori*, the only paper in Tirana, mentioned only those incidents that occurred at the very gates of the city—incidents about which the population would hear in any case. And then the Italians would maintain that the incident was the exception in a sea of tranquillity.[61] But to accompany these attempts at denial and obfuscation, Jacomoni and the other Italian officials continued the traditional reactive carrot-and-stick policy, which, although it had not achieved much success in the past, seems to have been the only policy they could envision.

The Italian authorities would have preferred to leave the suppression of resistance to Kruja, who had pushed since his appointment for the construction of an effective Albanian gendarmerie. But the Italians were reluctant to give too much to the Albanians, and even if they had given Kruja all the weapons and the training he requested, it would—in the estimation of many—have only constituted a half measure. But something had to be done for Italian prestige, particularly when incidents in Tirana itself began to increase. Tirana had always constituted something of a safe haven for Italian officials, particularly those assigned to outlying regions who came to the capital infrequently. Now this oasis, too, by the fall of 1942, was experiencing open gunfights in the streets.[62]

In any case, those units of Albanian forces that were constructed or armed by the Italians proved to be more trouble than they were worth. The Dibra bands that Kruja sent into southern Albania were—because of their atrocities—swelling the ranks of the partisans. To make matters worse, many of Kruja's police defected to the resistance, taking their weapons with them.

The Italians, then, were forced to rely on their own resources to combat the growing resistance. The first major operations that the Italians launched were against the Peza region in September and the Vlora region in December 1942.[63] Because the resistance was fighting a traditional guerrilla-style war, its members had no intention of confronting large Italian units. As a result, little fighting actually took place in these first operations, and the Italian actions degenerated into punitive expeditions in which many villages were burned and many civilians were killed. The net result in military terms was more volunteers for the resistance and of course increasing hostility on the part of the population—in particular the population of the south—to the Italian authorities and their Albanian puppets.

Italian authorities in Rome, in the meantime, decided to heed Ciano's persistent warnings and increased the size of their forces in Albania. Although Ciano's estimates of Italian troop strength in Albania were certainly low, an increase was warranted and the Italians hoped that they might overawe the Albanians with numbers. Significant reinforcements were sent, and by the end of February 1943 the Italians had at their disposal, at least on paper, over 100,000 troops. Of this number, however, close to 17,000 were Albanian troops,

12,000 were GAF *costieri presidiari* (coast guard) 11,000 were *intendénza* (commissariat), and 5,000 were territorial defense. This left a little more than 55,000 regular Italian troops.[64] But a secret report noted that half of these were unusable in operations. The military problem was aggravated, so the report continued, by the high degree of unreliability of the Albanian forces.[65]

Since the military option seems to have had little of the desired effect, the Italians hoped to placate the Albanians through political tinkering. The experiment with Kruja, after one year, had achieved none of the desired results. As a representative of a class other than the beys, his principal task had been to broaden the support that the Albanian puppet regime could command among the population. This had not happened. Indeed, the principal result of Kruja's appointment was to alienate the beys. By the end of 1942, this fact seems to have become clear to the Italian authorities. A SIM report concluded that the Italians had made a mistake in giving the government to the people—they should have left it to the beys. By early December Jacomoni seems to have come to a similar decision, concluding that Kruja had to go. He commented to Ciano that "here is a man who in our best interest we should have destroyed gradually."[66]

Instead, Jacomoni destroyed Kruja all at once, which helped to cause a political crisis that ended his own career. Kruja was forced to resign in early January 1943, and Jacomoni planned to construct a government of landowners, who Ciano—rather naively—believed still had considerable influence in Albania and were in a strong position to impact public opinion.[67] Jacomoni turned to Eqrem Bey Libohova, who had been Zog's minister of court and had stopped a bullet for the king during an assassination attempt in Vienna in 1931.[68] It was undoubtedly this unintended sacrifice that encouraged Zog to overlook the fact that Libohova spent most of his political career in the pay of the Italians. Jacomoni hoped that Libohova, while totally without scruples, would be able to bring around all of the southern landowning class (the beys), many of whom had been alienated following the appointment of Kruja.

This task proved to be somewhat more difficult than Jacomoni had anticipated. As Ciano complained in his diary on 1 February, "The men who were most faithful to us are trying to abandon ship. Even Vrioni. Even Vërlaci."[69] Reports circulated abroad that Vërlaci was even attempting to sell some of his vast estates. Jacomoni was having trouble finding southern landowners to fill Libohova's government. He was finding it necessary to depend too heavily upon men from new Albania, men who had more to lose with an Axis defeat. Jacomoni did manage, initially, to attract the Mirdita chief, but he drove a hard bargain. The chief demanded control of the entire government as the price for his cooperation. Jacomoni would not be blackmailed and ultimately was forced to appoint men who had no hope of placating any segment of Albanian society.

The Fall of Jacomoni and Ciano

This cabinet crisis convinced Ciano that Jacomoni himself had outlived his usefulness; he noted that "For a certain period he did very well, but now his policies are turning sour. We need a man who can talk about force and can also employ it. I propose Guzzoni or Pariani, two generals who know the country and are well regarded."[70] Within two days, however, on 5 February, Ciano himself was forced to resign. As a consolation Ciano was offered a list of options, one of which was the position of lieutenant general in Albania. He wrote in his diary, "I decisively reject the governorship of Albania where I would be going as an executioner and hangman of those people to whom I promised brotherhood and equality."[71] Paternalistic to the end, Ciano of course was refusing to take responsibility for a situation caused almost exclusively by his own policies and actions. Ciano's obsession with Albania hastened the collapse of his own career as well as that of Mussolini.

The Italian position in Albania was becoming increasingly desperate. Before Jacomoni could be replaced by anyone, the three-week-old government of Libohova was removed; Ciano complained just before his own ouster that the government was up to its "old tricks." Libohova was replaced by Maliq Bushati, who had served as minister of justice in Vërlaci's post-invasion government and yet had a reputation as a nationalist. Although Bushati had counted as a long-time opponent of Zog's, the two had corresponded since the invasion, something about which the Italians were certainly unaware. Albanian socialist historians maintain that Bushati was also a leader of the BK. The Italians were being forced to accept people who had little interest in maintaining Italian domination in Albania.

Aware of this, Bushati, who also became provisional head of the National Fascist Party of Albania, was carefully watched. His vice-premier was the Kosovar Iliaz Agushi, who had served a minister of the new territories in 1941. As minister of the interior, the Italians finally succeeded in recruiting the Mirdita chief Gjon Marka Gjoni, who would demonstrate considerable ruthlessness in his pursuit of the partisans.

But the Bushati government lasted only a few weeks. Problems between the premier and Marka Gjoni began immediately, principally with regard to the handling of resistance in the south. The government, composed primarily of northerners, had less chance than the previous two governments of convincing the southerners to cease their resistance, so the minister of the interior favored abandoning persuasion for force. Bushati disagreed. Bushati had also appealed to the Italian authorities to release many citizens of Korça who had been interned in the concentration camp at Durrës. The Italians refused. Bushati further annoyed the Italians by frequent complaints about Italian atrocities in southern Albania against the partisans.[72]

By this point, Mussolini had chosen General Alberto Pariani as Jacomoni's replacement. Pariani had considerable experience in the Balkans as governor of Corfu just prior to his Albanian appointment and as the head of the Italian military mission in Albania from 1927 to 1933. He gained the respect of his hosts, and even the Germans considered him to be one of the most competent senior Italian officers.[73] Zog, it will be recalled, had asked for Pariani as a mediator during the desperate final days of his regime. Pariani was a man of good reputation and extensive experience, thrust into what was rapidly becoming an impossible situation.

Pariani was not unaware of the challenge of the task that faced him. Upon accepting the appointment, he wrote a private note to Mussolini describing the situation as grave and chaotic.[74] He suggested that the Albanians be given back a substantial degree of their independence as a first step toward defusing the situation. The specifics of his program included (1) equality of rights for Albanians and Italians in both countries and diplomatic representation in each other's capitals, (2) restoration of a truly independent Albanian gendarmerie and army, (3) the establishment of an Albanian home guard with the express purpose of combating the inroads made by the Greeks and the Yugoslavs, (4) returning control of Albanian customs to the Albanian government, (5) dissolution of the Albanian Fascist Party and its replacement by a new organization called the Protection of Greater Albania.[75] Clearly, he did his utmost to play the nationalist card. At the same time, however, Pariani let it be known that he would not allow his work to be disturbed from any side, and as a demonstration of his resolve, he increased Italian troop strength to some five and one-half divisions.[76] Pariani, then, could do little more than continue the existing policy of concessions and repression.

Pariani's regime was not without its successes, not the least of which was a March 1943 agreement between Lorenzo Dalmazzo, the commander of the Italian Ninth Army, and Ali Këlcyra, one of the leaders of the BK. This so-called Dalmazzo-Këlcyra agreement, about which there is considerable controversy,[77] effectively neutralized a section of the BK. Albanian socialist historiography suggests that this agreement committed the BK to prevent any assault against Italian troops and to help the Italians in their punitive operations in southern Albania.[78] Since BK policy was based on a fear of reprisals, it is unlikely that much was done to assist in Italian punitive operations. But the BK did significantly reduce its military operations to prevent reprisals and to save its strength for the inevitable conflict with the NLM. This agreement was clearly of some benefit to the Italians, but since most of the actual resistance was being conducted by the NLM, that benefit was minimal.

The problems and failures of Pariani's regime, however, were substantially more important than his successes. To be sure, the obstacles in his way were formidable and few could have done better. Nevertheless, Pariani seemed to do little more than lurch from crisis to crisis. Not the least of his problems were generated by Bushati, who seems to have made some genuine efforts to protect Albanians while assuming greater responsibility for internal affairs. But given the increasingly anarchistic internal situation, Bushati's hopes and efforts were, of course, in vain. By the end of April his cabinet was in crisis, and it fell at the beginning of May. The cabinet—made up primarily of northerners—was, naturally, unsuccessful in controlling the south, despite Marka Gjoni's extensive use of repressive measures. Pollo and Puto suggest that dozens of villages were burned and hundreds slaughtered.[79] Pariani reluctantly approved of these measures, and Bushati continued to complain. Pariani ultimately fired Bushati.[80]

Pariani was hard pressed to replace him, however, since by the end of May 1943 most Albanians were convinced of the inevitability of an Italian defeat. It was two weeks before Pariani could round up Italy's fourth collaborationist regime. Eqrem Libohova was reappointed as prime minister, indicative of the shrinking pool of candidates. The cabinet was made up of the usual suspects, people who had served in one or more of the occupation regimes, and once again northerners dominated. Agushi once again became deputy prime minister as well as minister of public works and finance.[81] In what seemed to be little more than a pro forma action, the Italians dropped leaflets from planes encouraging Albanians to work together with the new government. The leaflets outlined yet another new program and threatened those who failed to cooperate with the usual dire consequences.[82] But the composition of this last collaborationist regime under the Italians made it clear that the Italians had finally given up expecting much from the Albanian collaborators. The fighting in the south had become more serious—schools were closed—at the end of May nonessential Italian personnel were being evacuated from Albania.[83] In addition to his increasing problems with the Albanians, by the spring of 1943

Pariani had the British to contend with as well—the British, who after nearly two years since their last involvement in Albania, had returned in an attempt to coordinate and stimulate the resistance.

The Return of the British

The British had done very little with regard to Albania since 1941 with the exception of dealing with competing groups of exiles and attempting to gather material upon which to base a policy. In this latter regard, the British had not been overly successful. The misconceptions that had generated the unsuccessful mini-invasion from Kosova in April 1941 had not been dispelled. And the British had no clear idea of the important events that had taken place in Albania since 1941. Their sources were limited to the occasional traveler's report and the predominantly anticommunist exile groups, which quite often—even when aware of internal developments, which was rare—misrepresented events for their own interests.

The Foreign Office did commission a few policy papers from Albanian specialists in Britain, but these people were generally limited to knowledge of prewar developments. As a result, their material was often misleading. Arnold Toynbee, for example, produced a lengthy paper on the territorial dispute between Albania and Greece, which was rather cavalier about Albanian claims.[84] In general, the British government questioned the viability of Albania's territorial unity and whenever possible supported the claims of their principal ally in the Balkans, Greece.

Perhaps the clearest summation of British policy toward Albania at the time is contained in a memo written by Pearson Dixon at the end of May 1942. Dixon reviewed the history of Britain's relations with Albania, noting that Britain originally condoned the Italian annexation of Albania when on 31 October 1939, the government announced in Parliament that it had appointed a consul general. With Italy's declaration of war in June 1940, the government announced publicly that it had regained its liberty of action. The British government did not define its position but declared itself free to do so. Dixon cited as reasons for this negative position (1) the assumption that Albania was not a viable state and that it would need some form of foreign protection, (2) the problem of Zog, who was deemed unpopular—his presence in Britain would make it difficult to avoid suspicion that Britain secretly supported him if Albania was recognized, and (3) Yugoslav and Greek claims on Albanian territory. Still, Dixon concluded that it was time for some sort of statement on

Albanian independence based upon both political and military considerations. The Albanian population would welcome it, resistance would be stimulated, and a possible Greek-Yugoslav conflict over what both considered spoils might be averted.[85] Lord Glenconner, head of SOE in 1942-43, went even further, announcing that he had a plan for subversion in Albania that would be aided by a declaration on the territorial integrity of prewar Albania.[86]

When foreign secretary Anthony Eden did finally make a statement on Albania, he did so not as a result of an appreciation of events in Albania but because of the war in general.[87] With the American landing in North Africa in November 1942, the Allies took the offensive in the Mediterranean. In light of this fact, Eden decided, after informing the Soviets and the Americans, to finally make a statement on Albania. The statement, made in Parliament on 17 December, expressed sympathy with the fate of Albanians and called for the restoration of Albanian independence, recognizing that the form of government would be left up to the Albanians themselves after the war. Following strenuous objections from the Greek government in exile, Eden added that the question of frontiers would be left to the peace settlement.[88] The Americans had made a similar statement—although without the qualification on the frontiers—several days earlier. A Soviet statement followed that of the British—despite Hoxha's contention that the Soviets came up with a more important statement earlier.

The statement had a good effect on the Albanians, but it still did not outline a clear British policy on the future of Albania. As Dixon minuted in March 1943, "We, however, interpret our declaration to mean that while we shall endeavor to reestablish an independent Albanian state after the war, we do not regard an Albanian state as now existing. Thus no question of recognizing any Albanian government in exile arises at present."[89] As the British prepared to become involved in Albania militarily, then, the Foreign Office still maintained a nonpolicy in relation to the country's existence as a state, its future frontiers, its future government, and its future place in the Balkans. The British officers who were dropped into Albania, then, were not only ignorant of political conditions in Albania but were backed up by nothing more than political emptiness.[90]

As suggested earlier, renewed military attention to Albania—like renewed political attention—came about less because of an understanding of Albanian conditions than as a result of the course of the war as a whole. Enver Hoxha maintains that the British renewed their interest in Albania out of alarm at the rise of the Communist Party's activities and because of news about the conference of Peza.[91] But this is simply not the case. Renewed British interest developed slowly, and those involved were motivated by somewhat more far-reaching ends. General Lord Glenconner must be given some credit for this renewed interest. Although he failed to convince the Foreign Office in June 1942 to make a statement to aid Albanian resistance, he was encouraged by Dixon to continue his plans for subversion in Albania.[92] These plans, however, were still in preliminary stages.

In December 1942 these plans were given further impetus. Joint British-American planners began drawing more extensive attention to subversive activities in the Balkans as a means of speeding the expected collapse of Italy. This would require that the Germans occupy the Balkans and Italy, thereby straining their resources in the Soviet Union. This was considered particularly significant, since the cross-channel invasion of France was ruled out for 1943, making it imperative that something be done for the Russians. Many of these ideas were included in the official memorandum on future strategy presented by the British Chiefs of Staff at the Casablanca conference in January 1943. The most significant elements of this memorandum were adopted at Casablanca, and resistance movements in the Balkans became of prime importance for the first time.[93]

In the meantime, as a result of a general agreement between SOE and the U.S. Office of Strategic Services (OSS) in June 1942, SOE was given priority over subversive operations in the Balkans.[94] The Albanian section of SOE, which initially had consisted of little more than Margaret Hasluck, the widow of a noted archaeologist who spent some ten years living in Elbasan, was enlarged and moved to Cairo.[95] Brigadier Keeble, head of MO4 in early 1943—which is what SOE Cairo was called at the time—recruited officers to drop into Albania to act as British liaison officers.[96] The task of these agents was to contact, coordinate, and direct the supply of those groups or individuals resisting the Italians. The instructions seemed clear, and despite Enver Hoxha's claims there was no political brief included. The mission was conceived as a strictly military one.

The first group was sent in in April 1943 and was under the command of Major Neil (Billy) McLean, a tall, fair-haired young officer of the Scots Grey Regiment. Hoxha, who would develop an intense personal dislike for McLean, described him as having a cold, clean-shaven face, and intelligent blue eyes with the look of a savage cat about them.[97] McLean was accompanied by an interpreter, a wireless operator, and his second in command, Captain David Smiley, whom Julian Amery described as someone who liked his friends and disliked his enemies, but otherwise was more interested in things than in people. Smiley lived for action alone and was happiest on a dangerous recon-

The Growth of Resistance and the Collapse of Italy

naissance or when "blowing things up."[98] Because of their ardent anti-communism, McLean and Smiley would become a considerable worry for Hoxha.

McLean's mission—code-named "Consensus"—arrived in Greece in April, because there was no real contact with Albanian bands at the time. Greek resistance fighters of the EAM supplied the British with guides, mules, and escorts and then handed them over to the nearest Albanian peasants on the frontier.[99] At first Albanian resistance leaders of all parties refused to deal with them, being suspicious of their Greek contacts and convinced that they had come to develop Greek bands on Albanian soil. The first partisan leader of stature that they encountered, Bedri Spahiu, required them to return to Greece.[100] Although they had more reason to be suspicious than did the BK, it was the partisans who first recognized the potential and accepted the British. Still, in was not until June that McLean succeeded in making contact with a representative of the NLM council. After a difficult trip, McLean first met with the council itself at the July meeting at Labinot, where the General Staff of the Albanian National Liberation Army (ANLA) was created.

Hoxha boasts at length in numerous works that he intentionally treated the British badly. He kept them waiting to make it clear to them that they could not just walk into Albania without first obtaining permission from the NLM. He failed to mention, however, how this could have been possible without first making contact. Because they were British, Hoxha also told them very little about the political situation in Albania and tried to do what he could to restrict their movements to keep them in the dark as well as to keep them as much as possible away from the rivals of the NLM. Hoxha writes that he did this because the British officers were sent to spy, to assist the British agents in Albania—read all those who opposed Hoxha—and to do their utmost to ensure, under the disguise of aid, that the people's revolution fail.[101]

While Hoxha's reception was certainly cool, as McLean readily confirms, much of the delay preventing McLean from contacting the NLM council more quickly can be attributed to poor communications and lack of organization. After all, in the first three months after contact—that is, June through August—the British dropped 19.5 tons of weapons, ammunition, and supplies to McLean and Smiley, of which the partisans received the lion's share.[102] Hoxha surely recognized this potential. As a pragmatist, he certainly would have made contact with the British at the earliest possible movement, not only for the supplies but also for the legitimacy such a connection would bring. This postwar reconstruction of Hoxha's, as with so many others, served a political purpose once the British were declared the enemy.

Once the connection was made, it rapidly became clear how fortuitous the presence of the British was for the partisans. The British arrived just at the time the NLM decided to organize larger permanent military units—brigades—as a major step toward the construction of a regular army, a move with both political and military significance. Albanian socialist historians argue that the principal source of arms and ammunition for the partisan movement came from raiding enemy supplies. The principal source of clothes and food was the supportive population and the careless Italians. These historians do admit, however, that the people gave supplies only gradually, that major political work was required to convince them to do this. As a result, the partisans suffered from major and daily deficiencies, no fixed ration of food, no hot meals, and no regular supply of clothes or health services.[103]

It is undoubtedly true that the partisans were able to live off the countryside while they remained divided into small guerilla bands. How they intended to arm equip and maintain brigades by these same means remains a mystery. Larger military organizations of this sort require a permanent reliable source of supply, which the Albanian peasants had no way of providing, even if they had wanted to. Smiley and McLean, then, as their first task were given the job of organizing, training, and equipping the First Partisan Brigade.[104] The British threw themselves into the task, and after several months of airdrops, in August the brigade was ready, commanded by perhaps the most experienced and effective Albanian military leader during the war, Mehmet Shehu.

Albanian socialist historiography and Hoxha rarely mention British supplies except when referring to them as "so-called" aid or aid to the enemies of the NLM, who, it is maintained, were given ample weapons.[105] Hoxha complained that McLean received chocolates by air, noting that "Perfidious Albion had aircraft for such things, but when it came to dropping weapons to us who were fighting fascism, aircraft were not available."[106] It certainly is true that Albania was a low priority and few planes were assigned, but much material did get through.[107] Some of it was clearly of questionable value: boots for left feet only, battle dress for midgets or giants, underpants big enough for Sumo wrestlers, ammunition of the wrong caliber, weapons without ammunition. Some of the material was certainly destroyed when parachutes failed to open, and some of it was carried off by local peasants when it was dropped too far from the drop zone. Still, the bulk of the material must have been weapons, ammunition, explosives, uniforms, blankets, and so on, put together to McLean's specifications.[108] But naturally it was never enough. Hoxha consistently complained—with some justification—that he was being asked to engage a vastly superior enemy with extremely limited resources. McLean tells

The Growth of Resistance and the Collapse of Italy

us, for example, that the armament for one armored Albanian brigade consisted of three 81mm mortars, one 45mm mortar, five Breda machine guns, one U.S. bomb thrower, six automatic Breda rifles, and individual rifles.[109] Though limited, what the British were giving the Albanians was by Albanian standards quite substantial, and it came at a critical time.

Apart from helping to supply the Albanian resistance, the British also hoped to facilitate resistance unity. It did not take McLean long to discover at least some of the divisions that existed in the resistance, and because these were not properly understood, the British believed that unity among the Albanian resistance was less difficult to achieve than under the Yugoslavs or the Greeks. Although Hoxha tells us in his memoirs that he successfully prevented contact between the British and the non-NLM resistance for a significant period, this seems not to be the case. In July and August six more missions were dropped and sent to various parts of the country. While the McLean mission had been considered an all-Albania mission, these later missions were assigned to specific regions; one went to contact the important Dibra chiefs, one was sent north of Tirana into the Kruja area, one was sent to the Vlora region, where the countryside was loyal to the BK, and one was sent to Myslim Peza's area.[110]

The Mukje Agreements

While the British were dispersing throughout Albania in the hopes of facilitating unity, representatives of the NLM and the BK were meeting at Mukje in what turned out to be the last serious attempt to unify the two groups. Almost every aspect of this important meeting—which took place near Tirana between 1 and 3 August—is racked with controversy. To begin with, the question about who initiated the meeting seems rather unclear. Albanian socialist historians and Hoxha argue that Hoxha and the central committee of the Communist Party were responsible, demonstrating their genuine interest in uniting all patriotic Albanians.[111] The historians Nicholas Pano, Bernhard Kühmel, and Stavro Skendi argue that British pressure was at least partly responsible for the meeting, although Reginald Hibbert—one of the British officers in Albania during the war—writes that the meeting took place without the knowledge of British officers.[112] McLean maintains that Kupi was responsible, and the historian Elizabeth Wiskeman argues that British officers and Kupi initiated the meeting.[113]

It is clear, at least, that both sides were interested in the meeting. The inevitable collapse of fascism in Italy made a free Albania—perhaps to be occupied by the Allies—at least possible. The BK began to realize that its relative inactivity might prove to be a significant disadvantage in such an eventuality, particularly since the partisans had not been hurt by Italian military action, as the BK had hoped. In June and July, therefore, the BK changed tactics, distancing itself from the collaborationist government, strengthening its armed units, and issuing more uncompromising propaganda, although this shift also seems to have been accompanied with less, not more, military activity.[114] For the BK it was the ideal time to come to terms with the NLM. It was also a good time for Hoxha, who too at least considered the possibility of an Allied landing, an eventuality that would principally benefit the pro-Western BK, to come to terms with that group. It was also more than likely that British officers made further shipments of gold and weapons contingent on some attempt at unity. Finally, Hoxha was still under insistent Comintern pressure to create a politically correct united front.

All of these pressures together resulted in an organizational meeting at Tapiza on 26 July. Here the BK representatives suggested the organization of a provisional government in Kruja, the city of the Albanian national hero Skënderbeg. The NLM representatives refused to agree to this suggestion but did send delegates to Mukje for further discussions. Representing the NLM were Kupi and two moderate communists, Mustafa Gjinishi and Ymer Dishnica. The BK sent, among others, Mithat Frashëri, still possessed of considerable diplomatic skill, and Hasan Dosti, an accomplished jurist who had moved from collaboration to opposition when he fled Tirana in June along with most of the BK central committee.

The agreement that the delegates worked out speaks to the skill of the BK negotiators. The Mukje Agreements called for the construction of a new national committee for the salvation of Albania, which would be made up of equal numbers of both organizations and would be headed by Hasan Dosti. The committee would function as a provisional government. The delegates supported the concept of an "ethnic Albania" based upon the enlarged frontiers of 1941. The delegates also proclaimed Albania's independence by annulling the decisions of the fascist assembly of 12 April 1939, which had constructed the first puppet Albanian government after the Italian invasion. Finally, the assembled delegates agreed immediately to take up arms against the Italians.[115]

That the BK got the best of this compromise agreement is clear. The NLM, as an organization, was not part of the provisional government. The Albanian Communist Party had failed to force the inclusion of any provisions outlining social change. The agreement also was to the disadvantage of the ACP in that the party's policy of linking resistance to a political revolution through the destruction of the existing system was not part of the program.

What happened next has been interpreted in any number of ways. What is clear is that first Hoxha, then the ACP, and finally the NLM rejected the Mukje Agreements. Albanian socialist historiography argues that the NLM delegates exceeded their authority and that Dishnica gave way to demagoguery, while Gjinishi came out of the meeting an ardent supporter of the reactionary claims of the middle class.[116] Nicholas Pano, relying on both Albanian and Yugoslav sources, convincingly argues that Enver Hoxha and the central committee of the ACP were ready to approve the agreements but were prevented from doing so by Svetozar Vukmanovic-Tempo, Tito's roving ambassador in the Balkans, who happened to be in Albania at the time. Hoxha hurls invective at Tempo in his memoirs, calling him a political gangster who was attempting to seize the leadership of all the resistance movements in the Balkans by the creation of a Yugoslav-controlled Balkan staff.[117]

This may indeed have been the case, but the principal problem here was again Kosova. Although the Yugoslav Communist Party had approved a resolution calling for self-determination in Kosova as recently as 1940, by 1943 the situation had changed. The party was now not nearly as far away from power and Tito was unwilling to alienate the Serbs, many of whom still considered Kosova sacred. The Yugoslavs themselves claim a role in the rejection of the agreements, criticizing Hoxha and the central committee—with the exception of Koçi Xoxe, one of the founders of the ACP from Korça, and the hard-liners, who always supported the Yugoslavs—and accusing them of deviationism and irredentism.[118]

That the Yugoslavs played an important role in these events is certain. Hoxha complained of continual attempts on the part of the Yugoslavs to interfere in Albanian affairs. He also argued, however, that he successfully prevented them from doing so. This is hardly likely. Hoxha's position on Kosova itself was made clear at the NLM Labinot conference in September. Although he had rejected the Mukje Agreements, he spoke of Kosova in terms similar to those used by the BK at Mukje. As Yugoslav influence increased and as Hoxha began to realize that maintaining control of Kosova might be an internal political disadvantage (Kosova was entirely Geg), he did eventually come into line on this issue.[119]

It is reasonable to conclude that neither side wanted to work with the other and that both looked for a way out while blaming the other. In this instance the NLM and the ACP were more forthright. Despite a momentary surge of BK resistance immediately following Mukje,[120] the BK was reluctant to resist because of the dangers of reprisals; there is no reason to believe that its position had changed. And Harry Fultz, who headed the Albania desk at the OSS and had considerable experience with Albania prior to the war, concludes that the BK might have been looking for a reason to break the agreement once it became clear that the organization would have a chance to work with the Germans.[121] The BK was saved the trouble by Hoxha's action and accumulated some political capital in the process. After all, the BK could not be held responsible for breaking the agreement.

Although the episode itself remains somewhat murky, the results are less so. Mukje constitutes a major turning point for the ACP and for the resistance in general. The collapse of the agreement marked the beginning, or at least a significant escalation in, the mutual animosity and distrust between Hoxha and the Yugoslavs. Internally, Mukje weakened the moderates within the party, such as Gjinishi, Dishnica, and Hoxha himself, who moved even further to the Left to save his own position. In terms of the resistance movement in general, the episode signaled two important events that will be discussed in more detail in chapter 7: the defection of Kupi and the beginning of the civil war, which further complicated the resistance picture in Albania.[122] But first the occupation picture changed as well, with the fall of Mussolini's regime at the end of July and, within six weeks, the replacement of the Italian occupation by a German one.

The Fall of Mussolini

Mussolini's regime had been battered by ever increasing military defeats and growing internal opposition. His armies had been humiliated and expelled from North Africa. His navy was destroyed through foolish policies. His parallel war against Greece had been a disaster. After Stalingrad, the Axis forces in general were forced on the defensive. And through it all, Mussolini did not make the trains run on time. The successful Allied invasion of Sicily on 10 July constituted the final blow to his waning political prestige. Internal opposition had, by this point, reached the Italian Fascist Grand Council and ultimately included Count Ciano, his son-in-law. The intrigues of Victor Emmanuel III and growing distrust and resentment within the Comando Supremo helped speed Mussolini's end. On 24 July 1943 members of the Fascist Grand Council, hoping to save their own skins, deposed Mussolini, who was soon arrested but quickly rescued on Hitler's orders. He was replaced by Marshal Pietro

Badoglio, who, while responsible for much of the fiasco, had some credibility with the Allies because he had resigned as chief of staff of the Comando Supremo in December 1940. Badoglio, it seems, was only waiting for the ideal time to surrender, which he did on 8 September.

Without a doubt, the Albanians contributed significantly to these events. The Italians had demonstrated early their inability to administer Albania effectively. Corruption and lack of financial accountability doomed their efforts. What little was accomplished was ruined by the failure of the war against Greece. Rudimentary nationalism—some of it instilled by Zog—combined with Italophobia and economic problems brought on by the occupation slowly aroused the Albanians to resistance. Once individual and scattered resistance was channeled by the NLM, the Italians found it necessary to augment significantly their security forces just to protect their garrisons in Albania's larger towns. By July 1943 the Italians had between seven and eight divisions stationed in Albania, although none was anywhere close to being at full strength. Although the Italians were in no danger of actually being thrown out of Albania, the fact that 100,000 troops could not establish even rudimentary security destroyed what little prestige Italian arms had and helped contribute to critical morale problems. All of this naturally contributed significantly to Mussolini's problems at home. Albania, then, deserves considerable credit for the fall of Mussolini and the surrender of Italy.

Mustafa Kruja becomes prime minister of Albania, 19 February 1942. (Jacomoni)

The Zogist resistance leader Abaz Kupi in exile in 1940. (Amery)

The independent resistance leader Gani Bey Kryeziu in 1927. (Amery)

The independent resistance leader Muharrem Bajraktari. (Amery)

British general Trotsky Davies (with hat, in foreground) and his staff in Albania in autumn 1943. Pictured from left: Smiley, McLean, Nicholls, Hare, Davies, Smythe. (Amery)

Hoxha posing with guards at General Headquarters, late 1943 or 1944. Such arranged photographs served as effective propaganda.

CHAPTER 6

THE GERMAN INVASION AND THE CONSTRUCTION OF A GERMAN ALBANIA

The Germans watched Italy's decline with some alarm, recognizing that in the event of a complete collapse, their own responsibilities would increase significantly. Italian-occupied territories everywhere, including Albania, would have to be invaded and held, straining an already overburdened Wehrmacht. The Germans also realized that they had perhaps been overcautious of Italian sensibilities with regard to interference in Albania, overcautious to the extent that, in July 1943, as action seemed increasingly imminent, the foreign ministry and the Wehrmacht realized that they knew next to nothing about Albania, a problem that had plagued the Italians—although Rome had no good reason for a dearth of information—and the British. Like the British and the Italians, the Germans lacked proper intelligence upon which to base policy decisions. This problem was never entirely resolved.

German Interests in Albania

Germany's connection with Albania during the twentieth century was marginal, although with a few exceptions. The first important exception was the appointment—by the Great Powers—of Prince Wilhelm of Wied, the grandnephew of Wilhelm II of Germany, as prince of the newly founded Albanian state in 1913. Although Wied, overwhelmed by circumstances, lasted a scant six months, it was long enough to leave a favorable impression on some in Albania.[1] During the various regimes of Zog, from 1922 to 1939, German interest in Albania was almost nonexistent, except for a short interlude during the six-month premiership of Mehdi Frashëri in 1936.

Mehdi Frashëri, who had sympathy for the Germans partly because he had studied in Austria, worked with the German minister Erich von Luckwald, in the hopes of establishing closer relations and to gain some protection for the Albanians from the Italians. The German Foreign Ministry was hesitant, particularly after the Italians became nearly hysterical upon learning of Frashëri's overtures.[2] King Zog, who found it prudent to placate the Italians in late 1936, jettisoned Frashëri, replacing him with Kostaq Kota, a pro-Italian yes-man who immediately reversed not only Frashëri's liberal internal policies but also swung Albania once again solidly behind Italy.[3]

Albanian-German relations during the last years of Zog's regime were, as a result, extremely limited. Hitler sent Zog a Mercedes on the occasion of his wedding to Geraldine in 1938, prompting Zog, who rarely missed an opportunity to irritate the Italians, to inquire of the Germans if they were not interested in Albanian oil. The German minister Eberhard von Pannwitz, who became head of the mission in 1937, seemed enthusiastic, but the Foreign Ministry in Berlin was cautious. Ciano, who seemed to be bribing every other prominent Albanian, learned of the overture immediately and informed Mackensen in Rome in no uncertain terms that the Italians considered Albania to be one of their provinces and that Pannwitz did not seem to appreciate that fact. Ciano had complained about Pannwitz prior to this incident; his crimes included an apparent unwillingness to attend Ciano's parties. Pannwitz was instructed to cool his ardor. The disappointed German minister reported, almost sadly, that Germany's influence was restricted to a modicum of trade and an occasional scholarship for an Albanian student to study in Germany. Pannwitz did manage to negotiate a new trade deal in 1938, but by this point Italian economic control was nearly complete, so the agreement included no important raw materials. And even this modest agreement came to nothing in light of the Italian invasion four months later.[4] Given this rather distant relationship, Zog's appeal to Hitler in March 1939 to protect him from Mussolini was clearly an act of sheer desperation.[5] Because Germany had no particular interest in Albania, Zog could not have seriously expected the Germans to act against the Italians on his behalf.

Although it is perhaps not surprising that because of Italian hypersensitivity German knowledge of Albania was limited in 1939, the Foreign Ministry had less of an excuse by 1943. Pannwitz, who stayed on as consul general following the invasion, sent regular reports concerning the deterioration of Italy's position.

Although the Foreign Ministry seems to have failed to anticipate an enlarged German civilian role in Albania, the Wehrmacht was more careful. Military planners, who feared a possible Allied landing in the Balkans, drew up plans for an invasion. While the Germans were aware that Churchill had pushed for Allied action in the Adriatic at the Casablanca conference in January 1943, they were unaware that General George Marshall had talked him out of it, and presumably they were also unaware that the idea was finally dropped at the Tehran meeting in November 1943.[6]

In anticipation of such an invasion, the Wehrmacht drew up a series of military plans for action against Italy—code-named "Alarich," later "Achse"—and for action against the Italian holdings in the Balkans—code-named "Konstanin."[7] And of a more direct nature, units of German Military Intelligence (Abwehr) Section II were sent to Mitrovica in April 1943 in an attempt to gain some influence among the growing number of Albanians disaffected with the Italians.[8] Even more directly, in July and August 1943, the German army occupied Albanian airports and ports, ostensibly to protect Italian Albania from the possibility of an Allied invasion. By the middle of August there were some six thousand German troops in Albania.[9]

But there had been surprisingly little preparation of a political nature and a great deal of misinformation. Much of the German problem in this regard stemmed simply from a lack of sources. Much of what was available in Germany in the 1930s concerning Albania was either superficial or catered to the romantic notion of the Albanians as a vital warrior mountain race, a notion that appealed to those imbued with Nazi racial theory. Hitler himself thought of the Albanians in the context of a Karl May novel.

What information the German Foreign Ministry was able to collect was often inaccurate. Martin Schliep, who replaced Pannwitz, sent reports that contained numerous important errors, including mistakes concerning the strength and makeup of the growing resistance groups. These mistakes often made their way into Foreign Ministry calculations.[10] To make matters worse, in March and June two of the three people in the Foreign Ministry who knew anything about Albania were relieved. The third, Franz von Scheiger, although still attached to the Foreign Ministry, was employed in matters not impacting Albania.[11]

The first political move made by the Foreign Ministry prior to the invasion was the appointment of Hermann Neubacher, a former mayor of Vienna, as Ribbentrop's special representative for southeastern Europe. Neubacher, already active in the Balkans as Hitler's representative for economic concerns, would become the key German figure in the Balkans during the second half of the war.[12] Although he was not officially assigned Albania as part of his responsibility until 10 September, he relates in his memoirs that he had at least done some reading on Albania during the three weeks prior to his appointment.[13]

Apart from the appointment of Neubacher, the only other concrete political step taken by the Foreign Ministry—and this on the recommendation of Schliep—was the dispatch of Major Franz von Scheiger to Mitrovica.

Scheiger had more Albanian experience than anyone else in the Foreign Ministry, indeed more than anyone else in Germany. Scheiger's first exposure to Albania was as an officer in the Austro-Hungarian army during World War I. After the war he returned to Albania, learned the language, set up a business, and eventually came to know many interwar politicians of influence on a personal basis. From 1936 to 1942 he served in the capacity of German trade attaché but was eventually relieved after the Italians complained that Scheiger was becoming too friendly with the locals.[14] But rather than being returned directly to Tirana, Scheiger was sent to German-occupied Mitrovica—where he was given a military function—so as not to alarm the Italians. He arrived on 2 September—armed with thirteen pounds of gold as well as Portuguese brandy and coffee—and instructions to contact and influence local Albanian leaders.[15]

Although the appointment of Neubacher and Scheiger constituted the extent of German political action prior to the invasion, Ribbentrop did scramble to catch up. He bombarded Schliep with requests for information and finally ordered Schliep to Rome for extensive consultations with Mackensen. Based upon the sometimes contradictory material Schliep forwarded—a problem about which Ribbentrop himself complained—the foreign minister sketched the basis of German policy toward Albania. The Wehrmacht made it clear to Ribbentrop that Albania was strategically important and had to be held against an anticipated Allied invasion but that the troops for traditional military occupation were simply not available.

The rugged terrain of much of Albania, which had for centuries protected the Albanians from the outside world, further discouraged a traditional occupation. German priorities included direct control of the coast as well as strategic areas inland, including the major towns and, most important, the major roads. To make this possible, Ribbentrop suggested that Schliep help draw up plans for the construction of an independent neutral Albania controlled by a government friendly to the Germans.[16] The foreign minister had few suggestions as to how this might be achieved but indicated that Schliep might start by identifying, contacting, and influencing "statesmen-like people" who, with German military and political support, might relieve the German army by taking control of a significant portion of internal security. In order for this to succeed, the Albanian government would need to produce a stable political system with widespread domestic support.

Schliep gave a general description of the political situation in Albania, which though not always accurate still managed to shed light on some of the problems the political implementation of Ribbentrop's plan might encounter. He attested to the popularity of the Germans, maintaining that Albanians, although the majority no longer believed in the victory of the Axis, were friendly toward the Germans and had respect for Hitler, but hated fascism because of its connection with the despised Italians. Schliep concluded, however, that the plan's chances for success were really not that good.

The question of a regime under German control presented the first problem for Schliep. Libohova's government was completely compromised because of its relations with Italy, and the NLM was ruled out because of its communist connection. Schliep frankly asserted that there were no statesmen of significance who had authority and popularity and had remained free of a connection with the Italians.[17] Schliep concluded, sensibly, that the Germans might be forced to rely on the Kosovars, whom he considered the most trustworthy of Albanians. The Kosovars were grateful to have been saved from the Serbs. Neubacher reinforced this line of reasoning by suggesting that Kosovars were not only the most politically and militarily united but that they would stand or fall with Germany and that they would be useful in the occupation of large parts of Albania.[18] It is perhaps not surprising that of the first two Albanian leaders Neubacher met in Belgrade just prior to the German invasion, one was the Kosovan bandleader Xhafer Deva, who had been working with the Abwehr for some time and offered his full support. The other, Vehbi Frashëri, also with long-standing Abwehr contacts, was the son of Mehdi Frashëri, who was still interned in Italy.[19]

The German Invasion

In the midst of this initial planning, the Germans were suddenly faced with the surrender of the Badoglio government. On 3 September Allied forces crossed the Strait of Messina and landed on the toe of Italy. On 8 September General Dwight D. Eisenhower announced the Italian armistice, which German radio reported at about 5 P.M. At 4 A.M. on 9 September units of the German army assigned to group F under Field Marshal Baron Maximilian von Weichs invaded Albania, carrying out a plan that had been completed only three days earlier.[20] Three divisions of the Twenty-first Corps under General Hubert Lanz overran Albania with considerable efficiency, encountering only minimal resistance from the nine Italian divisions stationed in Albania, or from the various resistance groups.[21] The 118th Jäger Division, the only unit to encounter resistance on 9 September, moved southwest from Niksic. The 100th Jäger Division occupied Elbasan and Struga, while its 92d Motorized Regiment took the territory between Tepelena and Vlora. The 297th Infantry Division reached Prishtina and Prizren, according to plan. On the next day the Germans took Pogradec, Tirana, Durrës, and Kukës. On 11 September the 118th reached the coast while a part of the 297th crossed the Drin River. These rapid movements were aided by a number of German units already stationed in southern Albania, plus German security forces the Italians had requested to assist in holding Albania's airports at Tirana, Shkodra, Vlora, Berat, Shijak, and Kërçova.[22]

Despite substantial numerical superiority, the only resistance offered by the completely demoralized Italian troops included a minor encounter south of Durrës and the shooting of a German lieutenant in Tirana. This collapse is perhaps not surprising given the state of Italian units in Albania and their status. In describing the Ninth Army under General Lorenzo Dalmazzo, which occupied much of Albania, a British officer noted that seldom in military history could an army have been so badly led and officered as the ninth, and the troops knew it. The leaders were described as weak, cowardly, and hesitant, and the officers in general failed to present any example or give any help to the troops, caring only for their own welfare.[23] Morale could hardly have been lower, and a general terror of Germans was widespread. Further, apart from vague suggestions to make for the ports, Italian units were completely without instructions. Badoglio gave no clear orders and did not declare war on Germany until the middle of October.[24] Italian units were on their own; even worse, they were at the mercy of their officers.

The Germans demanded their surrender. The Italians received instructions from the Allies as well. General Sir Henry Maitland Wilson, Commander in chief of British forces in the Mediterranean, broadcast a message encouraging the Italians to either hand over their weapons to the partisans or at least not to give them to the Germans. The Allied best-case scenario was to embroil the Germans and the Italians, and British liaison officers (BLO) were ordered to contact as many Italian commanders as possible in the hopes of influencing Italian decision making.[25] The BLO reports are a good indication of the chaos in which Albania found itself just prior to and during the German invasion and the overly optimistic attitude the British harbored concerning Italian cooperation. One of the British officers, Captain George Seymour, entered Tirana in an Italian staff car wearing an Italian great coat to negotiate with General Dalmazzo's chief of intelligence. Plans were discussed for the coordination of Italian, Allied, and partisan efforts to resist the Germans. Dalmazzo was to concentrate the entire Ninth Army around Tirana, then seize Tirana and Durrës in preparation for an Allied landing, while partisans blocked all German access to Tirana. It was later learned that at the very moment this conversation was taking place, Dalmazzo himself was in the next room of Zog's old palace making arrangements with senior German officers for the evacuation of himself and his family.[26]

Similar discussions were taking place elsewhere. Partisan units walked unopposed into Berat on 9 September to negotiate with the Italians there, but as talks dragged on the Germans swept in, causing the partisans to flee. The British put forward a plan involving the Firenze Division, located in Burrel north of Tirana, which was to join with the partisans in attacking and taking Tirana, while the Brennero Division, concentrated around Kavaja, was to protect the Tirana-Durrës road. BLOs, together with Mustafa Gjinishi, talked with Colonel Caligari, the chief of staff for general Princivalle, the Brennero divisional commander, who assured the British that the division was ready to cooperate. The division was still armed after having convinced the Germans that it would help against the partisans. After playing the Germans off against the partisans, the Brennero Division double-crossed both, made a dash for Durrës, abandoned its equipment, found ships, and bolted for Italy.[27] As with the vast majority of Italians, these troops were uninterested in supporting either side and just wanted to go home.

But the partisans and the other resistance groups did benefit somewhat. Officially, we are told that about 15,000 officers and men surrendered to the partisans, many from the Firenze Division, the only Italian division in which large numbers of troops actually cooperated with the Albanians. Of these 15,000, between 1,500 and 2,200 went so far as to constitute a resistance battalion named after Antonio Gramsci, the Italian communist of Albanian origin.[28]

What the BK and the tribes of the north got from the Italians is difficult to determine. Amery notes that Muharrem Bajraktari occupied Kukës for a short time before the arrival of the Germans. He certainly would have helped himself to Italian stores. Italian troops were attacked in northern Albania during this period, losing a good deal of equipment. It is safe to assume, however, that the partisans got more arms and equipment than the BK or the northern chiefs, simply because they were more active. British liaison officers argue that the partisans could have gotten even more if they had acted more decisively while the Italians were still in a state of hopeless indecision. Dalmazzo had apparently even expressed a willingness to arm the partisans, but the Germans got to him first.[29]

The Germans, it seems, reached most of the Italians first and avoided what might have become a dangerous situation. They moved quickly and treated the Italians as something less than a military threat. Germans in small groups of two and three were seen disarming large groups of Italians. By 10 September they had taken both General Ezio Rosi, commander of the Italian Army Group East, and General Dalmazzo, commander of the Ninth Army. Both generals ordered their troops to hand over their guns and equipment to the Germans. Both were immediately evacuated to Belgrade. Most of the rank and file in Albania complied. The Germans captured some ninety thousand Italians in Albania, while forty-five thousand avoided capture and disappeared into the country. The Germans announced that if the surrender and disarmament of those who had avoided capture were not complete by 24 September, they would shoot the Italian general staff.[30] This can only be interpreted as an indication that the Germans had no interest in any more Italians surrendering.

Of those who did not surrender or go over to the partisans, some initially constituted their own resistance unit under the command of General Azzi. But he proved to be a poor choice. Not only did he fail to organize any action against the Germans, but he abandoned his men and lived quite comfortably on the money given to him by the Allies. German documents note that some blackshirt units put up resistance.[31] Many thousands of Italians were shipped from the Allied staging area "Seaview" and made it back to Italy.[32] But most simply went to ground, some falling into a modern version of serfdom as they tried to survive in a hostile environment. The majority wandered in search of food or employment, generally with little success. Soon Albania was host to thousands of starving Italians, without clothes or boots, lice ridden, and without leaders. British documents tell us that during the winter of 1943-1944 the death rate among these unfortunates was estimated at one hundred a day.[33]

Italian soldiers continued to be a problem for all the principal parties in Albania for the remainder of the war. The partisans were on the whole tolerant toward the Italians—with the exception the members of the secret police, some of whom were executed. But partisan sources complained that the sheer number of Italians constituted a significant drain on scant resources. The British complained that news of evacuation from their Seaview base caused a flow of Italians toward the coast, including thousands from Greece. This gave away one of the British SOE headquarters and caused the capture of a number of British liaison officers by the Germans. The Germans themselves occasionally issued orders for the Italians to surrender. Many, out of desperation did, only to be turned away because the Germans ultimately could not handle all those willing to surrender. At the end of the war as many as twenty thousand Italian troops were still in Albania.[34]

The Italian civilian population proved to be less of a problem and was actually quite useful, first to the Germans and later to the Albanians. Numbers are difficult to estimate, but at the time of the Italian armistice there were perhaps twenty thousand Italians in Tirana alone, which before 1939 had a total population of well under forty thousand. By mid-December 1943 there were still one thousand Italian families living in apartments in Tirana.[35] Neubacher reported to the Foreign Ministry that he believed there to be approximately fourteen thousand Italian civilians in Albania, for the most part skilled workers whom the Germans were anxious to employ.[36] Indeed, the Germans discovered that the Italians were virtually irreplaceable if they hoped to avoid bringing in specialists from Germany. Many important trades were dominated by Italians, who constituted most of the auto mechanics, electricians, welders, and, perhaps most important the most useful road builders.[37] Many of these skilled workers were employed by Italian firms, including Marinucci, Ferrobeton, Simoncini, Tudini e Talenti, and others, which were persuaded by the Germans to remain and work without profit.[38]

The Construction of a German Albania

Before the invasion was complete, German political officials had already descended upon Albania to attempt to implement the Ribbentrop plan. On 10 September Neubacher was ordered to meet the German division at Elbasan, but discovering that there was no airport in the vicinity he decided on his own authority to fly directly to Tirana. Because the capital was still in Italian hands, Neubacher sent a company of paratroopers with sixty Abwehr II agents in three JU 52s. Landing soon thereafter, Neubacher and Scheiger, whom he had brought along, were met by Schliep. While driving through the city toward the German mission, Neubacher took notice of thousands of armed Italian troops who looked rather flustered and confused but showed him deference and respect because—he assumed—he was wearing an unfamiliar uniform.[39]

Neubacher found the political situation somewhat more complex than he had anticipated, but remained confident that he would be able to attract a large enough group of respectable Albanians to declare independence, organize a government, and unburden the Germans. He had good reason to make that assumption, because Germany possessed significant advantages over the Italians in attracting Albanian cooperation. To begin with, they understood the uses of propaganda. First, prior to the invasion, the Germans had covered the country with leaflets announcing that they had come to Albania to protect the Albanians from the enemy—here they emphasized the Italians rather than the Allies—and from communism—which was associated with the Russians and the Serbs. The leaflets reassured the Albanians that nothing would endanger Albanian independence from Italy "who robbed you and has betrayed us." Albanian youths were complimented for their struggle against fascist Italy.[40]

Soon after arriving in Tirana a German general took the trouble to make a speech in which he apologized first for having occupied the country at all and second for having done so "without first knocking at the door". He went on to explain that this occupation was necessary first to obtain possession of the material, arms, and equipment of the Italian forces in the country and second to prevent an Allied invasion of Albania and that time did not permit the usual formalities to be observed.[41] The Germans declared that they wished only the best for Albania, within its ethnic frontiers, a reference to Albania's enlarged frontiers.

Further, the Germans benefited from and capitalized on the good impression left by the Austro-Hungarian troops who had occupied much of Albania during World War I. Not only had these troops behaved well, but they assisted the economy. The Austrians had invested heavily in Albania's infrastructure, building roads as well as constructing a narrow-gauge Decauville railroad from Durrës to Elbasan and from Tirana to Durrës, although it was soon completely neglected and was by 1922 no longer salvageable. Perhaps most important, the Austro-Hungarians had protected the Albanians from the Serbs, for which the Albanians remained grateful.[42] Taking advantage of this connection, the Germans whenever possible appointed Austrians to important positions in Albania, including of course Neubacher and Scheiger, but also the SS chief, SS General Josef Fitzthum, who before the war had been the chief of police in Vienna.[43]

German troops, too, had made a good impression on the Albanians, not only as a result of German victories in other theaters but also as a result of their rapid success and generally good behavior in Albania. Neubacher noted in his memoirs, with some exaggeration, that the people of Albania, pleased that the Germans were in the process of disarming the Italians, committed no unfriendly acts against the German military. The German record was compared favorably to that of the Italians, who were held in low esteem militarily for abandoning their Albanian holdings under the pressure of Albanian bands in 1920, for their mauling at the hands of the Greeks in 1940, and for their inability to provide basic security during their occupation.

Although all foreigners made mistakes in Albania out of ignorance, not only did the Germans seem to make fewer, but they were quick to take advantage of those made by their enemies. Many Allied moves could have been scripted in Berlin. The Allies, for example, allowed Victor Emmanuel III to continue referring to himself as "king of Albania" until the beginning of December 1943. The Albanians themselves had deprived him of the crown six weeks earlier, with the goodwill and encouragement of the Germans. The Allies had allowed themselves to be put in a position in which an admitted wrong to a small nation had been righted with German cooperation.[44] Other Allied blunders included the BBC's praising known collaborators for their staunch resistance and the dropping of leaflets over Albania in Greek and Serbian, leaving, not surprisingly, the worst of impressions.[45]

Although the Italian reputation did not require much tarnishing, the Germans let no opportunity slip by. They did much to emphasize that Italy had little to do with the creation of a Greater Albania. Italy's role was dismissed as a simple act of colonialist annexation, the culmination of the long-standing Italian policy of controlling their "fifth shore."[46] The Germans created the impression that only now, with the coming of the Germans, would Kosova's real union with Albania be achieved. As we will see, the Germans even slightly enlarged Greater Albania. The Germans did not fail to bring to the attention of the Albanians that the Allies had been carefully silent on Kosova—indicating their intention to hand it back to the Yugoslavs—and had failed to recognize any Albanian government or committee in exile, leaving the entire question of the existence of an Albanian state in the postwar world unresolved.

Upon his arrival Neubacher immediately hoped to build on these advantages by avoiding the structuring of a conventional military occupation. Rather than a military governor, a "German General in Albania" (DGA), General Theodor Geib, was appointed. His official function was to "represent the interests of the Wehrmacht to the Albanian government," although as the structure took more definite shape, he seemed to have had only limited authority.[47] All relations with the Albanians, once a puppet regime was constructed, were to be conducted by Schliep, who would later be named German ambassador. This system won over many Albanians but seemed to exasperate and infuriate some elements of the German military command. Officers complained incessantly in their reports that there was no clear division of authority, allowing Albanians to play the German army off against German diplomatic representatives. The army complained that what they called the fiction of independence made their job, which itself seemed somewhat unclear, a more difficult one.[48] But Neubacher had his goal, and he intended to achieve it.

The Germans, then, had much working in their favor and some of them expected rapid success. Neubacher was considerably disappointed, then, with the lukewarm reception with which his schemes were met by the quality of Albanian leader he hoped to attract. This reluctance stemmed first from the obvious connection between Germany and Italy. Many Albanians remembered that Germany had staunchly supported the Italian invasion as well as the four and one-half years of Italian occupation. The general disdain for the Italians, as Schliep noted, was due in part to Rome's attempt to force fascism down the throats of the Albanians, an ideology clearly associated with the Germans.[49] But Neubacher also credits British propaganda for the cold reception, propaganda that had convinced many Albanians that Germany could not win the war. British propaganda was also effective, at least for a time, in keeping the specter of an Allied invasion alive. Even Hoxha believed that it was a question of when, not if.[50] Allied deception with regard to a major landing in the Balkans was resurrected in 1944 as "Plan Zeppelin," part of "Operation Bodyguard," which was intended to help cover the proposed landing in Normandy.[51]

Although disappointed, Neubacher moved ahead and worked with those who were willing to cooperate at this early stage. While initially he was not in much of a position to reject any Albanians with administrative experience, he did make a point of avoiding many who had collaborated with the Italians. Mustafa Kruja and Eqrem Libohova offered their services and were rejected, partly because of their Italian connections and partly because of their failure. Neubacher clearly was attempting to distance himself from the Italian past, hoping to create a government in which fascism, which he recognized was unpopular, played only a limited role. This attitude, of course, further restricted his choices.

But some Albanians demonstrated enthusiasm for the Germans. The first to lend the Germans unequivocal support, to no one's surprise, came from the new territories of Kosova and Çamëria. In Kosova, Scheiger and Deva, the latter of whom had returned to Prizren after his meeting with Neubacher in Belgrade, rallied local leaders through the creation of the Second League of Prizren, hoping to capitalize on the late-nineteenth-century Albanian nationalist organization of the same name. The second league had but one principal goal: the protection of Greater Albania. Many Albanian leaders in Çamëria, too, were quick to cooperate with the Germans, since their hopes of becoming part of the enlarged Albania were as dependent on Germany as were the hopes of the Kosovars.[52] These hopes, however, would never be realized. After considerable delay, Neubacher decided that the only viable solution to the problem was an exchange of population with the Greeks of southern Albania,[53] but even this policy was never carried out.

Neubacher believed that Germany's position would be further enhanced if he followed strictly constitutional procedures in structuring the new Albanian government. First, he declared that the Libohova government no longer existed, since Libohova had fled to Italy with Lieutenant General Pariani.[54] Some of Libohova's colleagues had remained and agreed to stand in until a new government could be formed, although Neubacher was loath to use them too openly.[55] Neubacher's next move was to convince those Albanians with whom he had been working, or with whom he had contact, to call for the creation of a national committee to declare Albania independent and put together a provisional executive committee. The principals in this process included Deva, Bedri Pejani, the rather ardent president of the Second League of Prizren, and Ibrahim Bey Biçaku, a major landowner from Elbasan, as the primary representative from old Albania. The Italians had tried and failed on several occasions to tempt Ibrahim Biçaku with the premiership, but he had consistently declined.[56] Although his refusal to collaborate with the Italians lent him some credibility, it was generally recognized that both he and the others from old Albania who rallied to the Germans at this early stage were politicians of the second rank.

Once these individuals had gathered, discussions began but just as quickly became bogged down. Neubacher, who never shied away from applying a heavy hand when he considered it appropriate, reminded his friends that they risked a traditional occupation regime if they could not come up with a government that recognized the necessity of the German presence. While pressing on the one hand, Neubacher withdrew to Belgrade on 12 September to give the impression that the Albanians were doing all this on their own.[57]

These tactics seem to have succeeded, because on 14 September the Kosovars and the few politicians from old Albania constructed a national committee of twenty-two, headed by Pejani, with an executive committee of six, headed by Biçaku, which functioned as a provisional government. Two of the six were Kosovars and one, Mihal Zallari, a staunch pro-German. The first task of the committee was to declare the independence of Albania. After carefully reviewing the wording with Neubacher, the committee issued a proclamation that briefly examined Albanian history to date, announced the end of slavery under the Italians, and called for the creation of a representative government. Neubacher was generally pleased with the declaration but found it necessary to remove a reference to the desire of all Albanians to expand Albania's frontiers to include Mitrovica, to the detriment of Serbia. Neubacher feared that this would immediately become the goal of all Albanian nationalists.[58] But the Germans did eventually relent and gave the Albanians some territory around Mitrovica that had been part of occupied Serbia.[59]

Representatives of the committee delivered the proclamation to Neubacher at the German Consulate, where, we are told, the always attentive hostess Frau Schliep had prepared refreshments for the "fathers of the Nation." Neubacher flew to Belgrade the next day and soon to Germany, where Hitler "who always had great interest in the last romantic corner of Europe" expressed himself to be very satisfied with developments.[60]

Again following careful constitutional forms, the committee next called for the election of a national constituent assembly to draw up a new constitution. The plan for this step was developed and published in the official government organ, *Kombi*, on 19 September. Every community in Albania would send three representatives, who, together with representatives from the district towns, would elect one representative per ten thousand people. In cases where this procedure was deemed not possible, people living in Tirana who had connections with the local area would act as representatives. The provisional executive committee would appoint representatives for the clergy, for "political personalities," and for the more inaccessible mountain regions.

Since much of the south was still essentially controlled by the resistance, and since much of the north had reverted to traditional forms of tribal anarchy, this system naturally could never have worked, particularly in a state with no democratic tradition. And all of this was scheduled to be completed in two weeks. The process, of course, allowed considerable room for creative manipulation, much of it left to Scheiger. On 16 October Scheiger duly delivered 243 deputies to Tirana, heavily representative of the north.[61] Tirana radio announced their names, although the Allies were convinced that most of these people were not actually present, their names being mentioned only to create the impression of wide support for and cooperation with the Germans.[62]

Although there certainly was a good deal of subterfuge, by October the Germans were having much better luck in attracting prominent Albanians. Circumstances, often beyond the control of the Germans, had convinced many Albanian politicians to abandon their earlier hesitancy. The fact that the expected Allied landing had not materialized was important, as was German military success against the NLM. The removal of many Italian prisoners, too, left a positive impression, but perhaps the most important factor was the increasing hostility between the NLM and the BK. BK leaders were convinced that the Germans would only stay for a short time, but they also recognized that the Germans were a fact and would not go away immediately. BK leaders reasoned that if the situation were handled carefully, the Germans could be used against the BK's domestic opponents, but only cooperation with the Germans would bring this about. Chieftains from the north, including leaders of the Catholic Mirdita tribe, became less obstructionist for the same reason.[63]

When the national constituent assembly met in October, then, Neubacher had reason to hope that his original plan, of attracting prominent Albanians to form an independent government that would relieve the Germans, could now go forward. The assembly elected Lef Nosi, a prominent member of the BK, as president. Nosi, an Orthodox Albanian from a well-to-do Elbasaner commercial family, had good nationalist credentials. He had participated in the declaration of Albanian independence in 1912 and served as a minister in the first government.

The Council of Regency

Still careful to adhere to traditional constitutional form, the assembly under Nosi passed a series of decrees that fundamentally altered Albania's Italian-established constitution. The union with Italy was officially dissolved; many of the laws passed after the Italian invasion were revoked; and Albania was declared free, neutral, and independent. At the same time, the assembly revoked the draft law of June 1940 that declared Albania to be a co-belligerent with Italy.[64] The assembly reaffirmed the decrees of 1 September 1928, which had declared Albania to be a royal dictatorship, a move calculated to attract Abaz Kupi. While clearly leaving the road open for the possible return of Zog, the assembly announced that Albania would be governed by a regency of four—one representative from each of Albania's four major religious communities—for the remainder of the war. The Germans, in this instance, were being quite thorough and quite sensitive. They had created a government similar to the one that had ruled after the retreat of Prince Wied in September 1914, demonstrating an appreciation for not only Albanian history but also for Albania's religious makeup. The Germans, like the Italians before them, would be less successful in gauging social needs.

Given the uninspiring nature of the national committee and the provisional executive, and the fact that with the restored constitution whatever power the Albanians would have would be exercised by the regents, the choosing of the regents took on added significance. Nosi was chosen as the Orthodox representative. Representing the Sunni Moslems, the Germans were able to attract Fuat Bey Dibra, a landowner from new Albania who, like Nosi, had a long and distinguished record. He had represented Albania at the Paris conference in 1920 and was appointed, but never served, as minister of the interior in the Vrioni government of 1920. Unlike the others, Dibra had served in the collaborationist cabinet of Mustafa Kruja, but in November 1942 he had been elected to the central committee of the BK and was therefore something of a catch for the Germans.[65] Albanian Catholics were represented by the prior of the Franciscans in Shkodra, Father Anton Harapi, who maintained connections with both the Kosovars and the NLM. Learning of his appointment, NLM emissaries unsuccessfully attempted to dissuade him from accepting. Neubacher seems to have developed a warm personal relationship with Harapi, in part because Harapi had received some of his education at the monastery school of Meran and Hall in the Tyrol.[66]

But the biggest prize for the Germans was Mehdi Bey Frashëri, who agreed to head the Council of Regency. Frashëri, a Bektashi Moslem, was one of the most respected living Albanians. His career was long and distinguished; he had served as governor of Jerusalem under the Ottomans, mayor of Durrës under Prince Wied, and minister of the interior in 1920. During the 1930s he held a myriad of significant posts, including prime minister from 1935 to 1936, when he constructed a relatively liberal regime made up of many young Germanophiles. As we have seen, after the Italian invasion he was interned in Italy, principally for having publicly castigated Mussolini for his destruction of Albanian independence. While held in Italy, British documents suggest, he was chosen as titular leader of the NLM. It is also likely that he was connected with the BK in its early stages of development.

The Germans were appraised of his significance—most probably by his son Vehbi—and began to search for him immediately after the invasion.[67] The venerable Albanian politician was found, and he agreed, on 16 September, to return to Tirana for talks with Neubacher, Scheiger, and Schliep. Frashëri, much to the chagrin of Neubacher, would not be rushed and drove a hard bargain. He made it clear to Neubacher that while he was in sympathy with the German position in Albania, he was concerned about his credibility with the nationalists, and at the same time he was under intense pressure from the NLM not to cooperate. While debating he negotiated for as much independence as he could extract and hoped to convince the Germans to recognize Albania's full neutrality. Neubacher finally agreed to recognize Albania's "relative" neutrality and "relative" sovereignty, congratulating Frashëri on discovering a new category in international law.[68] Frashëri had achieved for Albania a status similar to that of Croatia or Slovakia—the Germans were still clearly in control, but something had been saved.

Frashëri, who must certainly be counted as an Albanian patriot, agreed to serve as regent as well as head the council. The leadership of the council was originally designed to rotate, but Neubacher tells us that Nosi declined for health reasons and that Harapi argued that as a Catholic monk he could accept no position in which he would be forced to sanction the death penalty.[69] Frashëri explained soon afterward in a pamphlet published in Tirana that he had accepted the position fearing that resistance to the Germans and the growing conflict between the BK and the NLM would weaken Albania to the point that it would become an easy target for neighboring states that coveted Albanian territory. He and the BK leaders who joined with him also feared that the NLM had become little more than a communist front designed to camouflage the party's ultimate objective—the seizure of power.[70] The Germans themselves reported that despite his acquiescence, Frashëri's attitude toward the Germans remained ambiguous, demonstrated perhaps by the fact that throughout his tenure he continued to maintain feelers to the West through Ankara.[71]

The Government of Mitrovica

Once committed, the regency moved to form a permanent government, which would begin the process of ending the chaos and stabilizing Albania. Following hurried negotiations, on 5 November, a government headed by the Kosovar Rexhep Mitrovica was introduced. Mitrovica, too, boasted a long political career, having taken part in the declaration of independence at Vlora in 1912. A minister in 1921, he was forced to flee Albania in 1924 after standing with Zog's Kosovar opponents. He became a leader of the so-called Paris group, anti-Zog exiles, and then returned to Albania after the Italian invasion, assuming a relatively minor role as a member of the Council of State. In 1942 he joined the BK, and he was arrested by the Italians in 1943.[72]

The small cabinet, most of whom had credentials as nationalists as well as some German or Austrian connection, included Deva as minister of the interior and Rrok Kolaj, a Catholic from Shkodra who had studied at the University of Graz, as minister of justice. The regents announced that the veteran politician and diplomat Mehmet Konica, still in Rome, had accepted the portfolio of minister at the reinstated foreign ministry. It seems, however, that he never actually agreed; nor did he ultimately ever serve. The Austrian-educated Vehbi Frashëri was appointed provisionally in his stead.[73] The Orthodox Elbasaner Sokrat Dodbiba, the nephew of Nosi, became minister of finance. He had attended a business school in Vienna and had considerable experience in the Finance Ministry. Ago Agaj, a Moslem landowner from Vlora, who had studied agriculture in Austria, became minister of political economy, and Musa Gjylbegu, a Moslem from Shkodra, became minister of labor. Eqrem Çabej, who had studied linguistics in Austria and was a leading intellectual and educator, was offered the position of minister of education, but, like Konica, refused. The vacant post was later filled by Koço Muka, a member of the BK central committee who had collaborated with the Italians.[74]

The Germans had done reasonably well. They had attracted some significant people, although the group was predominantly from Kosova or northern Albania. Most also had some connection with the Germans: a full three-quarters of the government spoke German, most having spent some time studying either in Germany or Austria. They were, then, primarily Germanophile northerners and included few representatives of the Tosks in the south and few people outside the rather narrow landlord class to whom the Italians had appealed as well. Although far from "national," then, the government did include many national groups, including prewar influential politicians, both pro- and anti-Zog, representatives of the Catholic clergy, representatives of the Geg tribes in the north, some individuals with BK connections, and, of course, Kosovar nationalists.

But the nature of the government was perhaps more important than its makeup. This nature can perhaps best be characterized by a statement issued by Frashëri and published in the essentially uncensored Albanian press, which occasionally even published uncensored Allied communiqués. In his New Year's address, the head regent, while thanking Hitler for freeing Albania, announced that his social reforms would be based on "democratic principles that eliminate all dictatorships." Here we have a public official under German occupation who in the official press declared his support for democracy and opposition to dictatorships. This was certainly a far cry from the ingratiating attempts at fawning on military masters demonstrated by those who collaborated with the Italians. The Germans had succeeded, during a critical period, in attracting a group of people that included many who had known pro-Allied and democratic sentiments and who at the same time had rejected with scorn the chance to collaborate with the Italians.[75]

Even the Allies registered grudging admiration for this initial German achievement. Peter Kemp, a British liaison officer in Albania, noted in his memoirs that "it is a measure of their [the Germans'] success that when they set up a puppet government, they were able to induce Albanians of high principles and distinction to serve."[76]

Mitrovica's government, working through the constituent assembly that had simply declared itself the new national assembly, proved to be energetic in the early months of the German occupation. Not blind to the challenges, in his first address to the National Assembly Mitrovica noted that four and a half years of Italian domination had left anarchy and chaos in Albania. The pre-1939 state apparatus had been completely dismantled. The Italians had destroyed the army, the gendarmerie, the police, and the Foreign Ministry; they had changed the flag, altered personal greetings, renamed cities, and even reassigned family names. To reestablish the state, Mitrovica set down an ambitious plan that included reestablishing local government on the pre-1939 basis, gaining foreign recognition, reorganizing the economy, introducing effective agrarian reform, and creating a military force.[77] The general goal of the government, and this was repeated at every available opportunity, was to protect Albania's territorial integrity within its ethnic borders. The principal obstacle was the NLM and more specifically its communist core, which Mitrovica identified as un-Albanian. He argued that the "Albanians, as Aryans of Illyrian heritage, could not ignore tradition and would be saved from the hydra of communism."[78]

Mitrovica's program was reasonably progressive. Margaret Hasluck, who advised SOE in Cairo, was moved to exclaim that "the lines of government policy would meet with our warm approval if we were not at war with the country whose armed forces now occupy Albania."[79] Mitrovica's program, had it been successfully carried out, might have achieved what both the government and the Germans had hoped for: a stable regime, with enough popular support, or at least respect, and a loyal, effective security force to unburden the Germans. To the great disappointment of the Germans, Mitrovica, and his far less effective successors, failed in their efforts, ironically, at least partially as a result of German inaction.

International recognition would have lent the government considerable domestic legitimacy and might even have favorably impressed the Allies. German resistance and obstructionism in this regard showed that they were certainly fallible in their policy toward Albania, or at least that they were willing to go only so far. In late November the Albanian government asked the Germans to help them convince the Bulgarians to extend recognition. Schliep supported the request, suggesting that Bulgarian recognition would strengthen the government.[80] At the same time, Mehdi Frashëri began negotiations for the establishment of diplomatic relations with Switzerland and Turkey, which continued to show a paternalistic interest in its co-religionists in Albania. That he did so through Bulgaria, without consulting Schliep, caused some alarm at the German Foreign Ministry. Berlin argued that although the neutral states should not be approached, perhaps at least those states under German control might be asked to extend recognition. Neubacher seems to have agreed, but noted that there was no hurry.[81] But after these states were canvassed, the only regime willing to extend recognition to the Albanians was Ante Pavelic's Ustashi regime in Croatia. In the end Neubacher would not even go this far, arguing that the Croatians had little interest in Albania and that a Croatian representative in Tirana would only serve as a conduit for bad news. He was also apparently afraid of offending the Serbs.[82]

In a related matter, Vehbi Frashëri asked the Germans at the beginning of November to transform the German Consulate General into an embassy. In February, while in Berlin, Frashëri repeated his request, but again there seems to have been little immediate action.[83] Schliep was finally elevated to the level of ambassador, but since this did not happen until July 1944, any possible good effect the move might have had was squandered.

In the matter of land reform, one of Albania's most pressing needs, the Mitrovica government made a start, but ultimately settled for little more than a token gesture. Mitrovica announced that state land would be sold to twenty-five hundred "proletarian farmers" at prices they would be able to afford. While little of this land was actually distributed, the move certainly encouraged many landless rural laborers to think twice about joining the resistance, for fear of missing even the slightest chance of becoming one of the fortunate twenty-five hundred.[84] As agrarian reform, however, this was rather pathetic—but realistically, could the Germans have expected more? After all, the government consisted primarily of men who had little to gain by such a process. The Germans had attached themselves to the traditional elite, the large landowners and beys, those people who were the natural enemies of the communists and who had something in common with the Germans themselves, linguistically and culturally. The Germans, by tying themselves to the narrow European-educated elite, who had no ties to the common Albanian, denied themselves a knowledge of the needs of the average Albanian.[85] The Germans created a German ghetto and spawned an atmosphere of the "ugly German,"[86] similar to what the Americans created in Southeast Asia in the 1960s.

The Albanian Economy under the Germans

Economic stabilization remained another unattained goal. Without intending to, the Germans complicated Albania's economic picture and added considerably to the day-to-day hardship experienced by the average Albanian. The extent to which the Albanian economy had become dependent on Italian subsidies was evidenced by the last budget under the Italians. Expenditures for 1943 to 1944 were estimated at 147 million francs, with revenues of only 107 million. The deficit, one-third of the budget, was to be made up by the Italians.[87] The Germans had no intention of underwriting the Albania economy. And unlike the Italians, who had maintained their troops almost solely by the importation of food from Italy, the Germans hoped to live off domestic resources. The Germans had fewer mouths to feed than the Italians—no more than thirty-six thousand, a number that steadily decreased during the German occupation—but Albania had never really been able to take care of its own needs. The surplus from Kosova helped to avert disaster, but even with Kosova deliveries, prices rose, causing shortages. Exacerbated by poor weather, German policy even caused famine conditions in southern Albania during the spring of 1944. Although the situation never approached the grim reality of Greece, the difficult circumstances for which the Germans were at least partially to blame eroded Albanian patience.[88]

When Hitler was asked by Bulgarian prime minister Dobri Bojiloff what plans he had for Albania, he answered that he intended to keep its business in good order.[89] Not only did he not keep Albania's business in good order, but he did not have a plan. The German occupation of Albania began on a precarious economic footing precisely because the Germans did not have an economic plan. As with their political program, it was improvised and, as a result, often caused problems that might have been avoided.

The economic problems began within days of the German invasion. When the Germans entered Tirana they had hoped to find enough money in the National Bank of Albania to pay their troops. This was to be considered a loan. But they found only thirty million francs, and overhead expenses for the German army in Albania proved to be about forty million francs a month. With some degree of urgency they turned to the German authorities in Rome, where an SS commando raid had recently captured 120 million francs in notes, the plates, twenty-three sacks of gold coin, and twenty-nine cases of gold bars from the main branch of the National Bank of Albania. The gold was sent to Berlin, and the plates, which later turned out to be defaced, were sent to Belgrade, but most of the paper money was sent to Tirana.[90] The same plane that brought Mehdi Bey Frashëri back to Albania also carried—without Frashëri's knowledge—substantial sums, which were immediately transferred to the National Bank of Albania in Tirana.[91] The money was used to pay German troops in Albania and Montenegro. It was also used to finance German construction projects, airports, road repair, and coastal gun emplacements.

This seemingly wanton disregard for the Albanian economy soon bore bitter fruit. As early as 16 October Schliep told the Foreign Ministry that the money in possession of German troops was threatening the Albanian economy. The Albanian government complained bitterly that inflation was rampant, with prices reported to be some fourteen times what they had been in 1939. The population had begun to resent the Germans, Schliep was told.

Neubacher, who had assumed direction of economic policy in the Balkans through a direct order from Hitler, responded energetically. He asked the army, which disclaimed responsibility for Albania's economic morass, to restrict its purchase of domestically produced goods to a bare minimum. The army simply could not do without items such as oil, fruit, meat, fish, wool, and leather, and ultimately, of course, the needs of the German military outweighed the health of the Albanian economy. Still, the army made a serious effort to comply, by reducing consumption as well as importing gold (not that confiscated in Rome) and manufactured goods, both in short supply in Albania. The gold was sold on the free market to offset the National Bank of Albania's dearth of notes. The most important articles the Germans imported included sugar, medicine, chemicals, and spare parts.

But neither method satisfied Albania's needs or even paid Germany's debts in Albania, once the extensive exportation of raw materials was fully under way. To make matters worse, the German soldiers suffered from the level of inflation as well—their pay was rarely increased to account for inflation unlike the pay of the German police; the people who worked for the Todt Organization, a German construction agency active in Albania; and other civilians. In order to survive, a substantial black market developed, which German authorities were never able to control successfully.[92]

In an attempt to prevent the total collapse of the Albanian economy, a comprehensive agreement was negotiated between the Germans and their puppet regime in December 1943, which was intended to solve some of the economic problems the German invasion had caused. The German negotiators and the Albanian government agreed that Germany accept responsibility for financing the costs of the German army, for repairing the destruction caused by the invasion, and for financing strategic projects—although some Albanian financial participation in road construction was specified. The Germans admitted the use of 46.5 million Albanian francs during the early months of the occupation, which they agreed to repay as quickly as possible with 3 percent interest. (However, this apparently was never done. Indeed the sums the Germans owed to the Albanian government for support of the army increased to 81 million francs by August 1944. Some Albanian sources set the figure for the entire German debt at 430 million francs by November 1944.)[93] The agreements also set down some basic principles regulating trade, with secret protocols dealing with the exploitation of raw materials.[94]

But the Germans also took some practical steps to stabilize the Albanian economy. The Reichsbank disgorged more gold—Neubacher maintained at the Nuremberg trials that the final amount approached 0.3 tons.[95] The German military also began selling items such as bandages, medicine, and iron, which had been taken as spoils from the Italians, as well as large quantities of sugar taken from German stores. The Germans began growing their own animal feed, as well as vegetables and potatoes for the troops. The German army even became directly involved in Albanian light industry, producing among other things soap, cigarettes, olive oil, beer, cement, explosives, and various iron products.[96]

There was some mutual benefit from these arrangements. The National Bank of Albania reported that over the five months after the agreements were signed, inflation slowed somewhat, with prices increasing from 3,004.1 in January to 3,378.9 in May, based on a 1939 index of 100.[97] Nevertheless, it is perhaps not surprising that the Germans benefited the most from the financial arrangements, particularly in the extraction of raw materials.

The first problem confronting the Germans in raw material extraction was the lack of usable geological reports. The Zog regime had done little, and the Italians had been remiss as well. The Wehrmacht found the Austrian geologist Dr. Ernest Nowack, who had worked in Albania during World War I. He was assigned as an officer to the 501st Motorized Battalion and began work immediately. Still, it was not until May 1944, five months before the German withdrawal, that an effective raw material map was ready.[98] In the meantime, of course, the Germans actively exploited existing mines.

The second problem was to avoid the label of colonial exploiter. Neubacher addressed this problem at a meeting with representatives of German firms interested in Albanian raw material that took place as early as September 1943. He told agents from the mining concerns Neuhausen and Südostmontan that although there must be no interruption of raw material deliveries, the Albanian government must be given letters of credit for everything shipped since the collapse of Italy. The negotiations with the Albanian government must be regulated on the basis of the German firms acting as buyers, and all relations would function in strict accordance with the notion of an independent state.[99] While there was never a question of the Albanians looking for other buyers, Neubacher was again carrying out his instructions to the letter. The fiction of independence was maintained.

The Germans expressed an interest in a variety of raw materials and found important mineral deposits, but transportation problems prevented the exploitation of the copper southeast of Shkodra and the iron ore in the south. The Germans were able to take advantage of the lignite in Kosova and the zinc and lead mines in Trepça from which they were able to extract about 40 percent of their total lead requirements. Other coal sources around Tirana provided the city and the surrounding area with much of its fuel. High-quality magnesium was found at Godolesh, and despite the problem of water in the mine and the ever present transportation problems, significant amounts were extracted and shipped to Germany.[100]

Oil and chrome remained, as they had under the Italians, the two most important resources. While Albanian oil was less important than the chrome for the Germans, the Wehrmacht nevertheless maintained that Albanian oil was second only to Romanian oil in its importance. The first problem faced by the Germans with regard to oil was that in September Albania's most active fields at Devoll in the south were in partisan hands. But by the end of October the fields were cleared and technicians from "Oilcompany 33" were sent from the Ostmark to replace the Italian Azienda Generale Italiana Petroli (AGIP) technicians.

As the exportation of crude oil was deemed impractical, the next problem was refining. The Italians had piped the crude to Vlora, refined it in Bari, and sent the fuel back by ship. As the Allies controlled the Adriatic, this was no longer an option. The Germans decided to refine it in place. Devoll itself had only one small primitive refinery that produced enough fuel to run the fields. The Germans decided to build four small Heckmann refineries with the hope that at least the needs of the Wehrmacht in Albania could be met. Because of the difficulty of transporting heavy parts over Albania's inadequate roads, the first small refinery did not go into operation until May 1944.

It was not until July 1944 that an agreement with the Albanian government was worked out as to ownership and payment. The Wehrmacht argued for some time that the fields should be considered war spoils, since German troops had recovered and protected the fields. It is clear that not all elements of the German administration were as enthusiastic as Neubacher about maintaining the notion of Albanian independence. Still, as usual Neubacher got his way. The Wehrmacht surrendered control of the fields to the civilian Albanian Oil GmbH, a subsidiary of Continental Oil GmbH, which negotiated a deal with the Albanian government. German military sources maintain that during the period of operation, that is, until the middle of October 1944, approximately one million tons of crude were pumped, although there are no German figures concerning the amount of actual fuel produced.[101] Albanian figures suggest that both the needs of the military and the needs of the civilian population were met. By June 1944 there was apparently even a surplus, but by July Allied air attacks began to cause considerable damage.[102]

By far the most important resource the Germans found in Albania was chrome, indispensable in weapons production. Deposits were located at Bulqiz and Kukës in the north and Pogradec in the south. In a memo to Hitler in November 1943, Armaments Minister Albert Speer argued that if for no other reason, the Balkans had to be held for the chrome. Without it, he continued, supplies would be depleted in five or six months, and in another three to four months, production of aircraft, tanks, submarines, grenades, and artillery would stop.[103] Albanian supplies became even more important after Turkish chrome—Germany's principal source—was cut off in April 1944. The Germans found rich deposits of chrome, enough to satisfy a substantial part of their needs, in both old and new Albania. As with other Albanian resources, the Germans were hampered by pricing negotiations with the puppet regime and the perennial transportation problems. Of the two problems, pricing negotiations proved the less significant, since mining, often with the use of experienced Italian labor, and deliveries continued uninterrupted during the talks.

Transportation was a greater problem. The chrome was important enough for the Germans to contemplate the construction of a railroad from the mines at Djakova in Kosova to Pec. German planners correctly assumed that shipment by truck, given a lack of trucks and spare parts, not to mention the bad roads, could never keep pace with production. But a railroad proved impractical, because the Germans assumed that their stay was limited. Trucks appeared to be the only option. Neubacher negotiated a complex scheme with the Albanian government whereby the Albanians would provide funds to improve the mines and continue with the soon-to-be-abandoned railroad project, in exchange for 120 trucks and scheduled payments for the chrome. The Albanians agreed, but the Wehrmacht refused to give up any trucks. A prolonged paper war followed between the Foreign Ministry, the Reichswirtschaft minister, and the army, culminating in Hitler's being informed of the dispute. Subsequent to a strong letter from the Reichswirtschaft minister to Field Marshal Wilhelm Keitel, Albania received sixty trucks. As assumed, trucks were able to bring out just over half of the chrome being mined, but still, the Germans were able to export one-sixth of their total chrome requirements from these Albanian mines.[104] The Germans transported away more chrome than they could pay for, and at the time of the German withdrawal they owed the Albanians considerable sums. Economically, the Germans did well by the Albanians; the reverse was rarely the case.

Unlike the Italians, the Germans provided little employment, with the exception perhaps of the mines, the construction of coastal installations, and the roads. Although all three were important, the roads were perhaps the highest priority for the Germans. Given Albanian geography—an extensive Adriatic seacoast as well as good harbors—Albania had traditionally been dependent on seaborne transportation. Because the Adriatic was not secure for the Germans, other forms of transportation were needed. The Germans found virtually no railroads in Albania, with the exception of a narrow-gauge line from Struga over Tetovo to Skopje, which had been constructed for the chrome mines of Pogradec. Kosova possessed a line from Skopje through Kosova to Belgrade that became important in the German retreat but was of little significance in inter-Albanian transportation. There were no usable natural or artificial waterways with the exception of a short canal connecting Lake Shkodra to the Adriatic.[105]

This left only the roads, and taking, holding, and maintaining them became one of the central problems of the entire German occupation. The long distance roads, mostly built by the Italians, were the first priority. These included the north-south roads Himara-Shkodra over Durrës and Vlora and in the east from Florina over Korça-Struga to Kosova. The principal east-west roads ran over the southern line Bitolj-Struga-Elbasan-Tirana and in the north Urosevac over Prizren to Shkodra. Roads of secondary importance included the road to Devoll because of the oil and the Elbasan-Peqin-Kavaja-Durrës road, which played a crucial role in the German retreat.[106]

Once again, the Germans experienced relative success. Responsibility for maintenance and security of Albanian roads was divided between the regular army and the German military authority in Albania, or DGA. The regular army was assigned the strategically important thoroughfares, with the German military administration responsible for the rest. The military administration officials complained that the corps could and did avail themselves of the service of the Todt Organization, which had the funds to hire private companies and pay higher wages. To complicate matters further for the occupation authorities, when Todt pulled out suddenly in August 1944, it left without paying a substantial debt, and those owed money, both individuals and firms, directed their claims to the German military administration and not the regular army.

Still, the Germans considered their efforts with regard to the roads to be successful. Although the German military authorities in Tirana had only Albanian and Italian firms with which to work, and although their responsibilities were significantly increased in August 1944, the roads were generally kept secure and in good shape when the Germans needed them. This was possible partly because the Italian construction firms worked without pay and because of the efforts of the Albanian technical minister in charge, Hifzi Korça. A German report names Korça as a pro-German with remarkable abilities and energy.[107]

Although the principal roads remained basically under German control, much of the rest of the country did not, despite the best effort of the Germans and the puppet governments. The latter, for their part, hoped to contribute through a legal system. The government posted stringent laws against sabotage and set up a draconian court called the "Court for the Protection of the Nation." The court was given wide jurisdiction against what it called espionage and also against acts in "conflict with the orders of the High Council and orders of the government."[108] But this court could only have been effective with credible security forces behind it. This was perhaps the most significant failure of the Germans and their puppets. This was a crucial goal not only because it aimed to legitimize the government but also because it aimed to unburden the Germans, who by the fall of 1943 had even fewer troops to spare.

German Security Plans

The original plan for Albanian security, in Neubacher's words, was to effect a "national mobilization against the communists."[109] The Germans hoped to do this by a number of steps, including arming and using some nationalist bands, creating and maintaining an Albanian army and gendarmerie corps—something from which the Italians had shied away—and, finally, creating an indigenous SS division in Kosova. The original enthusiasm for these units quickly died, however, when it became clear that not only were they of questionable value militarily, but in many cases the Albanian units did much to alienate the population as a result of brutality and a penchant for plunder.[110]

The first part of the German plan, to arm and use existing bands, was set in motion within days of the German invasion. In the hopes of attracting the Gegs of the north, the Germans released many of those who had been imprisoned by the Italians and essentially allowed the governing of the region—with the exception of the sensitive coastal areas—to revert to its traditional state of tribal rule, with its blood feuds and bandit chiefs, no tax collection, and the only law the ancient code of Lek Dukagjini.[111] As we have seen, Italian neglect of the north encouraged this process as well, but German policy did so to a greater extent over a greater area. The goodwill produced by this hands-off policy was exploited by Captain Lange, Neubacher's military adjutant attached to Abwehr II. Lange's task was to attempt to build something of a national militia projected at some thirty thousand, to serve as a reserve.

Lange turned to the Catholic Mirdita and to the ever loyal Kosovars. The Mirdita were chosen for their significance in the north and because they had cooperated with the Austrians in World War I and with the Italians in World War II. Negotiations proved successful, and in exchange for money and weapons the Mirdita secured the crucial Prizren-Kukës-Puka-Shkodra road for the Germans. The situation in central and southern Albania was much more complex, although the Germans did win the cooperation of many BK *çetas*—often armed with captured Italian weapons—in the drive against the partisans. But the Germans were initially hesitant to attach themselves too closely to the BK, with Schliep notifying Berlin that in his estimate the BK were cooperating only in order to make off with German weapons.[112]

The most notable militia units proved to be a battalion of six hundred to seven hundred volunteers from Kosova whom Neubacher hoped, because of their loyalty, could be relied upon to secure German lines of communication and perhaps even occupy Tirana.[113] These troops, who were trained at Zemun and led by Lieutenant Colonel Adem Boletini, marched to Tirana at the end of September 1943 wearing their Italian uniforms.[114] Their behavior, however, did the Germans more harm than good, as they ravaged the countryside like a conquering army of old. The same was true of the twelve hundred armed gendarmes that Deva brought from Mitrovica to Tirana in December. With Fitzthum, the SS chief in Albania, directing operations, the unit "arrested communists" and "sacked unreliable officials" along the way.[115] They became a thoroughly undisciplined version of storm troopers for the regime. Lange was able to produce some results beneficial to the Germans, but it is questionable whether the benefit was worth the negative impact of Kosovar brutality, or the 14,000 rifles and 425 machine guns and extensive supplies and money the Albanians extracted from the Germans.[116]

The second phase of the German plans, the construction of a regular Albanian army and a gendarmerie under German supervision but Albanian control, proved to be even more difficult. Because nothing of what the Italians had constructed remained after the German invasion, the Germans were required to start anew. The task was assigned to General Fitzthum and to General Gustav Fehn, the commander of the Twenty-first Corps. The project was doomed from the beginning, partially because Fitzthum, who had been sent by Himmler to advise the Albanian government on police matters (without an actual command), disliked working with the Albanian authorities.[117]

Following considerable reassessment, the Germans decided, in April 1944, that any more than 8,250 troops for the army and 2,400 for the gendarmerie would be unrealistic. Even this figure proved to be very optimistic, and far fewer were ultimately enlisted. The problems, aside from Fitzthum's attitude, included a lack of instructors, a lack of Albanian officers and non-commissioned officers, and a failed recruitment program. Finally, those Albanian soldiers who successfully completed the program proved to be highly unreliable. After the operation turned into a fiasco, Fitzthum wrote angrily to Himmler that one battalion dissolved after being attacked by a few planes and the rest just disappeared.[118]

The final attempt to use Albanians as support troops, equally unsuccessful, was Fitzthum's notion of creating an Albanian SS division under direct German command. Himmler took personal interest in this project, recalling the legendary elite Bosnian-Herzogovinian regiments that had fought for the Habsburgs in World War I.[119] But Neubacher objected, arguing that an SS detachment was incompatible with the notion of an independent Albania. With the help of the Foreign Ministry, as well pressure from SS General Ernst Kaltenbrunner, Himmler was initially dissuaded. By February 1944, however, because of increasing pressure on the Germans and because the Albanian government itself favored the plan, Hitler gave Himmler his personal approval for the creation of the SS "Skanderbeg" Division. Although this formation would remain under direct German control, its advertised agenda was to remain entirely Albanian. The "Skanderbeg" Division was to serve only in Kosova and was to protect ethnic Albania.[120]

Although the SS had originally planned a division of ten thousand to twelve thousand, just over six thousand were recruited. The division ultimately consisted of approximately fifteen hundred prisoners of war, natives of Kosova who had served in the Yugoslav army, plus remnants of the failed Albanian army and gendarmerie, volunteers from both old and new Albania, and finally draftees, from families with more than two sons. Although the division proved to be the government's and the Germans' most useful tool, its success, too, was limited. Neubacher tells us that the division, during the early stages of training, was poorly led into an action against the partisans and performed rather badly. This was followed by some desertions, partially because Serb partisans were attacking Kosova northeast of Gusinje. Units of the division gained an unenviable reputation, apparently preferring rape, pillage, and murder to fighting, particularly in Serbian areas. The Germans were forced to disarm battalions at Pec and Prizren, arresting the Albanian officers and sending them to the camp at Prishtina. One commanding officer was sent to prison in Germany. The units that remained intact were sent against the Serbs, which is why many had joined, that is, to fight the hereditary enemy. By October 1944 some thirty-five hundred, or more than half the original force, had deserted.[121] Himmler was ultimately forced to disband the unit prior to the German exodus from Albania, with the more reliable members transferred to the 14th SS Mountain Regiment of the 7th SS Mountain Division.[122]

Like Neubacher, the Germans on the spot in Albania tended to blame the Albanians for the failure of their schemes. The German commander of the SS "Skanderbeg" Division, Major General August Schmidhuber, explained his failure by suggesting that Albanians had not developed culturally since the time of Skënderbeg in the fifteenth century. In his estimation, they had developed no concept of "state" or "nation," indeed, they had vegetated. He argued that the legend of Albanian military heroics was just a saga and that he personally could chase them all around the world with a light grenade launcher. They went on the attack only as long as there was something to steal.[123] The staff of the Twenty-first Corps came to very similar conclusions, blaming the lack of nation-state traditions and the impetuosity of the Balkan temperament for the failure to sustain an effective security force. General Fitzthum, a particularly arrogant racist who had always had trouble interacting with Albanians, blamed all his troubles on the Albanian officer corps, which he maintained was not only worthless but filled with pederasts.[124]

Later, somewhat more detached observers within the Wehrmacht argued that the principal problem may have rested with the Germans themselves. Fitzthum not withstanding, many German officials were more than willing to work with the Albanians but complained that the structure that Neubacher had set up restricted contact between Germans and Albanians. It would have been logical, German critics maintained, for the Germans to work with local officials, from prefects on down, in their efforts to keep the Albanians calm. But Neubacher's representatives resisted German interference in Albanian affairs, even as late as September 1944, just two months before the German withdrawal.[125] The German plan to extend a level of autonomy in Albania, while often successful, clearly was not without its difficulties, and it lost the Germans some indigenous support.

The precise level of support the Germans and their puppet regime enjoyed in Albania is, of course, difficult to gage. That it was higher than in other areas of occupied Europe is clear. In Greece, for example, popular support for the resistance was almost universal. This can be explained by the wretched conditions German actions produced. Because Greece was of little economic value to the German war machine, the Germans had little interest in the health of the economy. German troops were allowed to strip the country clean, and the Allied blockade prevented resupply. The result was famine conditions in Athens and on some of the islands in 1941 to 1942.[126]

In Albania the Germans made a genuine effort, often to their own disadvantage, to leave the people with the impression that they possessed at least some level of autonomy. Albania was also spared at least some of the brutality the Germans inflicted on most of the remainder of the area under their control. There was no effort to forcibly recruit labor from old Albania for the Reich.[127] German military authorities complained that an opportunity was lost here, particularly in light of the fact that more and more Albanians volunteered as the security situation degenerated. But this was deemed impractical, first, because it was incompatible with the notion of Albanian independence and, second, because the Germans in Albania were ultimately faced with a labor shortage in significant areas such as road maintenance. The German authorities broached the idea of a domestic labor service, but Deva maintained that it would not work. The Germans ultimately agreed that the coercive power of the state would not suffice, and the idea was dropped.[128]

For the most part, the Germans also refrained from hunting, deporting, and exterminating Jews there. The small Jewish population in old Albania, estimated at 200 by the Wannsee conference, was protected by the independent status the Germans had conferred on the Albanian state.[129] Indeed, Albania is certainly the only state in Europe where the Jewish population actually grew during the Axis occupation; it is estimated that there were 1,800 Jews in Albania at the end of the war.[130] Albania became a haven for small numbers of Jews who managed to escape the horrors the Jews of Greece and Yugoslavia experienced.[131] Albanians took them in and have since been honored by the Israeli government for their efforts. This policy did not, however, apply to the Jews of Kosova, where 281 were arrested by the SS "Skanderbeg" and were most likely sent to the camp at Prishtina before being transported into the Reich.[132]

In the same vain, Mehdi Frashëri was able to negotiate an agreement with the Germans in February of 1944 that stipulated that Albanian prisoners would not be transported out of the country. Three camps in old Albania were used, and a new one in Prishtina was constructed in the summer of 1944.[133] Although the Germans did not always live up to this agreement, particularly near the end of the occupation, it did make for effective propaganda in early 1944.

Given these considerations, a German historian has estimated that the first Albanian government under the Germans was received favorably by 25 to 30 percent of the population, leaving 30 to 35 percent neutral and 35 to 45 percent in opposition.[134] Numerous Allied sources give evidence of widespread support for the Germans and their government. In the north and northeast support was widespread, particularly after the Germans took up the defense of the area against attacks by the Çetniks of Colonel Draza Mihailovic. In October, for example, the Çetniks attacked Place and Gusinje. The inhabitants put up fierce resistance but were ultimately saved by the Germans. Even in the south the Germans were not always unwelcome, since they seem to have treated the Albanians better than had some of their previous Balkan occupiers.[135] It is probably not an overstatement to suggest that the German position actually improved from month to month until the end of June 1944, five months before the German withdrawal from Albania.

This surprising level of support inevitably began to erode, however, principally because of the continued growth of the resistance and the reprisals the Germans exacted as a result. The continued growth of resistance was the single most important factor explaining the failure of German plans at pacification of the country through the construction of an independent regime with prestige and its own military authority for fighting the NLM.

CHAPTER 7

RESISTANCE TO THE GERMANS

The story of Albanian resistance to the Germans is one of complexity and controversy. Although the resistance picture in Albania was by no means simple under the Italians, the arrival of the German forces contributed to the further splintering of the movement. And astute German policy did much to reduce the effectiveness of the many pieces as well as help insure the failure of various efforts aimed at reconciliation. The Germans succeeded in pitting the various elements of the resistance against each other, ultimately co-opting all but the partisans. It is reasonable to argue that in doing so the Germans did much to insure a partisan victory. But at the same time, German policy also allowed for the subjugation of Albania with a comparatively small number of second-level troops, often Russian former POWs. In a military sense, the strategy of the resistance can hardly be considered successful. In a political sense, the partisans were able to insure dominance in a postwar Albania.

Resistance to the Germans began rather tentatively, principally because of the German invasion's speed and effectiveness. The Italian collapse resulted in a momentary power vacuum that the resistance groups--partisans, nationalists, and independent chieftains—seem to have taken advantage of, each grabbing as much territory as possible in anticipation of an Allied invasion. Abaz Kupi took Kruja in the northwest, and Muharrem Bajraktari took Kukës in the northeast. The partisans, who were much more active, not only consolidated their hold on much of the southern countryside but also occupied Korça, Gjirokastra, Elbasan, and Berat. The BK, by now somewhat less prepared to pursue military activity, was active in the area around Vlora.[1] But this activity proved to be little more than a minor obstacle once German forces poured into Albania. Although the nationalist chiefs and the partisans could occupy virtually undefended towns, they were less willing to actively resist battle-hardened German troops.

There seem to have been a number of reasons why this was the case. First, most Albanians believed that with the Italian collapse, an Allied invasion was imminent. The Allies did much to spread this idea widely, in what was called operation "Bodyguard," an attempt to draw attention away from the projected Normandy landings.[2] None of the groups in Albania was willing to expend scant resources against the Germans, who they assumed would soon be removed by the Allies. And the Albanians had a much higher regard for German military prowess than they had had for the Italians. It is generally accepted, therefore, that the German invasion encountered little resistance, precisely how much will remain in dispute.

Hermann Neubacher maintains in his book, although he certainly is exaggerating, that the Germans encountered no unfriendly act on the part of the Albanians. He asserted that the BK did not resist the Germans,[3] and this is supported by Schliep, who accepted the assurances of Mithat Frashëri that although the BK had declared itself against the Axis during the Italian occupation, it would take no hostile act against the Germans.[4] While a British BLO argued that Kupi "fought like a lion," Neubacher reported that Kupi remained in the woods.[5] It seems, however, that both the BK and Kupi made some initial limited anti-German moves. Abaz Ermenji, a member of the BK central council, resisted the Germans briefly, and Kupi struck at the Germans once on 21 September but then decided to await developments before committing his forces. The discrepancy in accounts likely stems from the fact that the Germans were often unaware of who their attackers were.

But similar discrepancies can be found regarding partisan resistance. Socialist historiography suggests that the partisans fiercely resisted the German invasion, inflicting some 3,000 dead in one battle on 14 September.[6] While this is certainly an exaggeration, the partisans, as usual, did most of the fighting. The partisans had demonstrated their attitude toward the Germans early by attacking a German convoy on the road from Korça to Ioannina in July, prior to the invasion. The Germans responded by destroying the town of Borova near Korça and killing 107 civilians.[7] German documents mention some further hostile action in September, organized and carried out by communist bands.[8]

The Germans responded to this scattered resistance, as they had to the July attack, with swift and brutal reprisals, hoping to quickly discourage further resistance prior to the institution of their soft political program. This brutality was accompanied by the rather naive suggestion that the partisans simply go home now that the Italians had been ejected. Neither of these strategies was particularly successful, the resistance continued, although not, to be sure, in the same fashion and in the same form as it had under the Italians.

The German invasion had a profound impact on Albanian resistance, the most immediate manifestation of which was a further distancing between the

NLM and other real or at least potential resistance groups, as well as the splintering of the NLM, a process that began with the failure of the Mukje Agreements. The BK, which had long since ceased to oppose the occupation actively as a organization, was ordered on 7 October, by its central council, to cease hostilities—not to say that there was much—against the Germans, and most of the BK units complied.[9] As under the Italians, the BK hoped to avoid reprisals, a particular problem for the BK, since many of the strongest BK centers were in towns and exposed districts of the coastal plain, areas under strict German control. This, they hoped, would increase their political stock among Albanians. The BK also hoped that their general attitude would encourage the Germans to supply them with weapons for the inevitable showdown with the partisans.[10] At this point, much of the BK slipped into a more complete collaboration than they had committed to under the Italians. BK bands first began to inform on NLM activity to avoid reprisals; then they began to receive funds from the Germans and were allowed to purchase weapons both from the collaborationist government and the Germans. Soon they were administering large sections of the country for both. By the beginning of February 1944 BLOs reported that it was becoming increasingly difficult for the partisans to attack the Germans because German units were frequently being screened by the BK and that BK forces—who actively fought the partisans—had become a normal part of any German force.[11] This support for the Germans cannot be explained as an ideological shift. The organization had no illusions about a German victory, and much of it never disavowed its support for a democratic regime built on broad social and economic reform. The move was a calculated, tactical one that turned out to be disastrous.

Although the evidence of widespread collaboration is extensive, to condemn roundly all elements of the BK as quislings would be a disservice to many. The principal danger of explaining BK makeup and policy is the ease with which almost anything can be proved about them. Most BK members denounced collaboration and whenever a BK member collaborated, the organization would either deny that the offending party was even affiliated with the BK or denounce them openly, but keep contact with them clandestinely.[12] Some in the BK were dedicated to resistance to all invaders. On 21 November 1943 a BK pamphlet, probably the work of Skënder Muço, bitterly attacked the Germans and Albanian collaborators as the barbaric enemy. Muço, the BK chief of the Vlora area, and member of the BK council, offered to fight under direct British orders if London helped to control the partisans. In mid-November the council itself under Mithat Frashëri gave the British a signed document, to be discussed later, indicating that the BK would now actively fight the Germans.[13] This agreement, as with many others, was never honored by the BK. From the time of the German invasion, despite a number of exceptions, the rule for the BK was collaboration.

The Creation of the Legality Movement

Perhaps even more important than the further estrangement of the BK and the partisans was a break within the ranks of the partisans. In October 1943 Abaz Kupi returned to traditional forms of Albanian politics, which required that one maintain friendly relations with all sides. While he refused to allow the construction of NLM administrative units in his area, he still sent people to NLM meetings. At the same time, however, he consolidated his power base by organizing his own faction called Legality. Discussions had begun in September, and a Zogist declaration—signed by numerous northern leaders, including Muharrem Bajraktari, Cen Elezi, and Fiqri Dine—was issued. A Legality council was formed in October with Zog himself declared as titular leader.[14] Legality established links with the independent northern chieftains, the BK, the collaborationist government, and the Germans. Kupi's goal seems to have been to construct a broadly based nationalistic movement that favored some role for Zog in an ethnic, independent Albania. Ultimately Kupi cast his net too far and included many individuals who were compromised by both the Italians and the Germans.[15]

Even with this support, Kupi's numbers remained small. Although there were widely divergent views on how many men he could raise, even the most liberal estimates suggested that his maximum strength was under eight thousand, five thousand of whom came from his own tribal area.[16] The leaders were mostly drawn from former Zogist army officers and officials, and the rank and file included mostly Moslems not particularly interested in politics but attached by bonds of booty, sentiment, and tribal loyalty. Because they were mountaineers they exhibited a good deal more fighting ability than did the southerners—at least before the NLM trained its units—although Kupi's policy rarely allowed his troops to demonstrate their effectiveness.

Kupi's policies ran counter to his long history of resistance and proven patriotism. Indeed, his actions or lack thereof, ran counter to his stated program as set down in the newspaper *Atdheu,* or "Fatherland," which he founded to accompany his movement. Kupi's program, introduced at the first Zogist conference in November, included a call for war against the oppressor to free Albania from foreign occupation; the establishment of an Albanian nation with all of its ethnic rights (a reference to new Albania); the return of Zog under a democratic kingdom; and the implementation of significant social reforms, including significant agrarian reform and the institution of a social insurance system. Zog's role in delivering Albania from anarchy was emphasized, and the German propaganda suggesting that Zog was uninterested in Kosova was simply denied.[17]

This was fairly sophisticated stuff, perhaps as some Foreign Office observers suggested, the most subtle and clear to appear in Albania during the war.[18] Whereas the partisans and the collaborationists blackguarded each other with eighteenth-century invective couched often in terms of Oriental imagery, Kupi had presented a progressive coherent program. It is more than likely that Zog, by now an experienced and clever statesman, rather than Kupi, the illiterate tribal leader, was responsible for its inception. In any case, Kupi's program had the potential to attract wide support. But rather than act on it, Kupi continued his fence-sitting and non-belligerence.

The Nationalist Chieftains

Apart from Kupi, northern Albania was host to a series of other nationalist groups involved in constant realignment and maneuvering. Some were independent Zogists, like many of the Dibra chieftains. Most followed the traditional policy of frequently changing their position and attempting to insure their success by placing members of their families in every rival camp. The powerful Elezi family serves as a good example. Cen, the head of the family and generally considered to be a Zogist, accepted the rank and salary of colonel in the government forces. His brother Ersat was the principal NLM organizer in north Dibra, while his nephew was an important partisan commander. His two sons, Gani and Islam, maintained contact with Kupi and the other nationalists.[19]

The most important figures among the remaining northern nationalists were two who had already acquired some prominence: Gani Bey Kryeziu and Colonel Muharrem Bajraktari. Following the failure of the 1941 united front opposition, Kryeziu was arrested by the Italians and interned in the concentration camp at Ventotene. After the collapse of Italy, he was released and immediately returned to Albania, taking to the mountains to resist the Germans. Gani Kryeziu, with his two thousand retainers, continued to work for a united front and gave valuable assistance to the partisans. Kryeziu was consistently encouraged by the British to step up his efforts, which he agreed to do after receiving assurances of British material and political support. He would receive little of either.[20]

Muharrem Bajraktari was perhaps one of the most colorful of the nationalist chiefs and, like many of the other northern tribal chieftains, saw himself as the future of Albania and hoped to convince all interested parties, in particular the British, that there really was no alternative to his leadership. Again, like many of the other northern tribal chieftains, Bajraktari seemed totally out of touch with wartime conditions both in Albania and abroad. This is perhaps best illustrated by a curious "report" that he sent to Anthony Eden in January 1944. In it he maintained that Albania would be crucial to the future of British policy in the Balkans, which he suggested should be anti-Slav, anti-Serb, and anticommunist. Further, Bajraktari offered to foment a revolution against the Germans in exchange for an extensive shopping list of weaponry and up to one million pounds sterling. While this all seemed ludicrous, it is important to recognize that the only difference between Bajraktari and many of the other northern chieftains is that Bajraktari committed his thoughts to paper.[21]

As tribal leader of Lumë, Bajraktari controlled no more than one thousand men. He had fought against the Italians and participated in the founding of the Legality movement but signed a *besa* with the Germans that constituted a nonaggression pact. He upheld this pact until August 1944, when he attacked as the Germans were preparing to withdraw, far too little and far too late. Nevertheless, following this break with the Germans, Bajraktari was invited to a conference with the partisans, where he was told that he could either join them or die. He shot his way out of the meeting, losing at least one of his bodyguards, and returned to the mountains more determined than ever to pursue his independent and ultimately disastrous policies.[22]

The German invasion had helped convince Kupi and most of the northern tribal leaders to adopt a policy that most of the BK had adopted under the Italians: to avoid reprisals and possible destruction, to wait for the defeat of the Axis before encouraging a national uprising, and to preserve military strength for the inevitable confrontation with the communists. Kupi and some of the chiefs actually succeeded in obtaining weapons and material, usually in only small quantities, from both the British and the Germans. But this was their only success.

The nationalists, like their counterparts in Greece and Yugoslavia, were shortsighted in terms of both world affairs and the changing realities in Albania. They were unaware that anything but unrelenting opposition to the Germans would doom them in the postwar world. In terms of domestic politics, they made the mistake of attempting to protect a social order that the war was rapidly undermining.[23] Many of the BK leaders, Kupi, and the other Geg chieftains constituted the social and political ruling class of the vanishing old order. All of them felt that they could only pursue military operations as long as they could insure adequate protection for this order from enemy reprisals. Failure to insure this protection, they were convinced, would have led to rejection of their leadership by their own society. Prior to the Italian invasion, operations might have been possible, but the Italians had constructed an extensive road network that left few safe harbors into which to withdraw.

To complicate matters further, the highly regional northern nationalists stuck to their traditional rules of engagement, the basis of which made it nearly impossible, without a *besa*, for one leader to withdraw his forces into the territory of another. Under these conditions, small-scale guerrilla warfare of the partisan variety seemed out of the question for the Geg chieftains. A general uprising was really the only option, but as the occupation grew longer and the conservation of strength became more and more important, Kupi and the northern chieftains, like the BK, slipped slowly into collaboration. Kupi, like Bajraktari, eventually signed a *besa*, a nonaggression pact, with the Germans.[24]

Whereas the Italians had faced resistance from various quarters, the Germans, then, had only to contend with the increasingly communist-dominated NLM. The Germans were by no means unhappy with this situation; indeed, it was in their interest to threaten the nationalists with the prospect of a communist Albania. As long as the communist-dominated partisans remained a force, the nationalists would be coerced, to a greater or lesser extent, to orient themselves toward the Germans, who did much to protect the interests of the nationalists. It was, then, in the German interest to keep the partisans relatively strong, although not to the extent that serious damage could be done to German communications.

The German Winter Offensive

To insure that the partisans did not become too strong, the Germans launched a series of offensives against the partisans, powerful enough to inflict serious damage on them but not to destroy them completely. At the beginning of November 1943, when the Germans launched their first antipartisan operation, the resistance picture was as follows: northern Albania and Kosova were quiet; the middle of the country around Tirana was filled with many bands, including those of the BK, Kupi, Bajraktari, Peza, and the partisans—with increasing tension between the BK and the partisan units; and much of southern Albania's land and the town of Berat were controlled by the partisans. The Germans estimated that the partisans could muster sixteen thousand to eighteen thousand fighters, with the nationalist groups, not as well organized, controlling perhaps eight thousand.[25]

Against this background, the Germans in early November launched their first campaign against the partisans, operation "505." The Germans did not squander their resources on unnecessary operations; rather, they confined themselves to clearing areas potentially dangerous to their communications. The Germans would seldom molest partisans in areas where they were not dangerous. Operation "505," directed against the Peza region close to Tirana, aimed to remove the possible threat to the roads linking Durrës, Tirana, and Elbasan. Within eight days the Germans declared the campaign a success, having killed some 100 "bandits" and Italians and having taken 1,650 prisoners, who, by an earlier agreement, were turned over to the Albanian civil authorities. The Germans also reported the capture of a great deal of heavy and light infantry weapons.[26]

This operation, the beginning of what is often referred to as the winter campaign, had succeeded where the Italians had so often failed, for a number of reasons. The battle-hardened German troops employed in this operation proved to be quite effective, some brought in for the purpose from Greece. Perhaps more important, however, the Germans used tactics that stood a greater chance of success, given the Albanian terrain. While the Italians had used larger units—at least partially because they were afraid of the Albanians—the Germans used small units, which clearly had a better chance of maintaining the element of surprise. The Germans usually operated in small columns of 50 to 150, with light machine guns and small mortars.[27] Like the Italians, the Germans engaged in terror, although it seems to have been somewhat less indiscriminate.

The Peza campaign was quickly followed by two more, "Roter Mann" and "Edelweiss," which drove the partisans out of Berat and the area between Dibra and Peshkopi. In December a further series of operations was initiated, with the most important being "1828" against the NLM staff and groups of BLOs and "Bergkessel" against Mehmet Shehu commanding the First Partisan Brigade, which was rapidly becoming the elite unit among the partisans.[28] Both of these operations, too, experienced some success. Hoxha and other members of the NLM council were nearly wiped out, only to be saved at the last moment by Shehu and his first brigade in something similar to Mao's Long March.[29] The Germans were able, nonetheless, to shatter and disperse the partisans as a military and political force north of the Shkumbin River, where no more that two or three nondescript and poor-spirited partisan *çetas* remained in place.

Although they all feared communism, some northern chiefs, in particular Kryeziu and Bajraktari, gave the remains of the partisans in the north some shelter. Other northern chiefs at least did not attack them, for various reasons. Most chiefs believed that the British and the Americans would eventually arrive to drive the communists out and that it was therefore unnecessary to expend scant resources against the partisans. Others recognized that not only were the partisans Albanians but that in many cases the children of tribal leaders were active in partisan units. The principal motivation for this reticence to attack the weakened partisans, however, may have been the simple notion that the chiefs wanted quiet—their prestige depended on it.[30]

The British, too, were significantly impacted by the German winter campaigns. In early January 1944 Brigadier Edmund F. "Trotsky" Davies, the commanding BLO and highest-ranking British officer to take part in the resistance struggle, was shot and wounded by a BK band and handed over to the Germans. Kupi, demonstrating his increasing pro-British line, reacted strongly to this attack and went so far as to send people to kill Aziz Biçaku, the BK commander responsible for the attack.[31] In addition to Davies's capture, the British mission was essentially wrecked by the campaigns.[32] This was a serious blow to British prestige and, because Davies's diary was captured along with him, required some shift in plans. It was a blow to the resistance in general, as it deprived the partisans of needed material. The Germans recognized the significance of this event and reported it in the official *Völkischer Beobachter*.[33]

In January and February German ground operations, supported in the air by ME110s, shifted to the south. The principal goal was the control of the road network, important to the Germans as a secondary route from Greece, supplementing the primary road from Thessaloníki up the Vardar Valley to Skopje. The Germans were content to leave the mountains to the partisans. Indeed, neither the Germans nor the partisans seems to have seen the south as a main battlefield—the Germans pulled their punches on their attacks, and the partisans did not go after the roads as much as they might have. They did not overprovoke the Germans in the winter; they could not afford it.[34]

One of the principal reasons the partisans were in no position to push the invaders too hard was their increasingly violent struggle with the nationalists, another immediate result of the German invasion. Although Hoxha and Albanian socialist historians deny that these struggles were anything more than patriots fighting traitors, less subjective observers describe the clashes as a civil war. Although perhaps minor in scope, the partisan-nationalist struggle contained the bitterness and ferocity found when members of the same family fight on opposite sides. Traditional ethnic considerations, exacerbated by an occasional blood feud, quickly fell in line with political differences to make the war unstoppable. The various groups involved were willing to cooperate only when they felt unable to assume the responsibilities of power alone.

The Beginning of the Civil War

Prior to the German invasion, the partisan-nationalist struggle had been principally confined to a propaganda war, although skirmishes, some of them blood feud oriented, had occurred as early as March 1943.[35] But within weeks of the Italian collapse, more serious armed clashes were reported between the partisans and the BK. It seems clear that the principal responsibility for initiating these clashes must lie with Hoxha, who near the end of October ordered the liquidation of the BK. He assumed that the partisans could finish the BK in several weeks while holding their own against the Germans and developing a military presence around Tirana. These estimates proved to be overly optimistic.[36] Initially these clashes were limited in scope and took the form of raids on each other's villages, house burnings, and executions. As the struggle became more fierce, the Germans began to actively intervene on behalf of the BK. Once the partisans took a BK village, more often than not, the Germans—if their strategic interests were involved—appeared and handed it back to the BK. Once the German winter offensive demonstrated signs of success, BK units began to take an active part. By February Neubacher estimated that some ten thousand nationalists were aiding the Germans in one way or another, divided into approximately fifteen groups, with the BK making up half of that number.[37]

By late winter, then, the NLM found itself in considerable difficulty. Those units that had escaped the Germans and the nationalists were short on everything—food, clothing, and ammunition. Not only was the British ground effort in disarray, with the loss of personal and drop sights, but even if it were not, the weather would have prevented resupply from the air. The partisans further suffered from a lack of medicine and the impossibility of keeping reserves. The desertion rate was reported to be 20 to 30 percent, with many of these people defecting to Kupi.[38] Casualty figures were also quite high. Albanian socialist historiography maintains that the partisans lost more than 1,000 to death in the winter campaign.[39] German figures put the number somewhat higher and report 2,239 dead by the end of January, 401 dead in February, and 236 in March, at which point the Germans maintained that the government was in control of all prefectures except Gjirokastra in the south.[40] It is not surprising that the partisan ranks suffered considerable disillusionment. In an unusually candid moment, Hoxha, writing to Nako Spiru in March, conceded that "the situation is difficult, very difficult indeed.... But it is precisely under such difficult circumstances that we must try not to lose our bearing."[41]

Some of the British officers had by this point all but written the partisans off. In the middle of January the Foreign Office received a report arguing that the civil war had ended, that most of the country would go to the BK, and that Peza and Baba Faya would soon defect from the NLM. Other reports suggested that Kupi's fortunes were on the rise. One month later Colonel D. Talbot-Rice of the Ministry of Economic Warfare minuted that the NLM continued to reap the consequences of their folly in provoking hostilities with the BK. He concluded that in terms of the resistance picture in Albania as a whole, the north was completely tranquil, in the middle of Albania resistance had been reduced to a flicker, and in the south the Germans had cleared the road system.[42]

The nationalists reacted to these events in a number of ways. Some of the more clear-thinking elements began to show increasing interest in insuring their future by identifying more closely with the war effort against the Germans. Some members of the BK even began calling themselves Zogist in order to distance themselves from the collaborationist BK.[43] But the greatest number of nationalists took the opportunity to move closer to the collaborationist politicians. The government convinced the Germans to allow for the inclusion of more members of the BK. Neubacher agreed, although he made the limits of German tolerance quite clear. The government was able to broaden itself in January by the co-optation of three prominent BK members, but it was warned to avoid some of the less trustworthy elements among the BK, in particular individuals such as Skënder Muço in Vlora. Other neutral groups, including much of the leadership of the Moslems and the Orthodox Church, also moved closer to the government. Both the government and the Germans were clearly pleased. Mehdi Frashëri extended his control by using Deva to finally root out internal opposition to his regime in some Albanian towns. He also used his new prestige to increase his credibility among the population at large. He was able to raise the visibility of his government, which was further enhanced by the introduction of new, although not particularly effective, land reform programs.[44]

Partisan Resurgence

But the success of the German winter campaign proved to be quite momentary, and the partisans proved to be much more resilient than the Germans, the British, or many Albanians had anticipated. Despite the German blows, the partisans had certain long-term assets. The least tangible, but perhaps the most important, was described by Margaret Hasluck as "discipline, energy and clarity of aim."[45] The partisan goal of reestablishing an independent Albania under a social system based upon equality, which increasingly effective propaganda stressed, was something for which many were willing to sacrifice. Conversely, few were willing to make similar sacrifices for the reestablishment of the old social system under Zog, which had clearly failed.

More tangible considerations that help to explain partisan revival included some of the basic tactics of guerrilla war. As in most battles against German units, the partisans were often routed during the winter campaigns, but they were able to drift away and regroup. They were able to do this in part because many wore civilian clothes. This led to a growing German mistrust of civilians as well as increasing repression and atrocities against unarmed peasants and shepherds.[46] As during the Italian occupation, repression swelled the ranks of the resistance.

The government soon began to complain that following a short period of increasing prestige, its general situation was deteriorating because its credibility was slowing being undermined. The Germans, who never trusted the new BK people in the government, did not give the government the weapons they had hoped for, leading the population to assume, quite correctly, that the Germans did not trust their puppet regime. The government also complained that it was not given enough food nor the transportation to distribute it. This left many regions of Albania, particularly in the south, facing rapidly deteriorating conditions. This situation helped to convince the population that the government was unable to provide for the basic needs of the people, which of course was the case. The government complained that the Germans were continuing to ignore its request for foreign recognition, the establishment of a passport office, and upgrading Schliep's consulate to embassy status. The government argued that without the resolution of some or all of these problems, it could never hope to achieve legitimacy.[47]

Schliep added that the partisan revival could at least partially be traced to news from the east, including the significant German defeat at Stalingrad. Allied air attacks, which were stepped up in the spring, were helping to undermine the notion of German invincibility, as well as the notion that the puppet government had the power to protect the people.

The first Allied air attack from Italy occurred on 13 October 1943 and was directed principally against the Tirana Airport. Although the bombs damaged or destroyed eight planes, some fuel depots, and an electrical plant, many civilians were killed and houses destroyed. Following reports from British liaison officers that this had left a bad impression on much of the country, even the remote southwest, and a direct request from Hoxha to avoid a repeat of the October raid, the British Royal Air Force became more careful. In following raids (seven more through February 1944) the Allies hit principally military targets. British naval bombardment of Durrës was also primarily restricted to military installations.[48] With the onset of better weather, these raids increased and impacted many of Albania's major towns. Schliep told Berlin that now (in March 1944) the raids' principal effect was to turn the people against the Germans and the collaborationist government, which seemed powerless to prevent them. The collaborationist government was concerned enough to appeal to the Vatican for help, claiming that a neutral country was unjustly being victimized.[49] The British Foreign Office took little notice, with Michael Rose, a second secretary at the Southern Department, minuting "the answer is that the Albanians should kick the Germans out and then no one will trouble them anymore, except a few Greeks and a few Yugoslavs who want to swallow all their territory."[50]

Another factor that helped to facilitate a partisan revival was a significant change in the configuration of German troops in Albania. As Germany's general military situation continued to deteriorate, the experienced German troops in Albania were needed elsewhere. The 279th Infantry Division was withdrawn and sent to the Russian front in early March 1944, and the 100th Jäger Division was sent to Hungary at the end of the month. While they were replaced by units composed of nearly as many troops, the quality of the replacements was poor. One of the replacement units was the Second Brandenburg Division brought in from Greece, made up of static garrison troops containing large elements of Armenians and Moslem troops from Bulgaria, Russia, and the Caucasus region who had been recruited from POW and concentration camps. The Second Brandenburg, made up of individuals who had a reputation for not being particularly happy in the German army, was supported by a small mixed formation from army group F in Yugoslavia composed of Poles, Czechs, and French from the Rhineland. Although the Germans had planned further small offensives in April, they were called off partially because of the nature of the troops available.[51] It was not long before they began shooting their officers and defecting to the nationalists or partisans.

British Aid to the Resistance

The partisan revival was also aided by the resumption of supply drops by the British. In December 1943 the 334th Wing, the unit responsible for supplying the Albanians, was moved from Tocra in Cyrenaica to Brindisi, which considerably shortened the distance its C47s (Dakotas) had to fly. Despite the short distance, the weather naturally had an impact and reduced the amount of material the British could get to the Albanian resistance. In January 25.8 tons were dropped, of which 6.5 tons went to the nationalists in the north. In February 20.6 tons were dropped, of which 7.3 tons went to the nationalists. In March tonnage was increased to 29 and in April 27.8 tons were dropped, but this constituted a net increase for the partisans since they received all of it. Because this amount was little in comparison to the total requirements of the partisans, British material aid cannot be considered decisive. Still, much of it came at critical times and therefore constituted an important contribution.[52] How important it was remains a matter of considerable controversy.

The role played by the British in Albania during the German occupation, in general, is a matter of considerable dispute. For the British, the principal problem was determining a cohesive policy toward Albanian resistance, a decision made much more difficult as a result of the German invasion. Under the Italian occupation, when most resistance groups actually resisted, British policy was quite simple. McLean was ordered to arrange for the supply of all those groups resisting the Italians, while attempting to forge some degree of unity. With the German invasion, not only did Albanian resistance fragment further, but large sections of it, including groups that had resisted the Italians and received British supply drops, ceased resisting altogether. The British, then, found themselves facing the problem of whom to support. This issue was further complicated by political questions dealing with the future of Albania. The British and Allied statement of December 1942, which called for the reestablishment of an independent Albania, remained the basis of British policy. The question of the nature of this state, its government, and its borders remained a mystery both to the Albanians and, it seems, to the British. While the policymakers tried to sort these difficulties out, the ambiguity concerning support and the future of Albania adversely impacted the BLOs on the ground in Albania. Many began to resent their lack of instructions; in late October 1943 one asked somewhat plaintively of his government, "when will you do something to help us[?] . . . What is our policy?"[53]

Aware of these problems, and as a consequence of increasing Balkan resistance in general, the British chiefs of staff began paying more attention to the Albanians in October 1943. By this point the role of SOE was somewhat diminished, however. Changes in command arrangements in the Mediterranean and Balkan areas had transferred air operations and the execution of all special operations to the regular military and the Balkan Air Force, which had been created on 1 June 1943. Of course, the Foreign Office continued its major role in political policymaking. Although now thoroughly subordinate to the armed forces, SOE (which frequently changed its name and was known by different names in different areas) continued to provide technical assistance and advice, and its channels and agents continued to be used.[54]

In October 1943 SOE, in its new diminished role, was instructed to send Brigadier E. F. "Trotsky" Davies, with a large staff, to Albania to make recommendations about whether the recognition of any form of government in exile might be useful and about how to facilitate unity. In the meantime the British proposed to back any group that would fight. Davies, who after McLean, became the second of four British chief liaison officers in Albania, stated, "It had sounded so simple. In Albania I was to find the whole matter very complex and difficult."[55]

Davies first contacted Hoxha, who agreed to stop his recently initiated attacks on the BK if the BK agreed to attack the Germans. Hoxha assumed that his would never happen, and with Davies's first meeting with the BK leadership it seemed that Hoxha was right. On 8 November Davies made contact with the BK council, and during their first meeting it was clear to Davies that the BK had no intention of fighting the Germans and every intention of fighting the NLM. The council quickly reverted to traditional Albanian politics, however, and on 9 November—literally overnight—told Davies that they had seen the light. The council verbally agreed not to fight the NLM and produced a written agreement, signed by Mithat Frashëri, that the BK would now fight the Germans.[56] Davies brought this document to Hoxha, who refused to recognize the pledge, believing it to be little more than eyewash. Hoxha, of course, was right.

On the basis of these initial meetings and his personal observations, Davies recommended a number of courses of action to British policymakers. First, he suggested that an outside Albanian committee or government would be of little use. He gauged the influence of exiled leaders, such as Zog, to be minimal. Then he suggested that based on his signed agreement with the BK, the British should continue to support all groups until they demonstrated that they were unwilling to resist the Germans, which most, of course, had already done. Davies also issued a list of instructions for the BLOs then in Albania, which included (1) not intervening in the civil war, (2) assisting in organizing resistance against the Germans, and (3) gathering of all possible evidence of BK attacks on the Germans or collaboration with them. The Foreign Office cabled back that it would be guided by Davies's suggestions until he saw fit to make a change.[57]

Although Davies's memoirs fail to mention it, by December he did recommend a complete change in British policy. He wired that it was now imperative to denounce the BK and the Zogists. Although he found all sides in the Albanian resistance to be "incredibly narrow-minded, bigoted, biased, stupid and touchy," because the partisans had encountered mixed German-BK units and because Kupi had not moved, Davies recommended that the British quickly, finally, and openly declare for and exclusively support the partisans.[58] Davies was certainly right and he may have forced the Foreign Office to make a decision, but this was his last message. Within a week he was a prisoner and the Foreign Office was off the hook, refusing to make such a significant shift in policy on the strength of one unconfirmed message. With the removal of Davies, the British found themselves back where they had started and Hoxha, although he did not know it, had lost his best chance to construct a relationship with the British similar to that enjoyed by Tito.

The vacuum left by the capture of Davies was eventually filled by the official heads of mission Norman Wheeler and then Alan Palmer, in the south and by Billy McLean in the north. McLean, an enthusiastic anticommunist, had by this point developed an intense dislike for Hoxha and a genuine admiration for Kupi, with whom he spent most of his time. Unlike Davies, who had believed that the civil war was irrevocably started and that the partisans would certainly win, McLean believed that he had at least a 50 percent chance of reconciling the NLM and the nationalists and thereby preventing a complete communist takeover. In January 1944, on McLean's recommendation, the Foreign Office decided to refrain from immediately denouncing the BK and to continue support for the partisans, while at the same time building up Kupi as a political and military counterweight to the partisans and encouraging him to fight.[59] Consensus II, the mission to Kupi, was entrusted to Julian Amery, David Smiley, and McLean, the latter of whom began to act as something of an agent for Kupi. McLean and Smiley, who had been withdrawn after the arrival of Davies, were returned to Albania, along with Amery, in April 1944.[60]

Two months earlier McLean might have had a flicker of a reason to be optimistic. On 12 February a meeting took place in northern Albania between members of most groups involved in Albania's complex political picture. Several northern NLM representatives, who were out of touch with the NLM command in the south, met with Bajraktari, some Zogists, Kryeziu, and other band leaders. Before much could become of this, however, the Germans, who seemed to be aware of this meeting as well as the possible consequences, moved in and quiet was maintained in the north.[61]

But by April, when the Consensus II mission arrived, McLean's policy was not only unwise but entirely unrealistic. Despite the disasters of the winter, Hoxha had been able to continue the rapid formation of brigades. By May SOE (now called Force 266) estimated that partisan strength was close to 20,000, with 13,000 organized into twelve brigades. Hoxha claimed 35,000, but this figure undoubtedly included the territorials, who were essentially reservists. These figures indicate remarkable expansion. Partisan confidence was demonstrated by a complete structural reorganization. In April, perhaps prematurely and certainly for more political reasons than military ones, Hoxha transformed his partisan *çetas* into a conventional Albanian National Liberation Army, with traditional ranks, divisions, and corps. Shehu's first brigade became the center of the ANLA's first division.[62]

Not only were there more partisans, but they were also, by April, much better fighters. The first British appraisal of the fighting qualities of the partisans was, for the most part, quite negative, similar to the German evaluation of the nationalists. After witnessing an attack by 880 partisans on a village in 1943, and the rapid dispersal of those partisans by some 300 Germans, a British observer complained that the partisans were little more than "a thorough band of rascals, of no fighting ability whatsoever."[63] Although these comments can certainly be written off as pompous exaggerations, at least one official Albanian socialist view is no less preposterous. Lefter Kasneci, in his book *Steeled in the Heat of Battle*, would have us believe that every partisan was "a brilliant sharpshooter."[64] But it seems clear that the partisans left the impression in 1943 that there was room for improvement in their fighting capabilities. This impression may at least partially be explained, as Harry Fultz does, by the fact that the partisans often had little to fight with, in terms of guns and ammunition. But it is also clear that many of the early fighters, with their background as urban southerners, had little experience with this type of activity.[65]

Although partisan battle reports were almost always stunning exaggerations, by the spring of 1944 more objective evidence concerning partisan fighting qualities suggested an important increase in expertise. When Philip Leake, the head of the Albanian section of SOE visited Albania for two weeks in March 1944, he reported that the fighting qualities and skill of the partisans had greatly improved. The partisans were now capable of resisting German drives and could undertake coordinated offensive action. Although he found the central council of the NLM "inclined to be dilatory and oriental" and the training of the various brigades to be uneven, the partisans were again threatening German communications.[66]

Partisan morale and discipline had improved as well, partly because of the emphasis put on political and social instruction. When a brigade halted in camp, commanders oversaw military exercises while commissars, the heads of technical sections, organized educational activity and cultural events. Discipline, an important part of this educational system, was carried out at all military levels, and possible punishments included (1) a public analysis of the crime, conducted by the commissar in a unit assembly, (2) prohibition of the perpetrator from singing partisan songs, (3) removal of partisan badge and prohibition from making partisan propaganda and from joining partisan assemblies, and (4) death. Extra duty was imposed for minor faults, but only if some form of public disgrace could not be arranged. Fraternization between men and women, the latter making up some 9 percent of the partisan forces, was treated with particular severity. Observers credited this educational activity, propaganda, strict discipline, and emphasis on moral values with causing often halfhearted recruits to become enthusiastic partisans and with turning peasant volunteers into fighting units of first-class morale.[67]

The revived partisans began demonstrating their presence as early as March 1944, when Mehmet Shehu, with about two hundred men from the first brigade, marched into central Albanian regions controlled by Peza and Kupi. Although little fighting took place, the incursion made it clear that the NLM had not given up on Albania north of the Shkumbin River and that it intended to renew the struggle as quickly as possible. This essentially symbolic act was soon followed by the partisans' seizing the initiative in various areas in the south and then, on 15 April and somewhat prematurely, Hoxha's ordering the ANLA to take the offensive everywhere. The army made an effort to comply, and all the brigades began moving: the first in the mountains west and north of Korça; the fourth working in conjunction with the first around Pogradec and Lake Ohrid; the fifth around Vlora; the sixth south of Gjirokastra; the seventh around Berat. There was even some revival in the north, with the second brigade putting itself together again in Peza and a çeta resurfacing in Dibra.[68] Schliep reported on 11 April that there was quiet in the north and in the center to the Elbasan-Struga road. But the partisans again controlled much of the open country in the south and were pressing Vlora, Berat, and Korça.[69]

The government of Mitrovica and the Germans were forced to take notice and act. That there was concern was first indicated by stepped-up government anticommunist propaganda at the beginning of March.[70] The Germans stepped up their efforts as well, relying on the traditional arguments used since the beginning of the occupation. Of considerable impact was their propaganda line that while the partisans claimed simply to be reformist or even communist, they were in fact the advance guard of Pan-Slavism and as such the enemies of all

Albanians. Of course, Kosova continued to be a central feature of German propaganda. The Germans continued to maintain, and rightly so, that a partisan victory meant the certain loss of Kosova. When the Germans found it necessary to pressure the Zogist, their propaganda emphasized the fact—again rightly so—that Zog had cared little for the future of Kosova. In a global sense, the Germans maintained that England and Russia would eventually come to blows, at which point London would make some kind of a deal with the Germans. Alternatively, England was accused of having sold the Balkans to Tito and vilified as a traditional supporter of Greece. Albania, with the protection of the Germans, was independent and neutral and unlike under the Italians enjoyed a free press and gendarmerie, and the Germans rarely interfered in the daily life of the Albanians. British liaison officers reported that with the exception of the partisans most everyone believed German propaganda.[71]

But effective propaganda alone was not enough. The Germans concluded that coercive measures were again necessary to protect their positions, which did much to undermine the effectiveness of this very propaganda. In early spring 1944, responding to what was perceived as the continuing possibility of an Allied attack from the Adriatic, the commanding general of the Twenty-first Corps ordered the complete evacuation of three coastal zones. These included a small region directly around Vlora, the area behind Durrës—the port itself had already been evacuated—and an area around Shkodra, effecting in all some ten thousand Albanians. The Germans coordinated the evacuation with Deva and Ago Agaj, but left the accommodation and resettlement up to the Albanian regime. This was not handled particularly effectively, at least partially because of a lack of resources, and resulted in considerable resentment. Many of those displaced received no help whatsoever, so it should not be surprising that a significant percentage joined the partisans.[72]

The German Summer Offensive

Increased German coercion also took the form of renewed military action against the partisans. Recognizing that the garrison troops that the Germans now had in Albania were not equal to the task, the Germans pulled in some first-class units from Greece. Elements of the First and Twenty-fifth Mountain Divisions, the 297th Infantry Division, and the 104th Jäger Division attacked the partisans in the south and in central Albania. Because of the small number of German troops, the Germans found it necessary to rely on nationalist *çetas* and units of the Albanian army.[73] Although the Albanians again seemed of little use to the Germans, the "Junioperations" were not without some degree of success. The Germans drove the partisans away from the north-south roads in southern Albania and pinned large groups of partisans against the sea.

The fighting was quite fierce and was accompanied by considerable atrocity—many civilian deaths and many houses burned. Hubert Lanz, commander of the Twenty-second Corps ordered the evacuation of all Albanians from partisan-controlled areas, but it seems that cooler heads prevailed. Still, the Germans were clearly having a harder time of it. With better organization, larger numbers, more supplies coming from Italy, and occasional RAF fighter support, the partisans were able to mount spirited resistance. Although the partisans suffered heavy casualties, the units were able to avoid the various encircling maneuvers launched by the Germans.[74] As an indication of the level of partisan sophistication, while the bulk of the partisan forces were being pressured in the south, the First Partisan Division was able to initiate its own offensive in central Albania directed against both German positions and, essentially for the first time, against the heart of nationalist/Zogist Albania, Mati, and Dibra. The British attempted to forestall this escalation of the civil war by temporarily cutting off supplies to the partisans. This tactic was as least temporarily successful and the partisans—for lack of ammunition—withdrew briefly from Mati and Dibra in July.

Despite this momentary respite, the nationalists and the Zogists were faced with their worst nightmare, a scenario their tortuous policy since the founding of the Communist Party had been designed to avoid. The appearance of partisans in force in the center and north caused a crisis in the nationalist and Zogist camps and escalated an already existing crisis in the collaborationist government.

The Fall of Mitrovica

The government of Rexhep Mitrovica had been essentially paralyzed since May. While the fortunes of the government seemed to be on the rise during the first months of the year—in terms of prestige within Albania—the surprising and rapid revival of the partisans did much to undermine that prestige. The government was proving to be unable to influence the security situation or the economy. Although the north and the center of the country were experiencing tolerable conditions, life in much of the south by April 1944 can only be described as desperate. While Albania never experienced the famine conditions that affected much of Greece, times were extremely hard and the government could do little. Agriculture was interrupted, with frequent destruction of crops and with many of the men and women at war. Herds were depleted as a result of German, nationalist, and partisan confiscation. The BK proved to be particularly obnoxious in this regard, developing what amounted to a vast extortion ring—demanding money and food under the pain of death from already hard-pressed peasants in the areas they controlled. This practice began in early 1943 and continued until the Germans put a stop to it in the summer of 1944.[75] To add to the misery, many villages in the Gjirokastra-Korça area had been destroyed, leaving thousands without shelter. In May a typhus epidemic ran rampant with no medicine and with medical personal limited to a few Italian nuns. A similarly desperate medical situation existed in Kosova, as well, because all of the pharmacists were Serb and had been driven out. Malaria, the traditional scourge of Albania, also spread unchecked in the south. There was no electricity—Gjirokastra was in the dark—and there was little gasoline. It cost as much as five hundred Albanian francs to ride in an open truck to Tirana.[76]

Little was being done for these people. A committee for aid to war victims was formed in Tirana and concluded that it needed four million francs a month just to feed and cloth the desperate in the south. The committee had little money and no transport facilities. The government did nothing, except to continue passing laws that attempted to give the impression of normal conditions and social progress. It was a myth; by May the government had essentially ceased to function. It could not even pay what officials it had in the south, since money could not be sent over the roads and checks were useless because the banks had been closed for five to six months.

Mitrovica's popularity in the rest of the country was clearly also in eclipse. The general economy continued to deteriorate, partially as a result of expenditures on the not-very-effective security forces. The government continued to employ Italian administrative personnel against the wishes of many. The government was unresponsive to the needs of the people, and it was perceived as being corrupt.[77] As Hoxha had hoped, the integration of the BK members in February, rather than strengthening the government, had simply weakened the BK and undermined their influence throughout the country.

Mitrovica could possibly have withstood all of these problems but the Germans, too, it seems, had finally had enough of Mitrovica and his colleagues. Although at least partially to blame for Mitrovica's failure, the Germans complained that Mitrovica and his government were doing little or nothing to keep the south quiet. The Germans had also become dissatisfied with various individual members of the government, many of whom the Germans, too, accused of corruption. The Germans were particularly critical of Mitrovica himself, the minister of finance, Ago Agaj; the commander of the Albanian gendarmerie, Hysni Dema; and—perhaps most disappointing to the Germans—Deva, their principal support. Deva, the minister of the interior, was accused of releasing captured communists for money.[78]

Although quite long in coming, Mitrovica finally resigned in the middle of June 1944. Neubacher tells us that the principal reason was health related, and Mitrovica maintained that he was no longer able to work with Mehdi Frashëri, who constantly interfered with the functioning of his government. In reality, although Mitrovica was ill he had failed, and as the internal situation deteriorated, the Germans came to the conclusion that achieving their original goal of internal pacification carried out by Albanians might no longer be possible. The Germans hoped, as a backup plan, simply to divide and control the Albanians, which ultimately led them to continue to co-opt nationalist elements into the government. The German goal, then, had changed while the policy essentially remained the same. The policy achieved some success. A new, broader-based government was formed, although the rather complex process required a month to complete.

Although negotiations between the nationalists and Zogists (Kupi as well as Fiqri Dine and the Dibra chiefs) concerning their relationship with the Germans had been in progress for some time, the month-long period after the fall of Mitrovica witnessed these negotiations at their most intense. Both the fall of the government and the rapid increase in partisan activity acted to increase the urgency of the leaders meeting at the Hotel Dajti in Tirana. Neubacher, who was in Tirana for most of this period, wrote, "It was unforgettable. . . . Daily there were new combinations, new information, new opposing information, influence, counterinfluence. Politics came in high waves which continually rolled into my pleasant bungalow."[79] Neubacher believed the root of the problem to be either the basic nature of the Albanians or a conflict between Frashëri and Deva. The situation was considerably more complex and left both the Germans and the British, who often did well in discerning the intricacies of Albanian politics, in the dark.

The question of integrating at least the Zogists into the Mitrovica government was first broached by regents Anton Harapi and Mehdi Frashëri in April 1944, after it became clear that the injection of BK members in February had not been enough to stabilize the situation. Since February, the partisans were on the rise, famine threatened in the south and some sections of central Albania, and the BK was nearing collapse due to the immediate effect of increased collaboration. The regents wanted the Zogists for stability, and the Zogists were ready to do more than talk to the Albanians in Tirana. They had been talking with Tirana since the German invasion. Schliep reported that Kupi met with members of the Mitrovica government on 3 February, and at the end of March Schliep told Neubacher that Kupi was now in constant contact with government circles. At the same time talks were held among the Zogist Dine, Deva, Mustafa Kruja, Vërlaci, and Gjon Marka Gjoni.[80]

These discussions, particularly those between Kupi and the Albanians who had collaborated with the Italians, would have been unthinkable several months earlier, but the rapid resurgence of the partisans made all the northerners nervous. The failure of the meeting of the various opposition streams at Bilisht in February was further impetus for Kupi to soften his stance toward collaborationists. Although McLean and Amery were pushing hard to convince Kupi and the nationalists to fight the Germans, these groups were moving closer to the government in the hopes of creating a broad coalition to oppose the partisans. But in April the Germans themselves were not ready to include the Zogists in the government. The Germans saw the advantages but were hesitant, as they had been during the discussions leading to the inclusion of more members of the BK in February. The Germans considered the Zogists to be unreliable. Schliep laid down the German line on Kupi in August 1943, making it clear that Kupi would be treated as an enemy but that he should be used for German purposes whenever possible.[81]

But Mehdi Frashëri kept pushing, and the various anticommunist Albanians kept talking. A particularly important meeting took place at Tufine at the end of May, coinciding with the NLM Congress of Përmet. The meeting seems to have included Mehdi Frashëri, Lef Nosi, Mithat Frashëri, Kupi, Marka Gjoni, and the Dibra chieftain Fiqri Dine, and they were aimed at replacing Mitrovica with Dine. Dine had the trust of Kupi and was a Zogist, yet he was not an active member of the inner circle of Legality, which left Kupi, or so he thought, with some room to maneuver in the event that the entire scheme collapsed. Dine as prime minister, so the anticommunist scenario ran, would enable coordination of the military strength of all the noncommunists, including the Albanian army, the remaining active çetas of the BK, the forces of Kupi's Legality Party, the Albanians such as Kruja who had collaborated with the Italians—now calling themselves the National Independent Party—and the Dibra nationalist-Zogists.

Unlike in April, the Germans were now more willing to compromise. Although still distrustful of the Zogists, the Germans by the end of May felt they were left with few options. The Mitrovica government was moribund, and the BK was rapidly ceasing to function in the Albanian political landscape, leaving the various Zogists as the only organized political group in Albania outside of the NLM. The integration of the Zogist had become unavoidable, just as the integration of the BK had been in February. The Germans, including Fitzthum, who had been the most vocal opponent to Zogist integration, were in part persuaded by Mehdi Frashëri's guarantee that in case of the need for a rapid German withdrawal, Kupi's Legality Party pledged itself to not only create no difficulties, but actually protect the German withdrawal.[82] Because Kupi at the same time assured Julian Amery that he was about to attack the Germans, this appears to have been part of his traditional strategy of playing both sides.

But German acquiescence did not end the government crisis. Dine himself was still hesitant, in part it seems, because of the continuing effort by McLean and Amery to construct some unity among the Zogist-nationalists and convince them to break their contact with the collaborationists and attack the Germans. Kupi was the focus of this effort based on the erroneous assumption that he commanded extensive prestige throughout Albania and could muster—based on his own estimates—some twenty-five thousand troops. Both of these assumptions might have been true in late 1943, when McLean left Albania to report to London, but by May through June 1944 SOE was slowly becoming aware that neither assumption was now valid. On 11 May SOE reported to the Foreign Office that based on their latest information, Kupi's movement was less advanced than had originally been thought and consisted mainly of former officials of Zog's regime who had not been employed by the Italians and of some members of Zog's government and army who had originally fled with Kupi. On 9 June SOE further reported that rather than the twenty-five thousand troops Kupi had claimed to be able to put into the field in May, his forces numbered no more than five thousand and these were poorly armed and consisted mainly of personal retainers and Italians. The report concluded that after five months of attempting to build a political and military organization, Kupi had failed. The central committee of Legality was composed of unimportant people, Kupi's influence was strictly local, and he was moving closer to collaboration.[83]

But McLean, Amery, and certain elements within the Foreign Office refused to abandon the "Kupi option," regardless of the increasing ill-will continued British contact with Kupi was causing in the partisan ranks, particularly with Hoxha. Sensing that time was running out, McLean redoubled his efforts to unite the northerners and to convince Kupi to fight. Kupi, also aware that his position was rapidly becoming desperate, agreed to give up his neutrality and participate in the Geg meetings that had been taking place for some time. Kupi announced to the British that his aim was to bring about a united uprising against the Germans. Kupi was also willing to reduce his demands on the British, which had originally included the recognition of an Albanian government in exile under Zog.[84]

Now in May, he declared that he was willing to begin operations against the Germans upon the receipt of ten thousand gold sovereigns and sufficient automatic weapons and mortars to equip eight battalions of 250 men each. McLean would have been glad to oblige but recognized that the general British policy of first resistance, then supply, would not be changed to accommodate Kupi. McLean strongly encouraged Kupi to offer some gesture of good-faith resistance that would strengthen his case with SOE. McLean finally convinced Kupi to help David Smiley destroy the important Gjoles bridge on the Tirana-Shkodra road on 21 June. This act constituted the first anti-German operation carried out by Kupi since October 1943.[85]

The bridge was duly blown up, but the incident did not have the effect desired by Kupi and McLean. In the first instance, it left SOE in Italy entirely unconvinced about Kupi's willingness to resist and his eligibility for supplies. This opinion was reinforced by the discovery that Kupi had agreed to participate in the operation only if his name not be used in connection with the incident.[86] Clearly, Kupi was hoping not to jeopardize his negotiations with the collaborationists or the collaborationist negotiations with the Germans. McLean, by this point, had already appealed directly to Anthony Eden for a letter from Zog directing Kupi to resist. Some senior Foreign Office officials began to tire of the increasingly difficult question. Sir Orme Sargent, supervising deputy under the secretary of state, in exasperation questioned the value of doing anything at all in Albania, arguing that it was a complete backwater, and even if the entire country was ablaze it would cause very little inconvenience to the Germans.[87]

In general, however, the Foreign Office continued to push for Kupi, presumably from a strictly political standpoint, but received very little support from the British military or SOE in Bari. Smiley later maintained that McLean's position had been sabotaged and that certain officers in the Albanian section of SOE were well intentioned, if led astray by insidious communist propaganda; others were communist agents. Amery went even further, suggesting that "a genuine enthusiasm for the Communists and their works infected our headquarters, and responsible staff officers reveled with indecent and almost masochistic glee in the destruction of Chetniks and Zogists."[88] Smiley also charged that "certain" foreign sections of the BBC became influenced by communist sympathizers, causing much embarrassment to the BLOs attached to noncommunist resistance organizations.[89] Conspiracy or not, Kupi got nothing for the moment, and British policymakers once again avoided making a clear decision about whom to support in Albania.

Hoxha was of course aware of McLean's attempt to bring the nationalist-Zogists into a British anti-German coalition and was determined to undermine those efforts. He was able to do so in part by launching an offensive, at the end of June, spearheaded by the first brigade of the first division against Mati, the heart of Kupi's territory, and against Dibra, the home of some Zogist and some independent nationalist chiefs and a strong German garrison. The British, in response, temporarily cut off supplies to the partisans and sent in Major Victor Smith to attempt to stop the widening civil war. Smith, with orders from General Wilson, requested an armistice and talks in Bari between representatives for the partisans and Kupi. Kupi accepted immediately, as this would have put him on an equal footing with Hoxha. Hoxha naturally refused and continued his attack.

The Dine Government

A direct result of the partisan attack on the center and the north was Zogist Fiqri Dine's acceptance of the position of prime minister. In the middle of July, then, Dine became prime minister and constructed what Schliep referred to as a "moderately-Zogist" government, although Dine's Zogism was perhaps more a unifying theory to serve the existing social order in Albania than a deliberate attempt to bring back Zog himself.[90] In any case, if the Zogists and their nationalist supporters could not convince the British to help them resist the partisans, they would attempt to use the Germans.

Dine was possessed of a somewhat checkered political career in Albania. As the nominal leader of the Dibra chiefs, he was a man of some influence and—as with many other northern chiefs—was offered the rank and salary of colonel in Zog's gendarmerie and in 1927 was appointed gendarmerie commander in Tirana. Following the Italian invasion he was co-opted—at least to a certain extent—and was appointed first to the Italian-controlled Albanian Assembly and then became minister of interior in Libohova's short—one month—cabinet in early 1943. Dine managed to maintain some credibility, however, in that he was distrusted by the Italians for his nationalism and his rather pronounced sympathies for the resistance. He participated in the German drive against the partisans in his own area of Dibra at the end of 1943, but maintained a foot in both camps by informing local BLOs of the German approach.[91] Dine, then, was quite in the Kupi mold and could, in most cases, be counted as a Kupi adherent.

Although the Germans reluctantly accepted Dine, they refused to accept his, and Mehdi Frashëri's, proposed cabinet or Frashëri's choice to succeed Fuat Dibra, who died in February, as regent. Mehdi Frashëri hoped to use the crisis to make a clean sweep of all those he could not control. Following the refusal of Ibrahim Bey Biçaku to accept the post of regent, Frashëri hoped to appoint Rexhep Mitrovica, who, although often at odds with the head regent, was now quite ill and could be easily controlled. On 2 July, the Germans, who were becoming increasingly weary of Frashëri, forced the Parliament to elect Cafo Bey Ulqini, a Kosovar who could be counted on to support the Germans.[92]

Having lost that battle, Frashëri and Dine hoped at least to rid themselves of Xhafer Deva, whose brutality and corruption were proving to be a considerable liability. The two struck while Deva was out of Tirana and announced a cabinet without even consulting the Germans. Dine's government was to consist of Zogists, a supporter of the BK, and some members of the National Independent Party, the group around Kruja and the Mirdita chief Marka Gjoni.

The Germans were incensed that they had not been consulted and because most of the old BK people and Kosovars were excluded. And despite their own irritation with Deva, they objected to his exclusion from the new government. Both Neubacher, who was in Berlin, and Fitzthum would have none of it. Neubacher bluntly informed Frashëri that the German army represented the only order in Albania and that Albanian independence had certain limits, which included the security of the German army and the maintenance of German war aims. Fitzthum saw the move as the creation of a Frashëri dictatorship with Zogist dominance, which posed a threat to the creation of SS "Skanderbeg," for which Deva was recruiting. Schliep, following Neubacher's instructions, and Fitzthum both insisted on Deva's inclusion even if this drove Frashëri to resign. The Germans were loath to abandon their divide-and-rule strategy. Frashëri and Dine were again forced to capitulate.[93]

Having resolved these issues with the Germans, albeit unsatisfactorily, Frashëri and Dine turned their attention to the main task: the rather farfetched and somewhat desperate goal of a Geg coalition. The plan was to coordinate nationalist and Zogist strength and, in cooperation with the Germans, drive back the communists. At the same time, they hoped to convince the Allies that they were acting on behalf of an independent Albania and therefore deserved, if not direct Allied support, at least a respite from active Allied resistance. This entire scenario was based upon a series of misconceptions, including (1) the Germans would trust the Dine government to the extent that they would be willing to provide the government with significant military resources, (2) the partisans could be defeated with just one more serious effort, and (3) the Allies could be convinced that the government of a country that had been occupied by the Germans for more than one year could be genuinely neutral.

The first priority of the new government was to build an effective military force, coordinate it with the Germans, and attack the partisans. There was more than a little urgency here, since the partisans were now operating in and doing considerable damage to the ancestral land and principal residences of many of the northern chieftains who were cooperating with or actually a part of the new government. The brigades of the first division (partisan divisions in 1944 consisted of approximately four thousand to five thousand) were operating in the Dibra-Peshkopi area and in Mati. In August the first division, now commanded by Shehu, joined with the second division to form the First Army Corps of the ANLA under Dali Ndreu. This reorganization was more than smoke and mirrors. The partisans were continuing to grow at a rapid pace, with many of the new recruits coming from central and northern Albania, an ominous development for the northern chieftains.

Both Dine and Kupi appealed to the Germans for help, Dine directly and Kupi using his traditional backdoor tactics. Dine presented to the Germans what must have been perceived as a fantastic request. Neubacher tells us that Dine asked the Germans to supply him with enough weapons to form two mountain divisions to be supported by tanks.[94] Both Neubacher and Schliep saw this as a thinly disguised request from Kupi for arms, which the Germans believed might easily be used against their own forces. Kupi, meanwhile, had already made approaches to General Fehn, the commander of the Twenty-first Army Corps. Through the offices of General Gustav von Myrdacz, an elderly Austrian officer who had helped organize Zog's army and who during World War II served as liaison officer between the Albanian army and the Twenty-first Army Corps, Kupi hoped to obtain at least some ammunition.

Neither Dine nor Kupi did particularly well. Dine was given small quantities of equipment. Kupi was given access to transportation and some food. At the beginning of July, prior to the formation of the Dine cabinet, Kupi was allowed to move three hundred armed supporters through Tirana in trucks supplied by the government to engage partisan forces attacking his area.[95] At the same time Tirana bakeries supplied his forces with bread. The Germans were reluctant to go much further without tangible evidence of real cooperation. Scheiger tried to convince Kupi to come to Tirana for talks, but Kupi refused, recognizing that this would hopelessly compromise his position. As a result, Kupi's requests for heavy weapons and significant quantities of ammunition fell on deaf ears. It is probable, however, that Kupi did receive at least some ammunition and some small arms from the Germans.[96] It seems the Germans were willing to give Kupi just enough to compromise him but not enough to allow him to either effectively battle the partisans or threaten their own anticipated withdrawal. There is little question that Kupi was compromised, and as a result, as with the BK, his influence began to decline accordingly.

This attempt on the part of the government to supply nationalists and Zogist forces was accompanied by an administrative reorganization of these forces. Dine and Frashëri decided that a unified organization should be constructed with general command assigned to an Albanian directly responsible to two individuals: the prime minister and a German liaison officer. Existing forces would be supplemented by volunteer bands, strengthened by German officers. Once again without consulting the Germans, the regents on 17 August announced the construction of a "General Command of Active Forces." This move seems to have been about as successful as the attempt to convince the Germans to supply the nationalists with tanks. The only demonstrated result of this move was to enrage Schliep.[97]

And yet, initial military operations against the partisans were seemingly quite successful. Germans and Zogist forces, without directly cooperating, managed to drive the partisans from Mati at the end of July. Mehmet Shehu, whose first brigade was operating in Dibra, was driven into Macedonia, harried by the local populous once it became clear that they had been weakened. The Germans and the nationalist-Zogists were soon to discover, however, that these victories were much more the result of the partisans' having exhausted their supplies and ammunition. The British embargo on supply drops to the partisans proved to be the most significant factor explaining partisan withdrawal from the north.[98]

Kupi and Dine were soon faced with a resumption of the partisan offensive. British liaison officers attached to the partisans had convinced British headquarters in Bari that at least the Dibra battle was directed primarily against the Germans and based upon stated British priorities; this required the resumption of supply to partisan forces in the area. Much to the chagrin of McLean, who had rejoiced at the embargo, at the end of July the partisans were once again receiving drops from Bari. This allowed them to reenter Dibra, supported by RAF Beaufighter attacks on the town itself on 10 through 11 August. On 10 August the partisans also resumed their attack on Mati. Dine and the Germans began a counteroffensive on 18 August, using two

German regiments and an assorted group of Albanians—government troops; tribesmen from Mirdita; a nationalist *çeta* from Dibra led by Halil Alia, who had collaborated with both the Italians and the Germans; units of the "Skanderbeg" Division; and eight hundred to one thousand Kupi people, although Kupi once again refused to participate personally.

This operation, called "Fuchsjagd" in German documents, was a failure.[99] The collaborationist Albanian units fought badly, and there were simply not enough Germans. The offensive was halted on 27 August. The Germans were driven from the town and area around Dibra on 30 August, leaving possibly as many as four hundred dead as well as a considerable amount of equipment,[100] making the two-month Battle of Dibra perhaps the largest and most successful partisan operation of the war. At the end of the battle, the partisans were firmly established in central Albania and in a good position to rapidly overwhelm their domestic opponents. The battle also brought to an end the military portion of the complex, essentially hopeless plan concocted by Dine, Frashëri, Kupi, and some of the northern chieftains.

The other part of the plan, to convince the Allies of Albania's neutrality, was equally unsuccessful and speaks to the level of desperation and level of unreality apparent among the Albanian collaborators. Although Mehdi Frashëri had been unsuccessful in the past, he tried again to sell the concept of Albanian neutrality and gain some form of international recognition for his government. Frashëri was only marginally more successful this time. Of the states within the German orbit, the Croatians were willing to go as far as constructing a Croatian-Albanian society and the Bulgarians established a general consulate and sent a military attaché. In terms of neutral states, Frashëri was less successful. He had sent his son Raquip to Istanbul, but this came to nothing. Although the Germans were concerned that the goals of this trip included establishing contact with the British and the Yugoslavs, the Germans did not bother to intervene, being convinced that Frashëri's attempt would fail.[101] It did, as did the attempts on the part of Dine to explain to the Allies via telegraph that the government was neutral and that the Germans were there only as a necessity of war and to prevent anarchy and civil war. The only perceivable impact of this move was to enrage Ribbentrop personally. The government did, however, experience one minor success. It finally convinced the Germans to elevate Consul General Schliep to the status of ambassador. Rrok Geraj, who had been sent by Zog to treat with the Italians on the day of the Italian invasion and had simply joined them, was appointed Albanian ambassador to Berlin, but was never to assume his post. This meager activity was hardly enough to convince anyone of Albanian independence and neutrality.[102]

The nationalist-Zogist gamble had failed. A series of ominous international events during the last days of August made it abundantly clear to even the most pro-German Albanians that the German occupation of Albania would soon end. The rupture of German-Turkish relations had a significant impact in Albania, since the Albanians—despite having broken away from the Ottoman Empire in 1912—maintained close religious, cultural, and political ties with the Turkish republic. The fall of Romania to Soviet forces on 23 August and Bulgaria's desperate declaration of neutrality on 26 August were even clearer signs of impending doom.[103]

These events also helped to bring down Dine's government. Dine's position had become untenable. His military-diplomatic plans had failed, and the German withdrawal from the Balkans was in sight. By the end of August Dine's government was essentially nonexistent. Fewer than 10 percent of his officials were even bothering to report to work.[104] Dine quickly recognized the significance of all of these events, and following a scant forty days in office he resigned on 28 August. His resignation marked the end of the nationalist-Zogist plan to secure a noncommunist victory in Albania with the help of the Germans. It also marked the end of Germany's attempt to maintain order in Albania through the use of Albanian forces—it marked the end of the German version of an independent Albania.[105]

The leaders of the BK resistance movement: from the left Ekrem Peshkopi, Vasil Andoni, Mithat Frashëri, Ali Këlcyra, Koço Muka. (Amery)

German soldiers parade in Tirana prior to their departure. (Costa)

Street scene from the last stages of the Battle of Tirana, 1944. (Costa)

An American bomber in flyover of Tirana during the victory celebration. (Costa)

Victory celebration in Tirana with large American flag. (Costa)

Rare photo of Hoxha marching into Tirana with (from the right) partisan leaders Myslim Peza, Mehmet Shehu, Hoxha, and Koçi Xoxe, who was executed and became a non-person in 1949. (Costa)

CHAPTER 8

GERMAN RETREAT AND THE CONSTRUCTION OF A STALINIST ALBANIA

The collapse of Romania and the imminent fall of Bulgaria encouraged the German high command to finalize plans for the withdrawal of army group E and part of army group F from the Balkans. Headquarters in Belgrade ordered all units, including the Twenty-first Corps, to prepare for withdrawal, so as not to be caught between the advancing Soviets and the growing partisan forces. As the German military situation became more precarious, the veneer of a friendly occupation in Albania began to wear away, but only slowly. With Dine's resignation, Neubacher continued to insist that at least outwardly the Albanian political structure remain the same. Mehdi Frashëri declared himself ready to assist in forming a new government. The old former liberal must have realized that he was compromised beyond redemption. For his continued cooperation he did ask that when the time came to leave, he—along with his family and the other regents—be granted asylum in Germany or some safer place, along with some financial security.[1] The Germans agreed to his terms but concluded that Frashëri was more useful to them as regent than as prime minister.

The Biçaku Government

Following a week of negotiations, Ibrahim Biçaku agreed to lead a pathetically small and completely isolated new puppet government. Biçaku thereby demonstrated the validity of the German conclusion that although Biçaku was the perfect friend of Germany, he was nevertheless entirely without political instincts and quite incompetent. Tirana papers noted cynically that he had headed the provisional executive committee exactly one year earlier, prior to the construction of the Mitrovica government.[2] Biçaku had become, once again, the front man for the Germans, with very little to do. Julian Amery commented sardonically that the only remaining evidence of political activity in Tirana was Ambassador Schliep's daily game of Ping-Pong with Biçaku.[3] Biçaku's government of nonentities is distinguished only by the fact that Lefter Kosova, the new minister of labor, was shot dead in the streets of Tirana on the day he assumed office.[4] From the beginning of September, then, Albanians ceased to play any significant role in the administration of German authority in Albania. The Germans estimated that now considerably less than 10 percent of Albanian government officials, whom the Germans characterized as being corrupt, lazy, and inefficient in the best of times, actually showed up for work. And because Neubacher's staff still clung religiously to the doctrine of noninterference, Germans were often not allowed to assume the tasks of the missing Albanian bureaucrats.[5] As a result, much simply did not get done.

But not all German officials were willing to continue following the Neubacher plan. Obersturmführer Fitzthum had always considered it nonsense, and his power was increasing. The change of government was accompanied by a rather significant shift of power within the German camp in Albania. Authority until the fall of Dine had been shared among the German general in Albania, who did not actually command any troops; the Foreign Ministry, that is, Neubacher and Schliep; and Fitzthum of the SS. This authority was now quickly concentrated in the hands of Fitzthum. Amery maintains that the change dates from the attempt on Hitler's life at the Wolf's Lair on 20 July 1944. Although this event may have had an impact, German documents suggest that the change did not take place until the end of August, which would suggest that the collapse of Dine's government itself acted as the principle motivating factor for the change.

Other contributing factors include the increasing effectiveness of the partisans, who had by now demonstrated an ability to launch coordinated drives outside their traditional areas. The Germans, of course, were also much concerned about their own deteriorating military situation. Collaborators were leaving Tirana in large numbers. Prengë Previzi, the commander of the Albanian army, and Hysni Dema, commander of the gendarmerie and originally an active anti-Italian Zogist, fled, as did Halil Alia, commander of a—until now reliable—nationalist *çeta* in Dibra. Alia's defection was particularly irksome for Fitzthum, because his çeta had just been given a considerable amount of gold, weapons, and ammunition. With the exception of a few small units, the army and the gendarmerie had ceased to exist. Many of the gendarmes simply went home with their weapons and reportedly shot at both sides during the German withdrawal.[6] The Germans determined that even the Twenty-first SS Division "Skanderbeg" was by now of little use other than for simple guard duty.

The Germans, for the first time in Albania, also had to begin worrying about the effectiveness of their own troops. By September 1944 most of the three battalions of former Soviet troops in the 297th Infantry Division—who had deserted to the Germans or had been captured by them—had deserted again and gone over to the Albanians or the British. Julian Amery convinced thirty of these Tajiks, Kazaks, and Uzbegs, most of them Turkish speaking and therefore having something in common with many older Albanians, to kill their officers and join the Zogists. Amery expressed some surprise when the Kazak troops brought with them the ears of the dead officers, wrapped in a large green handkerchief. Amery was delighted, however, to finally be afforded the opportunity—somewhat in the tradition of Tamerlane—to ride at the head of a Turkoman horde.[7]

The Germans hoped to solve the problem by disarming the remaining central Asian battalions. But the morale of the German troops was being effected as well. General Ernst von Leyser, commander of the Twenty-first Corps, from the end of August began complaining about the undisciplined troops and a reduction in fighting capabilities. There were instances of German soldiers selling their equipment. One of the BLOs was told of a German who was willing to sell a tank.[8] Encouraged by these reports, Wing Commander Tony Neel, one of the BLOs in the north, sent a letter on 29 August to the divisional commander of the 181st Infantry Division headquartered in Shkodra. Neel offered surrender terms to the Germans whereby the Germans would be able to keep their weapons until the British could safely transport the Germans, with all military honors, out of Albania. He argued that he was motivated by a concern for German safety. Neubacher laughed this off in his memoirs, but Schliep advised the Foreign Ministry that it might be useful to maintain the connection to determine British political goals in the Balkans, something that seems to have been a mystery to all—all except Hoxha, who believed that Neel was attempting to develop a joint British-German scheme to crush the partisans, oddly similar to the contentions of McLean and Smiley, who believed that elements of SOE were attempting to crush the nationalists.[9]

The Germans in Albania were not ready to surrender to Neel or anyone else. Although there were reports that a few German officers had defected, widespread mutiny or even insubordination did not happen.[10] This may at least partially be explained by a significant decrease in partisan military activity in September owing to Hoxha's increasing concentration on political matters, to the absence of some partisans units that had been loaned to Tito, and to the fact that the First Partisan Corps ran out of ammunition during the last two weeks of September.[11]

But regardless of the actual level of danger to the German position, Fitzthum felt that more brutal measures were called for, but then when dealing with Albanians, Fitzthum always thought that brutal measures were called for. Fitzthum relieved the last DGA, General Otto Gullmann, sending him off to Bulgaria, and also had General Gustav Fehn of the Twenty-first Corps replaced. In conjunction with Neubacher's new special representative in Albania, Oberführer Dr. Karl Gstöttenbauer, Fitzthum rapidly reorganized the German administrative structure in Albania. This reorganization included the consolidation of the four field commands into one German field command in Albania, which conformed to the reality of the shrinking area of German control as well as to the fewer and fewer people with whom the Germans had to work.[12]

This consolidation was accompanied by an increase in terror directed against the civilian population in the hopes that this might ensure an orderly and painless German withdrawal. Some local officials participated with enthusiasm, including the prefects of Vlora and Durrës, Vizdan Resilia and Mehmet Çela respectively, and the police chief of Shkodra, Hasan Isufi. Through indiscriminate terror, these officials managed to maintain some order in their areas.[13] Fitzthum applied similar methods, although somewhat less indiscriminately, in those areas under his direct control. Amery tells us that among the first victims of this harder line were some forty pro-British members of the BK who were arrested and sent to the concentration camp of Semlin in occupied Yugoslavia. Skënder Muço, the BK *çeta* leader and central council member who had consistently pushed for active opposition to the Germans, was simply shot.

Kühmel argues that Fitzthum had always used terror, as evidenced by the Wehrmacht complaints in August. Regular army officers decried Fitzthum's rash of arrests as well as the transport of some 400 Albanian prisoners out of Albania, directly contravening existing agreements that Mehdi Frashëri had signed in February 1944.[14] And yet it seems clear that a general shift in German policy did take place after the promotion of Fitzthum. Beginning in September the Wehrmacht itself turned to increased terrorism. Prisoners were transported out of old Albania to a newly constructed concentration camp in Prishtina—instead of remaining interned in the three camps in Albania. While no definitive figures are available, the numbers could have been large. On the night of 17 to 18 September alone, some 600 Albanians were transported from Shkodra to Prishtina. To secure the Elbasan-Tirana road, all houses within three hundred feet were burned down and a section of the Tirana-Shkodra road was entirely evacuated. More seriously, Schmidhuber of the SS "Skanderbeg" issued orders to increase the burning of villages and killing of people. In keeping with these orders, between 19 September and 23 October 131 NLM prisoners—including women, which constituted a particular affront to Moslems—were shot or hanged in Kosova.[15] The image of the friendly occupation protecting the Albanians from their enemies had seemingly outlived its usefulness.

And yet at the same time German repression increased, cooperation with certain northern chieftains increased as well. Although all Albanians had reason to be apprehensive about the future, the nationalists and the northern chieftains were clearly in the most difficult position. As German evacuation of Albania became increasingly near, the nationalists remained disunited, their inactivity was undermining their authority even among their own followers, and the NLM had demonstrated its ability to strike at and hold any territory in Albania not considered vital to the Germans. To make matters worse, at the end of August, SOE (now called Force 399) signed military agreements with the NLM. Following protracted negotiations in Bari, in which Hoxha hoped but failed to extract some degree of political recognition, SOE, represented by Lord Harcourt, officially stated what had been clear for some time, that the NLM constituted the only force fighting the Germans in Albania. The agreement also included a series of operational decisions and Allied commitments in terms of further material support for the NLM.[16] This was an important document and lent the NLM some long-sought and much-needed legitimacy.

With good reason, the nationalists began to panic and many concluded that the only course of action open to them was to attack the Germans in the hopes of gaining the support of the British, who might protect them from the NLM. Mithat Frashëri, Hasan Dosti, Koço Muka, and Dine, along with Abaz Ermenji, left Tirana to join Kupi and created the so-called Mountain Government, a desperate organization destined to survive for approximately two weeks. Mithat Frashëri became prime minister and Kupi the military commander, the first instance of close coordination between the BK and Kupi.[17] Hurried meetings were held with McLean, the only British representative the nationalists could reach. On 8 September the BK leaders Abaz Ermenji and Mithat Frashëri, representing this new organization, met with McLean and offered to begin immediate operations against the Germans on the understanding that the Allies might be willing to reconsider their attitude toward the BK.[18] McLean has argued that he received assurances from SOE on 29 August that reconsideration toward the nationalists was still possible. On 5 September, SOE instructed him, once again, "to make Kupi fight."[19] McLean redoubled his efforts and Kupi, recognizing that time was running out, decided to attack the Germans. On 8 September, a Zogist band under Kupi's son Petrit attacked and overran the headquarters of a German battery killing ten and capturing some material. Zogist forces apparently carried out further operations over the next few weeks. Ermenji, with a force of two hundred, is reported to have attacked a German convoy on 10 September.[20] On the same day, Gani Kryeziu, who had been operating against the Germans for some time, attacked the chrome mines at Zogaj and Qafa e Rrërësit and captured them.[21] Muharrem Bajraktari, too, moved against the Germans in early September. The nationalists and Kupi asked that their efforts be registered by McLean and that he also transmit their requests for quantities of guns and money.

McLean was, of course, willing to oblige. His pleas came to nothing, however, principally because the various operations launched by the nationalists came to little. The Germans—based on their documents—never actually discovered that they were being attacked by the nationalists. The attacks were assumed to be of partisan origin and apparently failed to do much damage in any case. The British in Bari were suspicious, with some officers wondering if Kupi's reduced numbers constituted much of a threat to the Germans, and whether the actions reported by McLean could not actually be considered British operations supported by some Zogist troops.[22] It seems that the pro-NLM wing among British policymakers was finally gaining the upper hand in a process that frequently left the officers in the field bewildered and embarrassed. In the midst of this renewed nationalist activity, on the same day as the Ermenji attack, SOE Bari sent McLean a message making it clear that no supplies would be sent to the nationalists and that he and Smiley were to withdraw and report to headquarters in Bari. Amery, as interim head of the mission, was to remain with Kupi but only in the capacity of a neutral observer and was not to encourage Kupi to fight. McLean was more than reluctant to give in just as his heretofore failed mission was beginning to produce results, however meager. But once his instructions were confirmed twice by subsequent messages, McLean had no choice but to comply.[23]

Hoxha had by this point lost patience with McLean. Summoning Captain Marcus Lyon of the British mission attached to partisan headquarters, he complained that Consensus II was operating in conjunction with collaborators against the interests of the partisans. He ordered that McLean, Smiley, and Seymour (who had left Albania some two months earlier) evacuate within five days or face arrest and trial before a partisan military court. The British in Bari acted forcefully, requiring Hoxha to back down or face the cancellation of a recently signed military agreement between the British and the partisans.

Hoxha prudently retracted his allegations and threats, noting that they were made in a moment of anger, though the anger at this event may have been a falsehood, upon hearing of the death of Mustafa Gjinishi.[24]

The British Decide

Following years of indecision, which served to alienate most of the Albanian groups involved, particularly the NLM, British policymakers finally decided to accept what had been obvious to most liaison officers in Albania for some time—that the NLM constituted the only fighting force in Albania and that it was more than likely that the NLM would soon be in control of the entire country. On 19 September Foreign Office, War Office, SOE, and MI6 (military intelligence) chiefs in London met and grudgingly accepted this inevitability in an obscurely written memorandum.[25] Anthony Eden explained this new policy in a somewhat over-optimistic minute to Churchill on 26 September in which he concluded that "our policy should be to accept the probability of an FNC [NLM] government and on strengthening our position with them in order to offset Russian influence."[26]

While the nationalist cause had been lost for quite some time, these pronouncements and the fact that no weapons would be forthcoming sealed its fate. Many nationalists were willing to accept the probable outcome; some were not. By the third week of September a state of panic had seized many of the nationalists and collaborators, convincing many to flee Albania.[27] Mithat Frashëri and some one hundred leading members of the BK—including Ali Këlcyra, Hasan Dosti, Kadri Cakrani, and Koço Muka—managed to escape to Italy in a boat provided by the Abwehr.[28] Kupi had a more difficult time.

When McLean reluctantly told Kupi that he had been ordered out, Kupi received the news rather stoically, without recrimination. Interpreting Albanian politics in his traditional narrow tribalism he said, "Perhaps it is only just that they [NLM] should come to power. We Gegs have exploited the Tosks for 1,000 years, now it is their turn to exploit us."[29] Kupi concluded that only two options were open to him—either he could fight the partisans alongside the Germans, or he could disband his movement.[30] He considered the latter to be the only honorable course, and by the end of September had begun the process. Having done this he asked for some help from the British in evacuating himself, his two sons, and three close supporters.

McLean had hoped to bring Kupi out with him when he evacuated but was prevented from doing so by direct command of SOE Bari. Amery tells us that SOE Bari went so far as to send security officers along with the rescue vessel to insure that McLean did not try to bring Kupi along, fearing that this might further damage the rapidly deteriorating British relations with Hoxha.[31]

McLean and Amery, believing that their personal honor and the honor of the British government was at stake, made the rounds of senior British officials in Italy to arrange some help for Kupi. Both Harold MacMillian, the resident minister, and General Wilson agreed that something had to be done to help.[32] But elements within the Foreign Office argued that Kupi's record spoke against him, agreeing with elements of SOE Bari that any aid would compromise the British position with Hoxha. The issue was finally decided by Eden—to whom McLean had addressed angry telegrams. The foreign secretary ordered Kupi's rescue—which McLean was to personally conduct—"without it appearing that His Majesty's Government have been involved in the operation."[33] But once again, the British were too late as the ever resourceful Kupi had by this time managed to find his own way out, arriving in Brindisi during the first week of November.

Hoxha, of course, did all he could to facilitate the disintegration of the nationalists and the strengthening of his own position. Hoxha, too, like the Germans it seems, became more ruthless. This is perhaps best demonstrated by the death of Mustafa Gjinishi. Gjinishi had begun his resistance to the invader earlier than Hoxha and had demonstrated his courage in battle. Gjinishi had also consistently taken the line that some of the nationalists could be co-opted into the NLM. Indeed, Gjinishi himself had a hand in winning over some, such as Cen Elezi, who, along with other principal Dibra chiefs, joined the NLM in September 1944. Gjinishi certainly constituted a serious challenge to Hoxha's leadership within the NLM and the party.

At the end of August while on a march with Victor Smith, Gjinishi was "picked off accurately in two bursts of fire."[34] While Albanian socialist historiography argues that the Germans or the pro-German Albanians were to blame, both Schliep and the British BLOs believed that Gjinishi was assassinated by his own.[35] Hoxha, who rails against Gjinishi in his memoirs, was certainly well rid of him, and following his death the NLM established a harder line on the nationalists. At the beginning of September the general staff of the NLM issued orders that those nationalists not yet compromised would either be integrated into the NLM or liquidated. Under this new hard line, Muharrem Bajraktari, in a conversation with Shehu, was presented with these options. Bajraktari refused to submit and barely escaped with his life, turning to the Germans for protection. On 12 October the chiefs of twelve Geg clans, including Muharrem Bajraktari, with Marka Gjoni of Mirdita as the central figure, joined together in what they called the Mountain League, an organization supported and armed by the Germans.[36] The presence of Gjoni in this organization is perhaps not surprising, since he had been cooperating with the occupation authorities since the Italian invasion—cooperation that increased after the First and Fourth Partisan Brigades attacked his base at Orosh and burned down his house. But Bajraktari's adherence to this group was a political coup for Hoxha because one of the last remaining independent chieftains was now thoroughly compromised. Gani Kryeziu, too, in conversation with the head of the Second Partisan Brigade, was presented with the same options— his brother Said Kryeziu was arrested by the partisans along with the BLO assigned to Gani's headquarters. McLean reported that by the middle of October, Gani Kryeziu's organization had been suppressed.[37] Gani Bey and the remnants of his forces joined the NLM.

The Germans had by this point already begun evacuating nonessential personal and all women, an operation not without its problems. On 5 September a column of trucks carrying women civilians was attacked by partisans some twenty miles from Prizren. Of the forty women, twenty-two were killed or wounded—with the ambassador's wife among the wounded—and three were captured. Deva maintained that this act was retribution for the execution of women partisans in Kosova. For the release of the three captured women, the partisans first demanded one hundred pieces of gold for each plus the release of all communists in Kosova. Following German agreement to these conditions, the partisans decided they wanted Brigadier General Davies, who was in Germany. Negotiations dragged on, and the situation seems not to have been resolved by war's end.[38] A high-level German high command commission reported to Field Marshal Alfred Jodl, chief operations officer, who reported to the Foreign Ministry, that the commander of the convoy, Lieutenant Parisius, a veterinarian, would be court-martialed for failing to resist. The report also blamed both the German military personal in Tirana as well as the embassy for failing to adequately protect knowledge of German convoy movements.[39]

The episode had a significant impact on the relations between Fitzthum and Schliep, since they blamed each other. Of the two, Fitzthum proved to be the most experienced infighter and he ultimately eclipsed Schliep in influence. By cooperating, Neubacher's representative Gstöttenbauer further augmented Fitzthum's already-increased power. But Fitzthum had but little time to enjoy his empire. On 2 October, the Germans received orders to evacuate Albania and General Ernst von Leyser automatically assumed complete command. On 9 October Albania was declared an operational zone, and the Germans began moving their forces north. By the middle of October southern Albania had already been abandoned south of Berat, although German units from Greece, marching along the Florina-Korça-Struga road, entered Albania with little difficulty. In mid-October the Germans still controlled Korça, Elbasan, Struga, and Tirana as well as most of the towns and large territory in the north. But Gjirokastra and Berat were liberated in September, and the NLM moved its headquarters to the latter on 15 October. Prizren was liberated on 4 October and Vlora on the 15 October.[40]

On a number of occasions, British ground forces, which began small and limited action in Albania in June, participated directly in the partisan advance. The largest and most controversial of these actions involved the taking of the southern coastal town of Saranda on 9 October, an operation destined to become another milestone in the growing hostility between Hoxha and the Western Allies. The British were interested in Saranda primarily because of its location directly across the straits from Corfu, which could have afforded an escape route for the Germans on Corfu. Under Brigadier Tom Churchill (without informing Hoxha's headquarters) British commandos, with cooperation from local partisans under Islam Radovicka, took the town on 9 October and considered taking advantage of the success and pushing north to Vlora. Hoxha's headquarters—afraid that the British intended to maintain a permanent foothold—complained that British soldiers had looted Saranda. Once this issue had been resolved, the British HQ for land forces in the Adriatic decided not to pursue the matter further. The commandos were withdrawn, although some Long Range Desert Group patrols remained in Albania.[41]

Albanian socialist historiography presents several versions of this incident, ranging from the partisans' having taken Saranda well before the British arrival, to Hoxha's own version in which the partisans did most of the major fighting, having cleverly hemmed the British in. Hoxha, we are told, at this point handed the British an ultimatum to withdraw, which they did "with shame" ending their "diabolical intentions."[42] Much of this account is clearly inaccurate. Still, as with many of their dealings with the Albanians, the British might have handled the situation differently. They might, for example, have found some way to either inform Hoxha or the BLOs attached to him that the operation was planned. The fact that it came as a surprise did little to assuage Hoxha's fears of British designs. Perhaps more seriously, British War Office documents indicate that Greek Zervas forces took part in the Saranda operation, raising fears that the British, whose preference for the Greeks was clear to all Albanians, were attempting to establish Greeks in areas of southern Albania, which Greek nationalists claimed as rightfully theirs.[43] Although

Albanian fears were probably exaggerated, the British seem to have done everything in their power—inadvertently—to inflame them.

The partisan advance, of course, was made possible by the continuing German withdrawal. By the middle of October, German garrisons everywhere were shrinking. While the Twenty-first Corps had about sixty-five thousand men at its disposal, most of these troops were not in Albania but in Montenegro and others parts of the former Yugoslavia. And of those who remained, few were experienced fighters. The units of the Twenty-first Corps in Albania were mostly older, insufficiently armed, and without battle experience—militarily this was not the German army that had invaded Albania in September 1943.[44] Nevertheless, the evacuation proceeded smoothly and at remarkably little cost to the Germans. Much of the credit, or blame, for the successful withdrawal must go to the northern nationalists, who protected vital roads as well as large pieces of territory. Although the partisans certainly scored a political victory by driving northern chiefs firmly into the German camp, it was the Germans who scored the military victory. Units of the 297th Infantry Division with its HQ in Tirana secured old Albania to the area of Shkodra. But Shkodra—particularly important to the Germans, because they planned to leave in that direction—and the area south of the line Puka-Kukës were held—since the end of September—by Muharrem Bajraktari, Gjon Marka Gjoni, Halil Alia, elements of the BK, and small groups of Kupi supporters, all supported by the 181st Infantry Division. Most German observers agreed that without the pro-German clans of northern Albania, the northern route— the only way out—would have been closed to the Germans.[45]

The Battle of Tirana

The situation in Tirana during these last weeks of the occupation became increasingly desperate, and it is here that the largest battle of the war in Albania was fought. Amery, who ventured disguised into Tirana in September, leaves us a good description of the Germans in the capital: "We passed small groups of German officers and soldiers, hurrying to their offices with bulging brief-cases, or strolling towards the shops and cafes. Boyish in their tropical knit, pestered by peddlers and jostled by the oriental throng, they reminded me irresistibly of British troops in the Middle East. It is a new and perhaps healthy experience to see an army of occupation from the native's point of view."[46]

And now what had been the safest place in Albania for both the Italians and the Germans was under attack. Since the end of August, the capital had acted as a magnet for partisan forces, requiring tightened security. Following the not-altogether-successful evacuation of nonessential personal, the German army proceeded to construct something of a fortress. Certain sections of the city were blocked off, and a large security area was designated with the German mission at its center.[47]

Although the Germans continued to believe that Albanian political cooperation remained essential, collaborators in the capital were becoming increasingly difficult to find. On 7 September the prefect of Tirana, Qazim Muletti—whom German documents refer to as absolutely unreliable—panicked and fled to Germany. The position of mayor, after the flight of Omer Fortuzi to Allied-occupied Italy, was turned over to someone entirely unqualified. The German military authorities in Tirana suggested to Gstöttenbauer that the positions of mayor and prefect be united and given to Resilia, the prefect of Vlora, who had demonstrated his loyalty to the Germans, or to Mehmet Çela, prefect of Durrës, who was also considered reliable and effective. Gstöttenbauer rejected this suggestion and instead, in conjunction with Fitzthum, created a three-headed control committee for Tirana made up of General Gustav von Myrdacz, Previzi, who some Germans thought was a communist, and the head of the Albanian secret police. The plan failed, as the seventy-year-old general was captured and later shot by the partisans; the head of the secret police fled to Shkodra; and Previzi, once he had learned enough about German strength and tactics to make himself useful, defected to the partisans.[48]

Tirana remained without any effective Albanian authorities. Soon this was of little consequence for the Germans, however, since they too began to flee. On 15 October the German Ministry in Tirana was dissolved, and Schliep and Scheiger were evacuated to Germany. Within the next few days Fitzthum and Gstöttenbauer moved their headquarters to Prizren until Kosova, too, needed to be evacuated.[49] The German military command, part of the staff of the Twenty-first Corps, transferred its headquarters to Shkodra, where by the end of the month the bulk of the remaining German troops in Albania could be found, estimated at some fifteen thousand men.[50]

On the day before the corps staff left Tirana, the last Albanian collaborationist government of Biçaku, as well as the council of the regency, resigned. Radio Tirana issued a simple statement, noting that "the threats that existed when this government was formed, for various reasons within and without Albania have increased to the extent that they cannot be overcome, thus the High Council of Regency and government resigned on October 26. . . . All civilian officials and soldiers are advised to continue their duties."[51]

The orders for this act came from Gstöttenbauer and were delivered to the government, somewhat reluctantly, by the chief of staff of the Twenty-first Corps. German military authorities questioned both the constitutionality and the wisdom of this act. The same military officials who criticized the Foreign Ministry for adhering too rigidly to the notion of an independent Albania and respecting its neutrality now complained that the reckless dismissal of the government and regency was against stated policy, was carried out without reference to the military authorities, and constituted a black mark against the Germans. The military authorities were particularly concerned about the effect the dismissal of the government would have on order in the country. Perhaps giving Biçaku too much credit, the military authorities blamed the disintegration of authority and resulting anarchy on the removal of the government.[52] An attempt to rectify the situation—the construction of a National Committee in Shkodra, which included the former regent Harapi—predictably came to nothing.[53]

In the midst of the often unimpeded withdrawal, Hoxha determined to launch a final assault on Tirana, almost as if he felt it necessary to get in a few shots before all the Germans had gone. In October partisan forces had reached some forty thousand, and Allied airdrops were at a high as well, in excess of two hundred tons.[54] With new strength and confidence, Mehmet Shehu's first division—made up of the first, fourth, and twenty-third brigades—launched an all-out attack on the city on 29 October. Providing what proved to be valuable service were Stan Eastwood and his long-range desert patrols, who brought in RAF airstrikes. As a further indication of continuing deterioration of relations between the British and the Albanians, considerable dispute arose concerning the strike targets.[55] Nevertheless, on one day the RAF committed twenty-eight rocket-firing Beaufighters, which did considerable damage to the fortified barracks and gun positions the Germans had constructed.[56]

As the Germans were not yet ready to leave, the struggle for Tirana proved to be one of the longest and largest battles between the Germans and the Albanians during the war. Because of its significance in terms of the rapidly developing partisan legend, figures relating to the number of combatants and casualties vary widely. German documents suggest that the German garrison at the beginning of the attack consisted of between five hundred and seven hundred officers and men and some of the staff of the 297th Infantry Division, as well as some five hundred wounded. Albanian socialist sources are somewhat more vague concerning the number of German troops in Tirana, using terms such as "a reduced division."[57]

The first phase of the battle began when the partisans attacked from the south with some two thousand fighters, supported by artillery and armored cars. The Germans immediately withdrew to prepared positions in New Tirana, leaving the old city to the partisans. German military officials maintain that the partisans failed to take New Tirana and suffered heavy casualties in the process.[58]

The second and decisive phase of the battle began on 11 November. As the partisans renewed the attack, a German relief column from the south approached. Between 13 and 15 November the column—units of the Twenty-second Corps, which came from the direction of Struga-Elbasan and consisted of two thousand to three thousand supported by artillery—was itself attacked in the vicinity of the Kërraba Pass by units of the first and eighth brigades. While socialist Albanian sources maintain that the column was wiped out, German sources maintain that it was saved by the arrival of a small number of street tanks stationed in Tirana.[59] In either case, it was time for the German garrison to make for the north on the coastal road to Shkodra if it hoped to keep to the overall timetable for the withdrawal. After cleaning out the bank, on the morning of 18 November the first attempt to break out of what by now had become encirclement failed. Hoxha argues that the Germans in Tirana were completely smashed.[60] But German and British sources tell us that by the afternoon of 18 November battalions of the 297th Infantry Division from Durrës, with heavy artillery broke through to Tirana. The evacuation was certainly hurried. The British BLO who accompanied the partisans into the city noted that some intact vital installations were found.[61] Still, the final evacuation from Tirana seemed orderly, and with the German contingent from Durrës, the Tirana garrison continued north to Shkodra without significant losses.

German documents fail to mention casualty figures for the Battle of Tirana. Albanian socialist historiography maintains that two thousand Germans were killed and five hundred captured.[62] Although these figures are doubtless somewhat exaggerated, the fighting did constitute some of the heaviest in the war. There was heavy damage in those places where the Germans had strong points that were manned. But with the exception of extensive pockmarks from small arms fire, the city seems to have suffered little in the struggle. Zog's palace, for example, survived almost entirely intact—the only visible damage was a hole through the drawing room wall caused by an RAF Beaufighter.[63]

The Battle of Tirana ended on 18 November. The Germans remained in Albania for approximately another two weeks. By 20 November it was clear to the 297th Infantry Division command in Shkodra that the original plan to break out over Mostar was now impossible because of the growing strength of Montenegrin partisans. Instead, the command decided to march northeast through Visegrad to Sarajevo. This route, too, initially was blocked, but with the help of the Albanian nationalists, the troops had little difficulty reaching Montenegro-Bosnia. Once they arrived in Bosnia, further progress was made possible by help from blackshirt units and Montenegrin *çetniks*. The final push was facilitated by sending the Twenty-second Infantry Division from the other direction. In January 1945, following heavy mountain fighting and frequent air attacks—complicated by an early and hard winter, with considerable loss of men and equipment—the remnants of the German occupation forces in Albania joined the bulk of the remaining German forces in the Balkans in Sarajevo.[64] The German occupation of Albania had come to an end.

As a final act the Germans did what they could for some of the Albanians who had compromised themselves and could expect execution if captured by the partisans. In December 1944 the German Foreign Ministry opened a special office in Vienna to deal with those people. Mehdi Frashëri and Xhafer Deva were provided with aid to settle in Italy. Others relied on their own resources as Abaz Kupi had. The chief of the Mirdita and his sons were offered asylum by the pope. Mustafa Kruja and Said Kryeziu—following his release by the partisans resulting from British pressure—also found their way to Rome. Fiqri Dine and Prengë Previzi—although the Germans assumed the latter had been taken in by the partisans—escaped to Greece.[65] Many others, including Anton Harapi and Ibrahim Biçaku, failed to heed the German advice to withdraw. Neubacher tells us that Biçaku, impractical to the end, could not decide which of his opera records to take with him: he delayed too long and was taken.[66] Both Harapi and Biçaku were tried and executed by the new Stalinist government.

The War in Kosova

The war in old Albania had come to an end, except in the north, where forms of resistance to Hoxha continued well into the 1950s. But fighting persisted in Kosova, where Albanian partisans continued the struggle against the Germans and the nationalists. Because of Kosova's unique status, resistance to the Germans there grew much more slowly. Most Kosovar Albanians were willing to overlook the fact that German aggression had been responsible for their union with old Albania. Many Kosovar Albanians were principally preoccupied with driving out the Serbian minority, particularly those who had arrived since 1919. This attitude was at least partially in retaliation for the poor treatment they had received from the Serbs while Kosova was part of interwar

Yugoslavia. The wholesale expulsion of Serbs by the Albanians created special problems for the occupation, however, since the Serbs had performed important functions in Kosova. The Serbs had run most of the businesses, the mills, the tanneries, and the public utilities. Once the Serbs had gone, there were no pharmacists in Kosova. Serbian peasants, somewhat more technologically progressive than their Albanian counterparts, were responsible for much of the surplus agricultural production for which Kosova was so useful.[67] By April 1944, German documents tell us, 40,000 Serbs had been forced to leave, and Neubacher anticipated that the Germans might have to deal with as many as 150,000 Serbs leaving Kosova.

Neubacher complained that Bedri Pejani and the Second League of Prizren were at least partially responsible for these excesses. The formation of the league, in late 1943, had originally been welcomed by Neubacher because it provided the Germans with a Germanophile organizational focal point with which to deal. The excesses of Pejani and his group, however, were too much even for the Germans. Neubacher ultimately refers to Pejani as being mad or crazed, particularly after receiving Pejani's request for 150,000 weapons. Neubacher assumed, with good reason, that these weapons would be used to launch a modern St. Bartholomew's Day massacre of Serbs and Montenegrins. Neubacher was driven to the point of attempting to convince the regency that it would be in everyone's interest if Pejani were arrested.[68] Conscious of the support the league had in Kosova, the regency refused.

Because Pejani's rabid nationalism was far from unpopular among the Albanians of Kosova, it is not surprising that a communist or pro-Allied resistance movement was a long time in surfacing. Would-be resistance fighters had the additional challenge of the SS "Skanderbeg" Division, which operated principally in Kosova. Although hardly an observer sympathetic to the Albanians, the communist organizer Svetozar Vukmanovich-Tempo describes the problem quite accurately: "Conditions for armed resistance in Kosovo and Metohije were worse than in any other region of the country.... The Albanian population ... had an unfriendly attitude towards the partisans. ... Power is in the hands of the Albanians ... and this is all they see today."[69]

Under these adverse circumstances, the first conference of the People's Liberation Committee for Kosova-Metohija (or Kosmet) was not held until December 1943 to January 1944 at the town of Bujan. The meeting, chaired by Mehmet Hoxha and directed by Fadil Hoxha (neither related to Enver Hoxha), brought together some fifty delegates, mostly Albanian and mostly communist, although some nationalists hostile to the puppet Albanian regime were also in attendance. The conference adopted a resolution to fight on the side of the Allies on the basis of the Atlantic Charter, which guaranteed the right of national self-determination.[70] Those present clearly understood that without support for at least the prospect of an Albanian Kosova, the Kosmet committee stood little chance of gaining any level of popular support.

The declaration was essentially in line with Enver Hoxha's official position, which was to delay dealing with these delicate issues until the end of the war. But the conference further determined to send representatives to both Tito and the NLM. This move undermined what little support the declaration engendered. Indeed, the movement apparently was never strong enough and never received enough indigenous support to actually conduct any anti-German operations within its own area—although it was able to operate outside of Kosova and on the edges. Lack of supplies must also have been a major factor.[71] The British did send a liaison officer, Lieutenant Andy Hands, who was present at the Bujan meeting. Hands, however, was unable to supply much material and was ordered by Bari to confine his attention to operations within old Albania and to break off contact at the first sign of political complications and flee to territory controlled by Yugoslav partisans.[72]

Kosova, therefore, remained solidly within the Axis camp and was liberated with some difficulty. And it is fully understandable why it was in Kosova that Fitzthum and Gstöttenbauer made a last desperate attempt to forestall the inevitable. The two lent their support to the construction of an anti-communist Albanian government in Kosova under Xhafer Deva. While the political movement predictably led to nothing, the material support with which Deva was provided had significant later repercussions. Fitzthum and Gstöttenbauer apparently deposited large caches of weapons, ammunition, and food—and they have also been accused of leaving German agents behind—to support continued opposition to the NLM's and Tito's partisans. According to Yugoslav sources, these supplies were instrumental in the uprising of thousands of Kosovar Albanians.[73]

By September 1944, the Fifth Brigade, together with bolder units of the Kosmet group, were active against the Germans on the vital Kukës-Prizren road.[74] This brigade moved freely across the old frontier well before official socialist Yugoslav and Albanian histories suggest that, in response to an invitation from Tito, it crossed into Kosova; the official histories tell us that it was not until 13 October, following Tito's formal invitation, that the Third and Fifth Brigades entered Kosova to assist the Yugoslav partisans. At the end of November, the Twenty-fifth Brigade also moved into Kosova, joining with the Third and Fifth Brigades to form the Fifth division. Following the German retreat from Shkodra, these units were joined by the newly formed, and considerably less effective Sixth Division, which engaged the Germans around Podgorica and went on to participate in the liberation of Montenegro and Bosnia. While socialist Yugoslav sources of the 1950s tended to ignore the Albanian contribution to the liberation of Kosova and other areas of prewar Yugoslavia, socialist Albanian sources maintain that some three hundred Albanians were killed in the struggle.[75]

Why Tito, whose movement was considerably stronger than that of the NLM, needed Albanian participation for the clearing of Kosova is still debated. It is difficult not to conclude that his reasons were cynical. Tito was certainly aware of the unpopularity of his partisans in Kosova and assumed correctly that Albanian partisans would face somewhat less opposition from the local population. The Albanian units proceeded as usual to construct national liberation councils, at which point the Yugoslav General Staff ordered them north into Montenegro and Bosnia, where they certainly were not needed. Yugoslav partisans then replaced the Albanian partisans in Kosova, dismantling the councils they had constructed and proceeding administratively to reintegrate Kosova into the new socialist Yugoslavia. Once this was accomplished, the Albanian divisions were sent back to old Albania, without reentering Kosova.[76] Hoxha did not object, and his critics argue that he was so willing to give up Kosova because it is Geg and its incorporation would have meant an overwhelming Geg dominance in postwar Albania.[77] Yugoslav troops in Kosova treated the Albanians there like Axis collaborators, resulting in a full-scale revolt, which lasted from November 1944 to May 1945. It was only with difficulty, and some thirty thousand troops, that Tito was able to crush this uprising.[78] In a certain sense, of course, at least the spirit of the uprising continues to this day.

Zog's Final Attempt to Form a Government in Exile

As the war drew to a close in Albania, the question of a postwar political settlement—arguably the principal preoccupation of all Albanian groups during the entire wartime period—became even more acute. Zog, as the last legitimate ruler, who still controlled considerable financial resources, was certainly a contender for power. Although Zog had failed to convince the British to actively use him in the resistance, he never abandoned his claim to be Albania's rightful ruler. Despite the British insistence that he refrain from politics of any kind, Zog never entirely abstained, recognizing that if he did so his chances of returning to Albania after the war would be jeopardized. Zog did as much as he could, within the rather strict limitations imposed on him by the ever vigilant Foreign Office.

Zog's problem was one of legitimacy. No government officially recognized him either as the leader of an established government in exile or as the leader of the Albanian people. Zog hoped to solve this problem by convincing the British to change their policy, assuming that once the British had done so other Allied states would follow suit. Zog's campaign to convince the Foreign Office to change its mind included maintaining and expanding his contacts with Albanian groups both in and out of the country, rallying influential supporters in Great Britain and the United States, and taking advantage of opportunities—no matter how remote—whenever they happened to arise.

Examples of the latter include his appeal in 1942 to individual participants of a London wartime conference. He and his agents approached Canadian, American, Belgian, and Czech delegates to obtain help in gaining recognition. While the first two remained cool, the Belgians and the Czechs proved to be somewhat more receptive—presumably because they too had been forced out of their countries by Axis troops. But little came of this. The Belgians sent a sympathetic reply, and Eduard Benes went so far as to send a cordial one. Geraldine tells us that Benes became a frequent visitor at the Ritz, where Zog and his party were staying.[79] Although these people undoubtedly wished Zog well, none was willing to expend his own limited political capital to further the cause of Zog.

As the war progressed, Zog's schemes became more desperate, perhaps the most remarkable coming to light in an interview with members of the Anglo-Jewish Association in January 1944. Zog offered to sponsor a plan for a Jewish settlement in Albania if the Anglo-Jewish Association agreed to help him regain his throne. The association reported the interview to the Foreign Office and seems to have taken no other action in this regard.[80]

Zog seemed to be somewhat more successful recruiting influential nongovernmental foreign supporters, many of whom had served in the diplomatic corps in Albania during Zog's reign. Albania appears to be one of those states that casts something of a spell on those who come in contact with it, particularly Westerners. Few of these people seemed to be able to put Albania aside entirely. Many became directly involved as publicists for Albanian causes, including the resurrection of the monarchy under Zog. The former American minister Charles C. Hart serves as a good example. He organized a small group of Albanian enthusiasts called the Friends of Albania.

The most influential groups of this type, however, were active in London. The first group to devote its efforts to the cause of Albania during the war was the Friends of Albania (not connected to Hart's American group). This group, despite that it was formed under the auspices of Zog's rather obsequious secretary Qazim Kastrioti, nevertheless attracted some influential persons, including the philanthropist Miss Tildsley, as well as Harry Hodgkinson, a military organizer under Percy. This group was obviously very pro-Zog and ultimately cooperated with the larger and more influential Anglo-Albanian Association, founded by the Albanologist Aubrey Herbert. Following his death, the association went dormant but was revived by Herbert's widow in March 1943. Its membership included Viscount Cecil—who had played an important role in Western recognition of the new state of Albania—Jocelyn Percy, H. Hodgson, and the Albanologist Edith Durham. The secretary, Sir Edward Boyle, also served as the chairman of the Balkan Committee, a pro-Albanian, pro-Bulgarian, anti-Greek group with Lord Noel Buxton as president.[81]

Of the émigré Albanian groups, all of which founded Zogist committees, the largest communities could be found in the United States, Egypt, and Turkey. The latter two were of particular significance to Zog because they were located in states with Moslem governments quite sympathetic to him. This sympathy was such that Zog was allowed to maintain his old legations in Istanbul and Cairo, which provided him with a strong claim to legitimacy. While these legations accomplished little in practical terms, Zog was always willing to send them considerable sums of money for maintenance costs because of their symbolic importance.

The Albanian community in the United States—centered in Boston and Detroit—was also of considerable significance for Zog. The community was quite large—thirty thousand according to the Albanians themselves, fifteen thousand according to the U.S. Census Bureau.[82] The community contained some important figures, including Zog's long-time opponent Fan Noli, whose nominally democratic, Western-oriented government had been overthrown by Zog in 1924. Noli, founder and bishop of the Albanian Orthodox Church in the United States, was recognized as a principle community leader. The same held true for Zog's independently minded former minister to Washington, Faik Konica, who founded the Vatra organization and controlled the mildly republican newspaper *Dielli*. With Konica's death in December 1942, he was replaced by Peter Kolonja, an honest and quiet individual who was, however, considerably less astute politically than Konica had been. Kolonja quickly was completely taken in by Zog and began carrying out Zog's instructions, including his rather naive announcement to the State Department in January 1943 that he had been instructed to reopen the Albanian mission in Washington. The State Department had no interest in even discussing the possibility.[83]

The third principle force among the Albanians in America, and the most intransigent, was K. A. Çekrezi, a sworn opponent of Zog. During the 1920s, Çekrezi had been publisher of the *Telegraph,* one of Tirana's early newspapers. In that capacity he had become a virtual spokesman for Zog. By the 1930s, however, Çekrezi had turned against Zog and was arrested in 1932 in conjunction with a conspiracy to overthrow the king. Released in 1935, he immediately became involved in another more serious plot, and when it collapsed Çekrezi fled the country.[84] Once in the United States he organized a small, intensively anti-Zogist organization called the Free Albania Movement, with Tajar Zavalani, an Albanian employed by the BBC in London, as vice-president. Çekrezi founded his own newspaper, the *Liria,* and hurled invective against Zog and all those who would treat with him. Noli had a rather poor opinion of Çekrezi, noting in a letter that "Çekrezi is an irresponsible, unprincipled, unscrupulous juggler . . . who now represents a negligible misinformed minority in the United States and can be taken seriously as a champion of Albanian republicanism only by people who have no sense of humor."[85] The old Albanian adage that it is easier to collect a sack full of fleas than it is to find two Albanians who agree, seemed to have taken on a new meaning among the Albanians in the United States. Zog played an active role by funding Kolonja and *Dielli,* as well as sending three hundred dollars a month to Bishop Noli.[86]

Zog also attempted to maintain contact with Albanians of various political persuasions within Albania. How much actual contact there was is difficult to determine, but Zog told Ryan in 1941 that this group included many of his erstwhile staunchest opponents as well as some who had cooperated with the Axis. Among those who agreed to work with him, Zog counted Gani Bey Kryeziu, the powerful Kosovar chieftain, and Maliq Bushati, who had been minister of the interior in Vërlaci's first post-invasion government.[87] Zog's principal supporter, of course, was Kupi and his Legality movement, which constituted Zog's single most important claim to legitimacy in Albania.

In order to strengthen his claim among the émigrés and among the Allied powers, Zog hoped to do two things: first he hoped to create some degree of unity among the émigré groups, and then he hoped to be allowed to create some form of official government in exile. Both of these tasks proved to be significant challenges. In terms of Zog's first goal, he actually enjoyed some success. He was able to effect coordination between the Anglo-Albanian Association and the Friends of Albania in Great Britain. He was also able to convince Vatra and Noli to cooperate with him. Considering past relations between Noli and Zog, winning over Noli was a significant coup for Zog, and he was able to do so partly as a result of cash payments and partly as a result of Zog's declaration in Paris in 1940 and again in London in 1942 that once Albania was freed, a national assembly, elected freely and democratically, would be summoned to decide Albania's social and political future.[88] Zog, though naturally reluctant to make such a guarantee, seems to have had little choice.

Noli, for his part, had no illusions about Zog. He was described by Larry Post, the assistant editor of *Liria*, as considering Zog to be necessary only up to the peace conference, at which point Noli would conclude, "I've got across the river, to hell with you now." Noli apparently also recognized that Zog's money would be useful, noting that "At least we'll make him spend his stolen funds on a good cause."[89] In exchange, Noli expressed his willingness to cooperate with Zog in a united Albanian front, but he himself, because of his American citizenship, would only serve in an advisory capacity. Noli further suggested that some sort of official role be assigned to Çekrezi in order to gain his cooperation.[90]

Zog was willing to do this, but Çekrezi, it seems, found it difficult to forget the time he spent in Zog's jails. Çekrezi did, however, eventually soften his stand, motivated possibly by rumors that Zog's supporters circulated in Washington in the summer of 1942 to the effect that the British were on the verge of recognizing Zog.[91] Çekrezi was also being pressured by elements within his own small Free Albanian Movement to come to some accommodation with Noli and Zog, and he reluctantly relented.

Nothing came of this fragile unity, however, since Zog and Çekrezi failed to agree on the course the united front was to follow. Çekrezi suggested the formation of an Albanian national committee, consisting of Zogists, anti-Zogists, and guerrilla chiefs. Guerilla chiefs would act as minister of war and commander in chief, and Noli would be designated as honorary president. Zog rejected this plan, arguing that the proposed committee was not a government, and Albania would in effect be giving up what he considered to be its legal rights. This, Zog suggested, was incompatible with Albania's national interests.[92]

Zog wanted more. He hoped to rescue what Noli insisted he should demand, namely, official recognition as the legitimate and logical head of the Albanian government in exile, entitled to a seat at the peace conference.[93] Boyle, Percy, and Hodgson also encouraged Zog to act, suggesting that he attempt to play the Allies off against each other and appeal to Washington for recognition in light of the Atlantic Charter.[94]

But once the British government was informed of Zog's increased activities, he was quickly stopped. Ironically, it was Zog himself who informed the British of his plans, laying the whole scheme out for Ryan during one of their frequent conversations. Once the plans were out in the open, the Foreign Office acted quickly. Officials were sent to Boyle, requesting that he cease to encourage Zog. Zog himself was told that the government would not allow such activity on its soil and that Zog had violated his pledge not to become involved in politics.

Zog complained bitterly that Albania was being discriminated against and that he needed to do something, since he was being criticized by some Albanians in Istanbul for inactivity. Further, Zog argued, a small government was necessary as a focal point for the legations still open, for the Albanians abroad, and for those who had remained loyal in Albania proper.[95] The unfortunate Ryan was left to explain British policy to the embittered king. Ryan stated that the British government would not recognize Zog, because it had legally acknowledged the invasion and because Zog had not headed a democratic government. Britain, as a result, planned to preserve liberty of action.

A clear statement of British policy toward Zog was made in a Foreign Office minute in March 1943. The British government would not recognize a provisional government under Zog even if all Albanians in the United States and Great Britain united behind Zog, because (1) such an organization would not stimulate resistance, and it might even have the opposite effect because of Zog's unpopularity; and (2) it would create serious problems in British-Greek relations. The memo concluded that the British would not exclude Zog if the Albanian people expressed a desire for his return after the war.[96]

Because the Americans followed the British lead with regard to most Albanian matters, Zog had little hope. The Foreign Office was further reinforced in its decision by Brigadier Davies's report in December 1943 in which he concluded that an Albanian committee abroad would have no appreciable effect on the resistance situation within the country. The final blow to Zog's hopes came in early 1944 when the Foreign Office was told by BLOs that the strength of Kupi's movement had been significantly overestimated.[97] Zog would not be allowed to lead or join in a government in exile. This left only Enver Hoxha and the communist-dominated NLM and insured a communist takeover. As with many other aspects of Albania at war, this communist takeover was unique. It had no parallel in the other Balkan or Eastern European states where communism was installed, because Albania was not directly liberated by the Soviet Union. Neither the Soviets nor Tito's partisans sent war material or troops. Hoxha's revolution was the most indigenous of all.[98] And it had been very carefully prepared.

A Stalinist Albania

Since the founding of the Albanian Communist Party in November 1941, Enver Hoxha's moves and those of his party had been as much political as they had been military. His goal, although often hidden from the Western Allies, was to encourage the Germans to speed their withdrawal and then to insure the construction of a Stalinist state in Albania. As it became more and more clear that the Axis would be defeated, the political program consumed more and more of Hoxha's time and attention and by September 1944, a significant lull in partisan military activity occurred which can be attributed partly if not principally to Hoxha's preoccupation with politics.[99]

While Hoxha's most important wartime political moves were saved for 1944, the groundwork, fashioned principally on the Yugoslav model, was laid much earlier. The important milestones include Hoxha's bold stroke at Peza in September 1942, when he became a national figure by creating a national front of resistance in the NLM. This move, as with many others, corresponded with the policies of Tito and the Comintern. The meeting at Peza was a big step; because the communists were the only organized political party at the meeting, they were able to dominate. The *History of the Party of Labor of Albania* tells us that the Peza Conference laid the foundation for the new state power.[100] Apart from the general council, regional and local councils were constructed, which did much to spread Hoxha's influence, while at the same time gathering food and clothing for the fighters.

Parallel to the united front meetings, Hoxha convened meetings of the party to strengthen his own internal position. After receiving Comintern approval, Hoxha called the first national conference of the ACP in March 1943 at Labinot. Tito had sent a letter to the Albanian central committee, and its contents became the agenda for the conference. The letter, which summarized a message from the Comintern, instructed the Albanian party to beware of internal traitors, choose reliable leadership, and follow the Comintern popular front strategy by reaching out to the middle class and the peasants.[101] With these instructions, the conference condemned heresy and elected a permanent central committee with Hoxha continuing as first secretary. The conference also called for the creation of a regular army of national liberation to be controlled by the communists.[102] The General Council of the NLM quickly agreed, and Hoxha became the principal political commissar with the communist Spiro Moisiu as overall commander.

Although Yugoslav influence in the Albanian party increased as a result of this conference, this influence was still not strong enough to allow Tito's roving ambassador Vukmanovic-Tempo to convince the Albanians to accept his Balkan general staff idea. The communists in Greece, and even the weak communist organization in Bulgaria, also rejected the idea as a transparent attempt on the part of the Yugoslavs to gain control of all of the Balkan resistance movement.[103]

The next major step, in September 1943, was the second conference of the NLM at Labinot. Carefully monitored by the Yugoslavs, the NLM at Labinot rejected the Mukje Agreements and strengthened and expanded the local and regional councils, which, because of the collapse of the Italians, were briefly given the opportunity to function in urban areas, principally Gjirokastra and Kruja. Hoxha argued that while the tenure of these urban councils was limited, the experience was important because rather than being faced with confusion, Albanians were shown what the future leaders of the country could do. The councils went beyond their original function of collecting aid for the partisans and—at least in some areas—began to govern the towns and the districts. At the Peza conference, the councils had emerged as the nuclei of the future organs of state administration; at the Labinot conference, the tasks and activities of the councils were increased and were proclaimed to be the only people's power.[104]

As Axis defeat and the withdrawal of German troops from Albania became increasingly certain, Hoxha stepped up his political activity. At the end of May 1944 Hoxha called an NLM congress at Përmet, in a hard-hit area of the south that had traditionally remained under partisan control and where he was welcomed by the people. This would be one of the most important sessions prior to the end of the war. Motivated at least in part by the ultimately unsuccessful British efforts to bring about unity and resistance among the noncommunist Albanian groups, Hoxha hoped to use the congress first to insure his control over the NLM.[105] He also used the opportunity to move an important step closer to the formation of a government. We are told that some 186 delegates attended "a representative body democratically elected within the possibilities permitted by the war circumstances."[106] A new NLM council was elected, which was invested with executive and legislative powers. This group of 115 was declared provisional until a national election for a constituent assembly could be held. The council chose a standing committee of thirty, which, with Omer Nishani at its head, elected a committee of twelve, with Hoxha as president and supreme commander of the armed forces. This standing committee was said to possess "all of the attributes of a provisional government."[107] Hoxha tells us that a regular provisional government was not yet formed, because a good part of the country was still under German occupation, by May 1944 there was not yet a complete network of administrative organs, and the Allies would not have recognized the move.[108]

The congress changed the name of the NLM to the NLF (National Liberation Front), since Albania now had a government, and the movement ceased to perform executive functions.[109] The congress also approved a series of far-reaching decisions that in part comprised the basis of the future Albanian state constitution. The decisions included the following: (1) Albania was to have a democratic and popular government, according to the will of the Albanian people as expressed in the Anti-Fascist Council of National Liberation, the sole national authority to have arisen from the national liberation struggle; (2) King Zog was forbidden to return to Albania; (3) the formation of any other government in Albania or abroad was not to be recognized; and (4) all treaties and agreements concluded by the Albanian government with other countries before 1939 were to be examined and declared null and void if found to be incompatible with the people's needs.[110] Hoxha was not yet ready to liquidate the monarchy for fear of Allied reaction—a groundless fear—and in keeping with his pledge to allow the people as a whole participation in the decision on the future nature of the state.

In an attempt to reassure the citizens of Përmet that the worst was over, that he was firmly in control, and that peaceful pursuits were soon to return, Hoxha decreed that the congress end with a series of cultural events. Although the theater turned out to be of the socialist-realist variety, the songs and dances contributed to a lighter atmosphere. It was clear that the end of Albania's wartime experience was not far off.

Hoxha's committee did what it could to look like a government. Although the German summer offensive effectively hindered the normal business of the standing committee, once the German push receded in July, decisions and laws were again promulgated by the committee from its new base in Helmës, deep in the southern Ostrovica mountain range. These decisions concerned the organization and revival of the economy, education, and health services. In an attempt to demonstrate that the standing committee was more than just a paper authority, it began to register and administer the national assets, to bring into production those few industrial projects Albania possessed, to open schools, and wherever possible to provide the liberated areas with needed personal such as teachers and doctors.[111] Although these initial steps were undoubtedly extremely limited and had little real impact, their propaganda value was certainly important.

It was only a matter of months before Hoxha decided that another major step towards the creation of a new government was necessary. Hoxha relates that he was motivated by the fact that by October, with some three-quarters of the country free of Germans, a more permanent political structure was needed. Hoxha was certainly also concerned about the possibility of an Allied landing; the British had landed in Greece in October and were quickly followed by the Greek government in exile. The Yugoslavs again played a critical role at this juncture. Tito, too, was worried about the possibility of an Allied landing in Albania and urged Hoxha to confront the Allies with a provisional government.[112]

Berat, one of Albania's principal cities, in the center of the country, and with ancient historical traditions, was chosen. The city had been evacuated by the Germans only a few weeks earlier, and because it had suffered little during the war it presented a picture of normalcy. Hoxha, who was enthusiastically received, tells us about the shops being full and the restaurants and cafés remaining open late into the evening.[113]

In order to provide continuity, the meeting was called the second session of the congress of Përmet. The decisions taken, again closely following the Yugoslav model, were certainly as important, however, and included the transformation of Hoxha's committee into a provisional government. The most important members included Hoxha as prime minister; Moscow-trained Sejfulla Malëshova as minister of press, propaganda, and culture; and Koçi Xoxe, the creature of the Yugoslavs and the only worker in the top leadership, as vice-president of the council. Only two of the eleven members of the provisional government were noncommunists, although Hoxha made an attempt to disguise the fact, aware that Allied recognition would be jeopardized by overtly communist acts and that nationalists made up perhaps 25 percent or more of partisan forces.[114] Hoxha was not altogether unsuccessful here, with OSS agents reporting to Washington in December 1944 that Hoxha was not a communist. William Donovan, the OSS chief, was convinced and urged the state department to adopt a more encouraging attitude toward Hoxha because, Donovan reported, the Albanian leader was neither a communist nor a fellow traveler and was sincerely anxious to establish a Western-oriented democracy.[115]

The eight-point program which the provisional government released was the picture of reasoned Western democracy. The program included the following points: (1) after the complete liberation of Albania and after the situation is stabilized, the democratic government of Albania shall hold free elections on a democratic basis for a constituent assembly, which shall lay down the form of the state and promulgate a constitution; (2) the democratic government shall ensure and defend all the civil rights of its citizens (followed by an enumerated declaration of the rights of citizens); (3) the democratic government of Albania shall try to promote cooperation with the great allies: Great Britain, the Soviet Union, and the United States; and (4) the democratic government of Albania shall seek recognition as the sole government of Albania from the allied powers—Great Britain, the Soviet Union, and the United States—as well as from all other participants in the Anti-Fascist Coalition.[116]

Although this was little known either outside of or in Albania at the time, for clearer glimpses of Albania's future it was more important to watch the internal functioning of the Communist Party. Hoxha remained in Berat for a month after the Berat congress, and it was there, at the end of November, that the party held its important second plenum. At that point, divisions within the party, in conjunction with the growing difficulties between Hoxha and the Yugoslavs, threatened to oust Hoxha from his leadership role. Prior to the plenum, the pro-Yugoslav elements within the politburo—in particular Koçi Xoxe—had forced Hoxha to agree to allow Tito's representative to take part in politburo discussions.

Once in, Colonel Velimir Stojnic ardently pursued Yugoslav aims. These included transforming the Albanian party into a miniature version of its Yugoslav counterpart; weakening Hoxha, who had demonstrated determined nationalism; and pushing for the construction of some sort of confederal link between Albania and Yugoslavia. Stojnic, Xoxe, and Malëshova criticized Hoxha for sectarianism, for alienating important segments of the population—including noncommunist opposition groups, influential members of the bourgeoisie, and the churches—all of whom, according to the then current Yugoslav line, should be brought into the NLF.[117]

Hoxha argued that the ultimate goal of those orchestrating these determined attacks was his removal. He survived because of the support he had among many of the fighting cadres, some of whom were added to the politburo in Berat. Although Hoxha was certainly correct in his fears, it would have been surprising had his opponents succeeded in their goal in the midst of the wartime victory.[118] These attacks did, however, succeed in two things. First, they turned the next four years, until Hoxha was able to liquidate most of the pro-Yugoslav faction following the Soviet-Yugoslav break, into a trying time for Hoxha, a time when his position could never be considered fully secure. Second, and perhaps more important in the long run, Hoxha's experience in the last months of 1944 further encouraged him to jettison that part of him that contained liberal and Western elements. His rise to power had occurred during a time of struggle—he had maintained his position in late 1944 in light of that struggle.[119] He seems to have decided that to maintain his power, he must perpetuate the mentality of struggle and to perpetuate the notion of enemies everywhere, externally and internally. The state-of-siege mentality (similar to that used by the puppet Albanian governments under the Germans) that characterized Hoxha's regime until his death in 1985 can be traced, in part, to this plenum.

Immediately following the end of the plenum, Hoxha traveled to Tirana—which the Germans had evacuated on 17 November—in order to enter the capital on flag day, 28 November. Although his reception was somewhat less warm than those received in southern towns, Hoxha and his movement were firmly in control of most of the country. He moved rapidly to insure the continuance of that control, and through these first moves observers were able to identify some of the principal elements of the character of the regime to come.

Although the tasks of constructing an entirely new state, rebuilding the economy, and forming the basis of a new social order were daunting, Hoxha had advantages his predecessor Zog had not had. When Hoxha came to power, he had a relatively free hand as a result of the traditional right of conquest and by virtue of the growing partisan army. Equally as important, the war had either destroyed or completely discredited the traditional ruling classes in Albania. Either they had collaborated outright or had at least done nothing for the resistance.

Hoxha benefited from a number of other advantages as well. He had the example of Zog, which occasionally allowed Hoxha to avoid mistakes. To shape his policies Hoxha also had the legacy of failed interwar capitalism, the wartime fascist experience, and the sometimes manufactured but frequently real specter of capitalism encirclement.

Hoxha, then, was faced with the task of rebuilding Albania on the foundation, or what was left of it, laid by Zog. Like Zog, his main goal was predetermined. In its simplest sense Hoxha's principal task was the creation of a viable independent nation-state and what he colorfully described as "the monolithic unity . . . of the Albanian people."[120] Because his goals were often similar to those of Zog, it is perhaps not surprising that his policy priorities were often similar as well. Despite the violent Stalinist rhetoric Hoxha adopted and did follow through on to a certain extent, he essentially had little choice at the same time to become as ardent a nationalist as Zog had been, not particularly difficult for Hoxha, since he had strong nationalist tendencies in any case. Indeed, given the narrow base of the communist movement's support, extreme nationalism was the only means (added of course to the army and other security forces) by which Hoxha could remain in power and progress toward a modern Stalinist state. Nationalism proved to be the principal element in all of his policies.

The first priority—to gain legitimacy—was to construct an adequate political system rapidly. Building on Përmet and Berat, Hoxha used both intelligence and savage brutality to achieve his goal. The initial steps included the physical removal of those forces considered a danger to the construction of the new Stalinist state, forces initially identified only by the somewhat generic term *war criminal*. This was done in a number of stages, including the immediate execution of an undetermined number of people, estimated at forty to sixty, as soon as the provisional government established itself in Tirana in November 1944.[121] In December 1944 and January 1945 a number of Special People's Tribunals were established, the most notable of which was the Special People's Court of Tirana, headed by Koçi Xoxe, who was assigned to the task of dealing with the major war criminals in a series of show trials. As long as officials still hoped for Allied recognition, the work of these courts was reasonably circumspect. Despite the fact that neither Xoxe, nor the president of the court, nor any of the judges had any legal training, British military observers maintained that the accused, most of whom appeared to be genuine collaborators, received more justice than they might have expected.[122]

But once Allied recognition seemed less likely and after the West refused to extradite a long list of enemies, including Kupi, Hoxha allowed his courts more leeway. The terms *war criminal* and *noncommunist* rapidly became synonymous. While figures vary, the number of victims executed or imprisoned during these early years was certainly in the thousands. That significant excesses took place is clear. Hoxha himself related the story of an innocent Albanian who was tortured and put to death during this period. Hoxha indicted Xoxe, who was later purged and executed, for this crime, and he further suggests that these incidents were frequent.[123]

By these means Hoxha was able to eliminate or silence the remaining elements of the pre-war political elite. The general population was discouraged from opposition by the superior force of partisan security. Rather than demobilize the army at the end of the war, Hoxha rapidly increased the size of the armed forces, so soon Albanian security forces made up 3.5 percent of the population and cost between 10 and 11 percent of the GNP.[124] Other means of control included rigid checking of movement, billeting of large numbers of troops in private houses, and periodic raids on homes. Control was further enhanced by keeping partisan brigades on the move, requiring civilians to report at various times, and when necessary carrying out purges followed by imprisonment.[125] Despite these rigorous security measures, however, partisan troops generally behaved correctly, even in the north where they were never popular.

With the enhanced personal security these measures provided, Hoxha slowly moved toward the creation of a permanent government. While democracy and free elections had constituted an important part of Hoxha's propaganda, once he ascended to power these promises became considerably less important.[126] Provisional foreign minister O. Nishani, speaking to a member of the British mission, explained why: "These people do not understand democracy as you know it. . . . They have not yet received sufficient education to vote as you vote." He went on to say that voting would continue to be controlled by the army.[127] The outcome of the first postwar election, then, was not left to chance. Like the Yugoslavs, Hoxha had created a democratic front, as the successor to the NLF, but it was, of course, dominated by the communists. Unlike in much of the rest of Eastern Europe and the Balkans, Albania did not experience a coalition government, principally because no government in exile had ever been recognized.

Because only official Democratic Front candidates could run for office stand, the Front swept into office with 90 percent of the vote. When the new national constituent assembly met early in 1946, it formally abolished the monarchy, proclaimed Albania to be a people's republic within its prewar frontiers, and approved a new constitution along Stalinist lines, similar to the one in Yugoslavia.[128] Although much of Albania's Ottoman tradition remained, Hoxha had nevertheless succeeded in constructing, in a short time, a highly personal, reasonably stable regime, as totalitarian as any regime in Albania could be in 1945. Hoxha held the posts of general secretary of the party, president of the Democratic Front, prime minister, foreign minister, defense minister, and commander in chief. Although his dangerous rival Koçi Xoxe, who did much to insure the continuance of close ties to Yugoslavia, controlled the crucial post of minister of the interior, Xoxe's tenure came to an abrupt end in 1948, when he was shot during the early stages of the Soviet-Yugoslav break. This event allowed Hoxha to free himself from Tito and turn to Stalin, and it did much to cement Hoxha's extremism.

This new government and its developing state-of-siege mentality based on hard-line revolutionary ideology allowed Hoxha to turn quickly to reshape Albania's economic and social foundations. When Hoxha came to power, he faced the most difficult internal economic conditions in Eastern Europe. By 1944 Albania's economic condition had changed little since the mid-1920s. In 1938 industry accounted for only 4.4 percent of the national income.[129] Agriculture and stock-breeding methods remained primitive. Transportation and communication were still arduous. In 1939 there were still no railroads and only five hundred miles of roads, most of which were generally in a state of disrepair. Albania still found it necessary to import all needed manufactured goods, as well as significant quantities of wheat, corn, and rice.[130] The war and Axis occupation did not substantially alter Albania's economic condition.

Hoxha moved with speed and ruthless determination in addressing these problems. Initial government operating expenses were obtained through the confiscation of the property of "enemies," the levying of a crippling war-profits tax on the larger merchants, and forced subscription to internal loans. Many resisted and had their entire holdings nationalized, whereas others made every effort to make the first installments in the hopes that the regime would either change or soften its demands.[131] Hoxha, of course, did not soften his demands, with little regret. Because the small merchant class represented the alienated classes, he could easily afford to offend its members.

Further, in a sweeping resolution passed in December 1944, the government confiscated the goods of all Germans, Italians, and political refugees, and in effect it nationalized all goods of value. The decree declared that all industries and firms had become the property of the state; all food supplies and other needed material would be requisitioned after a fair payment. All trained persons were declared mobilized, and the exportation of metals of industrial value, precious stones, gold, jewelry, and ornaments was prohibited.[132] By 1947 nearly 100 percent of nationalization of industrial production had been achieved, dispersing the prewar archaic economy and ultimately destroying the remains of the prewar middle class.[133]

An even more important priority, given the overwhelming agrarian nature of the Albanian economy, was agrarian reform. Gaining some support among the essentially hostile peasant majority was crucial to the survival of the regime, and once again Hoxha moved quickly. His first steps in the direction of reform included cancellation of debts and a 75 percent reduction in rents, quickly followed in August 1945 by extensive land reform. Land belonging to individuals with other sources of income was expropriated outright, thereby destroying the economic power of the prewar landowning class. The expropriated land was redistributed among seventy thousand landless or poor families. All forests and pasturelands were nationalized. In the first year of reform some 50 percent of Albania's arable land was redistributed, thereby doing much to neutralize the peasant class' hostility toward the communists.[134] Although Hoxha would eventually follow Stalin and fully collectivize agriculture, he felt it prudent not to go too far too soon.

Possibly the greatest obstacle to the creation of a modern nation-state in Albania was its diverse religious and social structure and its primitive level of education. Apart from the Geg-Tosk division, Albanians adhered to four principal religions. But disunity was perhaps primarily fostered by the coexistence of three conflicting stages of civilization: the illiterate mountain clansmen in the north, who were primarily Geg and Moslem; the feudal beys and their repressed peasants in the south; and the more educated and urbanized population of the Orthodox Hellenic and Catholic fringes. Hoxha saw religion as not only divisive but also as a force for the perpetuation of foreign influence.

Hoxha began his religious repression with the Catholics. They were singled out because many Catholics had either collaborated with the Italians or at least had vigorously opposed the communist takeover. Hoxha subsequently determined that the Catholic Church was controlled by—as he defined them—reactionaries, subversives, and antinationalists, each of whom represented foreign interests. Even before the end of 1944 Hoxha attempted to close Catholic schools, associations, and periodicals in Shkodra, Albania's Catholic center. Because of the resistance these moves provoked, however, the orders were withdrawn, and Hoxha decided to move much more slowly.[135] By 1945 Hoxha had regained his nerve, and the persecution progressed. The church leadership was either executed; imprisoned, with the rank-and-file clergy pensioned off; or retained as carefully controlled civil servants.[136]

But Hoxha saw education as the principal means of weaning Albanians from their archaic social system and encouraging them onward in the struggle for the creation of monolithic unity and a Stalinist state. Hoxha had begun his crusade to eradicate Albania's 85 percent illiteracy rate during the war. When not fighting, the men and women of the partisan movement received instruction, including the basics of reading and writing, and some political education. Instructors connected all those not in the movement with fascism, and they blamed capitalism for the failed prewar economic system. They were careful, however, to avoid certain aspects of Marxism that simply would not be accepted in Albania, including Marxist internationalism.[137]

Once the war was over, education and culture received more serious attention. The major themes indicate the depth of Hoxha's nationalism. Extreme reverence was paid to the heroes of Albanian nationalism, whether or not they were politically acceptable. Skënderbeg received prominent attention but so did the meeting of the League of Prizren in 1878, the linguistic congress at Monastir in 1908, and an event in which Zog played a major role, the removal of the Italians from Vlora in 1920.[138] Particular homage was paid to Ismail Kemal Bey, who declared Albanian independence on 28 November 1912, despite being the head of one of Albania's great feudal families that later produced many reactionaries and collaborators.[139]

Despite this emphasis on history, the central focal point for education and culture continued to be, until Hoxha's death in 1985, the liberation struggle against the invader.[140] Although a cult of partisan warfare took hold everywhere in the Balkans except Greece, only in Albania did it reach feverish proportions. Textbooks, traditional histories, literature for children, general literature, drama, and film, were all limited to variations on the same theme. Albania's wartime experience, although lasting only about five years, became the focal point of Albanian existence for the next half century.

CONCLUSION

Albania's wartime experience began with the Italian invasion of April 1939 and ended with the German withdrawal of November 1944 and the construction of the Stalinist republic. The intervening five and a half years produced three different "Albanias"—Italian, German, and Stalinist—all of which were built, to a certain extent, on elements of artificiality. The war also produced considerable suffering and hardship, which were not soon forgotten. Even had the Albanians wanted to, Enver Hoxha would not have allowed it. He saw it in his interest to overemphasize the war to the point of creating a national myth, like the one from 1920, of Albanian arms having driven the Italians into the sea. Albanians were told that they had defeated the Italians and the Germans. They did not, although this should not reflect poorly on the Albanians; there were too few of them, and they did not have the equipment necessary for such an enormous undertaking.

But the war experience resulted in much more as well. In the process of pursuing their own goals, the Italians and the Germans produced a profound transformation and acceleration in social, economic, and political change. King Zog had begun the process of slowly forcing Albania out of the mists of the fifteenth century. The war forced the Albanians to speed up this process and insured that no return was possible. Whether the Albanians were perceivably better off for this change must be examined elsewhere. But everything had changed.

When Mussolini ordered the invasion of Albania in 1939 he was motivated by several considerations. In the short term he hoped to repay Hitler in kind for his lack of courtesy concerning the stationing of troops in Romania. In the longer term Mussolini hoped to add what he was convinced would be a grateful Albanian people to his enlarging new Roman empire, as well as gain a foothold on the Balkan Peninsula in anticipation of further expansion. Count Ciano also convinced Mussolini that Albania offered almost limitless economic benefit. Not only was there extensive mineral wealth to exploit— Ciano's Carthaginian figs[1]—but Albania also offered extensive cheap labor and agricultural wealth to sustain perhaps millions of Italian settlers. The invasion itself—relatively nondestructive because it was not resisted—encouraged Ciano and Mussolini to believe that their assumptions were correct, that taking Albania would provide a myriad of benefits with little cost. The Italians were to be disappointed.

Tens of thousands of settlers and workers flocked to Albania, many to escape the economic chaos over which Mussolini presided in Italy. But their numbers remained a tiny fraction of the millions that Ciano, with his usual overconfidence, had predicted. Nor would Albania, with its still primitive agriculture, have been able to sustain that number. Albania as a receptacle for Italy's excess population was a myth. Albania's mineral wealth came closer to fulfilling Italian expectations, but here again the gap between actual export and Ciano's optimistic assessment was wide. The exploitation of Albanian iron ore, bitumen, and copper was limited because of an inadequate transportation network. The Italians did somewhat better with oil, although transportation problems and the poor quality of Albanian oil made exploitation of it expensive. Most estimates suggest that Albanian oil never made up more than 10 percent of Italy's requirements. The Italians, however, were able to benefit extensively from Albanian chrome deposits, which provided 100 percent of Italy's needs.

In general, economic benefits for the Italians in Albania were meager when compared to the costs. In the four and a half years of Italian occupation, Rome committed itself to spending in Albania close to three times what it had spent between 1922 and 1939, when Mussolini was desperately attempting to subjugate the Albanian economy. Although Italian-owned companies earned some 142 million francs in profit during the occupation, the Italians imported into Albania a surplus of goods valued at some 640 million francs.[2]

The Italians also found it necessary to import considerable quantities of food to make up domestic shortages and even more to feed the army of occupation, quite the reverse of the anticipated surplus that Albanian agriculture under enlightened Italian direction was intended to produce. The Italian occupation failed economically and politically. Even the addition of Kosova did not produce the expected political capital. The Italians were unable to win the hearts and minds of the Albanian people. And in a broader sense, Mussolini's Albanian policy did much to hasten the collapse of fascist Italy. Denis Mack Smith goes so far as to suggest that the Italian invasion and occupation helped to bring together the coalition that would defeat fascism in general.[3]

A number of factors help to explain Italian failure, including a general, mutual lack of respect. The Italians in Albania made poor imperialists. After an initial burst of activity following the invasion, Italian administration succumbed to disorganization, superficiality, and corruption. The Albanian economy became a plantation economy in the 1930s, as Albania was incorporated into Italy's drive for self-sufficiency. With the invasion it was fully integrated into the Italian war economy, but Albania remained essentially a poorly organized, corrupt plantation. The extensive sums Italian officials in Albania could spend attracted the worst of Italy's adventurers and con men. Financial corruption in Albania reached the highest levels of the Italian government. Many Italians involved in Albania during the war added arrogance to their corruption, considering the Albanians—including the traditional landowning elite to whom the Italians attached themselves—to be inferior in every respect. Whereas some, such as Ciano, adopted a paternalistic attitude and treated the Albanians like children, others, such as Giovanni Giro, did little to hide their contempt.

And these sentiments were more than reciprocated by many Albanians. At least since the period following World War I, Albanians had viewed the Italians as being cowardly, dishonest, and unmanly. These views stemmed from Italy's rapid withdrawal from Albania in 1920 and from the impression left by the hundreds of Italians abandoned in Albania, often in poverty. During the interwar period, Albanians, always somewhat xenophobic, believed that Italian negotiators and specialists were there principally to prey upon them. By 1939, Albanian attitudes toward the Italians ranged from indifference, to suspicion, to passive antipathy, to hatred. The war years did much to reinforce the last of these sentiments.

This was particularly true as the occupation wore on. As the economic advantages of the early period slowly dissipated, even those who had welcomed the Italians for strictly venal reasons began to turn away. As the Italians began to compound their errors with the various excesses of fascism—as with the imposition of the new flag—more and more Albanians became alienated, leaving perhaps only a small minority of Catholics in the north as willing collaborators. Even the faith of these last supporters was shaken, however, when the Italians invaded Greece in October 1940. The Greek campaign, a disaster from its inception, did much to destroy what little goodwill the Italians had purchased in Albania since the 1939 invasion. The failed campaign resulted in the first Albanian military and civilian casualties of the war, apart from the few who died resisting the invasion of 1939. The Italian invasion of Greece and the rapid Greek counterattack also devastated parts of southern and central Albania, constituting the first extensive war-related destruction in

Albania. The invasion further dislocated the Albanian economy, which was already showing signs of shortages and inflation. The Greek war ruined much of what Italy had done in Albania and decisively ended the period of relative stability of the early period of the occupation. Overall, the Italian invasion of Greece constituted the beginning of the end of the Italian occupation of Albania; resistance, which had been only sporadic until late 1940, increased significantly. While this post-invasion resistance may have been little more than a minor irritant to the Italians, it added to the growing insecurity, particularly in the countryside, which further emphasized to the average Albanian the failure of Italian occupation policy.

Ultimately, the Italians spent much more than they received, and their continuing military adventurism destroyed what goodwill they were able to buy. Italian puppet governments were ridiculed from their inception. Mussolini hoped that the addition of Kosova would appeal to the growing nationalism of the Albanians—a sentiment for which Zog had been at least partially responsible. Indeed, many Albanians did rejoice in the annexation of Kosova. But Mussolini seems to have underestimated growing nationalism in general, a curious failing for a fascist. The same sentiment that encouraged many Albanians to welcome their conationals in Kosova home worked against the Italians. Growing nationalism—particularly among students, intellectuals, and many town dwellers—led these people to reject foreign occupation no matter what benefits that occupation brought. The Albanians were slowly becoming aware that perhaps it was better to be ruled badly by one's own. This rejection of the Italians grew in intensity from verbal opposition to armed insurrection directed primarily by the budding Communist Party. The Italians had assumed incorrectly that rudimentary Albanian nationalism was so weak that it could either simply be repressed or that it could at least be directed. The Italians had underestimated Zog's greatest, and perhaps only, achievement: the creation of an environment ideal for the growth of an Albanian national consciousness. It is perhaps not surprising that Zog was able to achieve this partly as a result of his resistance to interwar Italian economic and political penetration.

Although the more than eight divisions the Italians had stationed in Albania by 1943 were sufficient to withstand any military challenge from the resistance, Italian policy had clearly failed. The Italians had refused to give their Albanian puppet regimes enough authority to play a genuine role in the administration of the country. And the Italian carrot-and-stick policy had failed to win the Albanians over themselves. Italian efforts ended ignominiously with the collapse of Mussolini's regime in 1943.

The overthrow of Mussolini and the Italian collapse forced the Germans, essentially against their will, to invade and occupy Albania. The Germans had one major motive, and that was to prevent, with a minimum of troops, an Allied landing in Albania, which had the potential to threaten the German position in Eastern Europe as a whole. The military operation itself—involving fewer than three divisions—was much quicker and more efficient than the Italian invasion had been, despite that in this instance there was some actual resistance, even though the groups themselves were still in the formative stages of organization. Once this resistance was quickly and often brutally brushed aside, the Germans proceeded with their plan to reduce the required number of occupation troops to the barest minimum. The collapse of Italy had strained the already overburdened Wehrmacht, which could not spare the number of troops required for an effective occupation. The German high command decided that it could afford no more than two and a half divisions of second-level troops to protect the Adriatic coast and the vital Straits of Otranto.

These goals and the policy to achieve them were broadly laid out by Foreign Minister Ribbentrop, who recognized that given German needs internal security would have to be left to the Albanians themselves. The only way this could be achieved was with the construction of an independent, neutral, yet friendly government that would create a stable political system and a reliable security force, thereby engendering widespread domestic support. Ribbentrop instructed Schliep and Neubacher to find "statesmenlike people" to carry out this policy.[4]

Once the rumors of an imminent Allied invasion had subsided, and it became clear to the Albanians that the Germans intended to remain for a time, Neubacher was able to find the cooperation he was looking for. The Albanians of Kosova, not surprisingly, were the first to cooperate, motivated by Allied promises to return Kosova to a reconstructed Yugoslavia. But eventually some distinguished figures from "old Albania" came forward to offer their services or were persuaded by German threats and bribes to cooperate. To hold people of the caliber of Mehdi Frashëri and to present the image of continuity, the Germans agreed to a governmental structure—the resurrection of the 1928 monarchist constitution with a council of regency serving in place of King Zog—which left considerable authority in the hands of the Albanians. And Neubacher took great pains to live up to this fiction of an independent Albania, even at the cost of disputes with German military authorities in the Balkans and with Heinrich Himmler. Berlin had created the unique situation of a German occupation regime that enjoyed virtual freedom of the press and was without any overt signs of fascism. It was a good beginning for the Germans, and like Ciano they too expected that their policy might work.

Neubacher seemed willing to make most of the concessions necessary to give his first prime minister, Rexhep Mitrovica, the chance to establish actual Albanian authority in Albania. Mitrovica, who was not blind to the challenge, presented an ambitious program, which even some in the British camp reluctantly admitted they would support. With this program—which included land reform for the peasants—and very effective German propaganda emphasizing the return of Kosova, the Germans managed to extract considerable support for their puppet regime. If 30 percent of the Albanian people supported the Mitrovica regime, as B. Kühmel suggests, this was a remarkable achievement. And it allowed the Germans some time to take advantage of Albania's natural resources.

In this arena, too, the Germans proved to be more successful than the Italians. Granted that Italian planning was long term, the Germans benefited far more from their arrangements with the Albanians. The Germans began by commissioning a raw materials map, finding Italian studies completely inadequate. Prior to its completion the Germans exploited what was readily at hand, including coal from Kosova, coal sources near Tirana, and magnesium at Godolesh, but primarily oil and chrome. As we have seen, the Germans imported portable refineries with which they were able to satisfy the needs of the Wehrmacht in Albania—always the first priority—and the needs of domestic consumption moreover, in June 1944 they even produced a surplus.

Chrome, of course, was the big prize, and despite the mounting transportation problems the Germans were for a time able to extract and ship to Germany one-sixth of their total requirements. The Germans did well by the Albanians, at least in an economic sense. Unlike the Italians, they certainly took far more than they contributed, and when they withdrew, not only did they leave a debt but naturally they also kept Albania's gold reserves.[5]

But although the Germans reaped these economic benefits, they began to realize that their original political plan was not working out as they had hoped. Mitrovica's remarkable level of support began to erode quickly due to a number of factors. Despite its early popularity, the Mitrovica government failed to extend its legitimacy either at home or abroad. Because of German obstruction, no foreign state recognized Albanian independence. The domestic economy deteriorated. The collaborationist government, made up principally of the traditional landowning elite, had little to gain from land reform, which remained, as a result, on paper. To add to this disappointment, the German troops—who numbered some thirty-six thousand at the height of the German occupation—unlike the Italians who depended on imports, hoped to survive without extensive imports. This drove up prices and created shortages, which in some areas of the south resulted in famine conditions. Under the circumstances, Mitrovica's government not only lost its credibility and was faced with increasing armed opposition, but it could not raise and maintain an effective security force.

The Germans were not unaware of these problems and began to shift their policy as soon as it became clear that success through a collaborationist government was unlikely. When faced with failure in Albania, the Italians had tended to apply more of the same. The Germans proved to be more flexible. The new German strategy included occasional offensives against the partisans, which in the spring nearly succeeded in destroying the movement, although its complete destruction was probably never a German goal. The partisans proved quite useful to the Germans as a threat for extracting cooperation from Albania's noncommunists. Politically, the Germans began to emphasize a more traditional divide-and-rule strategy. Although this policy had been initiated as early as September of 1943, it gained momentum once it became clear to the Germans that their preferred option was essentially out of reach. The Germans realized that resistance would continue and that they could not—with their limited manpower—fight the NLM, BK, Zogists, and the chiefs. The British, too, understood this and as a result struggled for resistance unity, while the Germans worked to attach one group after another to their cause.[6]

The Germans were quite successful in their endeavors, using all the means at their disposal. They threatened to institute direct German control of the government in Tirana; they threatened more extensive use of the German army against the Albanians. But the Germans also bribed and cajoled. Their propaganda line, fear of communism and the loss of Kosova, was effective. Assiduous use of gold and weapons, mostly from what the Italians left, also proved quite effective.[7] Although they had initially fought harder than the *çetniks* of Yugoslavia ever did, one after another the BK, the Zogists, and many of the independent northern chieftains were seduced and corrupted by the Germans. They either collaborated outright—with some joining the puppet government—or at least failed to resist the Germans—hoping to use the Germans to obtain an arsenal for fighting the communists once the Germans had left. This was old-style Albanian politics, which proved disastrous for the Albanian noncommunists. One of the important results, of course, was that all of these groups lost their credibility and that the partisans—appealing to budding Albanian nationalism—continued to grow in strength. It is perhaps ironic that the so-called nationalists, like the Italians, seemed to misunderstand Albanian nationalism.

The policy had some drawbacks for the Germans as well. First, many of the nationalists who entered the puppet regimes—such as Dine—could not really be trusted by the Germans; their pro-Allied sympathies were known to all. Second, as soon as these groups had fully been compromised, they lost all credibility and support and were as a result worthless to the Germans to use against the partisans, who were increasing in strength.[8] The Germans, too, like the Italians and the nationalists failed to fully appreciate the growth of Albanian nationalism.

Ultimately, of course, the Germans, too, had to fail. If the central point of German policy was the pacification of Albania through the construction of an independent regime with prestige and its own military authority, then the Germans fell short of their goal. The Mitrovica government gained a degree of acceptance and was certainly taken more seriously than the regimes under the Italians, but those that followed his government failed to exert anything more than regional influence. So the Germans were unsuccessful, but this failure was not unqualified. The first priority, after all, had been to hold Albania with a small number of troops. Not only was the German army able to do this, but during the course of 1944 more troops were transferred out than replaced. And the German army was able to withdraw from Albania with only moderate losses.

So what explains the partial success the Germans enjoyed, and why did they do better than the Italians? There are a number of possible explanations. Divergent goals, of course, played a role. Ciano planned for outright annexation with a sham government that was to attempt to placate the Albanians. The Germans genuinely hoped that the Albanians would be able to administer themselves—naturally within the context of German wartime interests—and as a result, the Germans were initially perceived in a much more positive light. The Italians declared their occupation as permanent, whereas the Germans announced that they were essentially just passing through. The Germans were also able, through a better grasp of propaganda tactics, to take advantage of Italian and even British blunders. And then there was the element of perception. Albanians traditionally viewed the Germans with admiration and some awe. German military victories were respected—particularly in light of the addition of Kosova to old Albania. Many of the German troops, at least the invasion force, made a good impression. Omer Nishani, Hoxha's provisional foreign minister, suggested to a British officer in early 1945 that the Germans, while occupying Albania, behaved themselves, on the whole, very correctly. In Tirana they caused little trouble. Nishani said the Germans did get nasty when turned out of villages and then resorted to looting and shooting, but he concluded that unlike the BK's deportment, German behavior was not that bad.[9]

These advantages were augmented by a policy that even the Allies argued was applied with imagination, skill, and vigor.[10]

But like the Italians, the Germans made mistakes, often even similar to those made by Rome. Like the Italians, the Germans failed to understand the needs of the average Albanian. The Germans, like their predecessors, attached themselves to a small Westernized elite, most of whom spoke German. Because no more than ten of the tens of thousands of Germans involved in the occupation spoke Albanian, German contact with locals was severely restricted. The Germans created a German ghetto, which helped to create the notion of the "ugly German."[11] The Germans, too, failed to understand the importance of growing nationalism. And in a postmortem written by a Wehrmacht official in early 1945, German policy was faulted for having held on to the fiction of an independent Albania too long, and then within the last month of the German occupation for having abandoned it too abruptly.[12]

Both Italian and German policy contributed significantly to the victory of the communists, although there were certainly other factors involved. Socialist historiography argues that the liberation and communist victory were achieved by the Albanian people led by the party. Although this is certainly an oversimplification, that the communists contributed significantly to their own victory is clear. They gave direction and leadership to the resistance movement. They built an army, whose leadership they controlled, to resist the invader and destroy the enemies of the movement. The communists and the NLM contributed the only important resistance to the Axis powers, even though they could not engage the Germans in the open field or take and hold fortified objectives. And even though the partisan army might not have done extensive damage to the Axis, it was the only organized force once the Germans had gone. Like its Yugoslav counterpart, it was able to easily step into the vacuum and seize power. The communists were also the only indigenous group to develop and effectively use propaganda, both to influence the membership of the NLM and the people as a whole. Finally, the communists recognized the importance of developing a political, social, and economic program that differed significantly from Zog's failed interwar system. Moreover, they developed the institutions that began implementing aspects of this program even before the end of the war.[13]

Nicholas Pano reminds us that external factors were equally important in explaining Hoxha's victory.[14] Hoxha, once he broke with the West, was willing to recognize Red Army victories as an external contributing factor, but that was a far as he was willing to go.[15] This is by no means far enough. Other important external factors include the failure of the Allies to recognize Zog or some other government in exile. This made Hoxha's task simpler than the one faced by Tito. Although Hoxha was certainly loath to admit it, organizational help from the Yugoslavs plus the success of the resistance in Greece played important roles in the formation of the party; the formation of the NLM; and the organization, strategy, and tactics of the NLM.[16]

Hoxha also benefited from a series of military and strategic decisions made by the Allies during the course of the war. Included in this category are the decisions of the Tehran Conference of late 1943, which rejected Churchill's planned second front at the head of the Adriatic; the agreement between Britain and the United States of late 1944 to forbid the use of Allied troops in Italy in any second country other than Greece; and the August 1944 recommendation by the U.S. Joint Chiefs of Staff that American troops should be used in Albania only in connection with relief and rehabilitation.[17]

The moral and material backing of the United States and to a greater degree the British also played a significant if highly controversial role in Hoxha's victory. While lavish with his praise for British material deliveries during the war, once the cold war set in Hoxha either completely ceased to mention British aid or referred to it as the so-called aid or as the "insufficient, not to say non-existent" aid.[18] The aid the British supplied was certainly insufficient to maintain the rapidly growing partisan forces. To suggest that it was of no consequence, however, is unrealistic. At the high point of British drops, between mid-July and the end of August 1944, the partisans received between 150 and 160 tons of supplies as well as a considerable portion of the some thirty-two thousand gold sovereigns that the British distributed in Albania.[19] The amount of material the British gave Hoxha was certainly insufficient to determine the outcome of the war in Albania, and it is therefore a mistake to suggest—as many of the British liaison officers in their memoirs do—that Hoxha was brought to power by British weapons, supplies, and money.[20]

Nevertheless, the British contribution was important, particularly in three instances. First, the British supplied Hoxha with the material and the training for the first brigade in 1943, and it is from here that Hoxha was able to begin the construction of a power base. The second instance in which British aid played a particularly important role was during the German winter offensive, at which point the leadership of the NLM was almost captured and the movement itself was nearly destroyed. Without the gold sovereigns supplied by the British, Hoxha would have required much longer to recover. And finally, British material played a crucial role during the Battle of Dibra. The partisans had been forced to suspend their offensive because of a lack of ammunition. This situation was rectified as a result of increased British deliveries, allowing

Hoxha and Shehu not only to make a good showing against the Germans, but also to virtually destroy their nationalist-Zogist rivals in the north.[21] British deliveries certainly shortened the civil war, but the partisans would have won in any case, because of their significant base of support in the south and because of the strength of their Yugoslav allies.

British material and moral aid cannot be considered decisive then, but it nevertheless played an important role. The British inadvertently contributed to Hoxha's rise in at least one other way. Britain's rather confused policy with regard to Albania and its inability to make a clear decision about whom to support even after BK collaboration were clear to all and allowed Hoxha to solidify his claim to being a nationalist. At the same time, British refusal to denounce the BK in a timely manner discredited those opposition groups that perceived themselves to be pro-Western.

The most important factor, external or internal, leading to the victory of communism was the policy of the Germans. Although the Germans clearly benefited from their divide-and-rule policy, so did the partisans. Each time the Germans won over another group, one more obstacle to Hoxha's rise to power was removed. In the fall of 1943 the communists were a significant but not overwhelming power group in the midst of a number of power groups—including the BK, the Zogists, and the independent central and north Albanian and Kosovar chieftains. By attracting each of these power groups in turn, the Germans destroyed their political credibility and what military effectiveness they might have had. As each of these groups moved closer to the Germans, and budding Albanian nationalism did its work, they were removed from serious contention for power in the postwar setting. First, the BK was attracted to the Germans, then the Zogist—which allowed the communists to attack the Zogist even in the face of protests from the British. And these attacks helped the Germans to organize an anticommunist coalition among the independent chieftains, allowing the Germans to withdraw essentially unmolested in November, despite the more brutal policy German forces had followed vis-à-vis the Albanian population since September. In November 1944, then, the communist-dominated NLM remained the only antifascist group with political credibility. They had fought the Germans more or less consistently and often under difficult conditions, although they had by no means defeated the Germans. And the partisans had, by this time, a reservoir of officers with experience and were no longer restricted to a few former Zogist officers and a handful of Spanish Civil War veterans.[22]

The Albania Hoxha was handed by the Germans had changed considerably since the beginning of the war. The war had brought death, destruction, famine, and hardship to Albania. Casualty figures vary rather widely. One of the first postwar Albanian newspapers, *Luftari*, estimated Albanian dead at 17,000.[23] This figure was later revised upward by official Albanian government estimates and the United Nations Relief and Rehabilitation Administration (UNRRA) to between 28,000 and 30,000, mostly from the south, out of a total population of about 1,125,000, or about 2.58 percent of the population. Some 13,000 were left as invalids.[24] The loss of life was tragic, but the totals are well below the number of casualties inflicted on Albania's Balkan neighbors. Greece lost some 7 percent of its population, with Yugoslavia losing an estimated 11 percent, more than half of those killed by other Yugoslavs.[25] While Albanian per-capita losses were lower, as with the Yugoslavs, most of the casualties suffered were inflicted by other Albanians.

Axis casualty figures in Albania have been estimated by Albanian socialist historiography to be as high as 26,500 dead, 21,000 wounded, and almost 21,000 captured. These figures are credible only if all Italian losses to the Greeks are included. The Greeks claim 6,000 Italian battle casualties, with a much higher number—some 13,000 Italian soldiers succumbing to trench foot and the "white death" or "dry gangrene" of frostbite.[26] Elizabeth Barker, who during the war was attached to the British Ministry of Economic Warfare, suggests that the Germans lost between 6,000 and 7,000 killed and 500 captured.[27] Postsocialist Albanian sources suggest that the figure for German dead is closer to 3,600, with some 2,400 identified.[28]

The economic effect of the war on Albania was profound. Albania as a whole was, of course, an economic disaster area in 1944. Although the Germans were in Albania for only a little more than a year, they were responsible for by far the most economic damage. The Italians built and spent, whereas the Germans extracted and destroyed as they withdrew. One modern Albanian observer, a minister of finance in a 1991 transitional government, has even called 1936 to 1943 the golden age of the Albanian economy.[29] While this may be, at the end of the war Albania was in serious difficulty. The International Center for Relief to Civilian Populations, headquartered in Geneva, concluded that Albania, though not as badly off as Greece, was one of the most seriously devastated countries in Europe. The center observers reported high infant mortality, widespread malnutrition, and poor health care facilities. After visiting Greece, Yugoslavia, Austria, Poland, Czechoslovakia, and parts of Russia in April 1947, General Lowell Rooks, general director of the UNRRA, reported that Albania had the worst hunger conditions.[30] Although many of these conditions existed before the war, and while Hoxha's policy toward the UNRRA is responsible for exacerbating the situation (see the following discussion), the war clearly contributed. During the war, herds were reduced by as much as one-third, and much of the small amount of farming equipment was destroyed. Of Albania's minute industrial base little survived, and that which did lay idle for lack of raw materials. Mines and oil wells were damaged. Harbors, in particular Durrës, and bridges had been destroyed. Roads were damaged, one-third of Albania's houses were destroyed, and Albania's gold reserves, which might have helped in the recovery, were in Berlin later to be transferred to the Bank of England.[31]

But the destruction caused by the war varied from region to region. The south suffered disproportionately, principally because this area witnessed most of the fighting. We have seen that the Italian invasion of Greece and the subsequent Greek conquest of nearly one-third of Albania turned the south into a battleground. And since the NLM operated principally in the south, Italian and German reprisals did most of their damage there. We have been left with a representative picture of the devastation by an Albanian-speaking OSS agent who traveled in the region for over a month in late 1944. His travels included visits to Kurvelesh, Tepelena, Përmet, and the Gjirokastra area. Some areas had been completely devastated—particularly in the Kurvelesh region, where food supplies were limited due to livestock herds left unattended while the people hid in the mountains during heavy partisan, BK, and German troop activity. In the Tepelena area the food situation was also desperate, partly because the Germans had allowed horses and mules to graze on planted fields. Përmet seemed less desperate, and German prisoners were being used to harvest crops, which were subject to requisitioning from all sides.[32]

The agent reported that in the areas he visited—particularly in the villages—many houses had been burned. Pilur, a village of 60 houses, was completely burned. Kuç, a village of 250 to 300 houses, was also completely burned, although Gjirokastra, with its 1,000 houses, was virtually untouched. While most of the destruction was caused by the Germans, the Italian-Greek war, Italian reprisals, and BK brutality contributed substantially to the misery of the south.[33]

The center and the north, however, were much less effected. We have seen Hoxha's own description of Berat in October 1944 with its late-night restaurants and its full shops. British reports from December 1944 indicate that not only was there little damage done to Tirana but the food situation—except for a shortage of wheat—was not really bad. Butcher shops were said to be full, and the sale of fresh meat was unrationed and the prices controlled.[34] This must have been quite a surprise to English officers, who would have to deal with rationing in Great Britain well into the 1950s. In Shkodra, in the extreme north—with the exception of communications—there was little sign of war damage. The food situation was described by the head of the new British military mission as being very satisfactory. Bread was plentiful and cheap.[35] Certainly, the general situation outside of the major towns was considerably more difficult, but rarely could one find the level of misery prevalent in the south.

It is perhaps telling that Hoxha was able to reject UNRRA food aid for months until he could get it on his own terms. The UNRRA, headed in Albania by Colonel Dayrell Oakley-Hill, offered to provide aid if its own officials—the organization assumed that hundreds would be required—distributed the aid throughout Albania. Hoxha was suspicious both of Oakley-Hill and the UNRRA and insisted that no more than fifteen agents were needed. He also refused to give the British information about petroleum reserves. Finally, he hoped to use the UNRRA to push for long-awaited recognition. The British were aghast—their reaction can best be summed up by a margin note of O. T. Pink, a Foreign Office official, who minuted, "It seems to me absolutely intolerable that a pack of Communist Albanian brigands who are offered relief supplies free, gratis and for nothing, should have the impertinence to say that they will only accept our help subject to their own conditions. I should dearly like to leave them to starve."[36]

Hoxha was often willing to sacrifice the well-being of his people for his own political ends. But he also seems to have concluded that he did not need the aid that urgently. It was a full six months before the disagreement was resolved, only after both sides demonstrated a degree of flexibility and Hoxha's predicament became more serious. The UNRRA ultimately was responsible for crucial assistance, amounting to some twenty-six million dollars between August 1945 and early 1947. This included not only food, clothing, and medicine, but also livestock, vines to help the recovery of the wine trade, seed, fertilizer, and machinery.[37]

So the situation in Albania at the end of the war was bad, but it certainly could have been worse. This was the conclusion of the Paris Reparation Conference, to which Hoxha submitted a request for 1.5 billion dollars. Albanian socialist historians in the 1960s revised the bill upward to 1.6 billion, a figure that included some 8 million dollars for the maintenance of the ANLA during the war.[38] Albania was ultimately awarded 5 million dollars.[39] It is clear that politics were involved in this decision, but it is equally clear that the conference considered Hoxha's estimate to be somewhat high.

While the war resulted in considerable suffering, as with other periods of violent change some benefits accrued as well. The immediate benefits included thousands of relatively high-paying jobs, mostly in construction; a significant increase in the availability of health service; and fixed prices on rents, food, and utilities. As a British observer resident in Albania noted at the end of April 1939, there was a great improvement in the condition of the people, at least those with whom she came in contact in Tirana. The addition of Kosova to old Albania in 1941, although only temporary, contributed not only substantial mineral wealth (which certainly did not significantly impact the average Albanian) but also some badly needed agricultural goods. With the German invasion, Albania took advantage of tens of thousands of Italian workers and many Italian firms. Although these people had to be fed, the country benefited from considerable free agricultural, manual, and skilled labor. Hoxha would not allow the most vital workers to return home until they had completed the projects upon which they were working.[40]

There were also some long-term benefits, although many were perhaps less tangible. The Italians and the Germans—using their own and local labor—built hundreds of miles of roads and dozens of bridges, which opened up hither-to-inaccessible areas of Albania. The invaders enlarged harbors, enlarged existing airports, and built new ones of each. Government buildings and tourist hotels were built. Swamps were drained to control malaria and provide agricultural acreage for the landless—although this last contribution was perhaps more of a public relations stunt; certainly more could have been done in this respect. Wells were drilled for oil extraction, and the Germans went so far as to bring in portable refineries. Mines were enlarged and modernized for mineral extraction. There is little doubt that the occupation was beneficial for Albania's mining capacity.[41] The Italians also began pipeline and railroad construction to facilitate the export of Albania's mineral wealth. While a good many of these projects were destroyed during the war, including most of the bridges, it is generally less difficult and costly to repair than it is to build from the ground up. With the glaring exception of houses—tens of thousands, perhaps as many as sixty thousand,[42] were damaged or destroyed—much of what the Italians and the Germans had constructed was quickly put back in order once the war had ended. It is not without some degree of justification that the Italian official responding to Albania's reparations claims argued that the occupation was not without its economic benefit.

The war did much to drag Albania out of the mists of the fifteenth century in a social sense. Although the Italian occupation was of longer duration, its impact, as with economic destruction, was considerably less significant than that of the German occupation. In 1943, when the Germans arrived, Albania was still firmly in the grip of tribal-feudal social traditions. Zog had ruled in cooperation with the Geg chieftains of the north. Even so, he had been able to lessen their influence somewhat by extending the power of the central government, at least in terms of taxation, military recruitment, and the rule of law, to areas that had long and successfully resisted this type of central power intrusion.

The Italian occupation in many ways enhanced Albania's tribal-feudal traditions. Not only did the Italians rely almost exclusively on tribal leaders and feudal beys for leadership in their puppet governments, but they were comfortable with the existing political and social structure and therefore did little to change it. Indeed in many areas of the north, social retrogression took place. Because the Italians seemed to have little interest in maintaining order in some areas, Zog's expansion of central authority was often reversed. Large parts of Albania reverted to the traditions of isolation and blood feud justice, particularly in those areas of little military value to the Italians, where the construction of roads was considered unnecessary.

It was German policy that did much to destroy traditional Albania, both in a political and a social sense. The Italians had compromised some chieftains and some of the feudal Moslem landowners by including them in puppet regimes. But a general appreciation that collaboration was not in Albania's national interest grew slowly along with the armed resistance. Once the Germans assumed control of Albania, this idea—that collaboration was anti-Albanian—became more and more clear, and those who participated were roundly condemned. Under the Germans this meant not only the tribal chieftains and feudal beys whom the Italians had attracted, but virtually all noncommunist opposition groups as well. Each group that the Germans attracted —the collaborationist chiefs, the beys, the prewar liberals, the BK, the Zogists, and the independent chiefs—were in turn compromised and removed from contention for power in a postwar Albania. Albania would never be the same. Hoxha came to power at the head of a party and army inspired by a militant foreign ideology that rejected and ridiculed the old ways. Hoxha's followers came from the traditionally disenfranchised; they were principally Tosk and principally young. The average age of the partisans was twenty, and the average ages of the party Politburo and Central Committee memberships in 1948 were thirty-five and thirty-two respectively. Hoxha, who was thirty-seven in 1945, was one of the oldest of the party leaders.[43] The partisans were also about 90 percent peasant and contained a relatively high percentage (9 percent) of women.[44]

The women did much more than tend to the sick and wounded. They were active fighters and in the process took a step toward loosening Albania's rigid patriarchal and traditional Moslem society. Hoxha and his ideology emphasized equality for women, but it would be a difficult struggle, particularly because important individuals in his own movement, such as Myslim Peza, were opposed to what they considered to be unnecessary radicalism. Hoxha would complain some thirty years later that Albania had a long way to go before real equality in the mind of the average Albanian would compliment the legal equality that the new regime had granted women. Still, the war pushed Albania down the road toward equality, away from the 1920s, when the custom of simply shooting faithless wives was still common and generally went unpunished.[45]

The war also impacted such basic indexes as urbanization, which jumped from 15.4 percent in 1938 to 21.3 percent in 1945, indicating that the rate of urban growth had almost quadrupled from fifteen or twenty years earlier. This significant trend can be explained by problems in the agriculture sector, increased industrial expansion, and, one can assume, increasing insecurity from growing guerrilla warfare.[46] Less tangible but equally as important was the new self-image that Albanian peasants, and many Balkan peasants in general, developed during the course of the war. The partisan forces were essentially peasant armies, and they were told, again and again, that they had defeated the Axis powers. This new self-worth the peasants gained as a result would complicate the various agricultural collectivization programs that the Stalinist government instituted in the 1940s and 1950s.

Certainly one of the most important results of the war was the impact on Albanian nationalism. Modern nationalism in Albania is essentially a twentieth-century phenomenon, and King Zog did much to ingrain the concept into his fellow Albanians. Socialist historiography dismisses Zog as a completely negative force.[47] Although his achievements were certainly limited, this verdict is politically and ideologically motivated. Despite his many failures, by the 1930s the central government was recognized in most parts of the country. The political stability that resulted, though relative, created the environment necessary for the growth of a national consciousness. Zog's resistance to Italian economic and political penetration provided a focus, if negative, for this growing consciousness, which by the end of his reign had grown to the extent that the Axis invaders underestimated its significance.

The experience of World War II in Albania served both to reinforce and to submerge this growing nationalist sentiment. The ordeal of foreign occupation did much to reinforce Albania's distinctiveness, but it also had a divisive effect. Following the invasion and occupation, the Italians sought to integrate the traditional Albanian elite into Mussolini's new Roman empire. Some Italian efforts failed—particularly the creation of the Albanian Fascist Party. Still, many elements of the prewar political and social elite compromised themselves by cooperating with the fascists and thereby contributing to what had been called the process of denationalization.[48] The partial success of this fascist policy fostered class division, because many middle-class Albanians—a relatively small group—and many peasants resented Italian, and after 1943, German occupation. Further, the division between north and south was accentuated by the formation of resistance groups with regional agendas. So while nationalism continued to grow, the pace of growth was slowed, and much of Zog's work was at least jeopardized.

When Hoxha came to power he was faced with the task of rebuilding Albania on the foundations—or what was left of them—laid by Zog. Like Zog, his main goal was predetermined and was, in its simplest sense, the creation of a viable independent nation-state and the "monolithic unity" of the Albanian people. Hoxha did this with blood—perhaps less blood than Tito and probably even Milovan Djilas. But the difference is that Djilas saw the error of his ways, and even Tito mellowed. Hoxha's extremism and paranoia increased.[49] But despite the violence and violent rhetoric of Stalinism to which Hoxha would eventually resort, he had no choice but to become as ardent a nationalist as Zog had been. Indeed, given the narrow base of support the communist movement had, and given Hoxha's need to downplay the Kosova issue, extreme nationalism was perhaps the only means by which Hoxha could remain in power and progress toward a modern Stalinist state. Nationalism proved to be the principal element in all of his policies. He could not do otherwise, for the war had determined that state-of-siege nationalism, supported by the myth that Albanian arms had defeated the fascist invaders, would become the focal point of his regime. It is for the postcommunist democratic forces in Albania to determine whether the nationalism built on Zog's foundation and further inspired by Hoxha—as a direct result of Albania's wartime experience—will become a positive or negative force in the Balkan region.

NOTE ON SOURCES

The task of attempting to grasp even the basics of Albania at war is not a simple one. Albania's Stalinist past has made the researcher's work difficult. A basic problem is that the Albanian archives remained closed to foreign scholars until the early 1990s. Further, Enver Hoxha reports that what existed in the archives prior to 1944 was destroyed in the Battle of Tirana, although this is perhaps an exaggeration.[1] Though now open, the archives still suffer from extensive organizational difficulties that only time, money, and a great deal of effort can correct. Still, since this work does not benefit from that material, it cannot claim to be the definitive work on the subject. That work will have to come from Albania's new generation of historians who are now able to work outside of the rigid bounds of political correctness that until recently was required of all Albanian historians who dealt with this crucial period in Albanian history.

Documents from interested states, both published and unpublished, are, however, extensive and are an important source for this study. Perhaps the most useful are the British Foreign Office, War Office, and Cabinet Papers, because of Great Britain's long-standing interest in the area and because of the often high quality of foreign service personnel. Foreign Office files are useful for information on the invasion and the early period of occupation, as the British government recognized the annexation and replaced its minister with a consul-general. The reports from the minister on the invasion and the reports from the consul-general on the construction of the first occupation regimes are extremely useful. British Cabinet Papers are also of some use, although the Albanian situation was certainly not high on the cabinet's list of priorities.

By necessity, there is a gap in British documents from the beginning of the war through the end of 1942, because the British no longer had official representation in Albania. Once Albania became a field of operations for the British in early 1943, Foreign Office and War Office records are again extremely useful. The Special Operations Executive, which became the primary outside source of supply for the various Albanian resistance groups, sent weekly situation reports to both the Foreign Office and the War Office. Although some SOE files in Great Britain are still closed, and likely will remain so for some time, some of these closed files are obtainable at the National Archives in Washington D.C., since some of this material was shared with the Americans and has been released. Many SOE reports can also be found in Foreign Office files, because there was some coordination between the two services.

The National Archives also contain the U.S. diplomatic and intelligence holdings, which are less useful, as much of what the Americans in Albania reported seems to have come directly from British sources. The American minister seems to have been less well informed about the invasion than the British minister, and his reports are on occasion simply copies of British reports. The United States clearly considered Albania to be a post of little importance, in light of the quality of American ministers. American documents do not cover the earlier period of the occupation at all because the United States refused to recognize the occupation and therefore withdrew its minister in July of 1939. The Office of Strategic Services (OSS) did run a series of intelligence-gathering operations during the course of the war, manned by Albanian-American field agents who were the only Americans in Albania until the United States reestablished a physical presence in Albania with the formation of the American military mission under Harry Fultz in 1945. Their reports, and the research and analysis papers to which these reports contributed, are quite interesting and provide some general information and numerous summaries of various aspects of Albania at war.

German diplomatic and military documents are particularly useful for the last two years of the war in Albania. German material for the earlier period is useful but spotty since the Germans were careful not to arouse Italian suspicions by collecting too much data. German military and Foreign Ministry documents covering the German occupation period are voluminous and thorough, and they rank second only to the British material in terms of usefulness. As evidence of the seriousness of purpose with which the Germans approached the collection and maintenance of documents, a faceless (and unfortunately anonymous) Wehrmacht bureaucrat pounded out a one-hundred-page report on all aspects of the German occupation of Albania in March 1945 as Berlin burned. These documents are available on microfilm in England and the United States.

Many Italian documents are available, in the United States and also, of course, in Italy. Although they are often extremely useful the researcher must be careful, since their reliability is often questionable. When Count Ciano became Italian foreign minister and took control of the Palazzo Chigi in 1936, he introduced a new policy called the "Tona Fascista," which was intended to infuse new energy and a new spirit into the Italian diplomatic corps. The net result, unfortunately, was to encourage the traditionally thorough Italian diplomats, who before the fascists had had a good reputation, to report primarily those pieces of information Ciano wanted to hear. Oddly enough, Ciano, in his diaries, complained that the reports he received from Tirana often did more to obfuscate than to illustrate. While this was not always the case, it seems to have occurred with enough frequency to call into question the veracity of many of the available Italian military and diplomatic records. Given this qualification, however, Italian records, particularly those of the Comando Supremo and the Ministero della Guerra (some are available at the National Archives in Washington, D.C.) are invaluable for the period of 1939 to 1943.

Extensive published documents are also available. Useful from the Albanian perspective is *La lutte anti-fasciste de liberation nationale du peuple albanais, 1941-1944: documents principaux,* which, however, ignores the period prior to the formation of the Albanian Communist Party. Of particular interest, when the originals are not available, are the United States Diplomatic Papers, British Documents on Foreign Policy, the German Akten aus dem Auswärtigen Amt, and the Documenti diplomatici italiani. Needless to say, the material relating to Albania is limited, and the respective usefulness of these documents tends to mirror the unpublished records. The American documents concentrate on the invasion, whereas the others are more general and more useful. Because Albania played a small role in the war in Europe, the number of documents in these collections that touch on aspects of the war in Albania is not great.

Of the general literature available, the numerous diaries and memoirs are the most interesting and the most useful. Perhaps the most remarkable are the diaries of the Italian foreign minister Ciano, which count as perhaps the single most useful source on high-level Axis decision making in World War II.

Because the invasion and occupation of Albania became Ciano's special project, Albanian questions figure prominently in Ciano's works, principally *The Ciano Diaries, 1939-1943*, and *Ciano's Hidden Diary, 1937-1938*. Although Ciano does, of course, try to present himself as the one sane voice in the wilderness—along the lines of Albert Speer in *Inside the Third Reich*—the material he includes on the decision-making process is invaluable. Undoubtedly not intending his diaries for publication, Ciano seems to have been frank and objective, a side of himself he rarely displayed.

In general, the memoirs are less useful because the writers inevitably use them as a forum to justify their actions, demonstrate that theirs was the correct policy all along, or overemphasize their personal role in the momentous events of World War II. Indicative of this unfortunate genre is the work of Francesco Jacomoni, who served first as Italian ambassador to Albania and then as lieutenant general—amounting to ruler—of Albania until shortly before the Italian collapse. Jacomoni not only carried out the orders of Mussolini and Ciano but was responsible for much of Italy's policy in Albania. His testament, *La politica dell'Italia in Albania*, could have been illuminating but instead we are left with a self-serving, inaccurate, and very general treatise that sheds very little light on the invasion and occupation.

The exhausting memoirs—in all some fifty volumes—of Enver Hoxha, the partisan leader and Stalinist dictator of Albania, must be considered in the same vain. These memoirs were, of course, produced not as an accurate record of Hoxha during World War II but rather to serve a political purpose. This is perhaps best reflected by the fact that the memoirs have often been rewritten to conform to political changes in postwar Albania. Major players were written in or out, according to the shifting of Albania's rather violent political winds. The case of Mehmet Shehu, the chief military commander of the partisans and the prime minister of Stalinist Albania until his removal and still-mysterious death in 1981 stands as the most extreme example. The price of disagreement with Hoxha proved to be his position, his role in history at least as he appears in Hoxha's memoirs, the freedom of his family, and possibly his life. Finally, as Jon Halliday points out in his interesting book *Enver Hoxha, the Artful Albanian*, a one-volume condensation of some of the Hoxha memoirs, it stretches the imagination to believe that after an interval of some twenty years Enver Hoxha could reconstruct five years of conversations word for word.[2] Still, the memoirs are of some use, certainly at least as a clear indication of the ever-changing official position concerning events in Albania during World War II. This attribute also applies to the various memoirs of Albanian soldiers involved in the war, the most prominent of whom was Mehmet

Shehu, the commander of the first partisan division and author of *On the Experience of the National Liberation War and the Development of Our National Army,* among other works.

Also useful are the memoirs of foreigners involved in the Albania's political and military events during the war. Although there are many, the most useful include Hermann Neubacher's book *Sonderauftrag Südost, 1940-1945: Bericht eines fliegenden Diplomaten.* Neubacher, who was Ribbentrop's personal representative in the Balkans, was responsible for carrying out Germany's unique occupation policy from 1943 to 1944. He glosses over some of the difficult moments he had dealing with the Byzantine Albanian political situation as well as some of the serious disagreements between the German political and military authorities with regard to dealing with the Albanians, but his perspective is, of course, valuable. It would have been more valuable, however, had he been somewhat more frank. One often comes away with the impression, reading Neubacher's book, that the Germans were invited guests who enjoyed Albanian hospitality for a little over a year and then decided to go home. The only published record of a German common soldier's experiences in Albania is Hermann Frank's *Landser, Karst und Skiptaren, Bandenkämpfe in Albanien.* Unfortunately, this work does little but emphasize the continuing confusion regarding Albania's political and social makeup and development that seemed common among many Germans who spent time there.

From the Italian side, besides the works of Ciano and Jacomoni, there is considerable military memoir and diary material available. At the command end we have the memoirs of Marshal Pietro Badoglio, *Italy in the Second World War: Memories and Documents,* which give us some insight into Comando Supremo decision making. Most of the stories of common soldiers come, not surprisingly, from Italians. Although they are interesting from the point of view of trial and survival, what they add to our general understanding of the period is of a highly personal nature.

British participants have produced a considerable amount of interesting memoir material that invariably reflects the political orientation of the author and must, therefore, be used with some caution. Sir Andrew Ryan, the last British minister in Albania, includes in his book *The Last of the Dragomans* a chapter on his experience in Albania. Most of the British memoir material, however, comes from British officers who served as liaison officers attached to the Albanian resistance. The most useful and interesting is Julian Amery's *Sons of the Eagle: A Study in Guerilla War* and *Approach March: A Venture in Autobiography.* Brigadier E. F. "Trotsky" Davies, the ranking British officer in Albania, has produced a memoir called *Illyrian Venture: The Story of the British*

Military Mission in Enemy-Occupied Albania, which if nothing else demonstrates the weakness of such material. Davies's reports to the Foreign Office cataloguing nationalist collaboration with the enemy strongly encouraged the British to throw the full weight of their support behind the partisans, and yet Davies, in his book, ignores what many see as a significant turning point for which he was responsible. His motivation, presumably, stems from a desire not to be remembered as the British officer responsible for the communist victory in Albania.

Also of note are Peter Kemp's *No Colour, No Crest* and David Smiley's *Albanian Assignment.* The latter, although written by an officer with a strong conservative orientation, serves as the British counterpart to the stories of adventure that many Italian soldiers produced. The principal problem with the memoirs of British officers is that all of them are written by individuals attached to the noncommunist movements in the center and north, none with the partisans. Their approach tends to mirror the approach of their Albanian contacts, dealing principally with the civil war.[3] As a result, these works are less than objective and most erroneously blame the British government, because of its material support for the partisans, for "losing" Albania to the communists.[4] The only presently available exception to this trend in the fine book by Sir Reginald Hibbert, *Albania's National Liberation Struggle: The Bitter Victory.* Essentially a combination of personal memoir and careful research of principally English language resources, Hibbert's book is of immense value.

For the secondary source published material it would be useful first to consult the two excellent bibliographies available. Armin Hetzer and Viorel S. Roman, in *Albanien, ein bibliographischer Forschungsbericht mit Titelübersetzungen und Standortnachweisen,* list documents, books, and articles written in Albanian as well as in Western languages. William B. Bland's *Albania* though more limited in scope because of its principal concentration on English language material, includes a brief and useful abstract on each item listed. Bland's book was recently revised and expanded by the Albanian specialist Antonia Young. Also very useful is Klaus-Detlev Grothusen ed., *Südosteuropa-Handbuch: Albanien.*

While the secondary source material is by no means overwhelming, it is still extensive and therefore only the most useful for this study will be mentioned here. Given that the war experience is central to socialist Albanian literature, socialist Albanian historians have, of course, produced a considerable amount of material, much of which is available in translation. The quality of the material is, however, inconsistent. As one might expect, there is frequently an overemphasis on the central themes of postwar political reality, including a need to (1) focus on and overemphasize the forces arrayed against the Albanians, (2) overemphasize Albania's ability to confront these forces and overwhelm them without outside aid, and (3) delineate domestic politics in black-and-white terms, that is, the correct position of the party as opposed to the "traitor" organizations that refused to cooperate with the communist-dominated national liberation councils during the course of the war. Perhaps it is safe to say that Stalinist Albania has produced good historians but not always good history. The political climate in Albania under Enver Hoxha, who ruled Albania from World War II until his death in 1985, did little to encourage a balanced approach to history.

Most notable among these Albanian historians are Ndreçi Plasari and Shyqri Ballvora as military historians and the excellent historians Aleks Buda, Stefanaq Pollo, Arben Puto, and Luan Omari for the political aspects of the war. The military historians, however, pay scant attention to the noncommunist resistance and seem consistently to overestimate the strength of the German units against which the partisans fought. The political historians tend to focus narrowly on the organization and struggle of the party. One of the central themes here seems to be oversensitivity to the question of foreign, particularly Yugoslav, involvement in the organization of the Albanian Communist Party in 1941. Several other general problems are consistently evident. As the German historian Bernhard Kühmel has pointed out, Albanian historiography argues that by the fall of 1943 two clearly defined blocks had developed in Albanian politics.[5] The partisans represented the progressive elements, and all other political groups, referred to as the "reactionary elements," supported the German invader. This was not the case. Even Michael Schmidt-Neke, who comes as close to the politically correct position as a serious Western scholar should, finds problems with socialist Albanian historiography. He complains that socialist Albanian historiography tends, when dealing with people, to see things in black-and-white terms. When a person is considered positive, that is, patriotic and progressive, many transgressions are overlooked. For example, many of the reactionary feudal elements who opposed King Zog for personal reasons are lauded simply because of their opposition to Zog.[6] Often this tendency reaches curious proportions. By way of illustration, the otherwise excellent historian Arben Puto in his book *From the Annals of British Diplomacy: The Anti-Albanian Plans of Great Britain during the Second World War according to Foreign Office Documents of 1939-1944* berates the British liaison officers McLean and Amery for pursuing an "inglorious odyssey, . . . that was going to take them into the odious swamps and gloomy dens of reaction and treason."[7] Treason against whom? one might ask. In the same book Puto refers to British material aid to the Albanian partisans, which reached an average of one hundred tons a month and without which the partisans would have been hard pressed to continue effective resistance, as the "so called" British aid.[8]

Despite occasional flaws, socialist Albanian secondary source material is of considerable interest. Among other works, Shyqri Ballvora has produced an interesting work on the German occupation called *Das nationalsozialistische Besatzungsregime in Albanien*, and Lefter Kasneci has made a valuable contribution in *Steeled in the Heat of Battle: A Brief Survey of the History of the National Liberation War of the Albanian People, 1941-1945*. Luan Omari's most recent useful work is *The People's Revolution in Albania and the Question of State Power*. Stefanaq Pollo and Arben Puto, have written, among other works, *The History of Albania: From Its Origins to the Present Day*. Perhaps the most useful and exhaustive Albanian secondary source is the four-volume collective work produced by the Instituti i Studimeve Marksiste-Leniniste Pranë KQ të PPSH called *Historia e Luftës Antifashiste Nacionalçlirimtare të popullit shqiptar*. This work is often quite candid but once again lacks objectivity when it comes to questions relating to the noncommunist resistance and Western involvement. Many of these works were, of course, revised as wartime communist leaders—Mehmet Shehu is the most prominent example[9]—fell out with Hoxha and were purged. This problem in often illustrated, quite literally, in the official photographs of wartime partisan units that often accompany these works in which the heads of the subjects rarely match the bodies.

Western historiography is of course less extensive. For the period prior to the Italian invasion of April 1939, German historian Michael Schmidt-Neke has produced a fine book called *Entstehung und Ausbau der Königsdiktatur in Albanien (1912-1939)* The book is well researched but relies perhaps too heavily on published Albanian sources. Although Schmidt-Neke is aware of and indeed mentions the propensity of socialist Albanian historians to see political figures in polarized terms, it seems that he himself at least partially falls into the trap in his overly critical interpretation of King Zog. For this early period and for the Italian invasion, also see Bernd Fischer *King Zog and the Struggle for Stability in Albania*. Of mild interest for this early period, and for the years of Zog's exile, is Gwen Robyns's authorized biography *Geraldine of the Albanians*. Robyns, however, falls rather completely into the familiar trap of accepting Zog's wife's verbatim recollection of conversations that took place fifty years earlier. The queen's perspective, not surprisingly, is less than objective. It is, in fact, liberally laced with exaggerations and inaccuracies.[10] One is left with the impression from this book that World War II was actually centered around King Zog and his family. In a conversation with me, the queen's sister—with Geraldine in fervent agreement—once confided that King Zog was the modern Napoleon.[11] Although the queen is a very pleasant person, her material is useful principally for an occasional anecdote.

A number of notable works have appeared that deal with the Italian invasion and occupation of Albania. The noted English historian Denis Mack Smith has produced a several works that include important material on Albania, including *Mussolini,* and *Mussolini's Roman Empire.* The American historian MacGregor Knox, in his book *Mussolini Unleashed, 1939-1941: Politics and Strategy in Fascist Italy's Last War,* includes a very useful chapter on Italy's Albanian adventure. Knox confirms, amplifies, and adds considerable new material to support the argument that Italy's war-making capacity was exaggerated and able to overwhelm King Zog's wretched Albanian army only by the sheer weight of its numbers.

British strategy and participation, which is of particular significance because of the crucial role played by the British in serving as quartermaster for the resistance, is ably described and analyzed by several historians. David Stafford, in his book *Britain and European Resistance, 1940-1945: A Survey of the Special Operations Executive,* describes the formation and organization of SOE, which was to coordinate and carry out the supply of Albanian resistance fighters. Elizabeth Barker, in her book *British Policy in South-East Europe in the Second World War,* provides us with the unique perspective of the insider involved in British policymaking. Barker spent much of the war as an employee of the political warfare branch of the British Foreign Office.

Although the Albanians themselves, including Ballvora, have produced considerable material on the German period, the most balanced and complete account to date was produced by Bernhard Kühmel. Kühmel, in his unpublished doctoral dissertation "Deutschland und Albanien, 1943-1944: Die Auswirkungen der Besetzung und die innenpolitische Entwicklung des Landes," describes—in often excruciating detail—the course and impact of the German occupation on internal Albanian politics. And finally, a very useful recent addition to the literature is the soon-to-be published doctoral dissertation of Hubert Neuwirth, "Widerstand und Kollaboration in Albanien (1939-1944): Eine historische Analyse des kulturellen Musters von Freund und Feind." While suffering from stylistic and organizational problems, and narrower in scope than this work, Neuwirth's book is unique in that it is the first Western study of collaboration and resistance in Albania that makes use of Albanian archival sources, plus a small collection of selective British documents collected by the historical institute in Tirana. That study is important in that it encourages us to give more prominence to the early noncommunist resistance movements. It also helps to confirm what Western scholars have argued for some time—that the official Albanian socialist view of the war is politicized to the extent that it is of only limited value. Though these are but a few of the sources I found useful, they are the most important.

It is hoped that the information contained herein might be of use to later scholars of Albanian history who are able to take full advantage of the Albanian archives, in particular the new generation of Albanian historians.

NOTES

Chapter One: Count Ciano's Invasion of Albania

1. For a brief survey of Italian interest in Albania see Bernd J. Fischer, "Italian Policy in Albania, 1894-1943," *Balkan Studies* 26, no. 1 (1985).
2. Christo Dako, *Albania* (Boston: E. L. Grimes, 1919), p. 104; E. L. P. Dillion, "Albania," *Contemporary Review* (July 1914), p. 125.
3. Giovanni Zamboni, *Mussolinis Expansionspolitik auf dem Balkan* (Hamburg: Helmut Buske Verlag, 1970), p. xxvi.
4. For the full text of the declaration, see Joseph Swire, *Albania: The Rise of a Kingdom* (London: Unwin Brothers, 1929), pp. 369-370.
5. Bernd J. Fischer, *King Zog and the Struggle for Stability in Albania* (Boulder, Colo.: East European Monographs and Columbia University Press, 1984), pp. 89-92.
6. League of Nations, *League of Nations Treaty Series: Publication of Treaties and International Engagements Registered with the Secretariat of the League* (Lausanne: Imprimerie Reunies, 1927), vol. 60, pp. 16-21.
7. Zamboni, *Mussolinis Expansionspolitik auf dem Balkan*, p. lxxxi.
8. Michael Schmidt-Neke, *Entstehung und Ausbau der Königsdiktatur in Albanien (1912-1939)* (Munich: R. Oldenbourg Verlag, 1987), pp. 266-267. The author quotes the German minister in Albania in the 1930s who drew up a list of eighteen sources of Italian influence in Albania.
9. Denis Mack Smith, *Mussolini's Roman Empire* (London: Longman, 1976), p. 141.
10. Ibid.
11. Ibid., pp. 140-141.
12. Ibid.

13. USDS 765.75/366: Rome, no. 349, 4 May 1937.
14. Count Galeazzo Ciano, *Ciano's Hidden Diary, 1937-1938* (New York: Dutton, 1953), p. 4.
15. Ibid., p. 94. (The *Anschluss* refers to the German annexation of Austria in March 1938.)
16. Ibid., p. 107.
17. Marcia Fishel Lavine, "Count Ciano: Foreign Affairs and Policy Determination in Fascist Italy, January 1939-June 1940" (Ph.D. diss., Vanderbilt University, 1977), p. 17.
18. Galaezzo Ciano, *Ciano's Diplomatic Papers: Being a Record of Nearly 2000 Conversations Held during the Years 1936-1942*, ed. Malcolm Muggeridge (London: Odhams Press, 1948), p. 207; Lavine, "Count Ciano: Foreign Affairs and Policy Determination," p. 17; Mack Smith, *Mussolini's Roman Empire*, p. 150.
19. Lavine, "Count Ciano: Foreign Affairs and Policy Determination," p. 17.
20. Ciano, *Ciano's Diplomatic Papers*, p. 207; Lavine, "Count Ciano: Foreign Affairs and Policy Determination," p. 17.
21. Lavine, "Count Ciano: Foreign Affairs and Policy Determination," p. 18.
22. Ibid., pp 18-19.
23. Ciano, *Ciano's Hidden Diary*, p. 107.
24. Ciano, *Ciano's Diplomatic Papers*, p. 204.
25. Ibid.
26. Ciano, *Ciano's Hidden Diary*, p. 125.
27. Ibid., p. 114.
28. Conversations with Her Majesty Queen Geraldine of the Albanians, July 1981, Casa Ponderosa, Costa del Sol, Spain.
29. CGR, roll T120/313, Nr.4 362, Tirana, 15 April 1939; Schmidt-Neke, *Entstehung und Ausbau der Königsdiktatur in Albanien*, p. 340.
30. Ciano, *Ciano's Hidden Diary*, p. 202.
31. Ibid., pp. 184-185, 205.
32. Conversations with Queen Geraldine, July 1981, Costa del Sol, Spain; Gwen Robyns, *Geraldine of the Albanians* (London: Muller, Blond, & White, 1987), p. 81.
33. Schmidt-Neke, *Entstehung und Ausbau der Königsdiktatur in Albanien*, pp. 271-272.
34. FO 371/12710 R725/725/90, Durrës, 23 February 1939, FO 371/23710 R1272/725/90, Durrës, 22 February 1939, and FO 371/23714 R4454/1335/90, Durrës, 18 May 1939; CGR, roll T120/313, Nr. 362, Tirana, 15 April 1939.
35. Schmidt-Neke, *Entstehung und Ausbau der Königsdiktatur in Albanien*, p. 272.
36. FO 371/23711 R2065/725/90, Durrës, 16 March 1939; Mack Smith, *Mussolini's Roman Empire*, p. 149.
37. Leften Stavrianos, *The Balkans since 1453* (New York: Holt, Rinehart, Winston, 1958), p. 725.
38. Count Galeazzo Ciano, *The Ciano Diaries, 1939-1945* (New York: Doubleday, 1945), p. 31; FO 371/23711 R2065/725/90, Durrës, 16 March 1939.
39. Conversations with Queen Geraldine, July 1981, Costa del Sol, Spain.
40. Ciano, *Ciano's Diplomatic Papers*, p. 271.
41. Lavine, "Count Ciano: Foreign Affairs and Policy Determination," p. 23.

42. Jacob Hoptner, *Yugoslavia in Crisis, 1934-1941* (New York: Columbia University Press, 1962), p. 126.
43. Ciano, *The Ciano Diaries*, p. 23.
44. Lavine, "Count Ciano: Foreign Affairs and Policy Determination," p. 26; Mack Smith, *Mussolini's Roman Empire*, p. 151.
45. Ciano, *The Ciano Diaries*, p. 28.
46. Ibid., p. 47; Lavine, "Count Ciano: Foreign Affairs and Policy Determination," p. 29.
47. Ciano, *The Ciano Diaries*, p. 53.
48. Ibid., p. 51.
49. Lavine, "Count Ciano: Foreign Affairs and Policy Determination," p. 33.
50. Ciano, *The Ciano Diaries*, p. 52.
51. FO 371/23714 R4454/1335/90, Durrës, 18 May 1939.
52. FO 434/6 73262, p. 172.
53. Ibid.
54. Ciano, *The Ciano Diaries*, pp. 54, 56.
55. Ciano had little confidence in his commanders, as evidenced by his ridiculing Guzzoni for wearing a bad toupee.
56. Ciano, *The Ciano Diaries*, pp. 51, 55, 56.
57. USDS 765.75/444: Tirana, 6 April 1939.
58. Ciano, *The Ciano Diaries*, p. 57.
59. USDS 765.75/444: Tirana, 6 April 1939.
60. The Germans became aware of the plan even before the Italian army was informed.
61. David B. Funderburk, "Anglo-Albanian Relations, 1920-1939," *Revue Etudes Sud-Est Européennes* 13, no. 1 (1974), p. 6.
62. USDS 765.75/444: Tirana, 6 April 1939; FO 371/23714 R2951/1335/90, Durrës, 11 April 1939.
63. USDS 765.75/444: Tirana, 6 April 1939; FO 371/23714 R2951/1335/90, Durrës, 11 April 1939; American Council on Public Affairs, *The Greek White Book, Diplomatic Documents Relating to Italy's Aggression against Greece* (Agence D'Athenes: 1943), p. 25.
64. Lavine, "Count Ciano: Foreign Affairs and Policy Determination," p. 37.
65. FO 371/23713 R2953/1335/90, Rome, 13 April 1939.
66. WO 208/62, Report on Albania, chap. 9, Armed Forces; Hubert Neuwirth, "Widerstand und Kollaboration in Albanien (1939-1944): Eine historische Analyse des kulturellen Musters von Freund und Feind" (Ph.D. diss., University of Graz, 1997), p. 36.
67. FO 371/23713 R2953/1335/90, Rome, 13 April 1939.
68. USDS 875.00/520: Tirana, 24 May 1939.
69. Ciano, *The Ciano Diaries*, p. 62.
70. Mack Smith, *Mussolini's Roman Empire*, p. 153.
71. Ibid., p. 152.
72. FO 371/23714 R3060/1335/90, 14 April 1939, Whipple.
73. Ibid.
74. Ibid., p. 152.
75. Mack Smith, *Mussolini's Roman Empire*, p. 154.

76. USDS 765.75/459: Tirana, 8 April 1939.

77. Conversations with Queen Geraldine, July 1981, Costa del Sol, Spain. Zog himself maintained on more than one occasion that Yugoslavia was prepared to invade Albania; see FO 371/22110 R1799/867/90, 14 March 1942. Gwen Robyns repeats this version in her authorized biography of the queen.

78. Robyns, *Geraldine of the Albanians*, p. 89.

79. CGR, roll T120/313, Nr. 362, Tirana, 15 April 1939.

80. Luan Omari, *The People's Revolution in Albania and the Question of State Power* (Tirana: Nëntori, 1986), p. 17.

81. Stephen Peters, "Ingredients of the Communist Takeover in Albania," in Thomas Hammond, ed., *The Anatomy of Communist Takeovers* (New Haven, Conn.: Yale University Press, 1975), p. 274.

82. Ciano, *The Ciano Diaries*, p. 62.

83. Fischer, *King Zog and the Struggle for Stability in Albania*, pp. 171-172.

84. FO 371/23713 R2657/1335/90, Rome, 8 April 1939.

85. FO 371/23713 R2755/1335/90, Durrës, 11 April 1939

86. FO 371/23713 R2927/1335/90, Durrës, 16 April 1939.

87. Ciano, *The Ciano Diaries*, pp. 64-65.

88. George M. Self, "Foreign Relations of Albania" (Ph.D. Diss., University of Chicago, 1943), p. 178.

89. *Times (London)*, 7 April 1939, p. 3.

90. Ibid.

91. *New York Times*, 4 April 1939, estimated that Italian investments in Albania during the interwar period approached 1 billion lire. H. Gross suggests that between 1928 and 1939 the Italians contributed 280 million Albanian francs. See H. Gross, "Albanien zwischen den Machten: Ein Beitrag zur Erschliessung unentwickelter Gebiete," *Wirtschaftsdienst* 6 (1949), p. 4.

92. Lavine, "Count Ciano: Foreign Affairs and Policy Determination," pp. 42-43; FO 371/23717 R2333/1335/90, Rome, 4 April 1939.

93. FO 371/23717 R2333/1335/90, Rome, 4 April 1939.

94. FO 371/23713 R2759/1335/90, Budapest, 11 April 1939; FO 371/23717 R3219/3219/90, Durrës, 18 August 1939.

95. CGR, roll T120/313, Nr. 362, Tirana, 15 April 1939.

96. FO 371/23712 R2447/1335/90, Berlin, 8 April 1939, and FO 371/23712 R2449/1335/90, Berlin, 8 April 1939.

97. FO 371/23712 R2484/1335/90, Foreign Office Minute, 8 April 1939.

98. FO 371/23712 R2487/1335/90, Paris, 8 April 1939.

99. Christopher Andrew, *Secret Service: The Making of the British Intelligence Community* (London: William Heinemann, 1985), p. 590.

100. FO 371/23785 R2473/1/22, Rome, 8 April 1939; CAB 23/98 18A, 19 April 1939.

101. Ciano, *The Ciano Diaries*, pp. 61-62.

102. Stavrianos, *The Balkans since 1453*, p. 726.

103. Funderburk, "Anglo-Albanian Relations, 1920-1939," p. 7.

104. Jon Halliday, *The Artful Albanian: The Memoirs of Enver Hoxha* (London: Chatto Press, 1986), p. 21.

105. FO 371/23711 4816/725/90, League of Nations, Events in Albania: Various Communications Addressed to the Secretary-General, A.14, 1939, VII, 10 June 1939.
106. MacGregor Knox, *Mussolini Unleashed, 1939-1941: Politics and Strategy in Fascist Italy's Last War* (Cambridge: Cambridge University Press, 1982), p. 41.
107. Mack Smith, *Mussolini's Roman Empire*, p. 156.; USDS 741.68/28 GDG: Athens, 10 April 1939.

Chapter Two: The Construction of an Italian Albania

1. Stavrianos, *The Balkans since 1453*, pp. 727-728; Wayne S. Vucinich, "Communist Gains in Albania (I)," *Current History* 221, no. 122 (1951), p. 212.
2. Örjan Sjöberg, *Rural Change and Development in Albania* (Boulder, Colo.: Westview Press, 1991), p. 32.
3. Nicholas Pano, *The People's Republic of Albania* (Baltimore: Johns Hopkins University Press, 1968), p. 13.
4. Stavrianos, *The Balkans since 1453*, p. 729.
5. Ibid.
6. Sjöberg, *Rural Change and Development in Albania*, p. 34.
7. Julian Amery, *Approach March: A Venture in Autobiography* (London: Hutchinson, 1973), pp. 370-371.
8. Stavrianos, *The Balkans since 1453*, p. 730.
9. Neuwirth, "Widerstand und Kollaboration in Albanien," p. 28.
10. CGR, roll T120/313, Nr. 387, Tirana, Political Circular, 10 April 1939.
11. Lavine, "Count Ciano: Foreign Affairs and Policy Determination," p. 40.
12. Ciano, *The Ciano Diaries*, p. 62; FO 371/23712 R2471/1335/90, FO Minute, 8 April 1939.
13. FO 371/23712 R2489/1335/90, Rome, Perth, 9 April 1939.
14. FO 371/23712 R26631/1335/90, Rome, Perth, 10 April 1939.
15. FO 371/23712 R2712/1335/90, Rome, Perth, 11 April 1939.
16. Ciano, *The Ciano Diaries*, p. 63; Omari, *The People's Revolution in Albania and the Question of State Power*, p. 18.
17. Schmidt-Neke, *Entstehung und Ausbau der Königsdiktatur in Albanien*, p. 277.
18. Francesco Jacomoni, *La politica dell'Italia in Albania* (Roca San Casciano: Cappelli Editore, 1965), p. 133.
19. FO 434/6 R6606/6606/90, Durrës, Ryan, 16 August 1939.
20. Andrew Ryan, *The Last of the Dragomans* (London: Geoffrey Bles, 1951), pp. 336-338.
21. CGR, roll T120/313, Nr. 25, Tirana, 12 April 1939.
22. FO 434/6 R6606/6606/90, Letter from Ryan to FO, Report on Leading Personalities, 16 August 1939, and FO 371/23714 R3075/1335/90, Durrës, Ryan, 14 April 1939.
23. Ibid.
24. FO 434/6 R3517/1335/90, Durrës, Ryan, 25 April 1939, and FO 371/23714

R3824/3824/90, Durrës, Ryan, 3 May 1939; WO 204/9428, Reports and Memos, July 1944-February 1945.
    25. Anton Logoreci, *The Albanians: Europe's Forgotten Survivors* (Boulder, Colo.: Westview Press, 1977), p. 67
    26. Ciano, *The Ciano Diaries*, p. xvii.
    27. Ibid., p. 64.
    28 Ibid., p. 349.
    29. Ibid., pp. 64-65.
    30. Neuwirth, "Widerstand und Kollaboration in Albanien," pp. 14, 31.
    31. Raphael Lemkin, *Axis Rule in Occupied Europe* (Washington: Carnegie Endowment for International Peace, 1944), p. 99.
    32. FO 434/6 p. 188, Durrës, Ryan.
    33. Ciano, *The Ciano Diaries*, pp. 66-67.
    34. Ibid., p. 65.
    35. FO 371/23715 R5009/5009/90, Durrës, Ryan, 13 June 1939.
    36. Ciano, *The Ciano Diaries*, pp. 92-93.
    37. Robert M. W. Kempner, "The New Constitution of Albania: a Model Constitution for European Vassal States," *Tulane Law Review* 15 (1941), p. 434.
    38. CGR, roll T120/313, Nr. 427, Tirana, German Legation, 13 May 1939.
    39. FO 371/23715 R5009/5009/90, Durrës, Ryan, 13 June 1939.
    40. The king had so little to do with the constitution that he first asked Ciano who had drafted it and then complained that the new Albanian flag did not include a heraldic symbol of the dynasty. Ciano told Mussolini, who went into another of his many tirades against the monarchy; the Duce argued that the king "is a small man, grumpy and untrustworthy.... It is a monarchy which, by its idiotic gassing, prevents the 'Fascistification' of the Army." Ciano, *The Ciano Diaries*, p. 93.
    41. CGR, roll T120/313, Nr. 391, Tirana, 26 April 1939.
    42. FO 434/6 R3517/1335/90, Durrës, Ryan, 25 April 1939.
    43. FO 371/23113 R2767/1335/90, Durrës, Ryan, 11 April 1939.
    44. FO 371/23715 R6243/1335/90, Athens, Palairet, 24 July 1939.
    45. Lemkin, *Axis Rule in Occupied Europe*, p. 101.
    46. Lavine, "Count Ciano: Foreign Affairs and Policy Determination," p. 45.
    47. OSS, Research and Analysis Branch, No. 772, Survey of Albania, 15 July 1943.
    48. For a complete translation of the text of the statutes, see Lemkin, *Axis Rule in Occupied Europe*, pp. 267-271.
    49. Omari, *The People's Revolution in Albania and the Question of State Power*, pp. 25-26.
    50. Lemkin, *Axis Rule in Occupied Europe*, p. 105.
    51. Ibid.
    52. Omari, *The People's Revolution in Albania and the Question of State Power*, p. 23.
    53. FO 371/23716 R4659/2066/90, Durrës, Ryan, 6 June 1939; Ciano, *The Ciano Diaries*, p. 87.
    54. FO 371/23717 R5013/2066/90, Durrës, Ryan, 19 June 1939, and FO 371/23717 R5420/2066/90, Durrës, Ryan, 27 June 1939.
    55. FO 371/23717 R9376/2066/90, FO Minute, Margin Note, 27 October 1939.

56. WO 208/62, Report on Albania, chap. 9, Armed Forces.
57. FO 434/6 R4385/1335/90, Durrës, Ryan, 19 May 1939.
58. FO 371/23715 R5419/90, Durrës, Ryan, 27 June 1939.
59. Omari, *The People's Revolution in Albania and the Question of State Power*, p. 21; Lemkin, *Axis Rule in Occupied Europe*, p. 100.
60. FO 371/23714 R4377/1335/90, Durrës, Ryan, 22 May 1939, and FO 371/23715 R5419/90, Durrës, Ryan, 27 June 1939.
61. Omari, *The People's Revolution in Albania and the Question of State Power*, p. 24; Lemkin, *Axis Rule in Occupied Europe*, p. 102.
62. OSS, Research and Analysis Branch, No. 772, Survey of Albania, 15 July 1943; FO 371/37135 R4069/39/90, FO Research Department, 5 May 1943.
63. FO 371/23113 R2711/1335/90, Rome, Perth, 11 April 1939.
64. Stavro Skendi, *Albania* (New York: Praeger, 1956), p. 61.
65. See chapter 1.
66. FO 371/23714 R3824, Durrës, Ryan, 3 May 1939.
67. Lemkin, *Axis Rule in Occupied Europe*, p. 103.
68. FO 371/23715 R5800, Durrës, Ryan, 11 July 1939, and FO 371/23714 R3824, Durrës, Ryan, 3 May 1939.
69. FO 371/23715 R5800, Durrës, Ryan, 11 July 1939.
70. WO 208/62, Report on Albania, 14 May 1940.
71. OSS, Research and Analysis, No. 1202, n.d.
72. FO 371/24866 R6098/503/90, Athens, 10 May 1940.
73. FO 434/6 R3182/1384/90, Durrës, Ryan, 22 April 1939; CGR, roll T120/313, Nr. 431, German Legation, Tirana, 10 May 1939.
74. CGR, roll T120/313, Nr. 431, German Legation, Tirana, 10 May 1939.
75. Ibid.
76. Mack Smith, *Mussolini's Roman Empire*, p. 155.
77. Ciano, *The Ciano Diaries*, p. 71.
78. CGR, roll T120/313, Nr. 420, German Legation, Tirana, 3 May 1939.
79. FO 371/24868 R4027/1427/90, Durrës, 16 March 1940; OSS, Research and Analysis, No. 1202, 8 November 1943; and FO 371/23715 R4530, Durrës, Ryan, 25 May 1939.
80. Jacomoni, *La politica dell'Italia in Albanìa*, p. 183; Lemkin, *Axis Rule in Occupied Europe*, pp. 103-104.
81. FO 371/33118 R8936/7557/90/1942, Foreign Office, Research Department, 22 March 1944.
82. FO 371/13560 C2310/2310/90, Durrës, 26 March 1929.
83. FO 371/14304 C5425/5425/90, Durrës, 30 June 1930.
84. FO 371/18341 R2465/2465/90, Durrës, 3 April 1934.
85. See David J. Kostelancik, "Minorities and Minority Language Education in Inter-war Albania," *East European Quarterly* 30, no. 1 (spring 1996).
86. FO 371/23717 R6150, Durrës, Ryan, 17 July 1939.
87. FO 371/13560 C2310/2310/90, Durrës, 26 March 1929.
88. FO 371/13561 C1988/565/90, Belgrade, 13 March 1929.
89. Vandeleur Robinson, *Albania's Road to Freedom* (London: George Allen and Unwin, 1941), p. 98.

90. FO 371/12847 C2557/2557/90, Durrës, 27 March 1929, and FO 317/12844 C1351/146/90, Durrës, 3 February 1928.
91. FO 371/12068 2074/946/90, Durrës, 25 February 1927.
92. Ciano, *The Ciano Diaries*, p. 64.
93. FO 371/24868 R4027/1427/90, Durrës, Grafftey-Smith, 16 March 1940.
94. CGR, roll T120/340, Nr. 3185, Rome, 4 December 1941.
95. FO 371/33118 R8936/7557/90/1942, Research Department, Foreign Office, 22 March 1944.
96. Neuwirth, "Widerstand und Kollaboration in Albanien," p. 30.
97. FO 371/23717 R3219/3219/90, Durrës, Ryan, 18 April 1939.
98. FO 371/23716 R10123/1384/90, Durrës, Grafftey-Smith, 7 November 1939.
99. FO 371/24868 R2856/2856/90, Durrës, Grafftey-Smith, 22 February 1940.
100. Omari, *The People's Revolution in Albania and the Question of State Power*, p. 19.

Chapter Three: Italian Greater Albania

1. FO 371/23713 R2806/1335/90, Rome, Perth, 13 April 1939.
2. Ciano, *The Ciano Diaries*, pp. 62-63.
3. Ryan, *The Last of the Dragomans*, p. 333.
4. FO 371/23714 R3824/1335/90, Durrës, Ryan, Mitchell Letter of 26 April 1939, 3 May 1939.
5. FO 371/23714 R4451/1335/90, Rome, Dixon, 24 May 1939.
6. FO 371/24866 R503/503/90, Information from the Former Albanian Consul in Constantinople, 5 January 1940.
7. FO 371/23710 R2712/1335/90, Rome, Perth, 11 April 1939, and FO 371/23710 R2767/1335/90, Durrës, Ryan, 11 April 1939.
8. Lavine, "Count Ciano: Foreign Affairs and Policy Determination," pp. 40-41.
9. FO 371/23715 R6492/1335/90, Durrës, Gamble, 7 August 1939.
10. Ibid.
11. USDS, 875.00/507: Tirana, Grant, 6 May 1939.
12. FO 371/58482 R3068/191/90, Ryan to Slater, 21 February 1946, and in conversation with Queen Geraldine of the Albanians, July 1981, Costa del Sol, Spain.
13. FO 371/23714 R3825/1335/90, Durrës, Ryan, 3 May 1939.
14. Ciano, *The Ciano Diaries*, p. 65.
15. FO 371/23715 R6848/1335/90, Durrës, Gamble, 23 August 1939.
16. FO 371/23715 R5592/1335/90, Rome, Chancery to Southern Department, 5 July 1939.
17. FO 371/23715 R6492/1335/90, Durrës, Gamble, 7 August 1939, and FO 371/23715 R8487/1335/90, Durrës, Gamble, 25 September 1939.
18. FO 371/23717 R6150/6150/90, Durrës, Ryan, 17 July 1939.
19. CGR, roll T120/313, Nr. 620, Tirana, 10 July 1939.
20. Jacomoni, *La politica dell'Italia in Albania*, p. 186; FO 371/23715 R6242/1335/90, Athens, Palairet, 24 July 1939.

21. Jacomoni, *La politica dell'Italia in Albania*, p. 184.
22. FO 371/23715 R8487/1335/90, Durrës, Gamble, 25 September 1939.
23. FO 371/24868 R2855, Durrës, Grafftey-Smith, 15 February 1940.
24. Ciano, *The Ciano Diaries*, p. 65.
25. *Giornale d'Italia*, 12 October 1939.
26. Michael Kaser, "Economic System," in Klaus-Detlev Grothusen, *Südosteuropa-Handbuch, Albanien* (Göttingen: Vanderhoeck und Ruprecht, 1993), p. 299.
27. According to socialist Albanian statistics, Albania did not become self-sufficient in bread grains until the mid-1970s, and even this achievement was short lived.
28. FO 371/23737 R3900/2068/90, Phipps, 10 May 1939, and FO 371/25116 R4057/1385/90, R. Moore, 24 April 1939; Mack Smith, *Mussolini's Roman Empire*, p. 157.
29. FO 371/23715 R9525/1335/90, Durrës, Gamble, 24 October 1939. Gamble mentions a comment made by Jacomoni to Ryan in March 1939 in which he said that Italian exploitation of oil in Albania was a financial disaster and would always remain unremunerative.
30. FO 371/33118 R8956/7557/90, London, 22 March 1944; Ciano, *The Ciano Diaries*, p. 69. Ciano notes that he protested against the sum to be spent, although he does not tell us whether he believed it to be too high or too low.
31. FO 371/23714 R3824/1335/90, Durrës, Ryan, Mitchell Letter, 3 May 1939.
32. CGR, roll T120/313, Nr. 620, Tirana, Pannwitz, 10 July 1939.
33. FO 371/23714 R4451/1335/90, Rome, Dixon, 24 May 1939.
34. Ciano, *The Ciano Diaries*, p. 81; FO 371/23715 R8487/1335/90, Durrës, Grafftey-Smith, 25 September 1939.
35. FO 371/24866 R6808/6586/90, Hodgkinson Report, 19 June 1940.
36. CGR, roll T120/313, Nr. 427, Tirana, Pannwitz, 13 May 1939.
37. Mack Smith, *Mussolini's Roman Empire*, p. 157.
38. FO 371/24868 R2854/1426/22, Durrës, Grafftey-Smith, 10 February 1940; CGR, roll T120/313, Nr. 3821, Tirana, Pannwitz, 4 June 1940.
39. Lefter Kasneci, *Steeled in the Heat of Battle: A Brief Survey of the History of the National Liberation War of the Albanian People, 1941-1945* (Tirana: Naim Frashëri, 1966), p. 9; WO 204/9529, Various Files, Italian influence in Albania; Derek Hall, *Albania and the Albanians* (London: Pinter, 1994), p. 105.
40. CGR, roll T120/313, Nr. 620, Tirana, Pannwitz, 10 July 1939; FO 371/23715 R5204/1335/90, Athens, Palairet, 17 June 1939.
41. FO 371/23715 R5417/1335/90, Durrës, Ryan, 26 June 1939.
42. FO 371/24868 R5906/1426/90, Durrës, Grafftey-Smith, 29 April 1940.
43. Ciano, *The Ciano Diaries*, p. 254.
44. FO 371/24868 R1426/1426/90, Durrës, Grafftey-Smith, 19 January 1940.
45. Ciano, *The Ciano Diaries*, p. 93.
46. Ibid., pp. 69, 254.
47. Ibid., pp. 69-70.
48. Ibid., p. 112.
49. FO 371/23715 R5266/1335/90, Athens, Palairet, 28 June 1939, and FO 371/23715 R5416/1335/90, Durrës, Ryan, 24 June 1939.

50. CGR, roll T120/340, Nr. 33, Tirana, Pannwitz, 20 August 1939; FO 371/23715 R6599/1335/90, Durrës, Gamble, 17 August 1939, FO 371/23715 R6621/1335/90, Durrës, Gamble, 18 August 1939, FO 371/23715 R6625/1335/90, Durrës, Gamble, 20 August 1939, FO 371/23715 R6738/1335/90, Durrës, Gamble, Conversation with Greek Minister, 23 August 1939, FO 371/23715 R6846/1335/90, Durrës, Gamble, 23 August 1939, and FO 371/23715 R8916/1335/90, Durrës, Gamble, 11 October 1939.

51. FO 371/24866 R4452/503/90, Durrës, Grafftey-Smith, 1 April 1940.

52. Ciano, *The Ciano Diaries*, p. 254; FO 371/24868 R6153/6153/90, Rome, Loraine, 19 May 1940.

53. CGR, roll T120/313, Nr. 421, Tirana, Pannwitz, 20 June 1940.

54. DDI, 9th Series, Vol. 5, No. 139, p. 122.

55. Knox, *Mussolini Unleashed*, pp. 106-107.

56. Ibid., pp. 169-170.

57. Miranda Vickers and James Pettifer, *Albania: From Anarchy to a Balkan Identity* (New York: New York University Press, 1997), p. 207.

58. Ibid., p. 170.

59. CGR, roll T120/340, Nr. 657, Berlin, 13 August 1940.

60. FO 371/29843 R399/138/19, Athens, Palairet, Report on Greek White Book, 20 December 1940.

61. Ciano, *The Ciano Diaries*, p. 283. For more on the Italian invasion of Corfu in 1923, see Mack Smith, *Mussolini's Roman Empire*, pp. 5-6, 18, 48; and James Barros, *The Corfu Incident of 1923* (Princeton, N.J.: Princeton University Press, 1965).

62. Knox, *Mussolini Unleashed*, p. 171; Robert Lee Wolf, *The Balkans in Our Time* (New York: Norton, 1967). p. 148.

63. Ciano, *The Ciano Diaries*, p. 283.

64. Ibid., p. 284.

65. DDI 9th Series, Vol. 5, No. 442, 443, pp. 424-426.

66. Knox, *Mussolini Unleashed*, p. 176.

67. Ciano, *The Ciano Diaries*, p. 300.

68. DDI 9th Series, Vol. 5, Nos. 443, 642.

69. Pietro Badoglio, *Italy in the Second World War* (London: Oxford University Press, 1948), p. 27; Ciano, *The Ciano Diaries*, p. 301.

70. Jacomoni, *La politica dell'Italia in Albania*, p. 346.

71. DDI 9th series, Vol. 5, No. 728, pp. 700-701; Knox, "Fascist Italy Assesses Its Enemies, 1935-1940," in Ernest May, ed., *Knowing One's Enemies: Intelligence Assessment between the Two World Wars* (Princeton: Princeton University Press, 1984), p. 361.

72. Mack Smith, *Mussolini's Roman Empire*, p. 233; Knox, *Mussolini Unleashed*, p. 212.

73. Ciano, *The Ciano Diaries*, pp. 303-304.

74. FO 371/29843 R399/138/19, Athens, Palairet, 20 December 1940.

75. Knox, *Mussolini Unleashed*, p. 212.

76. Hanson W. Baldwin, *The Crucial Years, 1939-1941* (New York: Harper and Row, 1976), p. 188. For an extensive account of the Italian invasion of Greece, see Mario Cervi, *The Hollow Legions: Mussolini's Blunder in Greece, 1940-1941* (Garden City, N.Y.: Doubleday, 1971).

Notes to pages 77-80

77. Knox, *Mussolini Unleashed*, p. 233.
78. Mack Smith, *Mussolini's Roman Empire*, p. 233.
79. Stavrianos, *The Balkans since 1453*, p. 751.
80. F. H. Hinsley et al., *British Intelligence in the Second World War*, vol. 1 (London: H. M. Stationary Office, 1979), p. 376.
81. Martin Gilbert, *The Second World War: A Complete History* (New York: Holt, 1989), p. 143.
82. Ciano, *The Ciano Diaries*, p. 318.
83. Ibid., p. 328.
84. Knox, *Mussolini Unleashed*, pp. 269-270.
85. WO 208/691, Cables from British Military Mission in Athens, 0200 to War Office, 7 February 1941; Baldwin, *The Crucial Years*, p. 270.
86. Cervi, *The Hollow Legions*, p. xxiv.
87. *Hitler e Mussolini: Lettere e documenti* (Milan: Rizzoli, 1946), pp. 11-19; Ciano, *The Ciano Diaries*, p. 307.
88. See Bernd J. Fischer, "Albania and the Italian Invasion of Greece, October 1940," in *Greece and the War in the Balkans, 1940-1941* (Thessaloníki, Institute for Balkan Studies, 1992).
89. WO 208/62, War Office Report on Albania, Armed Forces; Stefanaq Pollo and Arben Puto, *The History of Albania: From Its Origins to the Present Day* (London: Routledge and Kegan Paul, 1981), p. 227; FO 371/29940 R6219/218/22, BBC Communicated, Benito Mussolini Speech, 17 June 1941.
90. FO 371/29940 R6219/218/22, BBC Communicated, Benito Mussolini Speech, 17 June 1941.
91. CGR, roll T120/340, Nr. 2159, Rome, 27 November 1940; Badoglio, *Italy in the Second World War*, p. 28; Knox, *Mussolini Unleashed*, p. 233.
92. Pollo and Puto, *The History of Albania*, p. 227.
93. FO 371/29712 R442/149/90, Athens, Palairet, Maitland Report, 21 December 1940.
94. The Institute of Marxist-Leninist Studies at the Central Committee of the Party of Labor of Albania, *History of the Party of Labor of Albania* (Tirana: Naim Frashëri, 1971), p. 76. This book and other similar material make much of the aid that Albanian communists gave to the Greek military.
95. Laird Archer, *Athens Journal, 1940-1941* (Manhattan, Kans.: MA/AH Publishing, 1983), pp. 9-10; John Bitzes, *Greece in World War II to 1941* (Omaha: University of Nebraska Press, 1981) p. 94.
96. FO 371/29712 R442/149/90, Athens, Palairet, Maitland Report, 21 December 1940.
97. FO 371/29712 R442/149/90, Athens, Palairet, Maitland Report, 21 December 1940, and FO 371/24868 R6153/6153/90, Rome, Loraine, 19 May 1940.
98. FO 371/24868 R8924/6586/90, Athens, Palairet, 14 December 1940, and FO 371/29711 R111/111/90, Athens, Palairet, 21 December 1940.
99. FO 371/29712 R442/149/90, Athens, Palairet, 21 December 1940.
100. FO 371/29710 R47/47/90, Cummings, BBC, Dixon Margin Note, 16 December 1940.
101. FO 371/29712 R442/149/90, Athens, Palairet, 21 December 1940.

102. CGR, roll T120/5580, Tirana, Pannwitz, 19 April 1941.
103. FO 371/29712 R442/149/90, Athens, Palairet, 21 December 1940, and FO 371/29710 R47/47/90, Cummings, BBC, 16 December 1940; Archer, *Athens Journal*, p. 34.
104. Archer, *Athens Journal*, p. 34.
105. Ciano, *The Ciano Diaries*, p. 319.
106. WO 208, 691 dispatch 1508, to Commander in Chief, Middle East, 1 February 1941.
107. FO 371/29924 R29/28/22, Madrid, Hoare, 28 December 1940, FO 371/29924 R72/28/22, Berne, F. Savery, 30 December 1940, FO 371/29924 R148/28/22, Belgrade, Campbell, 4 January 1941, and FO 371/29924 R518/28/22, Bucharest, 30 November 1940.
108. Ciano, *The Ciano Diaries*, p. 316.
109. Mack Smith, *Mussolini's Roman Empire*, p. 232.
110. Ciano, *The Ciano Diaries*, p. 340.
111. Ibid., p. 314; Badoglio, *Italy in the Second World War*, p. 30.
112. Bernhard Kühmel, "Deutschland und Albanien, 1943-1944: Die Auswirkungen der Besetzung und die innenpolitische Entwicklung des Landes" (Ph.D. diss., University of Bochum, 1981), pp. 89-90.
113. CIR, roll T821/207, Comando Superiore Forze Armate Albania, ufficio operazioni, 4 December 1940.
114. CGR, roll T120/340, Nr. 2159, Rome, Rinteln, 27 November 1940.
115. Mack Smith, *Mussolini's Roman Empire*, p. 232.
116. Knox, *Mussolini Unleashed*, p. 273.
117. Charles B. Burdick, "Operation Cyclamen: Germany and Albania, 1940-1941," *Journal of Central European Affairs* 19 (1959/1960); Kühmel, "Deutschland und Albanien," p. 91.
118. Noel Malcolm, *Kosovo: A Short History* (London: Macmillan, 1998), pp. 289-290.
119. CGR, roll T120/1299, Tirana, Peiffer, 3 May 1941.
120. Population figures are very difficult to determine because Serbian figures are unreliable. The figures quoted here come from Skendi, *Albania*, p. 18, and Sjöberg, *Rural Change and Development in Albania*, p. 34.
121. CGR, roll T120/5580, Tirana, Peiffer, 19 April 1941.
122. Kühmel, "Deutschland und Albanien," p. 93.
123. CGR, roll T120/340, Nr. 133, Tirana, Schliep, 3 March 1944, and CGR, roll T120/340, Nr. 263, Tirana, Schliep, 22 April 1944; Barbara Jelavich, *History of the Balkans, Twentieth Century* (Cambridge: Cambridge University Press, 1983), p. 257.
124. OSS, Research and Analysis, No. 968, A Pocket Guide to Albania, 6 July 1943; see also Michael Schmidt-Neke, "Geschichtliche Grundlagen," in Klaus-Detlev Grothusen ed., *Südosteuropa-Handbuch* (Göttingen: Vandenhoeck und Ruprecht, 1993), vol. 7, *Albanien*, p. 51.
125. WO 204/9558, H. Hodgkinson Report, July 1944; Schmidt-Neke, *Entstehung und Ausbau der Königsdiktatur in Albanien*, p. 333.

126. CGR, roll T120/340, Nr. 3081, Rome, 26 November 1941.
127. Kühmel, "Deutschland und Albanien," p. 93.
128. CGR, roll T120/340, Nr. 21, Tirana, 13 November 1941.
129. CGR, roll T120/340, Nr. 3018, Rome, 21 November 1941.
130. Ciano, *The Ciano Diaries,* p. 403; CGR, roll T120/340, Nr. 3170, Rome, 24 November 1941.
131. CGR, roll T120/340, Nr. 3170, Rome, 24 November 1940.
132. FO 371/33116 R8171/1335/900, Berne, Censored Letter to Edith Durham, 30 October 1942.
133. Alex Dragnich and Slavko Todorovich, *The Saga of Kosovo: Focus on Serbian-Albanian Relations* (Boulder, Colo.: East European Monographs, 1984), p. 123; CGR, roll T501/258, Abschlussbericht fur Albanien, and CGR, roll T120/340, Nr. 246, Fuschl, Neubacher, 25 April 1944.
134. Malcom, *Kosovo: A Short History,* p. 292.
135. Sabrina P. Ramet, *Social Currents in Eastern Europe: The Sources and Meaning of the Great Transformation* (Durham, N.C.: Duke University Press, 1991), p. 175. An interesting report called "The Expulsion of the Albanians" on Serbian policy in Kosova was drawn up by Professor Vaso Cubrilovic in 1937 and presented to the government of Milan Stoyadinovic.
136. Ramet, *Social Currents in Eastern Europe,* p. 175.
137. WO 204/9558, Hodgkinson Report, July 1944 and War Office objections to Hodgkinson's conclusions.
138. Pollo and Puto, *The History of Albania,* p. 228.

Chapter Four: Italian Repression and the Beginning of Resistance

1. CGR, roll T120/313, Nr. 620, Tirana, Pannwitz, 10 July 1939.
2. Mack Smith, *Mussolini's Roman Empire,* p. 157.
3. CGR, roll T120/313, Nr. 48, Tirana, Pannwitz, 20 January 1940; FO 371/24866 R784/503/90, Durrës, Grafftey-Smith, 9 January 1940.
4. Ciano, *The Ciano Diaries,* p. 254.
5. CGR, roll T120/5580, Nr. 624, Tirana, Pannwitz, 16 July 1941.
6. FO 371/23715 R4530/90, Durrës, Ryan, 25 May 1939.
7. FO 371/23715 R12113/1335/90, Durrës, Grafftey-Smith, 20 December 1939.
8. CGR, roll T120/313, Nr. 3821, Tirana, Pannwitz, 4 June 1940.
9. CGR, roll T120/340, Nr. 287, Tirana, Pannwitz, 20 April 1940.
10. Ciano, *The Ciano Diaries,* pp. 92-93.
11. CGR, roll T120/340, Nr. 23, Rome, Pfeiffer, 17 November 1941.
12. Kühmel, *Deutschland und Albanien,* p. 46.
13. See chapter 2.
14. Fischer, *King Zog and the Struggle for Stability in Albania,* p. 304; Pano, *The People's Republic of Albania,* p. 13; Pollo and Puto, *The History of Albania,* p. 226.
15. Raymond Hutchings, "Albania's Inter-war History as a Forerunner to the

Communist Period," in Tom Winnifrith, ed., *Perspectives on Albania* (New York: St. Martin's Press, 1992), p. 118.

16. Institute of Marxist-Leninist Studies, *History of the Party of Labor*, p. 67.
17. FO 371/24868 R2855/90, Durrës, Grafftey-Smith, 15 February 1940.
18. FO 371/24866 R5903/503/90, Durrës, Grafftey-Smith, 27 April 1940.
19. FO 371/24868 R2855/90, Durrës, Grafftey-Smith, 15 February 1940.
20. CGR, roll T120/324, Nr. 1172, Rome, Pfeiffer, 16 September 1942.
21. FO 371/24868 R4454/1426/90, Durrës, Grafftey-Smith, 2 April 1940, and FO 371/24866 R5807/503/90, Durrës, Grafftey-Smith, 4 May 1940.
22. Ramadan Marmullaku, *Albania and the Albanians* (London: C. Hurst, 1975), p. 42.
23. FO 371/24868 R2855/90, Durrës, Grafftey-Smith, 15 February 1940.
24. CGR, roll T120/324, Nr. 41g/41, Tirana, Pannwitz, 16 October 1941.
25. CGR, roll T120/1299, Rome, Pfeiffer, 4 June 1941.
26. Ibid.
27. CGR, roll T120/324, Nr. 41g/41, Tirana, Pannwitz, 16 October 1941.
28. Stavrianos, *The Balkans since 1453*, pp. 729-730; Skendi, *Albania*, p. 152; WO 204/9558, Hodgkinson Report, July 1944.
29. Nicholas J. Costa, *Albania: A European Enigma* (Boulder, Colo.: East European Monographs and Columbia University Press, 1995), pp. 44-45.
30. CGR, roll T120/340, Nr. 1646, Berlin, Steengracht, 21 August 1943, and Nr. 185, Rome, Mackensen, 10 May 1939.
31. Ciano, *The Ciano Diaries*, p. 64.
32. Ibid., p. 81.
33. FO 371/23715 R5204/1335/90, Athens, Palairet, 17 June 1939.
34. FO 371/24866 R783/503/90, Durrës, Grafftey-Smith, 30 December 1939.
35. Logoreci, *The Albanians*, p. 67.
36. Ciano, *The Ciano Diaries*, pp. 202-203.
37. FO 371/24866 R1636/503/90, Durrës, Grafftey-Smith, 3 February 1940, and FO 371/24866 R2020/503/90; Durrës, Grafftey-Smith, 6 February 1940; Kasneci, *Steeled in the Heat of Battle*, p. 13.
38. FO 371/24866 R2020/503/90, Durrës, Grafftey-Smith, 6 February 1940.
39. Neuwirth, "Widerstand und Kollaboration in Albanien," p. 40.
40. CGR, roll T120/313, Nr. 287, Tirana, Pannwitz, 20 April 1940; FO 371/24866 R6993/503/90, Durrës, Grafftey-Smith, 12 August 1940; WO 204/9558, Hodgkinson Report, July 1944.
41. Kasneci, *Steeled in the Heat of Battle*, p. 13.
42. Neuwirth, "Widerstand und Kollaboration in Albanien," p. 38.
43. Ibid.
44. Pollo and Puto, *The History of Albania*, p. 226.
45. Ibid., p. 227; Neuwirth, "Widerstand und Kollaboration in Albanien," p. 48.
46. FO 371/24866 R6271/503/90, Durrës, Grafftey-Smith, 14 May 1940.
47. WO 204/9477, Military Report on Albania, 24 September 1941.
48. Enver Hoxha, *The Anglo-American Threat to Albania* (Tirana: 8 Nëntori, 1982), p. 25.
49. FO 371 24866 R6891/507/90, *Manchester Guardian*, 11 August 1940.

50. Neuwirth, "Widerstand und Kollaboration in Albanien," pp. 52-55.

51. Elizabeth Wiskemann, "Albania, 1939-1945," in A. and V. Toynbee, eds., *Hitler's Europe* (London: Oxford University Press, 1954), p. 674.

52. Ciano, *The Ciano Diaries,* p. 353.

53. Marmullaku, *Albania and the Albanians,* p. 43.

54. CGR, roll T120/340, Nr. 2159, Rome, Rintelen, 27 November 1940; Kühmel, "Deutschland und Albanien," p. 106.

55. Reginald Hibbert, *Albania's National Liberation Struggle: The Bitter Victory* (London: Pinter, 1991), p. 31; Halliday, *The Artful Albanian,* p. 23.

56. For more on this, see Hibbert, *Albania's National Liberation Struggle,* p. 30; and FO 371/24866 R7677/503/90, Broad, Ministry of Economic Warfare, 13 September 1940, and FO 371/24867 R8992/503/90, Broad, Ministry of Economic Warfare, 19 December 1940.

57. Fischer, *King Zog and the Struggle for Stability in Albania,* pp. 105-114.

58. FO 371/48079 R4145/46/G90, McLean Report, 23 February 1945.

59. For more on Kupi, see Bernd J. Fischer, "Abaz Kupi and British Intelligence," in John Morison, ed., *Eastern Europe and the West* (London: Macmillan, 1992); and FO 371/48079 R4145/46/G90, McLean Report, 23 February 1945.

60. FO 371/48079 R4145/46/G90, McLean Report, 23 February 1945.

61. FO 371/24866, Section P Memorandum, 25 August 1940. Richard Clogg mentions that a Greek doctor was caught smuggling dynamite into Albania for SOE in July 1940. See Richard Clogg, "The Special Operations Executive in Greece," in John O. Iatrides, ed., *Greece in the 1940s: A Nation in Crisis* (Hanover, N.H.: University Press of New England, 1981), p. 110.

62. Neuwirth, "Widerstand und Kollaboration in Albanien," p. 54.

63. As quoted in Basil Kondis, "A British Attempt to Organize a Revolt in Northern Albania during the Greek-Italian War," in *Greece and the War in the Balkans, 1940-1941* (Thessaloníki: Institute for Balkan Studies, 1992), p. 114.

64. Fischer, *King Zog and the Struggle for Stability in Albania,* pp. 294-296.

65. FO 371/24868 R6817/6586/90, FO Minute, 12 July 1940.

66. FO 434/6 R6606/6606/90, Durrës, Ryan, 16 August 1939.

67. FO 371/24868 R8270/6586/90, Ryan Conversation with Zog, 8 November 1940, FO 371/24868 R6817/6586/90, FO Minute, and FO 371/24868 R8270/6586/90, Athens, 4 November 1940, 23 November 1940; Neuwirth, "Widerstand und Kollaboration in Albanien," p. 61.

68. For more on SOE, see David Stafford, *Britain and European Resistance, 1940-1945: A Survey of the Special Operations Executive* (Toronto: University of Toronto Press, 1980); and Elizabeth Barker, *British Policy in South-East Europe in the Second World War* (London: Macmillan, 1976).

69. Kondis, "A British Attempt to Organize a Revolt in Northern Albania during the Greek-Italian War," p. 115.

70. FO 371/29714 R1804/187/90, Athens, Palairet, 25 February 1941; Bernd J. Fischer, "Albania and the Italian Invasion of Greece," p. 100.

71. FO 371/24868 R8270/6586/90, Athens, 4 November 1940, and 23 November 1940.

72. FO 371/24868 R8639/6586/90, Dixon Minute, 26 November 1940, and Broad Minute, 23 November 1940.
73. Robyns, *Geraldine of the Albanians,* p. 121.
74. Conversations with Queen Geraldine, July 1981, Costa del Sol, Spain.
75. FO 371/24868 R8639/6586/90, Cairo, 29 November 1940, and Belgrade, 4 December 1940.
76. Barker, *British Policy in South-East Europe in the Second World War,* p. 53.
77. Hibbert, *Albania's National Liberation Struggle,* p. 46.
78. FO 371/24868 R8639/6586/90, FO Minute, 11 December 1940.
79. FO 371/29711 R2906/111/90, Belgrade, Campbell, 22 March 1941.
80. Hoxha, *The Anglo-American Threat to Albania,* p. 24.
81. FO 371/48079 R4145/46/G90, McLean Report, 23 February 1945; Barker, *British Policy in South-East Europe in the Second World War,* p. 54; Hibbert, *Albania's National Liberation Struggle,* p. 46.
82. FO 371/48079 R4145/46/G90, McLean Report, 23 February 1945.
83. Institute of Marxist-Leninist Studies, *History of the Party of Labor,* p. 79.
84. Nicholas Costa, "Invasion—Action and Reaction: Albania, a Case Study," in *East European Quarterly* 10, no. 1 (spring 1976), p. 59.
85. *New York Times,* 28 October 1941.
86. FO 371/24868 R2855/1426/90, Durrës, 15 February 1940.
87. Ciano, *The Ciano Diaries,* p. 81.
88. FO 371/23715 R5419 1335/90, Durrës, Ryan, 27 June 1939.
89. Neuwirth, "Widerstand und Kollaboration in Albanien," p. 62.
90. CGR, roll T120/313, Nr. 620, Tirana, Pannwitz, 10 July 1939.
91. Omari, *The People's Revolution in Albania and the Question of State Power,* p. 26.
92. Kasneci, *Steeled in the Heat of Battle,* p. 13.
93. FO 371/33116 R4917/3592/90, Censorship, 25 July 1942.
94. FO 371/33116, Political Memorandum, Source: Albanian Legation in Istanbul, 15 November 1942.
95. OSS, Research and Analysis, No. 1202, Albanian Gauleiters, Quislings, and Traitors.
96. CGR, roll T120/340, Nr. 3158, Rome, Mackensen, 4 December 1941.
97. FO 371/24866 R2018/503/90, Durrës, Grafftey-Smith, 26 January 1940.
98. Ciano, *The Ciano Diaries,* p. 366.
99. An uncle of Zog's, Esad Pasha played a significant, yet entirely self-serving, role in the early years of the new state. He was assassinated in Paris in 1920 by Avni Rustemi, who was later assassinated on the orders of Zog.
100. FO 371/10654 753/48/43, Durrës, Eyres, 31 December 1924.
101. Ciano, *The Ciano Diaries,* p. 405.
102. Ibid., pp. 421–423.
103. Ibid., p. 449.
104. Ibid., p. 481.
105. Kühmel, "Deutschland und Albanien," p. 107.
106. CGR, roll T120/324, Nr. 118, Tirana, Schliep, 30 January 1942.
107. Ibid.
108. Logoreci, *The Albanians,* p. 70.

Chapter Five: The Growth of Resistance and the Collapse of Italy

1. CGR, roll T120/340, Nr. 2159, Rome, Rintelen, 27 November 1940; Kühmel, *Deutschland und Albanien,* p. 106.
2. Hibbert, *Albania's National Liberation Struggle,* pp. 11-12.
3. Nicholas C. Pano, "Albania," in Joseph Held ed., *The Columbia History of Eastern Europe in the Twentieth Century* (New York: Columbia University Press, 1992), pp. 28-29.
4. Pollo and Puto, *The History of Albania,* pp. 226-229.
5. Wolf, *The Balkans in Our Time,* p. 218.
6. Institute of Marxist-Leninist Studies, *History of the Party of Labor,* pp. 72-76; Pollo and Puto, *The History of Albania,* p. 229.
7. Wolf, *The Balkans in Our Time,* p. 217.
8. Hibbert, *Albania's National Liberation Struggle,* pp. 16-17.
9. Institute of Marxist-Leninist Studies, *History of the Party of Labor,* p. 82.
10. Skendi, *Albania,* p. 19.
11. Costa, "Invasion—Action and Reaction: Albania, a Case Study," p. 61.
12. Pano, *The People's Republic of Albania,* p. 43.
13. Peter R. Prifti, "The Labor Party of Albania," in Stephen Fischer-Galati, *Communist Parties of Eastern Europe* (New York: Columbia University Press, 1979), p. 17.
14. Hibbert, *Albania's National Liberation Struggle,* p. 13.
15. Institute of Marxist-Leninist Studies, *History of the Party of Labor,* p. 72.
16. Pollo and Puto, *The History of Albania,* p. 230.
17. Wolf, *The Balkans in Our Time,* p. 219.
18. Peters, "Ingredients of the Communist Takeover in Albania," p. 281.
19. Institute of Marxist-Leninist Studies, *History of the Party of Labor,* p. 99.
20. Ibid., pp. 118-119.
21. Ibid., p. 97.
22. Stavrianos, *The Balkans since 1453,* p. 795.
23. Malcolm, *Kosovo: A Short History,* p. 302.
24. CGR, roll T120/296, Nr. 986, Tirana, 2 October 1941.
25. CGR, roll T120/296, Nr. 986, Tirana, 2 October 1941.
26. CGR, roll T120/5580, Nr. 385, Rome, 23 March 1942.
27. CGR, roll T120/324, Nr. 1172, Rome, 16 September 1942, and CGR, roll T120/5580, Nr. 385, Rome, 23 March 1942.
28. Kasneci, *Steeled in the Heat of Battle,* p. 21.
29. Ibid.
30. Neuwirth, "Widerstand und Kollaboration in Albanien," pp. 71-77.
31. There is some disagreement concerning this point. Neuwirth quotes an Italian source that seems to indicate that Mehdi Frashëri had influence in the creation of the nationalist group, the BK. See Neuwirth, "Widerstand und Kollaboration in Albanien," p. 102.
32. FO 371/43549 R17877/39/G39, Rice, 12 January 1944.
33. Institute of Marxist-Leninist Studies, *History of the Party of Labor,* p. 124.
34. Ibid., p.125.
35. Kasneci, *Steeled in the Heat of Battle,* p. 25.

36. Ibid., p. 27.
37. Neuwirth, "Widerstand und Kollaboration in Albanien," p. 73.
38. Institute of Marxist-Leninist Studies, *History of the Party of Labor*, p. 129.
39. Hibbert, *Albania's National Liberation Struggle*, p. 20.
40. Neuwirth mentions some shadowy nationalist organizations, such as "Oso Shqipnija," that distributed anticommunist leaflets under the appreciative eye of the Italians. See Neuwirth, "Widerstand und Kollaboration in Albanien," pp. 96-97.
41. Institute of Marxist-Leninist Studies, *History of the Party of Labor*, p. 131.
42. Milovan Djilas, *Rise and Fall* (New York: Harcourt Brace Jovanovich, 1985), p. 4.
43. Kühmel, "Deutschland und Albanien," pp. 56-57, and for a complete text of both plans, see page 570.
44. Hibbert, *Albania's National Liberation Struggle*, p. 21.
45. Kühmel, "Deutschland und Albanien," p. 60.
46. Wolf, *The Balkans in Our Time*, p. 213; Neuwirth, "Widerstand und Kollaboration in Albanien," pp. 162-163.
47. Neuwirth, "Widerstand und Kollaboration in Albanien," p. 111.
48. Kühmel, "Deutschland und Albanien," p. 58.
49. Pano, "Albania," p. 31.
50. Omari, *The People's Revolution in Albania and the Question of State Power*, p. 41.
51. Institute of Marxist-Leninist Studies, *History of the Party of Labor*, p. 133.
52. FO 371/33108 R9044/184/90, FO Minute, 29 December 1942.
53. CGR, roll T120/340, Nr. 1, Tirana, Wegner, 3 January 1943.
54. CGR, roll T120/340, Nr. 529, Rome, Bismarck, 3 February 1943, and CGR roll T120/340, Nr. 703, Rome, Mackensen, 13 February 1943.
55. Institute of Marxist-Leninist Studies, *History of the Party of Labor*, p. 156; Kasneci, *Steeled in the Heat of Battle*, pp. 38-39.
56. Kasneci, *Steeled in the Heat of Battle*, p. 41; Hibbert, *Albania's National Liberation Struggle*, p. 23.
57. Ciano, *The Ciano Diaries*, pp. 455-571.
58. Ibid., p. 455.
59. Ibid., p. 521.
60. Ibid., p. 571.
61. CGR, roll T120/324, Nr. 1172, Rome, 16 September 1942.
62. Ibid.
63. Pollo and Puto, *The History of Albania*, p. 234.
64. CIR, roll T821/250, Comando Supremo, 2 March 1943.
65. Ibid.
66. Ciano, *The Ciano Diaries*, p. 555.
67. Ibid., p. 570.
68. Fischer, *King Zog and the Struggle for Stability in Albania*, pp. 180-185.
69. Ciano, *The Ciano Diaries*, pp. 577-578.
70. Ibid., p. 578.
71. Ibid., p. 579.
72. CGR, roll T120/340, Nr. 1285, Rome, Mackensen, 2 May 1943.
73. CGR, roll T120/340, Nr. 2031, Rome, Mackensen, 19 March 1943.

Notes to pages 142-47

74. CIR, roll T821/128, Pariani Letter to Mussolini, 11 March 1943.
75. WO 204/9440, War Establishment General Policy, September 1943; Pollo and Puto, *The History of Albania*, p. 233.
76. Wiskemann, "Albania, 1939-1945," p. 676.
77. BK survivors and their supporters deny its existence. Neuwirth is skeptical but considers the existence of such an agreement likely. Neuwirth, "Widerstand und Kollaboration in Albanien," pp. 118-119.
78. Institute of Marxist-Leninist Studies, *History of the Party of Labor*, p. 140.
79. Pollo and Puto, *The History of Albania*, p. 234.
80. CGR, roll T120/340, Nr. 1285, Rome, Mackensen, 2 May 1943.
81. FO 371/37144 R1465/1067/90, Reuters Agency Communicated, 13 May 1943.
82. CGR, roll T120/340, Nr. 2273, Rome, Mackensen, 15 May 1943; FO 37144 R1463/1067/90, Reuters Agency Communicated, 13 May 1943.
83. FO 371/34144 R9236, FO Research, Review of Foreign Press, 14 September 1943.
84. Halliday, *The Artful Albanian*, p. 25.
85. FO 371/33113 R2125/2125/90, FO Minute, Dixon, March 30 1942.
86. Halliday, *The Artful Albanian*, p. 31.
87. Hibbert, *Albania's National Liberation Struggle*, p. 39.
88. The declaration provoked a violent reaction from vice-premier M. Canellopoulos, the representative of the Greek government in exile in Cairo. Canellopoulos argued that the declaration was a mortal blow to the Greek government's authority and prestige. He was just restrained from resigning. Eden, in exasperation, minuted that "this young man needs spanking." See FO 371/33108 R8608/184/90, FO Minute, 15 December 1943; Barker, *British Policy in South-East Europe in the Second World War*, p. 176; Arben Puto, *From the Annals of British Diplomacy: The Anti-Albanian Plans of Great Britain during the Second World War according to Foreign Office Documents of 1939-1944* (Tirana: 8 Nëntori), pp. 88-91; and CAB 66 WP 42 (555).
89. Hibbert, *Albania's National Liberation Struggle*, p. 40.
90. Ibid., p. 41.
91. Hoxha, *The Anglo-American Threat to Albania*, p. 25.
92. Barker, *British Policy in South-East Europe in the Second World War*, p. 174.
93. David Stafford, *Britain and European Resistance, 1940-1945*, pp. 104-105.
94. For a worldwide breakdown of subversive operations, see Stafford, *Britain and European Resistance, 1940-1945*, pp. 89-90.
95. Miranda Vickers, *The Albanians: A Modern History* (London: I. B. Taurus, 1995), p. 153.
96. SOE changed names a number of times: Force 133, 266, 299, and so on. The cover for the Middle East branch of SOE was MO4; see David Smiley, *Albanian Assignment* (London: Chatto Press, 1984), p. 7.
97. Halliday, *The Artful Albanian*, p. 35.
98. Amery, *Approach March*, p. 328.
99. As elsewhere in the Balkans, resistance in Greece was split between communists (EAM) and the nationalist (EDES). For a good brief description, see Stavrianos, *The Balkans since 1453*, pp. 785-795.

100. FO 371/43550 R/7779/39/G90, Bawker to Howard, 9 May 1944; Smiley, *Albanian Assignment*, pp. 11-13, 29.
101. Hoxha, *The Anglo-American Threat to Albania*, p. 27.
102. Hibbert, *Albania's National Liberation Struggle*, p. 53.
103. Kasneci, *Steeled in the Heat of Battle*, p. 52.
104. The Institute of Marxist Leninist Studies's *History of the Party of Labor* maintains that the first brigade consisted of 800 fighters, Krasneci 500, and the British about 150.
105. Hoxha, *The Anglo-American Threat to Albania*, p. 52.
106. Halliday, *The Artful Albanian*, p. 36.
107. Hibbert, *Albania's National Liberation Struggle*, pp. 48-49.
108. Ibid., p. 53.
109. FO 371/43549 R1787/39/G39, Rice to FO, 12 January 1944.
110. Hibbert, *Albania's National Liberation Struggle*, pp. 53-54.
111. Institute of Marxist-Leninist Studies, *The History of the Party of Labor*, pp. 165-166.
112. Pano, *The People's Republic of Albania*, p. 51; Hibbert, *Albania's National Liberation Struggle*, p. 56.
113. FO 371/48079 R4145/46/G90, McLean Report, 23 February 1945; Wiskemann, "Albania, 1939-1945," p. 676.
114. Pano, "Albania," pp. 31-32; Kühmel, "Deutschland und Albanien," p. 110; Instituti I Studimeve Marksiste-Leniniste Pranë KQ të PPSH, *Historia e Luftës Antifashiste Nacionalçlirimtare të popullit shqiptar*, vols. 1-4 (Tirana: 8 Nëntori, 1986-1989), vol. 1, pp. 502ff.
115. Institute of Marxist-Leninist Studies, *The History of the Party of Labor*, p. 167; Kühmel, "Deutschland und Albanien," pp. 114-115.
116. Institute of Marxist-Leninist Studies, *The History of the Party of Labor*, p. 166; Pollo and Puto, *The History of Albania*, p. 236.
117. Halliday, *The Artful Albanian*, p. 25.
118. Hibbert, *Albania's National Liberation Struggle*, pp. 56-57.
119. Ibid., p. 59.
120. Neuwirth, "Widerstand und Kollaboration in Albanien," p. 114.
121. OSS, 154, box 14, Harry Fultz report to Philip Adams, 24 February 1944.
122. Nicholas C. Pano, "The Last Bastion of Stalinism," in Milorad Drachkovitch, ed., *East Central Europe: Yesterday, Today, Tomorrow* (Stanford, Calif.: Hoover Institution Press, 1982), p. 193.

Chapter Six: The German Invasion and the Construction of a German Albania

1. For more on Prince Wied, see Fischer, *King Zog and the Struggle for Stability in Albania*, pp. 7-10.
2. Kühmel, "Deutschland und Albanien," p. 79.
3. Fischer, *King Zog and the Struggle for Stability in Albania*, pp. 244-246.

4. Kühmel, "Deutschland und Albanien," p. 82.

5. Fischer, *King Zog and the Struggle for Stability in Albania,* p. 270.

6. Pano, "Albania: The Last Bastion of Stalinism," p. 195; Kühmel, "Deutschland und Albanien," p. 126; Wolf, *The Balkans in Our Time,* p. 249.

7. Kühmel, "Deutschland und Albanien," p. 126.

8. Paul Leverkühn, *German Military Intelligence* (London: Weidenfeld and Nicholson, 1954), p. 152.

9. Martin Seckendorf, *Die Okkupationspolitik des deutschen Faschismus in Jugoslawien, Griechenland, Albanien, Italien und Ungarn, 1941-1945* (Berlin: Hüthig Verlagsgemeinschaft, 1992), p. 77; Neuwirth, "Widerstand und Kollaboration in Albanien," p. 139.

10. Pannwitz was finally replaced on the repeated insistence of Ciano. Pannwitz, like so many other Westerners to come in contact with Albania, had essentially "gone native." He was certainly not the only diplomat to do so. The U.S. representative Charles C. Hart is another example.

11. Kühmel, "Deutschland und Albanien," p. 126.

12. Christoph Stamm, "Zur deutschen Besetzung Albanien, 1943-1944," *Militärgeschichtliche Mitteilungen* 2 (1981), p. 102.

13. Hermann Neubacher, *Sonderauftrag Südost, 1940-1945: Bericht eines fliegenden Diplomaten* (Göttingen: Musterschmidt Verlag, 1956), p. 105.

14. Kühmel, "Deutschland und Albanien," p. 128.

15. CGR, roll T120/340, Nr. 4193, Tirana, Schliep to Ribbentrop, 23 August 1943, and CGR, roll T120/340, Nr. 4193, Wolfschanze, Sonnleithner, 1 September 1943, and Kühmel, "Deutschland und Albanien," p. 141.

16. CGR, roll T120/340, Nr. 1250, RAM to Schliep, 21 August 1943. A similar occupation strategy had already been implemented by both the Germans and the Italians, with varying degrees of success, in much of the rest of Europe.

17. CGR, roll T120/340, Nr. 4893, Tirana, Schliep to RAM, 23 August 1943.

18. CGR, roll T120/340, Nr. 942, Tirana, Neubacher, 12 September 1943.

19. Neubacher, *Sonderauftrag Südost,* p. 106.

20. Neuwirth presents a good brief overview of the German command structure in the Balkans. Weichs was the principal military commander, commanding Army Group F. Subordinate to Weichs was Army Group E, commanded by Alexander Löhr in Thessaloníki, whose responsibility included Greece and Serbia, and the Second Panzer Army under Lothar Rendulic in Belgrade, whose responsibility included Croatia, Montenegro, and Albania. Weichs also directed the activities of various military representatives, including the "German General in Albania." Neuwirth, "Widerstand und Kollaboration in Albanien," pp. 140-141.

21. Albanian sources say seventy thousand German troops participated in the invasion, although this estimate is certainly too high.

22. Kühmel, "Deutschland und Albanien," pp. 151-152.

23. FO 371/43553 73862, B8/1/264, SOE Report, 24 August 1944.

24. Martin Clark, *Modern Italy, 1871-1982* (London: Longman, 1984), pp. 303-304.

25. FO 371/37144, SOE Report, Nr. 60, 16 September 1943.

26. FO 371/43553 B8/1/277, SOE Report, 26 August 1944.

27. Ibid.

28. Institute of Marxist-Leninist Studies, *History of the Party of Labor*, p. 173; Pollo and Puto, *The History of Albania*, p. 237; WO 9529, Report, Italian Influence in Albania, April 1945; Hibbert, *Albania's National Liberation Struggle*, p. 60.

29. FO 371/43553 73862, B8/1/264, SOE Report, 24 August 1944.

30. FO 371/43553 73862, B8/1/277, SOE Report, 26 August 1944; Kühmel, "Deutschland und Albanien," p. 157.

31. CGR, roll T501/258, Final Wehrmacht Report on Albania.

32. Fitzroy Maclean, *Eastern Approaches* (New York: Time, 1964), p. 383.

33. WO 9529 B8/14/PL/302, Report on Italian Troops in Albania, 26 February 1944.

34. WO 9529 B8/14/PL/302, Report on Italian Troops in Albania, 26 February 1944, Report on Italians in Albania, 21 December 1944, and Report on Italian Influence in Albania, April 1945.

35. FO 371/43550 R7779/39/G90, FO Minute, Bawker to Howard, 9 May 1944.

36. CGR, roll T120/340. Nr. 942, Belgrade, Neubacher, 12 September 1943.

37. CGR, roll T501/258, Final Wehrmacht Report on Albania.

38. WO 204/9529, Report on Italian Influence in Albania, April 1945.

39. Neubacher, *Sonderauftrag Südost*, p. 106.

40. OSS, Research and Analysis Branch, Nr. 1475, Survey on Albania, p. 20, December 1943; Omari, *The People's Revolution in Albania and the Question of State Power*, p. 50.

41. FO 371/43553 B8/1/277, SOE Report, 26 August 1944.

42. Neubacher, *Sonderauftrag Südost*, p. 108; Kühmel, "Deutschland und Albanien," p. 80; CGR, roll T120/313, Nr. 652, Tirana, Pannwitz, 13 September 1940.

43. Kühmel, "Deutschland und Albanien," p. 418.

44. FO 371/43550 R7779/39/G90, FO Minute, Bawker to Howard, 9 May 1944.

45. FO 371/43550 R7779/39/G90, FO Minute, Bawker to Howard, 9 May, 1944, and FO 371/33108 R8770/184/980, 21 December 1942.

46. Omari, *The People's Revolution in Albania and the Question of State Power*, p. 50.

47. Neubacher, *Sonderauftrag Südost*, p. 110.

48. CGR, roll T501/258, Final Wehrmacht Report on Albania, and CGR, roll T120/340, Nr. 1000, Belgrade, Neubacher, 23 September 1943.

49. Kühmel, "Deutschland und Albanien," pp. 166-167.

50. Ibid., p. 164.

51. CGR, roll T120/340, Nr. 942, Belgrade, Neubacher, 12 September 1943; Stafford, *Britain and European Resistance, 1940-1945*, pp. 146-147.

52. For more on this, see Kühmel, "Deutschland und Albanien," pp. 168-170.

53. Hagen Fleischer, "Kollaboration und deutsche Politik im besetzten Griechenland," in Werner Röhr, ed., *Europa unterm Hakenkreuz: Okkupation und Kollaboration (1938-1945)*, p. 387.

54. Pariani was quickly sent by Badoglio to assume the rather sensitive position of Italian ambassador in Berlin.

55. CGR, roll T120/340, Nr. 33, Tirana, Schliep, 10 September 1943.

Notes to pages 169-77

56. OSS, Research and Analysis, Nr. 1475, The Problem of Albania, 20 December 1943.
57. Neubacher, *Sonderauftrag Südost*, p. 109.
58. CGR, roll T120/340, Nr. 1466, Westfalen, BRAM, 19 September 1943; Kühmel, "Deutschland und Albanien," p. 173.
59. Schmidt-Neke, "Geschichtliche Grundlagen," p. 55.
60. Neubacher, *Sonderauftrag Südost*, p. 110.
61. Kühmel, "Deutschland und Albanien," p. 194.
62. OSS, Research and Analysis Branch, Nr. 1475, The Problem of Albania, 20 December 1943.
63. Kühmel, "Deutschland und Albanien," p. 192.
64. Omari, *The People's Revolution in Albania and the Question of State Power*, p. 51.
65. Schmidt-Neke, *Entstehung und Ausbau der Königsdiktatur in Albanien*, p. 333.
66. Neubacher, *Sonderauftrag Südost*, pp. 120-121.
67. CGR, roll T120/340, Rome, Ritter, 11 September 1943.
68. Neubacher, *Sonderauftrag Südost*, p. 113.
69. Ibid., p. 112.
70. Pano, *The People's Republic of Albania*, p. 54
71. CGR, roll T501/258, Final Wehrmacht Report on Albania.
72. Schmidt-Neke, *Entstehung und Ausbau der Königsdiktatur in Albanien*, pp. 345-346; CGR, roll T120/340, Nr. 9, Tirana, Scheiger, 9 November 1943.
73. Kühmel, "Deutschland und Albanien," p. 198; CGR, roll T120/340, Nr. 755, Rome, Moellhausen, 8 December 1943.
74. CGR, roll T120/340, Nr. 9, Tirana, Scheiger, 9 November 1943; *Bashkimi i Kombit*, 8 February, 1944.
75. FO 371/43550 R7779/39/G90, FO Minute, Bawker to Howard, 9 May, 1944; OSS, Research and Analysis Branch, Nr. 2500.1, German Military Government over Europe, Albania, 1 December 1944.
76. Peter Kemp, *No Colours, No Crest* (London: Cassell, 1958), p. 131; Kühmel, "Deutschland und Albanien," p. 206.
77. Omari, *The People's Revolution in Albania and the Question of State Power*, p. 53.
78. Kühmel, "Deutschland und Albanien," pp. 200-201.
79. Hibbert, *Albania's National Liberation Struggle*, p. 64.
80. CGR, roll T120/340, Nr. 179, Tirana, Schliep, 24 November 1943.
81. CGR, roll T120/340, Berlin, Vermerk, 28 November 1943.
82. CGR, roll T120/340, Belgrade, Neubacher, 6 March 1944; Kühmel, "Deutschland und Albanien," pp. 394-396.
83. CGR, roll T120/340, Nr. 144, Tirana, Schliep, 8 November 1943, and Nr. 365, Belgrade, Neubacher, 18 February, 1944.
84. FO 371/43550 R7779/38/G90, FO Minute, Bawker to Howard, 9 May 1944.
85. CGR, roll T501/258, Final Wehrmacht Report on Albania.
86. Kühmel, "Deutschland und Albanien," p. 456.
87. FO 371/43550 R7779/38/G90, FO Minute, Bawker to Howard, 9 May 1944.
88. Kühmel, "Deutschland und Albanien," pp. 212-213, 345; CGR, T120/340, Nr. 88, Tirana, Schliep, 16 October 1943. Money was requested for fifty-seven thousand troops, but some for troops outside of Albania.

89. Kühmel, "Deutschland und Albanien," p. 313.
90. CGR, roll T120/340, Nr. 23, Rome, Ritter, 16 September 1943; FO 371 48093 R744/361/6/90, OSS report, 21 December 1944.
91. Kühmel, "Deutschland und Albanien," pp. 227-228.
92. CGR, roll T501/258, Final Wehrmacht Report on Albania; Kühmel, "Deutschland und Albanien," p. 229.
93. Kühmel, "Deutschland und Albanien," pp. 247-248. M. Kaser quotes a lower figure of just over 200 million Albanian francs using Albanian socialist sources. See Kaser, "Economic System," p.299.
94. Kühmel, "Deutschland und Albanien," p. 249.
95. Ibid., p. 326.
96. Ibid., p. 329.
97. Ibid., p. 317.
98. Ibid., p. 238.
99. CGR, roll T120/340, Nr. 1060, Belgrade, Neubacher, 30 September 1943.
100. CGR, roll T501/258, Final Wehrmacht Report on Albania.
101. Ibid.
102. Kühmel, "Deutschland und Albanien," p. 341.
103. Stamm, "Zur deutschen Besetzung Albaniens," p. 114.
104. CGR, roll T501/258, Final Wehrmacht Report on Albania; Kühmel, "Deutschland und Albanien," pp. 330-336.
105. CGR, roll T501/258, Final Wehrmacht Report on Albania.
106. Ibid.
107. Ibid.
108. FO 371/43550 R7779/38/G90 FO Minute, Bawker to Howard, 9 May 1944.
109. Kühmel, "Deutschland und Albanien," p. 214.
110. Bernd J. Fischer, "German Political Policy in Albania, 1943-1944," in Richard Spence and Linda Nelson, eds., *Scholar, Patriot, Mentor: Historical Essays in Honor of Dimitrije Djordjevic* (Boulder, Colo.: East European Monographs, 1992), p. 226; Kühmel, "Deutschland und Albanien," p. 220.
111. FO 371/48079 R4145/46/G90, McLean Report, 23 February 1945.
112. Kühmel, "Deutschland und Albanien," p. 220.
113. CGR, roll T120/340, Nr. 941, Belgrade, Neubacher, 2 September 1943.
114. FO 371/43550 R7779/38/G90, FO Minute, Bawker to Howard, 9 May 1944.
115. CGR, roll T120/340, Nr. 1490, Belgrade, Ringelmann, 9 December 1943.
116. Ibid.; Kühmel, "Deutschland und Albanien," p. 220.
117. CGR, roll T501/258, Final Wehrmacht Report on Albania, and roll T120/340, Nr. 1702, Sonderzug for Neubacher, 25 October 1943.
118. Kühmel, "Deutschland und Albanien," pp. 303-305.
119. Neubacher, *Sonderauftrag Südost,* p. 116.
120. OSS, Research and Analysis Branch, Nr. 2500.1, German Military Government over Europe, Albania, 1 December 1944; Neubacher, *Sonderauftrag Südost,* p. 116; Fischer, "German Political Policy in Albania," p. 227.
121. Stamm, "Zur deutschen Besetzung Albaniens," p. 111.
122. WO 204/9428, Reports and Memos, July 1944-February 1945; Samuel W.

Mitcham, Jr., *Hitler's Legions: The German Army Order of Battle, World War II* (New York: Dorset Press, 1985), pp. 461-462.

123. Kühmel, "Deutschland und Albanien," p. 452.
124. Ibid., p. 205.
125. CGR, roll T501/258, Final Wehrmacht Report on Albania.
126. Stavrianos, *The Balkans since 1453*, p. 786.
127. Although many Albanians from Kosova seem to have been transported to Germany for work, reliable figures are unavailable.
128. CGR, roll T501/258, Final Wehrmacht Report on Albania.
129. Ibid.; Kühmel, "Deutschland und Albanien," p. 504.
130. *Illyria*, 6-8 February 1995; and see WO 204/9428, Reports and Memos July 1944-February 1945, for material on Jewish refugees from Yugoslavia in Korça.
131. For more on the Jewish experience in Albania, see Katherine Morris, ed., *Escape through the Balkans: The Autobiography of Irene Grünbaum* (Lincoln: University of Nebraska Press, 1996); and Harvey Sarner, *Rescue in Albania* (Cathedral City, Calif.: Brunswick Press, 1997). The first of these two accounts leaves the reader with the impression that the war had a limited impact on the lives of many urban Albanians.
132. Kühmel, "Deutschland und Albanien," p. 504.
133. Ibid., pp. 421-422.
134. Ibid., p. 448.
135. Robert T. Brewer, "Albania: New Aspects, Old Documents," *East European Quarterly* 26, no. 1 (March 1992), p. 34; FO 371/43549 R39/39/G90, Steel to Southern Department, 24 December 1943.

Chapter Seven: Resistance to the Germans

1. Logoreci, *The Albanians*, pp. 76-77; Kühmel, "Deutschland und Albanien," pp. 155-156.
2. Stafford, *Britain and European Resistance, 1940-1945*, p. 171.
3. Neubacher, *Sonderauftrag Südost*, p. 108.
4. Kühmel, "Deutschland und Albanien," p. 124; CGR, roll T120/340, Tirana, Neubacher, 8 October 1943.
5. Fischer, "Abaz Kupi and British Intelligence in Albania," p. 131; Hibbert, *Albania's National Liberation Struggle*, p. 61.
6. Marmullaku, *Albania and the Albanians*, p. 52.
7. Kühmel, "Deutschland und Albanien," p. 125; Schmidt-Neke, "Geschichtliche Grundlagen," p. 55.
8. CGR, roll T120/340, Nr. 49, Tirana, Neubacher, 25 September 1943.
9. FO 371/43549 R63/39/G90, Cairo, Lord Killian, 1 January 1944. This central council order was confirmed at the first BK Congress in Berat in January 1944. See Neuwirth, "Widerstand und Kollaboration in Albanien," p. 161.
10. Fischer, "German Political Policy in Albania," pp. 228-229.
11. FO 371/43549 R1718/39/G90, 22 January 1944, and FO 371/43549 R7167/39/G90, 7 February 1944.

12. FO 371/43553 B8/1/277, SOE Report, 26 August 1944.
13. FO 371/43550 R7779/39/G90, Bawker to Howard, 9 May 1944.
14. Neuwirth, "Widerstand und Kollaboration in Albanien," pp. 169-170.
15. FO 371/43550 R4244/39/G90, 1 March 1944.
16. CGR, roll T120/340, Nr. 148, Tirana, Schliep, 9 November 1943; FO 371/43551 R12381/39/G90, 1 August 1944.
17. FO 371/43550 R7779/39/G90, Bawker to Howard, 9 May 1944; Kühmel, "Deutschland und Albanien," pp. 257-262.
18. FO 371/43550 R7779/39/G90, Bawker to Howard, 9 May 1944.
19. CGR, roll T120/340, Nr. 88, Tirana, Schliep to Neubacher, 16 October 1944; FO 371/43553 R14615/39/G90, 24 August 1944.
20. FO 371/48079 R4145/46/G90, McLean Report, 23 February 1945.
21. Hibbert, *Albania's National Liberation Struggle*, p. 100.
22. CGR, roll T120/340, Nr. 148, Tirana, Schliep to Neubacher, 9 November 1944; FO 371/48079 R4145/46/G90, McLean Report, 23 February 1945.
23. Hibbert, *Albania's National Liberation Struggle*, p. 63.
24. CGR, roll T120/340, Nr. 148, Tirana, Schliep to Neubacher, 9 November 1943; FO 371/48079, R4145/46/G90, McLean Report, 23 February 1945.
25. CGR, roll T120/340, Nr. 148, Tirana, Schliep to Neubacher, 9 November 1943.
26. CGR, roll T120/340, Nr. 165, Tirana, Schliep, 13 November 1943.
27. FO 371/43553, B8/1/264, SOE Report, 24 August 1944.
28. Kühmel, "Deutschland und Albanien," pp. 267-269.
29. Hibbert, *Albania's National Liberation Struggle*, p. 80.
30. Ibid., pp. 89-90.
31. FO 371/43550 R3684/39/G90, SOE Review, 19 February 1944.
32. Hibbert, *Albania's National Liberation Struggle*, p. 81.
33. *Völkischer Beobachter,* 18 April 1944.
34. Hibbert, *Albania's National Liberation Struggle*, p. 81.
35. Neuwirth, "Widerstand und Kollaboration in Albanien," pp. 106-107.
36. FO 371/43553 B/8/1/277, SOE Report, 26 August 1944; Hibbert, *Albania's National Liberation Struggle*, p. 116.
37. CGR, roll T120/340, Nr. 227, Belgrade, Neubacher, 1 February 1944.
38. FO 371/45550 R3684/39/G90, SOE Review, 19 February 1944, and FO 371/43549 R1718/39/G90, SOE Report, 22 January 1944.
39. Institute of Marxist-Leninist Studies, *History of the Party of Labor*, p. 191.
40. CGR, roll T120/340, Nr. 161, Tirana, Schliep, 16 March 1944; Kühmel, "Deutschland und Albanien," p. 271.
41. Ibid., p. 120.
42. FO 371/43549 R1289/39/G90, Steel to Southern Department, 14 January 1944, and FO 371/43550 R2806/39/G90, Rice, 18 February 1944.
43. FO 371/43550 R3684/39/G90, SOE Review, 23 February 1944, and FO 371/43550 R4244/39/G90, SOE Review, 1 March 1944.
44. Kühmel, "Deutschland und Albanien," pp. 276-278.
45. Hibbert, *Albania's National Liberation Struggle*, p. 120.
46. Kühmel, "Deutschland und Albanien," pp. 292-293.

47. CGR, roll T120/340, Nr. 230, Tirana, Schliep, 17 April 1944.
48. FO 371/37145 R12213/1067/90, Pearson to Howard, 20 November 1943, and FO 371/43549 R364/39/G90, Djakova Letter, 4 January 1944.
49. CGR, roll T120/340, Nr. 161, Tirana, Schliep, 16 March 1944, and CGR, roll T120/340, Nr. 230, Tirana, Schliep, 17 April 1944; FO 371/43557 R279/279/90, Holy See, Osborne, 1 January 1944.
50. FO 371/43557 R279/279/90, Rose Minute, 1 January 1944.
51. WO 204/9453, Brocklehurst's Report, April 1944, and Hibbert, *Albania's National Liberation Struggle*, p. 121.
52. Hibbert, *Albania's National Liberation Struggle*, p. 113.
53. FO 371/37145 R10812/1067/G90, Boxhall to Rose, 28 October 1943.
54. Stafford, *Britain and European Resistance, 1940-1945*, p. 170.
55. Barker, *British Policy in South-East Europe in the Second World War*, p. 178.
56. FO 371/37145 R12213/1067/G90, Pearson to Howard, 20 November 1943.
57. Ibid.
58. FO 371/37145 R12213/1067/G90, Pearson to Howard, 20 November 1943; Barker, *British Policy in South-East Europe in the Second World War*, p. 178. Neuwirth tells us that Zogists in contemporary Albania blame Davies for their fate (see Neuwirth, "Widerstand und Kollaboration in Albanien," p. 240), a position that is hardly supportable given that British policymakers did not listen to Davies.
59. Stafford, *Britain and European Resistance, 1940-1945*, p. 172; Barker, *British Policy in South-East Europe in the Second World War*, p. 179.
60. For more on the Concensus II mission, see Smiley, *Albanian Assignment*, chap. 8.
61. Kühmel, "Deutschland und Albanien," pp. 356-357.
62. Institute of Marxist-Leninist Studies, *History of the Party of Labor*, pp. 151-163.
63. FO 371/43550 R7779/39/G90, Bawker to Howard, 9 May 1944; Kühmel, "Deutschland und Albanien," pp. 452-453.
64. Kasneci, *Steeled in the Heat of Battle*, p. 29.
65. OSS, 154, box 14, Fultz to Philip Adams, 24 February 1944; FO 371/43550 R7779/39/G90, Bawker to Howard, 9 May 1944.
66. FO 371/43551 R8574/39/G90, Boxhall to Rose, 24 May 1944.
67. Hibbert, *Albania's National Liberation Struggle*, p. 146.
68. Ibid., pp. 119-122.
69. CGR, roll T120/340, Nr. 230, Tirana, Schliep, 17 April 1944.
70. FO 371/43550 R4283/39/G90, SOE Report, 8 March 1944.
71. FO 371/43561 R9003/1474/90, McLean on Propaganda, 7 June 1944.
72. CGR, roll T120/340, Nr. 1619, Athens, Neubacher, 28 May 1944, and CGR, roll T501/258, Final Wehrmacht Report on Albania.
73. Hibbert, *Albania's National Liberation Struggle*, 152, maintains fifteen thousand Germans, but Kühmel, "Deutschland und Albanien," p. 387, maintains that there were fewer. Albanian socialist historians, as usual, produce the least credible figures, maintaining that in excess of fifty thousand Germans took part. Institute of Marxist-Leninist Studies, *History of the Party of Labor*, p. 213.
74. Kühmel, "Deutschland und Albanien," p. 386.
75. Neuwirth, "Widerstand und Kollaboration in Albanien," p. 162.

76. WO 204/9453, Brocklehurst Report, April 1944, WO 204/9558, H. Hodgkinson report, July 1944, and WO 204/9446, Intelligence Reports, 1944-1945.
77. WO 204/9428, Reports and Memos, July 1944-February 1945.
78. Kühmel, "Deutschland und Albanien," p. 373.
79. Neubacher, *Sonderauftrag Südost*, p. 117.
80. Kühmel, "Deutschland und Albanien," pp. 346-347.
81. Ibid., p. 392.
82. Ibid., pp. 375-376.
83. FO 371/43551 R8718/39/G90, Bari, Broad, 11 May 1944, and FO 371/43551 R9175/39/G90, Rice, 9 June 1944.
84. Hibbert, *Albania's National Liberation Struggle*, p. 159.
85. FO 371/43551 R10289/39/G90, Bari, 28 June 1944, and FO 371/48079 R4145/46/G90, McLean Report, 23 February 1945.
86. FO 371/43551 R10061/39/G90, SOE Report, 22 June 1944.
87. Hibbert, *Albania's National Liberation Struggle*, p. 160.
88. Amery, *Approach March*, p. 403.
89. Smiley, *Albanian Assignment*, pp. 27, 152.
90. FO 371/43551 R12381/39/G90, Deakin, 1 August 1944.
91. Schmidt-Neke, *Entstehung und Ausbau der Königsdiktatur in Albanien*, p. 333; WO 204/9446, Intelligence Report, 1944-1945.
92. Kühmel, "Deutschland und Albanien," p. 380.
93. Ibid.
94. Neubacher, *Sonderauftrag Südost*, p. 118.
95. Kühmel, "Deutschland und Albanien," p. 391.
96. Ibid., pp. 391-392; FO 371/43551 R12650/39/G90, Bari, Broad, 8 August 1944.
97. Kühmel, "Deutschland und Albanien," p. 388.
98. Hibbert, *Albania's National Liberation Struggle*, p. 180.
99. Kühmel, "Deutschland und Albanien," pp. 389-390.
100. Hibbert, *Albania's National Liberation Struggle*, p. 189.
101. CGR, roll T120/340, Nr. 1163, Ankara, Fusch, 1 June 1944.
102. CGR, roll T501/258, Final Wehrmacht Report on Albania.
103. Kühmel, "Deutschland und Albanien," p. 403.
104. CGR, roll T501/258, Final Wehrmacht Report on Albania.
105. Kühmel, "Deutschland und Albanien," p. 404.

Chapter Eight: German Retreat and the Construction of a Stalinist Albania

1. Kühmel, "Deutschland und Albanien," p. 410.
2. CGR, roll T501/258, Final Wehrmacht Report on Albania; Kühmel, "Deutschland und Albanien," p. 411.
3. Julian Amery, *Sons of the Eagle: A Study in Guerrilla War* (London: Macmillan, 1948), p. 270.

Notes to pages 224-31

4. Kühmel, "Deutschland und Albanien," p. 411.
5. CGR, roll T501/258, Final Wehrmacht Report on Albania.
6. Ibid.
7. Amery, *Approach March*, p. 382.
8. FO 371/43553 73862, B8/1/264, SOE Report, 24 August, 1944.
9. CGR, roll T120/762, Nr. S155, Tirana, 8 September 1944; Neubacher, *Sonderauftrag Südost*, p. 118; Hibbert, *Albania's National Liberation Struggle*, p. 154; Kühmel, "Deutschland und Albanien," p. 432.
10. Kühmel, "Deutschland und Albanien," p. 414.
11. Hibbert, *Albania's National Liberation Struggle*, p. 211.
12. CGR, roll T501/258, Final Wehrmacht Report on Albania.
13. Ibid.
14. Kühmel, "Deutschland und Albanien," p. 421.
15. Ibid, pp. 422-423.
16. For text, see FO 371/43553 R14317/39/G90, Bari, 30 August 1944.
17. Neuwirth, "Widerstand und Kollaboration in Albanien," p. 194.
18. FO 371/43553 R14412/39/G90, Bari, 14 September 1944.
19. FO 371/48079 R4145/46/G90, McLean Report, 23 February 1945.
20. FO 371/43553 R14412/39/G90, Bari, 14 September 1944; FO 371/43553 R15054/39/G90, Bari, 15 September 1944; Amery, *Approach March*, p. 385.
21. FO 371/43553 R/15054/39/G90, Bari, 15 September 1944.
22. Hibbert, *Albania's National Liberation Struggle*, p. 203.
23. FO 371/48079 R4145/46/G90, McLean Report, 23 February 1945.
24. Smiley, *Albanian Assignment*, pp. 135-136; Hibbert, *Albania's National Liberation Struggle*, pp. 199-200.
25. Hibbert, *Albania's National Liberation Struggle*, p. 206.
26. FO 371/43555 R16104/71/90, FO Minute, Eden to PM, 26 September 1944. The NLM was renamed the FNC in May 1944 in conjunction with the Congress of Përmet, which created a national assembly and a government.
27. FO 371/43553 R15131/39/G90, Bari, 21 September 1944.
28. FO 371/48091 R269/269/90, Bari, Deakin, 14 December 1944, and FO 371/48091 R2678/269/90, FO Minute, 7 February 1945.
29. FO 371/48079 R4145/46/G90, McLean Report, 23 February 1945.
30. FO 371/43566 R16503/9513/90, Bari, 10 October 1944.
31. Amery, *Approach March*, p. 400.
32. Ibid., p. 403.
33. Barker, *British Policy in South-East Europe in the Second World War*, p. 181; FO 371/43566 R17390/9513/90, to Bari, 28 October 1944.
34. Hibbert, *Albania's National Liberation Struggle*, p. 201.
35. Ibid.; Kühmel, "Deutschland und Albanien," p. 426; Amery, *Sons of the Eagle*, p. 266.
36. Kühmel, "Deutschland und Albanien," pp. 429-430.
37. Ibid., p. 427; FO 371/43564 R16955/2179/90, Bari, 13 October 1944.
38. CGR, roll T120/762, Nr. s.144, Tirana, 5 September 1944, and CGR, roll T120/762, Nr. 2151, Belgrade, Neubacher, 22 October 1944, and CGR, roll T120/762, Nr. 2151, Tirana, Schliep to Neubacher, 26 October 1944.

39. CGR, roll T120/762, Tirana, Schliep to Neubacher, 26 October 1944.
40. FO 371/43554 R16502/39/G90, Bari, 18 October 1944, and FO 371/43553 R14938/39/G90, Bari, 18 September 1944.
41. Hibbert, *Albania's National Liberation Struggle*, p. 215; and see WO 204/9486, "top secret plan for landing in Albania," 1 October 1944.
42. Kasneci, *Steeled in the Heat of Battle*, p. 85; Hibbert, *Albania's National Liberation Struggle*, p. 215; Enver Hoxha, *The Anglo-American Threat to Albania*, p. 346.
43. WO 204/9428, Reports and Memos, July 1944-February 1945.
44. CGR, roll T501/258, Final Wehrmacht Report on Albania.
45. Ibid.; Kühmel, "Deutschland und Albanien," p. 430.
46. Amery, *Approach March*, p. 373.
47. CGR, roll T120/762, Tirana, Schliep, 31 August 1944.
48. CGR, roll T501/258, Final Wehrmacht Report on Albania.
49. CGR, roll T120/762, Nr. 213, Tirana, Schliep, 10 October 1944, and CGR, roll T120/762, Nr. 233, Tirana, Gstöttenbauer, 16 October 1944; Kühmel, "Deutschland und Albanien," p. 433.
50. FO 371/43554 73862, HQ Force 399, 10 November 1944.
51. FO 371/4356 R16733/1471/90, PWE, 18 October 1944.
52. CGR, roll T501/258, Final Wehrmacht Report on Albania.
53. FO 371/43561 PWE/44/24/5, PWE to BBC, 24 November 1944.
54. Hibbert, *Albania's National Liberation Struggle*, p. 216. Some Albanian sources claim the number to be seventy thousand, but these figures probably include reservists.
55. Brewer, "Albania: New Aspects, Old Documents," p. 46.
56. Hibbert, *Albania's National Liberation Struggle*, p. 215.
57. Pollo and Puto, *The History of Albania*, p. 241.
58. CGR, roll T501/258, Final Wehrmacht Report on Albania.
59. Instituti I Studimeve Marksiste-Leniniste Pranë KQ të PPSH, *Historia e Luftës Antifashiste Nacionalçlirimtare të popullit shqiptar*, vol. 4, p. 799; Enver Hoxha, *Laying the Foundations of the New Albania* (Tirana: 8 Nëntori, 1984), p. 512; Kasneci, *Steeled in the Heat of Battle*, p. 89; CGR, roll T501/258, Final Wehrmacht Report on Albania.
60. Hoxha, *Laying the Foundations of the New Albania*, pp. 503-515.
61. FO 371/43554 R19192/39/G90, Bari, 22 November 1944.
62. Instituti I Studimeve Marksiste-Leniniste Pranë KQ të PPSH, *Historia e Luftë Antifashiste Nacionalçlirimtare të popullit shqiptar*, vol. 4, p. 807.
63. CGR, roll T501/258, Final Wehrmacht Report on Albania; FO 371/48078 R1781/46/90, Black Report, 11 January 1945.
64. CGR, roll T501/258, Final Wehrmacht Report on Albania; Kühmel, "Deutschland und Albanien," pp. 434-435.
65. Kühmel, "Deutschland und Albanien," p.438.
66. Neubacher, *Sonderauftrag Südost*, p. 120.
67. CGR, roll T120/340, Neubacher to Tirana, 25 April 1944, and CGR, roll 501/258, Final Wehrmacht Report on Albania.
68. CGR, roll T120/340, Neubacher to Tirana, 25 April 1944, and CGR, roll T120/340, Salzburg, Neubacher to RAM, 2 May 1944.

69. Dragnich and Todorovich, *The Saga of Kosovo*, pp. 140-141.
70. WO 204/9428, Reports and Memos, July 1944-February 1945; S. Repishti, "The Bujan Resolution," *Illyria*, 14-16 February 1994.
71. WO 204/9428, Reports and Memos, July 1944-February 1945.
72. Ibid.
73. CGR, roll T120/762, Nr. 213, Tirana, Schliep, 10 October 1944; Kühmel, "Deutschland und Albanien," pp. 436-437.
74. Hibbert, *Albania's National Liberation Struggle*, p. 211.
75. Institute of Marxist-Leninist Studies, *History of the Party of Labor*, p. 225; Pollo and Puto, *The History of Albania*, p. 243; Hoxha, *Laying the Foundations of the New Albania*, p. 515.
76. Hibbert, *Albania's National Liberation Struggle*, pp. 212-213.
77. Lyman H. Legters, *Eastern Europe: Transformation and Revolution, 1945-1991* (Toronto: D. C. Heath, 1992), p. 529.
78. Vickers, *The Albanians*, p. 161.
79. Robyns, *Geraldine of the Albanians*, p. 134.
80. FO 371/43559 R1219/616/90, FO Minute, 21 January 1944.
81. WO 204/9440, War Establishment, September 1944.
82. WO 204/9428, Reports and Memos, July 1944-February 1945.
83. FO 371/37136 R1161/52/90, Chancery, Washington to Southern, 27 January 1943.
84. Fischer, *King Zog and the Struggle for Stability in Albania*, pp. 138-140, 235, 241, 300.
85. FO 371/37136 R93/52/90, Censorship, 18 December 1942.
86. FO 371/37136 R2783/52/90, Censorship, 18 March 1943.
87. Fischer, *King Zog and the Struggle for Stability in Albania*, p. 298.
88. FO 371/37136 R3231/52/90, FO Minute, Laskey, Zog Telegram to Peter Kolonja, 8 April 1939.
89. FO 371/37136 R2817/52/90, Censorship, 15 March 1943.
90. FO 371/37137 R5945/52/90, Censorship, Noli to Martini, 1 July 1943.
91. FO 371/29709 R5733/390/90, Washington, 24 August 1942, FO 371/22110 R4497/867/90, Washington, 8 July 1942, and FO 371/33109 R4470/390/90, FO Minute, 3 July 1942.
92. WO 204/9440, War Establishment, September 1943.
93. FO 371/37136 R93/52/90, Censorship, 18 December 1942.
94. FO 371/29709 R4190/390/90, FO Minute, 25 June 1942.
95. FO 371/33110 R4493/867/90, Ryan Conversation with Zog, 6 July 1942.
96. FO 371/37138 R2127/61/90, FO Minute, 9 March 1943.
97. FO 371/43559 R5595/616/90, FO Minute, 8 February 1944, FO 371/43559 R7439/616/90, FO Minute, 8 May 1944, and FO 371/43559 R21222/616/90, Ryan Conversation with Zog, 12 December 1944.
98. Peters, "Ingredients of the Communist Takeover in Albania," p. 292.
99. Hibbert, *Albania's National Liberation Struggle*, p. 211.
100. Institute of Marxist-Leninist Studies, *History of the Party of Labor*, p. 211.
101. Peters, "Ingredients of the Communist Takeover in Albania," p. 276.
102. Pano, *The People's Republic of Albania*, pp. 50-51.

103. Ibid., pp. 277-278.
104. Omari, *The People's Revolution in Albania and the Question of State Power*, p. 63.
105. Pano, *The People's Republic of Albania*, pp. 55-56.
106. Omari, *The People's Revolution in Albania and the Question of State Power*, p. 74.
107. Ibid., pp. 76-77.
108. Hoxha, *Laying the Foundations of the New Albania*, p. 481.
109. Hibbert, *Albania's National Liberation Struggle*, p. 147.
110. Marmullaku, *Albania and the Albanians*, p. 56.
111. Hoxha, *Laying the Foundations of the New Albania*, p. 476.
112. Peters, "Ingredients of the Communist Takeover in Albania," p. 288.
113. Ibid., p. 485.
114. FO 371/43571 R17111/13194/90, Bari, 21 October 1944.
115. FO 371/43554 R20087/39/G90, Halifax, 4 December 1944.
116. Marmullaku, *Albania and the Albanians*, p. 56.
117. Hibbert, *Albania's National Liberation Struggle*, p. 220.
118. Ibid.
119. Ibid.
120. Hoxha, *Laying the Foundation of the New Albania*, p. 5.
121. FO 371/48079 R3670/46/90, Caserta, 13 February 1945; Logoreci, *The Albanians*, p. 81.
122. FO 371/48079 R3670/46/90, Caserta, 13 February 1945.
123. Hoxha, *Laying the Foundations of the New Albania*, p. 53.
124. Marmullaku, *Albania and the Albanians*, p. 70.
125. FO 371/48079 R3174/46/90, Caserta, 5 February 1945.
126. FO 371/4356 R1471/1471/90, Political Warfare Executive, 24 November 1944.
127. FO 371/48079 R1970/46/90, Bari, 13 February 1945, and FO 371/48079 R3174/46/90, Caserta, 5 February 1945.
128. Logoreci, *The Albanians*, p. 86.
129. Pano, *The People's Republic of Albania*, p. 13.
130. Stavrianos, *The Balkans since 1453*, p. 729. Immediately following the war, Hoxha complicated the food situation by significantly delaying and then accepting only limited quantities of United Nations Relief and Rehabilitation Administration (UNRRA) food. He was motivated by his growing hostility to the West.
131. FO 371/48081 R9255/46/90, Tirana, 29 May 1945.
132. FO 371/48078 R320/46/90, Bari, 22 December 1944.
133. FO 371/43561 R1471/1471/90, London, 24 November 1944; Peter Prifti, *Socialist Albania since 1944* (Cambridge Mass.: MIT Press, 1978), p. 53.
134. Logoreci, *The Albanians*, p. 85; Pano, *The People's Republic of Albania*, p. 61.
135. FO 371/48078 R321/46/90, Bari, 22 December 1944, and FO 371/48078 R463/46/90, London, 8 January 1945.
136. Marmullaku, *Albania and the Albanians*, p. 76; Logoreci, *The Albanians*, p. 154.
137. FO 371/48078 R1919/46/90, Bari, 12 January 1945.
138. Prifti, "The Labor Party of Albania," p. 8.
139. Schmidt-Neke, *Entstehung und Ausbau der Königsdiktatur in Albanien*, p. 302.
140. As an example, see Ismail Kadare, *Doruntine* (New York: New Amsterdam

Books, 1988), *Chronicle in Stone* (New York: New Amsterdam Books, 1987) and others. The major theme of these books relate to with the dangers of foreign entanglements.

Conclusion

1. See chapter 1.
2. Kaser, "Economic System," p. 299.
3. Mack Smith, *Mussolini's Roman Empire*, p. 156.
4. CGR, roll T120/340, Nr. 1250, Wolfschantze, Ribbentrop, 21 August 1943.
5. The gold was transferred to London at the end of the war and kept by the British, who refused to return it unless Hoxha's government paid the fines imposed by the World Court for its role in the sinking of British vessels in the Corfu Channel. The gold was finally returned to Albania in 1996. See *Illyria*, 24 February 1996.
6. Kühmel, "Deutschland und Albanien," p. 458.
7. Ibid.
8. Ibid., pp. 472-473.
9. FO 371/48078 R1781/46/90, Deakin to Howard on Views of Captain Black, 4 January 1945.
10. OSS, Research and Analysis Branch, No. 1475, Survey of Albania, 20 December 1943.
11. Kühmel, "Deutschland und Albanien," p. 456.
12. CGR, roll T501/258, Final Wehrmacht Report on Albania.
13. Pano, "Albania: The Last Bastion of Stalinism," p. 192.
14. Ibid.
15. Soviet historians maintain that the Albanians would not have been able to defeat Italian and German troops in Albania. Albanian socialist historians accuse Soviet historians of slander. As an example, see Omari, *The People's Revolution in Albania and the Question of State Power*, p. 102.
16. A good deal of controversy surrounds this question. For the Yugoslav position, see Vladimir Dedijer, "Albania, Soviet Pawn," *Foreign Affairs* 30 (1951), pp. 103-111.
17. Pano, "Albania: The Last Bastion of Stalinism," pp. 194-195.
18. Hoxha, *Laying the Foundations of the New Albania*, p. 497.
19. Hibbert, *Albania's National Liberation Struggle*, p. 193 and appendix 4.
20. Hibbert, in ibid., pp. 236-238, suggests that most of those who wrote memoirs—including Smiley, Amery, and Bethal—spent the war in the north among the nationalists and saw only the nationalist perspective. Smiley argues that their efforts were sabotaged by communists in SOE.
21. Hibbert, *Albania's National Liberation Struggle*, pp. 193, 238.
22. Kühmel, "Deutschland und Albanien," p. 473.
23. FO 371/48082 R13586/46/90, Caserta, Broad, 3 August 1945.
24. Logoreci, *The Albanians*, p. 83; Kasneci, *Steeled in the Heat of Battle*, p. 91.
25. Singleton maintains that Yugoslavia lost 1.75 million, and Stavrianos maintains that Greece lost 500,000. See Fred Singleton, *Twentieth-Century Yugoslavia* (New

York: Columbia University Press, 1976), p. 86; and Stavrianos, *The Balkans since 1453*, p. 787.

26. Baldwin, *The Crucial Years*, p. 270.
27. Barker, *British Policy in Southeast Europe in the Second World War*, p. 183.
28. *Illyria*, 25-27 May 1995.
29. Kaser, "Economic System," p. 298.
30. E. E. Jacques, *The Albanians: An Ethnic History from Prehistoric Times to the Present* (Jefferson, N.C.: McFarlan, 1995), pp. 426-427.
31. Pollo and Puto, *The History of Albania*, p. 247.
32. OSS, file 120, GB2129, 20 October 1944; Brewer, "Albania: New Aspects, Old Documents," pp. 32-33.
33. Brewer, "Albania: New Aspects, Old Documents," p. 33.
34. FO 371/48078 R1781/46/90, Deakin to Howard on Views of Captain Black, 4 January 1945.
35. FO 371/48081 R8567/46/90, Caserta, Broad, 6 May 1945.
36. WO 204/9471, Termination of Military Liaison in Albania, 5 July 1945; FO 371/48096 R1147/1101/90, Caserta, MacMillian, 15 January 1945.
37. Vickers, *The Albanians*, pp. 166-167.
38. Shyqri Ballvora, "Die Kriegsschaden Albaniens, 1939-1944," *Wissenschaftlicher Dienst Südosteuropa* 20, no. 1/2 (1981), p. 35.
39. FO 371/58473 R757/24/90, Caserta, British Military Mission report, 6-8 January 1946.
40. FO 371/23714 R3824/1335/90, Durrës, Ryan, Mitchell Letter of 26 April 1939, 3 May 1939.
41. Adi Schnytzer, *Stalinist Economic Strategy in Practice: The Case of Albania* (Oxford: Oxford University Press, 1982), p. 17.
42. Jacques, *The Albanians*, p. 426.
43. Pano, "Albania," p. 35.
44. Institute of Marxist-Leninist Studies, *History of the Party of Labor*, p. 221; OSS file 120, GB2129, 20 October 1944.
45. See Fischer, *King Zog and the Struggle for Stability in Albania*, p. 103.
46. Sjöberg, *Rural Change and Development in Albania*, pp. 34-35.
47. Schmidt-Neke, *Entstehung und Ausbau der Königsdiktatur in Albanien*, p. 302.
48. Arshi Pipa, *Albanian Stalinism: Ideo-political Aspects* (Boulder, Colo.: East European Monographs and Columbia University Press, 1990), p. 3.
49. Legters, *Eastern Europe: Transformation and Revolution, 1945-1991*, p. 526.

Note on Sources

1. Costa, *Albania: A European Enigma*, p. 121.
2. Halliday, *The Artful Albanian*, p. 4.
3. Hibbert, *Albania's National Liberation Struggle*, p. 185.
4. Ibid., pp. 236-238.
5. Kühmel, "Deutschland und Albanien," pp. 9-10.

6. Schmidt-Neke, *Entstehung und Ausbau der Königsdiktatur in Albanien*, p. 302.
7. Puto, *From the Annals of British Diplomacy*, p. 190.
8. Quoted in Barker, *British Policy in South-East Europe in the Second World War*, p. 157.
9. Mehmet Shehu was the most gifted Albanian partisan commander during World War II, eventually becoming commander of the first division. As part of Hoxha's small trusted inner circle, Shehu eventually rose to become prime minister and hoped to succeed Hoxha. But Hoxha harbored doubts about Shehu's capability to lead the nation and had him purged in 1981, resulting in the death of Shehu and many in his family.
10. Geraldine's account includes, for example, the assertion (page 121) that while in exile in Great Britain, Zog had several meetings with Winston Churchill. I can find no reference to such meetings. On page 122 Geraldine argues that the Greek strongman General Metaxas asked that Zog be flown to Greece to take part in the war. Metaxas, who hoped to annex parts of southern Albania, would never have done such a thing. Even more remarkable is the assertion, on page 121, that Greek soldiers fighting the Italians in Albania were given pictures of King Zog.
11. Conversations with Queen Geraldine, July 1981, Costa del Sol, Spain.

BIBLIOGRAPHY

Archival Sources

Germany. Akten aus dem Archiv des Auswärtigen Amtes (AA). Bonn.
———. Captured German Records (CGR), files of the Foreign Ministry and the Wehrmacht high command. National Archives, Washington, D.C.
Great Britain. Cabinet Papers (CAB). Public Record Office, London.
———. Foreign Office Archives (FO). Public Record Office, London.
———. Nash Papers. School of Slavonic and East European Studies, University of London.
———. War Office Archives (WO). Public Record Office, London.
Italy. Captured Italian Records (CIR), files of the Comando Supremo. National Archives, Washington, D.C.
United States. Department of State (USDS), Records of the Department of State. National Archives, Washington, D.C.
———. Department of State, Records of the Office of Strategic Services (OSS). National Archives, Washington, D.C.

Interview

Conversations with Her Majesty Queen Geraldine of the Albanians, 22 July–27 July 1981, Casa Ponderosa, Costa del Sol, Spain

Published Documents

Ciano, Galaezzo. *Ciano's Diplomatic Papers: Being a Record of Nearly 2000 Conversations Held during the Years 1936-1942.* Edited by Malcolm Muggeridge. Translated by Stuart Hood. London: Odhams Press, 1948.

Germany. *Documents on German Foreign Policy, 1918-1945, from the Archives of the German Foreign Ministry.* Washington: Government Printing Office, 1949.

Great Britain. *Documents on British Foreign Policy, 1919-1939.* London: H. M. Stationery Office, 1946.

Greece. American Council on Public Affairs. *The Greek White Book: Diplomatic Documents Relating to Italy's Aggression against Greece.* Washington: Agence D'Athenes, 1943.

Italy. Ministero delgi Affair Esteri. Commissione per la pubblicazióne dei documenti diplomatici. *I documenti diplomatici italiani* (DDI). Rome: La libreria dello stato, 1952 ff.

League of Nations. *League of Nations Treaty Series: Publication of Treaties and International Engagements Registered with the Secretariat of the League.* 205 vols. Lausanne: Imprimerie Réunies, 1920-1946.

United States. *Foreign Relations of the United States, Diplomatic Papers, 1939.* Washington: Government Printing Office, 1956.

War of National Liberation. *La lutte anti-fasciste de libération nationale du peuple albanais, 1941-1944: Documents principaux.* Tirana: 8 Nëntori, 1975.

Secondary Sources

Academy of Sciences. Institute of Marxist-Leninist Studies, Tirana University. *The National Conference of Studies on the Anti-fascist National Liberation War of the Albanian People.* Tirana: 8 Nëntori, 1975

Amery, Julian. *Approach March: A Venture in Autobiography.* London: Hutchinson, 1973.

———. *Sons of the Eagle: A Study in Guerrilla War.* London: Macmillan, 1948.

Andrew, Christopher. *Secret Service: The Making of the British Intelligence Community.* London: William Heinimann, 1985.

Archer, Laird. *Athens Journal, 1940-1941.* Manhattan, Kans.: MA/AH Publishing, 1983.

Badoglio, Pietro. *Italy in the Second World War.* London: Oxford University Press, 1948.

Baldwin, Hanson W. *The Crucial Years, 1939-1941.* New York: Harper and Row, 1976.

Ballvora, Shyqri. *Das nationalsozialistische Besatzungsregime in Albanien.* Munich: DAFG, 1979.

———. "Die Kriegsschaden Albaniens, 1939-1944." *Wissenschaftlicher Dienst Südosteuropa* 20, no. 1/2 (1981).

Barker, Elizabeth. *British Policy in South-East Europe in the Second World War.* London: Macmillan, 1976.

Barros, James. *The Corfu Incident of 1923.* Princeton, N.J.: Princeton University Press, 1965.

Bitzes, John. *Greece in World War II to 1941.* Omaha: University of Nebraska Press, 1981.
Bland, William B. *Albania.* Oxford and Santa Barbara: CLIO Press, 1988.
Brewer, Robert T. "Albania: New Aspects, Old Documents." *East-European Quarterly* 26, no. 1 (March 1992).
Burdick, Charles. "Operation Cyclamen: Germany and Albania, 1940-1941." *Journal of Central European Affairs* 19 (1959/1960).
Cervi, Mario. *The Hollow Legions: Mussolini's Blunder in Greece, 1940-1941.* Garden City, N.Y.: Doubleday, 1971.
Ciano, Count Galeazzo. *The Ciano Diaries, 1939-1943.* New York: Doubleday, 1945.
———. *Ciano's Hidden Diary, 1937-1938.* New York: Dutton, 1953.
Clark, Martin. *Modern Italy, 1871-1982.* London: Longman, 1984.
Clogg, Richard. "The Special Operations Executive in Greece." In John O. Iatrides, ed., *Greece in the 1940s: A Nation in Crisis.* Hanover, N.H.: University Press of New England, 1981.
Costa, Nicholas J. *Albania: A European Enigma.* Boulder, Colo.: East European Monographs and Columbia University Press, 1995.
———. "Invasion—Action and Reaction: Albania, a Case Study." *East European Quarterly* 1, no. 1 (spring 1976).
Dako, Christo. *Albania.* Boston: E. L. Grimes, 1919.
Davies, Edmund F. *Illyrian Venture: The Story of the British Military Mission in Enemy-Occupied Albania.* London: Bodley Head, 1952.
Dedijer, Vladimir. "Albania, Soviet Pawn." *Foreign Affairs* 30 (1951).
Dillion, E. L. P. "Albania." *Contemporary Review,* July 1914.
Djilas, Milovan. *Rise and Fall.* New York: Harcourt Brace Jovanovich, 1985.
Dragnich, Alex, and Todorovich, Slavko. *The Saga of Kosovo: Focus on Serbian-Albanian Relations.* Boulder, Colo.: East European Monographs, 1984.
Fischer, Bernd J. "Abaz Kupi and British Intelligence, 1943-4." In John Morison, ed., *Eastern Europe and the West.* London: Macmillan, 1992.
———. "Albania and the Italian Invasion of Greece, October 1940." In *Greece and the War in the Balkans, 1940-1941.* Thessaloníki: Institute for Balkan Studies, 1992.
———. "Fan Noli and the Albanian Revolutions of 1924." *East European Quarterly* 22, no. 2 (June 1988).
———. "German Political Policy in Albania, 1943-1944." In Richard Spence and Linda Nelson, eds., *Scholar, Patriot, Mentor: Historical Essays in Honor of Dimitrije Djordjevic.* Boulder, Colo.: East European Monographs, 1992.
———. "Italian Policy in Albania, 1893-1943." *Balkan Studies* 26, no. 1 (1985).
———. *King Zog and the Struggle for Stability in Albania.* Boulder, Colo.: East European Monographs and Columbia University Press, 1984.
———. "Kollaborationsregimes in Albanien 1939-1944." In Werner Röhr, ed., *Europa unterm Hakenkreuz: Okkupation und Kollaboration 1938-1945.* Berlin: Hüthig Verlagsgemeinschaft, 1994.
———. "Resistance in Albania during the Second World War: Partisans, Nationalists and the S.O.E." *East European Quarterly* 25, no. 1 (March 1991).
Fleischer, Hagen. "Kollaboration und deutsche Politik im besetzten Griechenland." In Werner Röhr, ed., *Europa unterm Hakenkreuz: Okkupation und Kollaboration (1938-1945).* Berlin: Hüthig Verlagsgemeinshaft, 1994.

Frank, Hermann. *Landser, Karst und Skiptaren, Bandenkämpfe in Albanien.* Heidelberg: K. Vowinckel, 1957.
Funderburk, David B. "Anglo-Albanian Relations, 1920-1939." *Revue Etudes Sud-Est Européennes* 13, no. 1 (1975).
Fusco, Gian Carlo. *Guerra d'Albania.* Rome: Feltrinelli, 1961.
Gilbert, Martin. *The Second World War: A Complete History.* New York: Holt, 1989.
Gross, H. "Albanien zwischen den Mächten: Ein Beitrag zur Erschliessung unentwickelter Gebiete." *Wirtschaftsdienst* 6 (1949).
Grothusen, Klaus-Detlev, ed. *Südosteuropa-Handbuch: Albanien.* Göttingen: Vandenhoeck und Ruprecht, 1993.
Hall, Derek. *Albania and the Albanians.* London: Pinter, 1994.
Halliday, Jon. *The Artful Albanian: The Memoirs of Enver Hoxha.* London: Chatto Press, 1986.
Hetzen, Armin, and Viorel Roman. *Albanien: Ein bibliographischer Forschungsbericht mit Titelübersetzungen und Standortnachweisen.* Munich: K. G. Saur, 1983.
Hibbert, Reginald. *Albania's National Liberation Struggle: The Bitter Victory.* London: Pinter, 1991.
Hinsley, F. H., E. E. Thomas, C. F. G. Ransom, and R. C. Knight. *British Intelligence in the Second World War.* Vol. 1. London: H. M. Stationery Office, 1979.
Hitler e Mussolini: lettre e documenti. Milan: Rizzoli, 1946.
Hoptner, Jacob. *Yugoslavia in Crisis, 1934-1941.* New York: Columbia University Press, 1962.
Hoxha, Enver. *The Anglo-American Threat to Albania.* Tirana: 8 Nëntori, 1982.
———. *Laying the Foundations of the New Albania.* Tirana: 8 Nëntori, 1984.
———. *Vepra* (Works). Tirana: Naim Frashëri/8 Nentori, 1968-1985.
Hoyt, Edwin P. *Mussolini's Empire.* New York: John Wiley, 1994.
Hutchings, Raymond, "Albania's Inter-war History as a Forerunner to the Communist Period." In Tom Winnifrith, ed., *Perspectives on Albania.* New York: St. Martin's Press, 1992.
Institute of Marxist-Leninist Studies at the Central Committee of the Party of Labor of Albania. *History of the Party of Labor of Albania.* Tirana: Naim Frashëri, 1971.
Instituti I Studimeve Marksiste-Leniniste Pranë KQ të PPSH. *Historia e Luftës Antifashiste Nacionalçlirimtare të popullit shqiptar* (History of the antifascist war of national liberation of the Albanian people). Vols. 1-4. Tirana: 8 Nëntori, 1986-1989.
Jacomoni, Francesco. *La politica dell'Italia in Albanìa.* Roca San Casciano: Cappelli Editore, 1965.
Jacques, E. E. *The Albanians: An Ethnic History from Prehistoric Times to the Present.* Jefferson, N.C.: McFarlan, 1995.
Jelavich, Barbara. *History of the Balkans, Twentieth Century.* Cambridge: Cambridge University Press, 1983.
Kadare, Ismail. *Chronicle in Stone.* New York: New Amsterdam Books, 1987.
———. *Doruntine.* New York: New Amsterdam Books, 1988.
Kaser, Michael. "Economic System." In Klaus-Detlev Grothusen, ed., *Südosteuropa-Handbuch: Albanien.* Göttingen: Vanderhoeck und Ruprecht, 1993.
Kasneci, Lefter. *Steeled in the Heat of Battle: A Brief Survey of the National Liberation War of the Albanian People, 1941-1945.* Tirana: Naim Frashëri, 1966.

Kemp, Peter. *No Colours, No Crest.* London: Cassell, 1958.
Kempner, Robert M. W. "The New Constitution of Albania: A Model Constitution for European Vassal States." *Tulane Law Review* 15 (1941).
Knox, MacGregor. "Fascist Italy Assesses Its Enemies, 1935-1940." In Ernest May, ed., *Knowing One's Enemies: Intelligence Assessment between the Two World Wars.* Princeton, N.J.: Princeton University Press, 1984.
―――. *Mussolini Unleashed, 1939-1941: Politics and Strategy in Fascist Italy's Last War.* Cambridge: Cambridge University Press, 1982.
Kondis, Basil. "A British Attempt to Organize a Revolt in Northern Albania during the Greek-Italian War." In *Greece and the War in the Balkans, 1940-1941.* Thessaloníki: Institute for Balkan Studies, 1992.
Kostelancik, David J. "Minorities and Minority Language Education in Inter-war Albania." *East European Quarterly* 30, no. 1 (spring 1996).
Kühmel, Bernhard. "Deutschland und Albanien, 1943-1944: Die Auswirkungen der Besetzung und die innenpolitische Entwicklung des Landes." Ph.D. diss., University of Bochum, 1981.
Lavine, Marcia Fishel. "Count Ciano: Foreign Affairs and Policy Determination in Fascist Italy, January 1939-June 1940." Ph.D. diss., Vanderbilt University, 1977.
Legters, Lyman H. *Eastern Europe: Transformation and Revolution, 1945-1991.* Toronto: D. C. Heath, 1992.
Lemkin, Raphael. *Axis Rule in Occupied Europe.* Washington, D.C.: Carnegie Endowment for International Peace, 1944.
Leverkühn, Paul. *German Military Intelligence.* London: Weidenfeld and Nicholson, 1954.
Logoreci, Anton. *The Albanians: Europe's Forgotten Survivors.* Boulder, Colo.: Westview Press, 1977.
Luckwald, Erich von. *Albanien: Land zwischen gestern und morgen.* Munich: F. Bruckmann, 1942.
Mack Smith, Denis. *Mussolini's Roman Empire.* London: Longman, 1976.
―――. *Mussolini.* London: George Weidenfeld and Nicolson, 1981
Maclean, Fitzroy. *Eastern Approaches.* New York: Time, 1964.
Malcolm, Noel. *Kosovo: A Short History.* London: Macmillan, 1998.
Marmullaku, Ramadan. *Albania and the Albanians.* London: C. Hurst, 1975.
Mitcham, Jr., Samuel W. *Hitler's Legions: The German Army Order of Battle, World War II.* New York: Dorset Press, 1985.
Morris, Katherine, ed. *Escape through the Balkans: The Autobiography of Irene Grünbaum.* Lincoln: University of Nebraska Press, 1996.
Neubacher, Hermann. *Sonderauftrag Südost, 1940-1945: Bericht eines fliegenden Diplomaten.* Göttingen: Musterschmidt Verlag, 1956.
Neuwirth, Hubert. "Widerstand und Kollaboration in Albanien (1939-1944): Eine historische Analyse des kulturellen Musters von Freund und Feind." Ph.D. diss., University of Graz, 1997.
Omari, Luan. *The People's Revolution in Albania and the Question of State Power.* Tirana: 8 Nëntori, 1986.
Pano, Nicholas. "Albania." In Joseph Held, ed., *The Columbia History of Eastern Europe in the Twentieth Century.* New York: Columbia University Press, 1992.

———. "Albania: The Last Bastion of Stalinism." In Milorad Drachkovich, ed., *East Central Europe: Yesterday, Today, Tomorrow*. Stanford, Calif.: Hoover Institution Press, 1982.

———. *The People's Republic of Albania*. Baltimore: Johns Hopkins University Press, 1968.

Peters, Stephen. "Ingredients of the Communist Takeover in Albania." In Thomas Hammond, ed., *The Anatomy of Communist Takeovers*. New Haven, Conn.: Yale University Press, 1975.

Pipa, Arshi. *Albanian Stalinism: Ideo-political Aspects*. Boulder, Colo.: East European Monographs and Columbia University Press, 1990.

Pollo, Stefanaq, and Arben Puto. *The History of Albania: From Its Origins to the Present Day*. London: Routledge and Kegan Paul, 1981.

Prifti, Peter R. "The Labor Party of Albania." In Stephen Fischer-Galati, ed., *Communist Parties of Eastern Europe*. New York: Columbia University Press, 1979.

———. *Socialist Albania since 1944*. Cambridge, Mass.: MIT Press, 1978.

Puto, Arben. *From the Annals of British Diplomacy: The Anti-Albanian Plans of Great Britain during the Second World War according to Foreign Office Documents of 1939-1944*. Tirana: 8 Nëntori, 1981.

Ramet, Sabrina P. *Social Currents in Eastern Europe: The Sources and Meaning of the Great Transformation*. Durham, N.C.: Duke Univerity Press, 1991.

Robinson, Vandeleur. *Albania's Road to Freedom*. London: George Allen and Unwin, 1941.

Robyns, Gwen. *Geraldine of the Albanians*. London: Muller, Blond, & White, 1987.

Ryan, Andrew. *The Last of the Dragomans*. London: Geoffrey Bles, 1951.

Sarner, Harvey. *Rescue in Albania*. Cathedral City, Calif.: Brunswick Press, 1997.

Schmidt-Neke, Michael. *Entstehung und Ausbau der Königsdiktatur in Albanien (1912-1939)*. Munich: R. Oldenbourg Verlag, 1987.

———. "Geschichtliche Grundlagen." In Klaus-Detlev Grothusen, ed., *Südosteuropa-Handbuch: Albanien*. Göttingen: Vandenhoeck und Ruprecht, 1993.

Schnytzer, Adi. *Stalinist Economic Strategy in Practice: The Case of Albania*. Oxford: Oxford University Press, 1982.

Seckendorf, Martin. *Die Okkupationspolitik des deutschen Faschismus in Jugoslawien, Griechenland, Albanien, Italien und Ungarn, 1941-1945*. Berlin: Hüthig Verlagsgemeinschaft, 1992.

Self, George M. "Foreign Relations of Albania." Ph.D. diss., University of Chicago, 1943.

Shehu, Mehmet. *On the Experience of the National Liberation War and the Development of Our National Army*. Tirana: 8 Nëntori, 1978.

Singleton, Fred. *Twentieth-Century Yugoslavia*. New York: Columbia University Press, 1976.

Sjöberg, Örjan. *Rural Change and Development in Albania*. Boulder, Colo.: Westview Press, 1991.

Skendi, Stavro, ed. *Albania*. New York: Praeger, 1956.

Smiley, David. *Albanian Assignment*. London: Chatto Press, 1984.

Speer, Albert. *Inside the Third Reich*. New York: Macmillan, 1970.

Stafford, David. *Britain and European Resistance, 1940-1945: A Survey of the Special Operations Executive.* Toronto: University of Toronto Press, 1980.

Stamm, Christoph. "Zur deutschen Besetzung Albaniens, 1943-1944." *Militärgeschichtliche Mitteilungen* 2 (1981).

Stavrianos, Leften. *The Balkans since 1453.* New York: Holt, Rinehart, Winston, 1958.

Swire, Joseph. *Albania: The Rise of a Kingdom.* London: Unwin Brothers, 1929.

Vickers, Miranda. *The Albanians: A Modern History.* London: I. B. Taurus, 1995.

Vickers, Miranda, and James Pettifer. *Albania: From Anarchy to a Balkan Identity.* New York: New York University Press, 1997.

Vucinich, Wayne S. "Communist Gains in Albania (I)." *Current History* 21, no. 122 (1951).

Wiskemann, Elizabeth. "Albania, 1939-1945." In A. and V. Toynbee, eds., *Hitler's Europe.* London: Oxford University Press, 1954.

Wolf, Robert Lee. *The Balkans in Our Time.* New York: Norton, 1967.

Zamboni, Giovanni. *Mussolinis Expansionpolitik auf dem Balkan.* Hamburg: Helmut Buske Verlag, 1970.

Newspapers

Albania
Bashkimi i Kombit, Fashizmi (later *Tomori*), *Kombi, Luftari, Zëri i Popullit*

France
Ere nouvelle

Germany
Völkischer Beobachter

Great Britain
Manchester Guardian, Times

Hungary
Pester Lloyd

Italy
Giornale d'Italia, Lavoro fascista, Popolo di Roma

United States
Illyria, New York Times

Vatican
Osservatore romano

INDEX

Abid, Mehmed, 31
Abwehr, 159, 161, 165, 184, 229
"Achse," 159
Adriatic Sea, 1, 9, 15, 28, 31, 159, 180, 182, 207
Agaj, Ago, 174, 207, 210
AGIP technicians, 180
Agostinucci, Christino, 43
Agricultural Bank, 48
Agushi, Iliaz, 87, 141, 143
"Alarich," 159
Alarupi, Vasil, 14
Albania/Albanians, 25-29, 57-58, 63, 73-75, 77, 80-83, 121, 140, 141, 219; WWI, 5, 6; Italian economic involvement, 6-8, 11, 47, 48, 56, 57, 65-70; Ciano plans invasion, 8-20; relations with Italy, 14, 18; Italian invasion, 21-25, 31, 122, 133, 150, 195, 214, 218, 231; Zog's attempts to re-establish control, 31, 105-10, 240-45; sentiment after invasion, 26, 27; international reactions, 29-32; resources, 33, 34; social conditions, 34; government under Italy, 35-46, 141-44; education, 49, 51; religion, 52-57; social development, 62-65; irredentism, 70-73, 83-85; anti-Italian sentiment, 86-97, 126, 132, 140; in Italian military, 75-80; relations with Germans, 89, 92, 96, 157, 158; non-violent resistance to Italians, 97-100; armed resistance to Italians, 101, 102, 104, 107, 109, 111-15, 129, 202; relations with British, 102-11, 144-50, 194, 197, 200-205, 208, 225, 227-30, 232, 233, 249; Albanian Communist Party, 121, 123-29; early communism, 121-23; organized resistance to Italians, 129-39, 142, 143, 147-49; relations among resistance groups, 134-36, 149-52, 198, 199; collapse of Italy, 152, 153, 247; German invasion, 159-65, 194; government under Germans, 165-76, 186-88, 208-12, 214-17, 223, 224; organized resistance to Germans, 170-73, 188-91, 199-208, 212, 213, 216-18, 235-40; German economic involvement, 176-83; in German military, 183-86, 215-18; German collaboration with resistance, 191, 192, 198-200, 203, 209-14, 227; splinter resistance groups, 192-95; German reaction to resistance, 195-98, 206-8, 217, 218; German decline, 223-27; German retreat, 231-35, 237, 239, 240, 246, 247, 249, 251; Hoxha assumes control, 246-51; under Hoxha, 248, 249, 251-56; notes on sources, 275-84
Albanian Communist Party (ACP), 111, 121, 123, 124, 127, 128, 137, 150-52, 246, 250, 277, 281
Albanian Fascist Party, 42, 45, 46, 49, 79, 97, 114
Albanian National Committee, 244
Albanian National Liberation Army (ANLA), 147, 205, 206, 216
Albanian Oil GmbH, 180

Albanian Orthodox Church, 26, 242
Albanian Parliament, 37, 43, 45, 58
Albanian Synod, 52, 53
Albanian Telegraphic Agency, 49
Alexander, King of Yugoslavia, 15
Ali, Ramiz, 100
Alia, Halil, 218, 224, 233
Alizoti, Fejzi Bey, 37, 49
Allies, 6, 73, 83, 126, 136, 145, 150, 152, 161, 162, 164, 166, 167, 170, 174, 175, 180, 189, 200, 201, 215, 216, 218, 227, 232, 239, 244, 246, 248-50
"Altesse Serenissme," 41
Amery, Julian, 163, 204, 211-13, 223, 225, 226, 228-30, 233, 279, 281
Anfuso, Filippo, 23
Anglo-Albanian Association, 242, 243
Anglo-Jewish Association, 241
Ankara, 32, 173
Anschluss, 9, 10, 12, 67
Anti-Fascist Coalition, 250
Anti-Fascist Council of National Liberation, 248
Apulia, 18
Archbishop Vissarion, 26, 39, 53, 54, 56, 101
Archer, Laird, 81
Armenians, 201
Arta, 84
Aryans, 175
Atdheu, 192
Athens, 32, 72, 79-81, 85, 107, 187
Atlantic Charter, 239, 244
Austria/Austrians, 6, 47, 67, 98, 103, 158, 166, 173, 174, 184
Austro-Hungarians, 160, 166
Avenol, Joseph, 31
Axis, 80, 83, 126, 134, 136, 140, 152, 161, 187, 190, 194, 239, 241, 243, 246, 277
"Azienda Strada Albania," 66
Azzi, 164

Badoglio, Pietro, 18, 71, 75-77, 82, 153, 161, 162, 279
Bajraktari, Muharrem, 102, 111, 163, 189, 192-97, 204, 228, 230, 231, 233; photograph of, 155
Balilla, 51
Balkan Air Force, 202
Balkan Committee, 242
Balkan Communist Federation, 121
Balkans, 5, 10, 30, 31, 34, 52, 72, 73, 75, 96, 107, 135, 142, 144, 146, 151, 158, 159, 168, 178, 181, 194, 207, 219, 223, 225, 237, 253, 256, 279
Balli Kombëtar (National Front, BK), 132-36, 141-43, 149-52, 163, 170-74, 184, 189-92, 194, 195, 197-200, 203, 204, 209-12, 215, 217, 226, 227, 229, 233; photograph of, 220
Ballvora, Shyqri, 281-83
Bank of Italy, 47
Bank of Naples, 48
Bari, 64, 180, 213, 214, 217, 227, 228, 230, 239
Barker, Elizabeth, 283
"Battaglioni Scanderbey," 64
Battle of Leskovik, 137
Battle of Metsovo, 77
Battle of Stalingrad, 136, 152
BBC, 80, 108, 110, 136, 167, 213, 243
Beca, Andon, 37
Bektashi, 55
Belgians, 241
Belgrade, 25, 53, 71, 86, 101, 109, 110, 161, 164, 168-70, 177, 182, 223
Benes, Eduard, 241
Benini, Zenone, 41, 66, 116
Berat, 66, 68, 137, 162, 163, 189, 195, 196, 206, 232, 250, 252
"Bergkessel," 196
Berlin, 75, 158, 167, 175-77, 184, 201, 215, 218, 277
Biçaku, Aziz, 169, 197
Biçaku, Ibrahim Bey, 215, 223, 224, 234, 235, 237
Bilisht, 85, 211
Bishop Victor, 53
Bitol, 84
Bitolj-Struga-Elbasan-Tirana road, 182
BK. *See* Balli Kombëtar
Bland, William B., 280
Bojiloff, Dobri, 177
Boletini, Adem, 184
Bonaparte, Napoleon, 104, 283
Boris, King of Bulgaria, 85
Borova, 190
Bosnia, 237, 240
Bottai, Giuseppe, 71
Boyle, Sir Edward, 242, 244, 245
"Brennero" division, 163
Brindisi, 23, 201, 230
Britain/British, 16, 22, 30-32, 43, 69, 101-10, 121, 144-50, 157, 162-64, 168, 172, 191, 193, 194, 197-99, 201-4, 208, 210, 212-14, 218, 225, 227-30, 232, 233, 235, 239, 240, 241, 243-45, 249, 250, 275-77, 279-81, 283, 284. *See also* England
British Chiefs of Staff, 146
British Consul-General, 91, 94, 99, 101, 110
British Liaison Officers (BLO), 162, 163, 190, 196, 197, 200, 202, 203, 214, 215, 225, 230-32, 236, 245
British Royal Air Force (RAF), 201, 208, 217, 235, 236

Index

Buda, Aleks, 281
Budapest, 10
Bujan, 238, 239
Bulgaria/Bulgarians, 37, 43, 83-85, 95, 98, 175, 201, 218, 219, 223, 226, 242, 247
Bulquiz, 181
Burrel, 101, 163
Bushati, Maliq Bey, 37, 141-43, 243
Buxton, Lord Noel, 242

Çabej, Eqrem, 174
Cairo, 108, 109, 146, 175
Cakrani, Kadri, 229
Caligari, 163
Çamëria, 70, 72-75, 79, 85, 168
Çami, Skënder, 128
Campbell, Sir Ronald, 101, 109, 110
Canadians, 241
Canevari, Emilio, 24
Captain Lange, 184
Carabinieri, 95, 96, 99
Carrara, 90
Casablanca, 146, 159
Casablanca Conference, 146
Catholics, 51-57, 63, 84, 95, 96, 101, 172, 255
Caucasus region, 201
Çekrezi, K. A, 243, 244
Çela, Mehmet, 226, 234
Central Council, 42
Central Council of the Corporative Economy, 42
Çetniks, 188, 213
Chamber of Fasces and Corporations, 28, 78
Chamberlain, Neville, 20, 30
Churchill, Tom, 232
Churchill, Winston, 108, 159, 229
Ciano, Count Galeazzo, 30, 31, 33, 39, 40, 48, 57, 69, 75, 79, 90-92, 97, 115, 140, 141, 152; background, 7, 8; plans invasion, 8-20; disappointed with invasion, 23, 26, 27; explanations, 28, 29; attitude toward Albanians, 34, 62, 85, 91; creates political structure, 35, 36, 39, 41-43, 112, 116; disappointed with new government, 37, 38; Albanian Fascist Party, 45; and Moslem community, 55; attempts to win over Albanians, 61-65, 68, 70-72, 83, 84; analyses Albanian resources, 65, 66; plans invasion of Greece, 73-76; invasion of Greece, 77, 78; blame for failure of invasion of Greece, 81-82; problems with Germans, 85-87, 158; beginning of resistance, 98, 99, 102; reaction to resistance, 112, 113, 137-39; resigns, 141; notes on sources, 277-79
Comando Supremo, 138, 153, 277, 279
Comintern, the, 121-23, 135, 150, 246

Concensus, 147
Concensus II, 204, 228
Conference of Ambassadors, 6, 70
Conference of Peza, 129, 130, 132, 145
Congress of Berat, 52
Congress of Permët, 211, 249
Constitution of 1876, 40
Corfu, 30, 32, 74, 76, 142, 232
Council of the League, 31
Croatia/Croatians, 46, 172, 176, 218
Curri, Bajram, 121
Cvetkovic, Dragisa, 15, 16
Cyprus, 108
Cyrenaica, 201
Czechoslovakia/Czechs, 17, 47, 201, 241

Dalmazzo, Lorenzo, 138, 142, 162-64
Dalmazzo-Këlcyra Agreement, 142
Davies, E. F., 197, 203, 204, 231, 245, 279, 280; photograph of, 156
Declaration of the Rights of Citizens, 249
Deda, Nijaz, 114
Dema, Hysni, 210, 224
Democratic Front, 253
Deva, Xhafer, 161, 168, 169, 173, 184, 187, 199, 207, 210, 211, 215, 231, 237, 239
Devoll, 66, 180, 182
DGA, 182, 226
Dibra, 84, 134, 193, 196, 206, 208, 214, 216-18, 224
Dibra (tribe), 102, 136, 139, 149, 193, 210, 214
Dibra, Fuat Bey, 134, 171, 172, 215
Dielli, 242, 243
Dine, Fiqri, 192, 210-12, 215-19, 223, 224, 227, 237
Dino, Xhemil, Bey, 37, 40, 43, 85
Directorate of the Albanian Fascist Party, 42
Dishnica, Ymer, 129, 150-52
DiVecchi, 75
Dixon, Pearson, 80, 105, 144-46
Djakova, 181
Djilas, Milovan, 133
Dodbiba, Sokrat, 173
Donovan, William, 249
Dopolavoro, 13, 41, 62; photograph of building under construction, 118
Dosti, Hasan, 116, 134, 150, 227, 229
Drin River, 162
Drita, 49
Dukagjin, 54
Dukagjini, Lek, 183
Duke of Bergamo, 41
Durham, Edith, 242
Durrës, 14, 19, 21-24, 26, 27, 34, 36, 61-68, 82, 94, 101, 103, 110, 128, 142, 162, 163, 166, 172, 182, 196, 201, 207, 226, 234, 236; photograph of reconstruction, 118

EAM, 147
Eastwood, Stan, 235
Ecole Normale (Elbasan), 50
Ecumenical Patriarchate (Patriarch), 52, 53
"Edelweiss," 196
Eden, Anthony, 109, 145, 194, 213, 229, 230
Egypt, 92, 106, 108, 109, 112, 242
"1828," 196
Eisenhower, Dwight, 161
Elbasan, 37, 50, 65, 68, 111, 128, 146, 162, 165, 166, 169, 182, 189, 196, 232, 236
Elbasan-Peqin-Kavaya-Durrës road, 182
Elbasan-Struga road, 206
Elbasan-Tirana road, 226
Elezi Family, 193
Elezi, Cen, 192, 193, 230
Elezi, Ersat, 193
Elezi, Gani, 193
Elezi, Islam, 193
England, 105, 106, 207. *See also* Britain
"Ente Assistenza Fascista," 46
"Ente Turistico Alberghiero Albania," 68
Epirus, 75, 80
Ere Nouvelle, 30
Ermenji, Abaz, 190, 227, 228
Ethiopia, 17, 41, 89
Europe, 277, 283

Falo, Dhimitër, 134
Fashizmi, 49, 63, 67, 69, 72, 113, 115
Faya, Baba, 199
"Federazione della Gioventu Albanese del Littorio," 51
Fehn, Gustav, 184, 216, 226
Ferrobeton, 100
"Firenze" division, 163
Fischer, Bernd, 282
Fitzthum, Josef, 166, 184-86, 212, 215, 224, 226, 231, 234, 239
Florina, 84, 85, 182
Florina-Korça-Struga road, 232
Foggia, 83
Fortuzi, 234
France/French, 16, 30, 32, 43, 69, 78, 105, 111, 123, 133, 146, 201
Franciscans, 50, 172
Frank, Hermann, 279
Frashëri, Mehdi Bey, 27, 113, 130, 133, 157, 158, 172, 173, 175, 177, 187, 199, 210-12, 215, 217, 218, 223, 226, 237
Frashëri, Mithat, 133, 150, 190, 191, 203, 211, 227, 229; photograph of, 220
Frashëri, Raquip, 218
Frashëri, Vehbi, 161, 172-74, 176
Free Albania Movement, 243, 244
French Communist Party, 125

Friends of Albania, 241
Friends of Albania (London), 242, 243
"Fuchsjagd," 218
Fultz, Harry, 152, 205, 276

Gabrielli, 107
Gayda, Virginio, 28
Gegs, 34, 174, 183, 194, 195, 213, 215, 229
Geib, Theodor, 167
Geloso, Carlo, 73
General Command of Active Forces, 217
Geraj, Rrok, 24, 35, 113, 218; photograph of, 59
Geraldine, Queen of the Albanians, 9, 12-14, 17, 20, 21, 24, 25, 62, 63, 108, 158, 241; photograph of, 59
Germany/Germans, 10, 11, 13, 47, 63, 69, 75, 87, 98, 102, 110, 111, 123, 142, 146, 152, 194, 209, 219, 227, 229, 230, 247, 254; relations with Zog, 14; relations with Italy, 16, 20, 29, 76, 78, 82-86, 158, 159; relations with Albania, 89, 92, 96, 157, 158; collaboration with resistance, 130, 191, 192, 198-200, 203, 211; interest in Albania, 157, 158; invasion of Albania, 159-65, 194, 202, 211; government, 165-76, 186-88, 209-12, 215-18, 223, 224; resistance, 170-73, 188-91, 193, 195-201, 205-8, 213, 216-18, 227, 235-40; economic policy, 176-83; Albanian military, 183-86; relations with British, 197, 202; decline, 224-27; retreat, 231-37, 239, 240, 246, 249; notes on sources, 276, 277, 279, 281-83; soldiers, photograph of, 220
Giornale d'Italia, 28, 43
"Giovenezza," 99, 100
"Gioventu Femminile del Littorio," 51
"Gioventu Italiana del Littorio," 64
"Gioventu Universitaria Fascista," 64
Giro, Giovanni, 11-14, 18, 45, 90, 91, 114
Gjinishi, Mustafa, 104, 111, 126, 129, 130, 150-52, 163, 229, 230
Gjirokastra, 62, 65, 68, 78, 80, 124, 126, 134, 137, 189, 198, 206, 209, 232, 247
Gjoles bridge, 213
Gjoni, Gjon Marka, 141, 143, 211, 230, 231, 233
Gjylbegu, Musa, 174
Gleiwitz, 75
Godolesh, 180
Göring, Hermann, 28
Graftey-Smith, Lawrence, 110, 112
Gramsci, Antonio, 163
Gramsh, 136
Grandi, Dino, 8, 78

Index

Grant, Hugh, 21, 24
Grazzi, Emanuele, 76
Greater Albania, 84, 86, 88, 116, 167, 168
Greece/Greeks, 6, 25, 31, 32, 43, 46, 51-53, 70-85, 88, 91, 96-98, 100, 104-11, 117, 134, 137, 142, 144, 147, 149, 152, 153, 164, 166, 169, 177, 186, 187, 194, 196, 197, 201, 207, 209, 232, 237, 247, 249, 256
Grothusen, Klaus-Detlev, 280
Gstöttenbauer, Dr. Karl, 226, 231, 234, 239
Gullman, Otto, 226
Gusinje, 185, 188
Guzzoni, Alfredo, 18, 21, 23, 24, 26, 35, 44, 91, 141; photograph of, 59

Halliday, Jon, 278
Hamid II, Abdul, 40
Hands, Andy, 239
Harapi, Fr. Anton, 172, 173, 210, 235, 237
Hart, Charles C., 241, 242
Hasluck, Margaret, 146, 175, 200
Helli, 72
Helmës, 248
Herbert, Aubrey, 242
Hetzer, Armin, 280
Hibbert, Sir Reginald, 149, 280
High Council of Regency, 234
High Court of Justice, 13
Himara-Shkodra road, 182
Himmler, Heinrich, 75, 184-86
Hitler, Adolf, 8, 12, 14, 17, 32, 73, 75, 78, 82, 83, 85, 87, 110, 152, 158, 159, 161, 170, 174, 177, 178, 181, 185, 224
Hodgkinson, Harry, 242
Hodgson, H., 242, 244
Hotel Dajti, 34, 210
House of Savoy, 17, 37, 38, 41, 92, 116
Hoxha, Daout, 72, 75
Hoxha, Enver, 31, 101, 104, 110, 111, 123, 132, 145, 146, 168, 197, 199, 203, 209, 212, 227, 235, 236, 238, 239; Albanian Communist Party, 124-26, 129; background, 124, 125; National Liberation Movement, 129, 130, 196; relations with Balli Kombëtar, 133, 135, 136, 149-51, 198; National Liberation Army, 137, 205-7; relations with British, 147-49, 201, 204, 214, 225, 228-30, 232, 249, 252; rejects Mukje agreements, 151, 152; harsh tactics, 230, 231, 251, 253; assumes control of Albania, 245, 251; government, 248, 249, 251-56; advantages over Zog, 251, 252; notes on sources, 275, 278, 281, 282; photographs of, 156, 222
Hoxha, Falil, 238

Hoxha, Mehmet, 238
Hristic, Bozko, 15
Hungary/Hungarians, 10, 201

Illyrians, 175
Institute of Albanian Studies, 49
Instituti I Studimeve Marksiste-Leniniste Pranë KQ të PPSH, 282
"Instituto Fascista Albanese pegli infortuni sul Lavoro," 68
"Instituto Nazionaleper i cambi con l'estero," 47
Ioannina, 84, 85, 190
Istanbul, 52, 53, 103, 107, 162, 218, 242, 245
Isufi, Hasan, 226
Italy/Italians, 10, 15, 25, 30, 39, 46, 54, 58, 61, 73-75, 86, 106, 116, 117, 122, 140, 142, 146, 148, 150, 153, 161, 168-71, 174, 175, 177, 182-84, 189-91, 193-96, 207, 211, 212, 214, 218, 230, 233, 234, 237, 254, 255; motivation for invasion, 5, 6; economic involvement in Albania, 6, 7, 11, 47, 48, 56, 57, 65-70; Ciano's plan for invasion, 8-13, 15-20; relations with Albanians, 13, 18; preparations for invasion, 18-21; propaganda, 21, 23, 24, 27, 48, 49, 62, 63, 143; invasion of Albania, 21-24, 28, 31, 111, 133, 150, 158, 171-73, 195, 214, 218, 231; explanations, 28-30; relations with Germans, 29, 30, 75, 78, 82-87, 158, 160-62, 164-68; creation of Italian Albania, 34-46; education, 49-51, 119 (photograph); religion, 52, 55-57; social development, 63-65; irredentism, 70-72, 84, 85; invasion of Greece, 76-83; anti-Italian sentiment, 79, 86-97, 112, 126; non-violent resistance, 97-99; armed resistance, 101-3, 107, 109, 112-15, 129, 136-39, 143, 163, 164, 202; Greece, 104, 106; government, 115, 116; relations with communists, 126-29; collapse, 135, 141, 143, 146, 150, 157, 164, 165, 171, 179, 189, 193, 247; notes on sources, 276-80, 282, 283
Italian Fascist Grand Council, 38
Italian Fascist Party, 45, 68
Italo-Albanian Skënderbeg Club, 49
Iulia, 77

Jacomoni, Francesco, 11-14, 16, 18, 19, 40-44, 47, 49, 55, 56, 65, 71, 73-76, 78, 79, 82, 84, 91, 97, 115, 116, 136-41, 278, 279
Jerusalem, 172
Jesuits, 50
Jews, 46, 187
Jodl, Alfred, 231

Juka, Musa, 14

Kaloshi, Murat, 102
Kaltenbrunner, Ernst, 185
Kasneci, Lefter, 205, 282
Kastrioti, Qazim, 106, 242
Kavaja, 163
Kazaks, 225
Keeble, 146
Keitel, Wilhelm, 181
Këlcyra, Ali, 133, 142, 229; photograph of, 220
Kemal, Ismail, 255
Kemp, Peter, 174, 280
Kërçova, 162
Kërraba Pass, 236
Kissi, Bishop Kristopher, 53, 56, 57, 96
Koçi, Jak, 12, 13
Kodheli, Marco, 27
Koka, Sami, 24
Kolaj, Rrok, 173
Koliqi, Ernest, 37, 40, 51, 64, 71
Kolonja, Peter, 242, 243
Kombi, 170
Konica, Faik, 242
Konica, Mehmet, 173, 174
"Konstanin," 159
Korça, 50, 51, 62, 65, 68, 71, 77-80, 99, 111, 122-25, 128, 136, 137, 142, 189, 190, 206, 232
Korça, Hifzi, 183
Korça-Struga road, 182
Kosmet, 238, 239
Kosova/Kosovars, 15, 29, 70-73, 84, 86-88, 95, 103, 107, 109, 110, 122, 123, 133, 134, 144, 151, 161, 167-69, 172-74, 177, 180-92, 184, 193, 195, 207, 209, 215, 227, 231, 234, 237-40, 243,
Kosova Committee, 122
Kosova, Lefter, 224
Kota, Kostaq, 116, 158
Kotor, 53
Kruja, 101, 104, 111, 117, 149, 150, 189, 215, 247
Kruja, Mustafa, 13, 20, 115-17, 128, 129, 134, 136, 139, 140, 168, 172, 211, 237; photograph of, 154
Kryeziu, Ceno Bey, 103
Kryeziu, Gani Bey, 103, 104, 109, 110, 193, 197, 204, 228, 231, 243; photograph of, 155
Kryeziu, Said, 103, 104, 231, 237
Kühmel, Bernard, 149, 226, 281, 283
Kukës, 62, 109, 162, 163, 181, 189, 233
Kukës-Prizren road, 239
Kupi, Abaz, 22, 27, 101, 103, 104, 111, 117, 129, 130, 149, 152, 171, 189, 190, 192-95, 197, 198, 204, 206, 210-18, 227-30, 233, 237, 243, 245, 252; photograph of, 154
Kupi, Ibrahim, 101
Kupi, Petrit, 228

Labinot, 246, 247
Laçi, Vasil, 102
Lake Ohrid, 206
Lake Prespa, 85
Lake Shkodra, 182
Lampson, John, 109
Lanz, Hubert, 161, 208
Lavoro Fascista, 28
League of Nations, 7, 31
League of Prizren (1878), 255
Leake, Philip, 205
Leka, Crown Prince of Albania, 24
Lenin, V. I., 130
Leshi, Haxhi, 102
Leyser, Ernest von, 231
Lezhë, 11
L'Humanité, 125
Libohova, Eqrem Bey, 113, 140, 141, 143, 161, 168, 169, 214
Libya, 64
Liria, 243, 244
List, Siegmund, 83
London, 8, 30-32, 37, 91, 105, 110, 229, 241, 244
Long Range Desert Group, 232, 235
Lord Glenconner, 145, 146
Lord Halifax, 30, 106, 108, 109
Lord Harcourt, 227
Lord Perth, 8, 29, 30, 35
Luckwald, Erich von, 158
Lumë, 111, 194
"Lupi di Roma," 13
Lyon, Marcus, 228

Macedonia, 70, 77, 84, 85, 217
Mackensen, Hans Georg von, 20, 86, 87, 102, 158, 160
Mack-Smith, Denis, 283
MacMillian, Harold, 230
Madrid, 20
Malëshova, Sejfulla, 249, 250
Mao Zedong, 196
Marinucci, Ferrobeton, Simoncini, Tadini e Talenti, 165
Marko, V., 52
Markovic, Jovan, 71
Marshall, George, 159
Martanesh, 111
Martaneshi, Baba Mustafa (Baba Faja), 111, 112, 130
Marxism, 255
Mati, 63, 208, 214, 216, 217

Index

Mborja, Tefik, 45, 46, 114
McLean, Neil (Billy), 146-49, 202-4, 211-14, 217, 225, 227-31, 281; photograph of, 156
Mediterranean Sea, 145, 162, 202
Menton, 77
Meran & Hall school, 172
Metaxas, John, 72, 76, 80, 81, 107-9
Metohija, 238
Metsovo, 77
Middle East High Command (Br.), 104
Mihailovic, Draza, 129, 134, 188
Military Intelligence (R) (Br.), 102, 104
Ministero della Guerra, 277
Mirdita, 63, 101, 112, 140, 141, 171, 184, 230, 237
Mirdizu, 17
Mitchell, Ruth, 61, 67
Mitrovica, 86, 87, 92, 159, 160, 169, 170, 184
Mitrovica, Rexhep, 84, 133, 173, 175, 176, 206, 208-14, 215, 223
Moisiu, Spiro, 137, 246
Monastir, 255
Montenegro/Montenegrins, 6, 70, 84, 95, 98, 128, 177, 233, 236-38, 240
Moscow, 128, 249
Moslem Bektashi, 111, 114
Moslems, 34, 52, 54-56, 84, 92, 93, 128, 192, 199, 227, 255
Mostar, 236
Mountain League, 231
Muço, Skënder, 191, 199, 226
Mugosa, Dusan, 123, 125, 135
Muka, Koço, 174, 227, 229; photograph of 220
Mukje, 149, 151, 152
Mukje Agreements, 150, 151, 191, 247
Muletti, Qazim, 234
Mussolini, Benito, 5-11, 13-17, 20-22, 24, 28-41, 45, 46, 51, 55, 61, 62, 64-66, 68, 70, 72-76, 78, 80-82, 84, 89, 90, 99, 100, 110, 113, 115, 116, 138, 141, 142, 152, 153, 158, 172, 278, 283; photograph of, 120
Myrdacz, Gustav von, 216, 234

National Archives, 276, 277
National Assembly, 175
National Bank of Albania, 47, 48, 94, 177-79. *See also* Albanian National Bank
National Committee, 235
National Independent Party, 211, 215. *See also* Party of National Independence
National Liberation Army, 137
National Liberation Movement (Lëvizje Nacionalçlirimtare, NLM), 130-37, 143, 147-51, 153, 161, 170, 172, 173, 175, 188, 191-93, 195, 196, 198, 199, 203-6, 211, 212, 227-32, 239, 240, 245-48. *See also* Partisans

Ndreu, Dali, 216
Near East Foundation, 81
Neel, Tony, 225
Neubacher, Hermann, 159-61, 165-69, 171-73, 176, 178-81, 183-86, 190, 198, 199, 210, 211, 215, 216, 223-26, 231, 237, 238, 279
Neuhausen, 179
Neuwirth, Hubert, 283
New Tirana, 236
New York Times, 112
Nigris, L., 56
Niksic, 162
Nishani, Omer, 247, 253
Noble, Sir A., 29, 30
Noli, Fan, 45, 52, 115, 122, 242-44
Normandy, 168, 190
North Africa, 101, 145, 152
Nosi, Frederick, 81
Nosi, Lef, 171, 173, 211
Novi Pazar, 84
Nowack, Dr. Ernest, 179
Nuremberg, 179

Oakley-Hill, Dayrell, 110, 111
Observatore romano, 29
Ohrid, 84, 85
"Oilcompany 33," 180
Omari, Luan, 57, 58, 281, 282
"Operation Bodyguard," 168, 190
"Operation Cyclamen," 83
"Operation 505," 196
Orosh, 231
Orthodox, 39, 52-54, 56, 57, 79, 84, 96, 110, 128, 199, 255
Ostmark, 180
Ottomans, 5, 6, 40, 103, 172, 219, 253

Palairet, Sir Michael, 107, 109
Palandri, Enrico, 44
Palazzo Chigi, 8, 43, 277
Palestine, 108
Palmer, Alan, 204
Pannwitz, Eberhard von, 67, 73, 82, 158, 159
Pano, Nicholas, 124, 149, 151
Papagos, Alexandros, 77, 80
Pariani, Alberto, 18, 20, 23, 143-44, 169
Parini, Piero, 73, 91
Paris, 13, 30, 31, 122, 123, 125, 133, 173, 244
Paris Conference (1920), 172
Parisius, 231
Partisans, 131, 132, 135, 137, 139, 141, 147, 148, 150, 162-64, 184, 185, 189-201, 204-8, 210, 211, 214, 216-18, 224, 228, 229, 231-40, 245, 247, 278-82. *See also* National Liberation Movement
Paul, Prince of Yugoslavia, 15, 83

Index

Pavelic, Ante, 176
Pec, 181, 185
Pejani, Bedri, 84, 169, 238
Percy, Sir Jocelyn, 105, 107, 242, 244
Permët, 137, 247, 248, 252
Peshkopi, Ekrem, 196, 216; photograph of, 220
Pester Lloyd, 29
Peza, 139, 196, 206, 246, 247
Peza, Myslim, 102, 111, 117, 129, 130, 149, 195, 199, 206; photograph of, 222
Piedmont, 71
Place, 188
Plan Zeppelin, 168
Plasari, Ndreçi, 281
Podgorica, 84, 240
Pogradec, 78, 99, 162, 181, 182
Poland/Poles, 75, 201
Pollo, Stefanq, 100, 143, 281, 282
Popolo di Roma, 28
Popovic, Miladin, 123, 125, 129, 132
Porto Edda, 62, 68, 78
Post, Larry, 244
Prague, 16
Prasca, Sebastian Viscounti, 73-78, 81, 82
Prevesa, 85
Previzi, Prengë, 224, 234, 237
Princivalle, 163
Prishtina, 87, 162, 185, 187, 226
Prizren, 162, 168, 169, 182, 184, 185, 231, 232, 234
Prizren-Kukës-Puka-Shkodra road, 184
Puka, 233
Puto, Arben, 100, 143, 281, 281

Qafa e Rrërësit, 228
Qyku, Faik, 134

Radio Athens, 108
Radio Tirana, 234
Radovicka, Islam, 232
Ramadan, 92
Ravenna, 64
Reichsbank, 179
Reichswirtschaft minister, 181
Reislia, Vizdan, 226, 234
Ribbentrop, Joachim von, 85, 159-61, 165, 218, 279
Rinia Balliste, 134
Rinteln, Enno von, 82
Ritz Hotel, 106, 241
Roatta, Mario, 76
Robyns, Gwen, 282
Roman, Viorel, 280
Romania/Romanians, 32, 43, 46, 75, 86, 219, 223
Rome, 5, 6, 14-16, 19, 20, 25, 27, 29, 38, 41, 43, 45, 54, 55, 63, 65, 67, 68, 74, 83, 84, 90, 102, 113, 116, 139, 157, 158, 160, 168, 177, 178, 237
Roosevelt, Franklin, 32
Rose, Michael, 201
Rosi, Ezio, 164
"Roter Mann," 196
"Royal Guard of Finance," 44
Russia/Russians, 146, 166, 201, 207
Ryan, Sir Andrew, 14, 18, 27, 29, 36, 40, 45, 61, 106, 107, 243, 245, 279

Sarajevo, 237
Saranda, 21, 62, 232
Sargent, Sir Orme, 213
Sazan, 5
Scheiger, Franz von, 159, 160, 165, 166, 168, 170, 172, 216, 234
Schliep, Martin, 159-61, 165, 167, 168, 172, 175, 176, 178, 184, 190, 200, 201, 206, 211, 214-18, 224, 225, 230, 231, 234
Schmidhuber, August, 186, 226
Schmidt-Neke, Michael, 281, 282
Scotland, 20, 30
Scots Grey Regiment, 146
"Seaview," 164
Second League of Prizren, 168, 169, 238
Secret Intelligence Service (SIS), 30, 103
Section D (Br.), 103, 104
Selenica, 100
Semlin, 226
Serbia/Serbs, 6, 15, 64, 70, 87, 98, 128, 151, 161, 166, 167, 169, 176, 185, 237, 238
Serreqi, Zef, 27, 35, 40
Servizio Informazioni Militare (SIM), 113, 140
Shehu, Mehmet, 137, 148, 196, 205, 206, 216, 217, 230, 235, 278, 279, 282; photograph of, 222
Shëngjin, 15, 21, 22
Sherko, Mihal, 27, 35
Shijak, 162
Shkodra, 14, 15, 38, 50, 52-54, 62, 68, 99, 100, 115, 122, 123, 162, 172-74, 180, 182, 225, 226, 233, 234-36, 239, 255
Shkumbin river, 196, 206
Shtylla, Tahir, 116
Shtypi, 49
Sicily, 152
Simopoulos, Charolambos, 29
"Skanderbeg" division, 185-87, 215, 218, 224, 227, 238
Skënderbeg Foundation, 49
Skënderbeg, Gjergji Kastrioti, 5, 86, 150, 186, 255
Skendi, Stavro, 124, 149
Skopje, 182, 197

Index

Slovakia, 172
Smiley, David, 146-48, 204, 213, 225, 228, 280; photograph of, 156
Smith, Victor, 214, 230
Soddu, Ubaldo, 78
Sofia, 85
Soviet Union/Soviets, 123, 124, 126-28, 145, 146, 219, 223, 245, 250. *See also* Russia/Russians
Spahiu, Bedri, 147
Spain, 89
Spanish Civil War, 16
Special Operations Executive (SOE), 107, 109, 145, 146, 164, 175, 202, 203, 205, 212, 213, 225, 227-30, 276, 283
Special People's Court of Tirana, 252
Special People's Tribunals, 252
Speer, Albert, 181, 278
Spiru, Nako, 199
SS, 166, 177, 183-87, 224, 227
Stafford, David, 283
Stalin, J., 126, 253, 254
Stalingrad, 200
Starace, Achille, 45
Statuto Fondementale, 40
Stefani News Agency, 41, 49, 72
Stirling, Wilfred, 109
Stojadinovic, Milan, 13, 15
Stojnic, Velimir, 250
Straits of Messina, 161
Straits of Otranto, 5
Struga, 162, 182, 232, 236
Struga-Dibra Highway, 137
Südostmontan, 179
Sunni, 52, 171
Superior Fascist Corporative Council, 42
SVEA, 7
Switzerland, 173

Tajiks, 225
Talbot-Rice, D., 199
Tamurlane, 225
Tapisa, 150
Taraboshi, 78
Tashko, Koço, 122, 126, 129
Tehran Meeting, 159
Telegraph, 243
Tepelena, 14, 128, 137, 162
Tetovo, 182
Thesprotia, 85
Thessaloniki, 15, 46, 107, 197
Tirana, 8, 9, 19-22, 25-29, 34-36, 38, 41, 42, 49, 50, 53, 55, 62, 63, 65, 66-68, 73, 77, 81, 82, 86, 87, 91, 92, 94, 98-102, 104, 107, 111, 113, 114, 117, 122, 123, 125, 127, 129, 138, 139, 149, 150, 160, 162, 163, 165, 166, 170, 172, 173, 176, 177, 180, 182, 184, 195, 196, 198, 200, 209-11, 214-16, 223, 224, 227, 231-36, 243, 251, 252, 275, 277; photographs of, 221, 222
Tirana-Durrës Road, 163
Tirana-Shkodra Road, 213, 226
Tito, 130, 135, 151, 204, 207, 225, 239, 240, 245, 246, 249, 250, 253
Tocra, 201
Todt Organization, 178, 181
Tomori, 49, 55, 114, 115, 128, 138
Tomori Battalion, 77, 78
Toptani, Esad Pasha, 115, 116
Tosks, 34, 174, 229
Toynbee, Arnold, 144
Treaty of London, 6
Trepça, 86, 87, 180
Tripartite Pact, 83
Tufine, 211
Turkey/Turks, 30, 37, 43, 46, 64, 92, 93, 102, 103, 106, 112, 175, 219, 242
Tyrol, 172

Ulqini, Cafo Bey, 215
Uniate Movement, 56, 96
United States/Americans, 43, 50, 52, 69, 106, 145, 197, 241-43, 245, 250, 276, 277; in Tirana, photographs of, 221, 222
University of Graz, 173
University of Montpellier, 124
University of Rome, 40, 81
Unthi, 17
U.S. Census Bureau, 242
U.S. Office of Strategic Services (OSS), 146, 152, 249, 276
U.S. State Department, 242, 249
Ustashi regime, 176
Uzbegs, 225

Valle, Giuseppe, 26
Vardar valley, 197
Vatican, 54, 55, 201
Vatra organization, 242, 243
Venice, 12
Ventotene, 193
Vërlaci, Shefqet, 37-40, 44, 45, 47, 48, 73, 86, 115, 116, 140, 141, 243; photograph of, 120
Victor Emmanuel III, King of Italy, 12, 17, 35, 36, 38-40, 45, 51, 55, 80, 84, 92, 99, 100, 102, 152, 167; photographs of, 60, 120
Vienna, 71, 140, 159, 166, 174, 237
Vienna Awards, 85, 87
Viscount Cecil, 242
Viscount Halifax, 30
Visegrad, 237

Vitetti, Leonardo, 17
Vlora, 5, 21, 22, 34, 62, 64, 65, 67, 68, 99, 100, 112, 136, 139, 149, 162, 173, 174, 180, 182, 189, 191, 199, 206, 207, 226, 232, 234, 255
Völkischer Beobachter, 29, 197
Vrioni, Qemal, 49, 140, 172
Vukmanovic-Tempo, Svetozar, 151, 238, 247

Wannsee Conference, 187
War Office (Br.), 102, 105, 107
Washington, 242, 244, 249, 276, 277
Wavell, Archibald, 109
Wehrmacht, 157, 158, 160, 167, 179-81, 186, 226, 277
Weichs, Baron Maximillian von, 161
Weltanschauung, 89
Wheeler, Norman, 204
Wilhelm II of Germany, 157
William of Wied, 86, 157, 171, 172
Wilson, Sir Henry Maitland, 162, 214, 230
Wilson, Woodrow, 6
Wiskeman, Elizabeth, 149
World War I, 5, 6, 34, 52, 89, 103, 160, 166, 179, 184, 185
World War II, 121, 184, 277-79, 281, 282

Xhuli, Reuf, 27
Xoxe, Koçi, 151, 249, 250, 252, 253; photograph of, 222
XXI Corps, 161, 184, 186, 207, 216, 223, 225, 226, 233, 234, 235
XXII Corps, 208, 236

Young, Antonia, 280
Ypi, Xhafer Bey, 26, 35, 36, 99; photograph of, 60

Yugoslavia/Yugoslavs, 13, 15, 16, 25, 28, 29, 31, 43, 70-73, 83, 84, 86, 103, 104, 109-11, 123-25, 134, 142, 149, 151, 167, 187, 194, 201, 218, 226, 233, 238, 240, 246, 247, 249, 250, 253, 281
Yugoslav Communist Party (CPY), 121, 123, 124, 151
Yugoslav General Staff, 240

Zallari, Mihal, 169
Zara, 115
Zavalani, Tajar, 243
Zemun, 184
Zëri i Popullit, 129
Zervas, Napoleon, 134, 232
Zjarri, 123, 126, 133
Zog, King of the Albanians, 9, 10, 16, 31, 33, 35-37, 41, 42, 44-46, 49, 67, 68, 73, 76, 89, 90, 92, 93, 96, 98, 101, 103, 104, 111-13, 115, 122, 124, 125, 129, 130, 133, 135, 140-42, 144, 145, 153, 157, 163, 171, 173, 179, 200, 203, 212-14, 218, 236, 251, 255; rise to power, 6, 57, 242; relations with Italians, 7, 12-15, 17-20, 24, 158; appeals to Germans, 14, 158; Italian invasion, 19-21, 24, 25; as object of blame, 26-28, 35; attempts to re-establish control of Albania, 31, 105-10, 240-45; early political success, 34; financial success, 48; education, 50, 51; religion, 51-56; anti-Zog campaign, 62, 63, 117; irredentism, 70, as head of Legality movement, 192, 193; exiled from Albania, 248; notes on sources, 281-83; photograph of, 59; palace, photograph of, 119
Zogai, 62
Zogaj, 228
Zogists, 225, 244